# OWN OUR OIL
## THE FIGHT FOR IRISH
## ECONOMIC FREEDOM

First published in 2014 by
Liberties Press
140 Terenure Road North | Terenure | Dublin 6W
Tel: +353 (1) 405 5701
www.libertiespress.com | info@libertiespress.com

Trade enquiries to Gill & Macmillan Distribution
Hume Avenue | Park West | Dublin 12
T: +353 (1) 500 9534 | F: +353 (1) 500 9595 | E: sales@gillmacmillan.ie

Distributed in the UK by
Turnaround Publisher Services
Unit 3 | Olympia Trading Estate | Coburg Road | London N22 6TZ
T: +44 (0) 20 8829 3000 | E: orders@turnaround-uk.com

Distributed in the United States by
IPM | 22841 Quicksilver Dr | Dulles, VA 20166
T: +1 (703) 661-1586 | F: +1 (703) 661-1547 | E: ipmmail@presswarehouse.com

Copyright © Own Our Oil Ltd, 2014
The author asserts his moral rights.

ISBN: 978-1-909718-22-7
2 4 6 8 10 9 7 5 3 1

A CIP record for this title is available from the British Library.

Cover design by Liberties Press
Internal design by Liberties Press

# OWN OUR OIL
## THE FIGHT FOR IRISH ECONOMIC FREEDOM

GENERAL EDITOR: EDDIE HOBBS

ASSISTANT EDITOR: DOMINIC SHERLOCK

TECHNICAL EDITOR: DR AMANDA SLEVIN

# TABLE OF CONTENTS

1. Own Our Oil | Eddie Hobbs     7

2. Without a Shot Being Fired | Padhraig Campbell     17

3. What Lies Beneath | Paddy Fahy     38

4. The Oil Industry and the Environment | Jack O'Sullivan     67

5. Voice of Youth | Patrician Secondary School Students     117

6. Can the State Sell the Nation? | Diarmuid Rossa Phelan, SC     120

7. Resource Nationalism and the Public Trust Doctrine | Vincent Salafia     129

8. A History of Irish Servitude | Bill McSweeney     168

9. The Norwegian Experience | Helge Ryggvik and Aileen Canning     201

10. Planning and Environmental Regulatory System | Dermot Flanagan     213

11. The Economic Impact of Getting It Right | Anna Hayes     227

12. Pricing: How Much Will We Get? | Eilis Quinlan and Eddie Hobbs     241

13. My Oil and Gas Filming in Norway | Scott O'Connor     265

14. Strategic Considerations | Chris Sanders     285

15. By Their Words You Shall Know Them | Press Cuttings     310

16. Epilogue | Eddie Hobbs     331

17. Ode Our Oil: A Poem | Dominic Sherlock     334

18. Sources     338

# DEDICATION

This book is dedicated to the memory of Justin Keating, veterinary surgeon, government minister, broadcaster, writer and humanist, for reasons that become eminently clear as you read into its content and listen to the remarkable interview with him on Ownouroil.ie recorded in 2009, the year he died. Here, his daughter, well-known accountant Eilis Quinlan, who co-authors the key chapter on pricing, comments:

> *Own Our Oil* is dedicated to the memory of Justin Keating, my father.
>
> I believe he would have been very proud of this work, and also ecstatic that finally somebody managed to both 'get it' – and do something about it!
>
> I also feel extremely privileged to be associated in my own small way with this book, this *cause*.
>
> It was often said, both before and after my father's death, that he was ahead of his time. Perhaps especially in politics, but also as a scientist, a veterinary professor, and a thinker.
>
> This book is not just a dedication to my father, but to those of his mindset, or as he would often like to say, 'Those of our ilk.'
>
> And above all, he would have loved the debate.

# 1.

## OWN OUR OIL
### Eddie Hobbs

'Goddammit, we're being misinformed, misled and exploited – all over again.'

Words to that effect summed up my own moment of epiphany in September 2012. Until then, I'd assumed that all of the hot air about offshore oil and gas was generated by a dolly mixture of extremists, lefties, and planet-before-people types who grasped little about economics, business and risk taking. It was uninformed. It was wrong. It was arrogant.

A small group involved with Dublin Bay Concern, horrified at the thought of an oil rig just 6 km off the Dublin coast, asked for a meeting. Bluntly, I told them that an organisation focusing purely on the prevention of an energy project off Dalkey and Sandymount, amongst the wealthiest real estate in the country, wouldn't have the aerodynamics to fly nationally. The likelihood was that most Irish people would quietly gloat at the thought of an oil spill spoiling their expensive sea views. The discussion moved on to the bigger picture – how in heaven's name could an oil rig get planning permission on Dublin's front door, at a distance from the shoreline of a capital city that simply could never be countenanced just about anywhere, other than a banana republic?

Still, I wasn't convinced purely by bizarre planning being cause for unprecedented concern, believing in the doctrine of encouraging risk-taking to harvest results over the long term for the Irish economy and, like many I guess, deeply sceptical of nimby-ism being used to hinder progress. From a distance I'd wrongly perceived the rumpus in Mayo about the gas pipe as a distraction hijacked by the stereotypical protestor types, Tricolour tattoos, lots of spare time, Celtic jerseys at the weekend. I'd swallowed the soft-focus media that occasionally passed for analysis in the popular press, not realising how much it reflected, almost verbatim, the industry position which, in turn, is official state policy. I didn't ask questions; that policy felt about right. After all, isn't callow corporation tax the centrepiece of Irish success in getting multinationals to drop into Dublin Airport in their executive jets? Weren't we the lucky ones that anyone would bother sinking their precious cash into holes off the Irish coast?

I'd well remembered the speculative fever as people borrowed from banks on the South Mall in Cork to buy Atlantic Resources shares in the early 1980s. Enthusiastic for insider information before loading up on more Atlantic Resource shares, punters interrogated oil rig workers coming off helicopters at Cork Airport – sadly there was more oil found under a Morris Minor sump. I'd thought economic rent exploitation was really a matter for emerging Africa and that Ireland, as a modern EU economy, was largely protected. I had not placed sufficient value in our natural resource endowment and to my shame I hadn't undertaken any reading of the reports and events that characterised the history of Ireland's offshore oil and gas over the past forty years. It was a yawn. I was sceptical, apathetic, uninterested.

But a few weeks later, after reading just about every report then available on the subject, I discovered just how much of a fool I'd been. I'd swallowed the government and industry line that Ireland was an extremely difficult exploration location – that, most likely, there was little hydrocarbon out there and in order to encourage private industry to undertake exploration risks we needed to adopt a soft taxation policy. What I didn't know then is that we'd be better off leaving it in the ground rather than continue the current policy, which is to give it away for nothing or next to nothing.

I now see industry and government PR for what it is: a great game of hypocrisy, greed and betrayal where the public are indoctrinated with the idea that they're getting a great favour afforded to them by companies prepared to take the gamble of drilling in resource-barren Irish waters while stock market analysts, shareholders and the oil majors are told the complete opposite. Tony O'Reilly Jr, CEO of Provident Resources, who planned the rig in Dublin Bay, announced to an international oil conference on 16 February 2012: 'I always say that if the oil price was thirty bucks I wouldn't be standing here, but the fact is it's a hundred bucks. But we don't need $100 pricing to make the Irish model work, we certainly do feel we need $40.'[1] Today oil is two and a half times that price despite the global turmoil since the Lehmann Brothers collapse in September 2008.

We are being exploited. It is not a conspiracy. It is a combination of an embedded attitude of servitude, an utter failure of ambition and competence by the State, and some good old-fashioned Irish corruption from the bad old days. This is not a conclusion I came to lightly, nor should you.

This book contains the views of an eclectic group of multi-disciplined experts who do not share the groupthink that characterises current Irish policy and opinion. The objective of *Own Our Oil* is to alter public opinion on the expectation that the political establishment will eventually follow given its propensity to lead from behind. In the swirl of media and politics, sometimes we lose sight of the truth that the people and the nation are separate from the State, from the political and permanent establishment which often does not act in the best interests of the people.

## CAN THE STATE SELL THE NATION?

That's a question posed by Diarmuid Rossa Phelan SC, an expert on constitutional law, succinctly capturing the difference between the people and the State. Read it through your fingers. Let's remember that the State, comprised of the political and permanent establishment, preserved for itself all of the entitlements during the economic emergency and demands over 50 percent of workers' pay once it goes over the average wage – at a level four times faster than that of our nearest neighbour, the UK, crushing the link between productivity and reward.

Taxation rates one-quarter those of tax on workers' wages are afforded to corporates and ineffective rates for licences to exploit offshore oil and gas are given devoid of production sharing, royalties or ambition. Industry expert Padhraig Campbell writes that the existence of a multi-billion-euro gas processing facility owned by the Shell consortium in County Mayo positions it to control the distribution network of multiple gas fields likely to exist off Irish waters. The irony from a taxation perspective, as outlined by Eilis Quinlan, is that all of the huge additional costs caused by the protest movement in County Mayo will be a write-off against Shell's future profits and will be borne by the people in lost tax revenue. We've also borne the cost of all the Garda overtime. Jack O'Sullivan brings us back through the forgotten details of recent environmental accidents, of weak and non-existent state agency oversight, of disregard for the Irish coastline, marine life, human safety and local culture. It's a timely reminder, given that the implicit state policy is to follow discovery and extraction with a new regime and resources to back it and not the other way around for fear of frightening the horses.

Vincent Salafia, with jaw-dropping irony, writes about resource nationalism globally and what international law has to say about the ownership of natural resources, highlighting the international agreements to which Ireland is a party, and identifies the Ugandan regime as far superior to ours – a regime modelled on a report financed by Irish taxpayers.

## TALK UP THE RISKS AND TALK DOWN THE PROSPECTS

There is little oil and gas out there – Ireland will never be a hydrocarbon producer. The Norwegians were told the same thing about their prospects in the late 1960s. Much like Ireland today, Norway's Department of Energy had become industry-captive but, sensing that the people of Norway were being set up to be robbed of their economic rent, the incoming Labour-led government decided to act in 1972. This was the pivotal moment for the Norwegians, changing them from a fishing economy with one oil field dominated by US 'big oil' to the Norway of today, which has a sovereign wealth fund three times the size of the Irish national debt. It was a close-run thing and it wasn't easy. Norway had just joined

NATO and facing down the big oil lobby with little evidence of the discoveries yet to come while lacking industry expertise meant risking radical departure from the culture that had dominated Norway's efforts since the early 1960s.

Unlike today's Irish Department of Communications, Energy and Natural Resources (DCENR), the Norwegians knew that a strategy is not merely a pricing policy but needed to be something much bigger, founded on a set of principles which became known as the 10 Commandments, chief among which was:

- that the development of offshore oil and gas should lead to a qualitatively better society

- that power could only be exercised through the establishment of a national oil exploration company (which became known as Statoil)

- that state governance and control must be secured, and that Norway should become independent in oil supply

Such are the crucial lessons from Norway that Aileen Canning has condensed 'The Norwegian Experience', by Oslo-based expert in economic history Helge Ryggvik, into a chapter in this book. The similarities to the current situation in Ireland are striking – you'd find it hard to separate DCENR press from the oil industry press, such is the groupthink that has developed from industry captivity, which is why the appendix contains quotes and media cuttings selected by Dominic Sherlock.

## CHALK AND CHEESE – KEATING AND BURKE

This book is dedicated to the memory of Justin Keating (7 January 1930–31 December 2009), a Labour politician, broadcaster, journalist, lecturer and veterinary surgeon. From March 1973 to July 1977, Justin Keating was Minister for Industry and Commerce. Learning from the Norwegian experience, he reserved 50 percent of all production of oil and gas for the Irish people. In addition to production sharing, royalties of between 8 and 16 percent were to be paid from sales revenues by exploration companies, and corporation tax was set at 50 percent.[2]

Thankfully we can delve past Justin Keating's pricing policy into the mind that drove it, into his grasp of economic rent and why it was important to stand up to big oil. There is a remarkable interview on the Own Our Oil website,[3] filmed just before he died by Richie O'Donnell, producer and director of IFTA award-winner *The Pipe*.

Months after becoming minister responsible for energy in 1987, Ray Burke TD (who would subsequently serve a jail sentence for tax offences and a betrayal of trust[4]) changed the rules of the game, after meeting oil industry reps, where he went unaccompanied by his civil servants. Production sharing and royalties were abolished. A few years later in 1992 the then minister for finance, Bertie Ahern TD, reduced corporation tax from 50 to 25 percent.

Ireland's offshore territory is remarkable in scale and estimated to contain 10 billion barrels[5] of oil equivalent (boe),[6] representing assets potentially worth one trillion US dollars at market prices at the time of writing.[7] The extent of the recoverable oil and gas cannot be ascertained and Ireland's vast offshore territory, representing 660,000 square kilometres, potentially holds multiple oil- and gas-bearing zones. The industry is quick to point out that only 6 percent is already reserved by licences and options available from the DCENR for a few thousand euros, but rarely admits to the fact that these are regarded as the 'sweet spots' based on available seismology.

Unpicking existing licence terms given the right to private property protected by the Constitution, would prove difficult, according to Diarmuid Rossa Phelan, SC. However, there may be scope to alter the taxation rules by tightening up on tax write-offs, and changing the rate of corporation tax itself as outlined in our chapter on taxation. Anna Hayes provides some indication of the economic transformation possible in one future, a future where the Irish strategy has changed and where the estimates provided by the DCENR come to pass. Senior Counsel Dermot Flanagan, an expert on infrastructural planning, outlines how the Irish model could be reformed into a cohesive, transparent and centralised system, de-risking it for industry players, removing the scope for political interference and providing the Irish people with greater clarity, consultation and control.

## THE JOC REPORT

Own Our Oil is not currently engaging with the political establishment, favouring direct engagement with the people first. This isn't just because of the long legacy of political incompetence, the captive nature of the DCENR and the whiff of corruption from Ray Burke's tenure but because there is no point – yet. A Joint Oireachtas Committee (JOC) reviewed the issue as recently as May 2012, coming nowhere near the 1972 radical pivot in Norway.[8]

The report was compiled by a cross-party committee comprised of fifteen TDs and six senators, none of whom had a background in the hydrocarbon industry.[9] It consulted nine agencies, and did not receive submissions from independent international industry experts in oil and gas. These agencies were the industry lobby group the Irish Offshore Operators Association (IOOA), civil servants from the DCENR itself, SIPTU, four local lobby groups (most of which are associated with the dispute in Mayo), Norway's ambassador and its deputy energy minister, and a representative from the Portuguese energy ministry.

The report made few of the recommendations outlined in this book, nor did it robustly challenge State strategy and policy. The report used consensus-forming language such as 'the

Minister should consider' throughout its recommendations. Pointedly, it specifically states that there should be no change to existing licence terms because of potential 'reputational damage'. This is opposite to the position taken by the Norwegians in 1972. Neither does it take account of the scope to tighten up on the tax write-offs associated with petroleum industry taxation.

In 2007, Green energy minister Eamon Ryan TD adjusted the rate of corporation tax of 25 percent, introduced by Bertie Ahern in 1992, by adding an additional tax rate of a potential extra 15 percent depending on the ratio of costs to profits associated with individual fields, known as Profit Resource Rent Tax (PRRT). Thanks largely to the input of people like Padhraig Campbell through the SIPTU submission, the committee recommended that this aspect of current taxation should be increased so that the total take moves to between 60 and 80 percent for medium to large commercial discoveries – but only for future licences. The JOC work was little reported and, ultimately, ignored. It was a year before Minister Pat Rabbitte responded publicly. The tenure of Minister Rabbitte, who campaigned in the early 1970s as a student activist for the nationalisation of the oil and gas industry, has proved to be a disappointment, content to tell the public that drilling holes costs the type of money we don't have. We didn't have much in the 1970s either, and neither did the Norwegians.

But the real reason the people have learned so little about the JOC report is because it did not advocate a new strategy, it merely suggested an incremental increase in pricing. It neither identified nor challenged the groupthink that dominates government policy. Of the twenty-one members of the committee there were no economists, geologists, accountants, or any member with a background in the hydrocarbon industry. The committee represented a cross-section of what constitutes the Irish Oireachtas: farmers, journalists, trade unionists and a postmaster. It sits comfortably into the pattern of defeatism outlined by history teacher Bill McSweeney in 'A History of Irish Servitude'.

## THE BIGGER PICTURE

The State has managed to break the Irish economy several times since the end of the Civil War in 1923, most recently by carrying forward the reckless economic policies enshrined in the 2007 manifestos of all political parties. The result is a massive national and personal debt overhang that is poised to weigh down the Irish economy for years to come while the educated young leave in large numbers. Wresting control once again of our offshore oil and gas is not merely a matter of reducing the national debt from its peak of 123 percent of debt to GDP, it has more profound implications in a world which is reaching resource limits and because it directly influences the strategic positioning of Ireland in the EU.

In his chapter entitled 'Strategic Considerations', Chris Sanders explores the bigger picture of limited natural resources, and why conventional economic thinking is dangerously wrong, since it assumes the continued availability of resources at affordable prices. Global population growth can be tracked directly with the availability of oil since it was first discovered in Pennsylvania. Hydrocarbons took over from coal to drive forward the Industrial Revolution, but look back into history as Professor Ian Morris has done in his bestselling book, *Why the West Rules – For Now*, and the cycle of development ceilings, followed by reversals, becomes clear, pock-marking the story of dynasties and empires from China to the West over millennia.

Technological breakthroughs that have increased worker productivity have dug us out of economic slumps over the past hundred years but cannot be taken as a given for the future. Neither can we foresee the X-factor of human invention and what technological leaps lie just around the corner. But what is clear is that the ownership and control of Ireland's offshore oil and gas endowment will be crucial, not just to improving national economics but potentially in revolutionising Irish society itself and positioning Ireland to become more independent, with the resources to exit the EU from a position of strength if the Irish people ever decided to do so.

Ireland, as the westernmost part of the EU, owns the largest proportion of its offshore waters and thus its offshore oil and gas endowments. There are rising concerns about security of gas, especially from Russia, together with declining production from the North Sea. Norway is expected to reach peak production in 2014.[10] A new frontier for European hydrocarbons must be found while, across the Atlantic, the US manufacturers are gaining competitive advantage from the US oil and gas revival.

Not only does Ireland enjoy a substantial proportion of the wind energy potential of Europe, but it may be sitting on a vast store of its future hydrocarbons. Without an alteration in Irish strategy preceded by a change in the groupthink which has dominated it, Irish hydrocarbons will be lost, like our fisheries. This must change.

## 'IF NOT ME, WHO?'

It doesn't take long to figure out what direction looks most sensible. One of our northwest Europe neighbours, Norway, cracked it in the early 1970s at a time when they knew little about offshore oil and gas exploration, industry monitoring and auditing, regulation, health and safety, refining distribution and retail products. But the Norwegians learned. They learned because they stitched into the licence agreements the requirement to pass the knowledge to Norway.

The Irish and Norwegian governments could come to an agreement much like the Norwegians did with private industry in the early 1970s. Norway, through Statoil, comes to the table with capital, know-how and expertise; Ireland comes with the licences and ownership of the oil and gas deposits. Terms are reached which provide the Norwegians with a rate of return appropriate to the risks being taken in Irish waters, tapering these down as discoveries are made, reducing the risk/reward relationship but still leaving an appropriate profit incentive.

Nominally, the maximum Irish tax take from a combination of corporation tax or RRPT is 40 percent. However, in practice the effective tax rate would be in the small single digits. Ireland will get nothing or next to nothing from existing licences. This must not continue. With excess capital chasing limited hydrocarbon resources globally, national governments have been tightening up on their take, raising this on average to between 70 and 80 percent.

Standard Chartered Bank, in *Global Crude Oil – A Compass for Fiscal Change,* reported that, globally, even with national governments taking between 70 and 80 percent of what is available, private companies are getting an internal rate of return on profits of between 20 and 30 percent per annum.[11] In undertaking its study, Standard Chartered analysts ran a model calculating rates of return sensitive to the level of corporation tax, production sharing and royalties associated with different regimes globally.

When the Irish regime was run through the model by one of the report authors contacted by me, it calculated that the average internal rate of return on profits which would be achieved under the Irish regime would be at least 46 percent per annum, doubling the level of profit every nineteen months! This ignores the scope for aggressive creative accounting on costs over twenty-five years. It is clear that the economic rent is flowing to shareholders of oil and gas companies and not to the owners of the assets – the Irish people.

The message from Helge Ryggvik is clear: the time to act is now, not later. He is unequivocal: don't give away too much in the first round, take time to set up a legal framework flexible enough for the State to tighten rules when conditions change, and strategic agreements and decisions made in the early phase in an oil region's development have decisive implications.

Ireland needs to radically revise its overall strategy, mimicking the steps taken in 1972 by Norway. This means beginning by establishing a set of principles much like the Norwegians did:

- A qualitatively better society

- A slow rate of extraction

- A target to become independent in oil and gas supply

- State governance and control of the sector

- Petroleum to be brought ashore

- Development of a domestic service industry

- Ownership and control of distribution

- Establishment of a national oil exploration company

Government ministers may duck behind Ireland's lack of financial resources, but as the Norwegians showed in 1972, financial resources are not the barrier. The barrier is a lack of ambition, savvy and courage.

You can help change that, first by engaging with the material in this book and by recommending it to your family and friends. Secondly you can join Own Our Oil, helping in the grassroots campaign to tell the story to audiences throughout the country, schools, communities and businesses using the videos and slides available on Ownouroil.ie. Thirdly, as the momentum of public opinion changes, you can add your voice to the rising chorus and say 'never again'. Never again must we give away our financial independence and natural resources to outsiders. That means not being passive, fulminating in frustration from the sidelines. It means campaigning. The founding slogan of Own Our Oil is 'If not me, who?' Once you've had a chance to read this book, have a think about that and get in touch.

Many thanks.

Eddie

## ABOUT THE AUTHOR

Eddie Hobbs is best known for writing and presenting RTE's 2005 blockbuster *Rip-Off Republic*, a hard-hitting polemic that closely examined how Ireland is run. He has also presented RTE's award-winning personal finance series *Show Me the Money*, entertainment programme *30 Things to Do With Your SSIA, The Consumer Show, My Civil War* and *The Give or Take Club*. He has written four bestsellers on finance and writes regularly for the *Sunday Independent* on matters related to economic management, competition, natural resources and personal finance. His business interests include clean energy, on-line marketing technologies and overseas property management. He is patron of The Jack & Jill Children's Foundation and is married with four children, living in County Kildare. In 2012 he co-founded Own Our Oil. He was made an honorary member of the Trinity Philosophical Society and UCD's Law Society in recognition of his public contributions

## NOTES

1.    50th Oilbarrel Conference sponsored by BDO, London, 16 February 2012

2.    www.siptu.ie/media/media_14689_en.pdf

3.    ownouroil.ie/keating

4.    www.rte.ie/news/2005/0124/59078-burker

5.    www.siptu.ie/media/media_14689_en.pdf

6.  www.investopedia.com/terms/b/barrelofoilequivalent.asp

7.  www.oil-price.net

8.  Joint Committee on Communications, Natural Resources and Agriculture Report Offshore Oil and Gas Exploration, May 2012.

9.  www.oireachtas.ie/parliament/media/Report-on-Offshore-Oil-and-Gas-Exploration.pdf

10. www.worldoil.com/Norway_oil_lobby_sees_investments_falling_after_2014_peak.html

11. Standard Chartered Bank, 'Global Crude Oil – A Compass for Fiscal Change,' 15 November 2012

# 2.

# WITHOUT A SHOT BEING FIRED

## Padhraig Campbell

In autumn 1997, an oil tanker, after taking four days to be loaded with 'light sweet' crude oil, left the licensed blocks in the Connemara Field, 100 miles west of Galway, to be refined outside this jurisdiction. The oil was produced by the Norwegian state-owned oil company Statoil after a drilling programme using the J. W. McLean oil rig. To date, this information has failed to fully emerge in the consciousness of the Petroleum Affairs Division (PAD) of the Department of Communications, Energy and Natural Resources, or the office of the present or former ministers.

Subsequent to this shipment, Statoil suddenly decided to cease drilling and test-production at the well, citing 'well difficulties'. With today's technology, this oil can be produced. In 2013, Natural Resources Minister Pat Rabbitte quipped in the Dáil that the only oil he knew about in Ireland was the spare pint of oil that he kept in the boot of his car. What follows is the story of how a nation gave away the wealth of future generations as a result of being canvassed, conned and tricked by the international oil companies.

## HOW IT BEGAN

The story of Ireland's oil and gas goes right back to the 1950s, when a company called Madonna Oil was registered in Dublin and obtained the rights to explore for oil and gas in Ireland from then Minister for Industry and Commerce Sean Lemass. Ambassador Oil were the first to drill, with their first wild-cat well at Rathmoylan, County Meath, using a land drilling rig operated by Loffland Brothers Drilling INC out of Tulsa, Oklahoma, on 15 August 1962. Their first hydrocarbon test was at a drilling operation near Granard, County Longford, in January 1963. Ambassador Oil drilled during the 1960s. By 1975, after the Kinsale Head discovery in 1970 by Marathon Oil, the lease was valued at £31 million. By

1977, the natural gas was valued at £700 million. Throughout the 1960s, there had been some oil and gas shows, and also dry wells in various parts of onshore Ireland, including Clare, Meath and Cavan.

The discovery of the Kinsale Head gas field, following on from wild-cat exploratory drilling by the Glomar North Sea drill ship by Marathon Oil, provided a huge economic boost to the Cork area. Other early drilling in the Celtic Sea included operations by the Norjahl semi-submersible rig from Norway. From 1970 to 1978, when the Kinsale Head gas field went into production, many Irish businesses either were formed or branched out into the gas service and support industry. The two Kinsale gas field permanent production platforms, Alpha and Bravo, were constructed in Cork Harbour and New Ross in Wexford. High-grade jobs were created onshore for welders, steel workers and crane operators, and in transport, engineering, fabrication, pipeline construction, administration, gas terminal construction, shipping and docks.

As well as onshore, many offshore jobs on semi-submersible drilling rigs, drill ships, supply ships and standby boats were negotiated for Irish-based workers by the then ITGWU (Irish Transport and General Workers Union), now SIPTU, with the oil companies, drilling companies and shipping companies. Throughout the mid to late 1970s, drilling took place at many locations in the Celtic Sea along Ireland's south coast, with various hydrocarbon 'shows' (oil and gas and discoveries).

The information, however, was controlled by the oil companies, which supplied their drilling reports, without any official department offshore monitoring, to the Energy Department. Policy developed on an ad hoc basis in terms of the State's approach to the development of Ireland's natural hydrocarbon resources. As a result of what was seen as a very poor deal for Ireland in terms of favourable tax and terms and conditions for the oil companies, there was mounting public pressure, spearheaded by the Resources Protection Campaign (RPC) from 1974 on. The aim of the RPC was to change the terms back in Ireland's favour. The RPC campaigners included present-day (2013) Minister for Communications, Energy and Natural Resources Pat Rabbitte, who was the driving force behind the RPC, and Tánaiste Eamon Gilmore, both of whom were previously in Official Sinn Féin, along with campaigner Noel Dowling, who went on to become the National Organiser for SIPTU trade union throughout the 2000s. Other members included Una Claffey and David Nelligan.

In 1975, as a result of this pressure, the then Energy Minister, Justin Keating, who was philosophically well disposed to Ireland securing a much greater return from the exploitation of her own oil and gas resources, and had a high regard for the Norwegian model of hydrocarbon development/taxation, introduced terms that included a 50 percent corporation tax on profits; a 'no cost to the state' 50 percent half-share in any discovery, and production-related royalties of between 8 and 16 percent. These changes were based on what became known as the 'Keating principles'.

With drilling and production activity in the Kinsale gas field and the drilling of the production wells from the Alpha and Bravo production platforms, many offshore jobs came on stream for roughnecks, roustabouts, derrick men, platform operators, maintenance roustabouts, riggers, crane operators, motormen, drillers, seamen, painters, scaffolders, divers, mechanics, subsea engineers, geologists, radio operators, engineers, mud loggers, cooks, stewards and medics. Many shore-based jobs in logistics, transport, supply, dock labour and administration were also created.

The Cork area developed a highly effective oil/gas service industry firmly based on the implicit understanding, particularly from Minister Justin Keating and his Department Secretary General, Joe Holloway, that the oil companies would use Irish-based jobs, goods and services. The main impetus for the genesis and development of an Irish-based rig and supply boat workforce (which in turn led to the development of an Irish offshore hydrocarbon services sector) came mainly from Cork branches 3 and 5 of the ITGWU.

Many highly skilled rig workers and seamen returned from overseas to work in Irish waters. Workers with transferrable skills, such as fishermen, mechanics and steel riggers, were trained up as roustabouts and roughnecks. Offshore supply companies, such as Doyle Offshore and Mainport in Cork, benefited from the job numbers negotiated by the union with the drilling companies and oil companies. Economic spin-offs to the Cork city and county area greatly increased from this developing, locally based industry.

After seismic mapping of large areas of the much deeper west coast of Ireland, the oil companies commenced their west coast drilling operations in 1977. The Zapata Lexington rig (owned by George Bush Senior) commenced drilling for the German company Deminex Oil west of Galway in the Porcupine Basin. Shows of natural gas after deep drilling on the Lexington raised much excitement among the American crew.

The time was not yet right for potential production of any commercial hydrocarbon discoveries. However, the oil industry plays the long game. These waters were much deeper than the waters of the south coast Celtic Sea. The average well depth was 10,000 feet under the sea-bed, which was often 1,500 to 2,000 feet below the ocean surface, and often 100 to 150 miles from shore. This deeper water posed significantly more challenges than shallower waters. The Lexington was serviced out of Galway Port, where the economic benefits from the drilling activity were very significant, with a large number of offshore and onshore jobs being created. There was great hope at the time in Galway, along with Foynes Port in Limerick and Fenit in Kerry (each involved in offshore service operations), that big economic benefits would come from the service activities related to the offshore oil and gas work.

The union structure in the ITGWU had offshore sections in the local branches of the union. As the drilling activities continued throughout the late 1970s and into the early 1980s, offshore firefighting and survival courses were set up by AnCO (subsequently FÁS), the state training agency, following lobbying and pressure from the union. In the absence of a full awareness by the State of the importance of developing a native oil/gas services industry, the ITGWU pushed hard to increase the number of Irish-based skilled oil-rig workers. Up to 900 Irish-based offshore workers did these courses, and they were mandatory for working offshore on rigs such as the Sedco 707, Sedneth 701, Pacnorse 1 drill-ship, Zapata Ugland, Western Pacesetter 2, Pentagone 84, Sedco 700 and the many other rigs and drill ships that drilled in the Atlantic from north of Donegal to south of Kerry in the Goban Spur.

There was also drilling in Dublin Bay using jack-up rigs (for water depths of up to four hundred feet) on the Zephyr 1 in 1977 and Pernod 81 in 1979. Although the semi-submersible rigs and drill-ships could drill in the deep waters of the western Atlantic in areas where seismic surveys had shown geological structures where oil and gas could potentially be found, the production technology to develop deep-water wells was still in the early stages of development.

## Irish Civil Servants Conned

Unlike other jurisdictions that have full-time oil specialists representing their country, there were no specialist officials representing the State in Irish waters. Irish rig workers who worked on the various offshore installations began to develop an awareness that the oil companies were well able to deal with any Department officials who occasionally visited the drilling operations offshore. The hard-bitten American oil veterans used to joke dismissively about the wide-eyed Department officials who were being shown around the drilling operations aboard whatever rig they were visiting, that 'they might as well have been looking up an elephant's arse' for all that they understood about the process!

This was in sharp contrast to other developed countries that had drilling operations in their waters, where experts representing these countries would be fully aware of the drilling process. At times of well-testing, Irish roughneck and floormen drill crews were often moved to other parts of the rig on maintenance work, while other crews were flown in as so-called 'specialists' to do the testing, even though Irish rig workers were well capable of handling the procedures involved.

During actual drilling on a rig (the drill-bit drilling), the well is lubricated and spun by a highly pressurised fluid pumped down the drill-pipe string (the full length of the drill pipe) called drilling 'mud'. This is a highly versatile liquid made from a cocktail of chemicals including barytes, bentonite, caustic and sometimes an oil-based additive. This drilling fluid lubricates, contains well pressure, keeps the unlined section of the open hole from collapsing and circulates the drill cuttings up to the shaker room inside the rig. In the shaker room, there are large mesh screens that clean the drilling mud and recirculate it back through the pumps and back down the drill string to the drill-bit drilling-down hole, thousands of feet below.

When the hole is cased with vertical steel piping (the process of running the vertical pipeline into the drilled well is called casing), the drilling mud acts to keep the pressure in the well and contain a 'kick' (blowout) prior to the Blow Out Preventer valve stack (BOP) shutting down the well and containing a blowout. Periodically, these rock cuttings are analysed by the geological mud logger to determine if there are any hydrocarbon 'shows'.

On occasion, Irish roughnecks who worked in the shaker rooms of some rigs became aware of a fairly common place practice of swapping cuttings that had 'shows' of oil or gas for inert cuttings kept in a plastic bucket, in the sample bags that were to be sent to the Department of Energy in Dublin for the State's own independent analysis. These samples were split into three approximately half-pound bags: one bag for the rig geology lab, one bag for the oil company, and sometimes a third, dud bag for the Irish Department of Energy PAD. This practice was subsequently pointed out to Department officials by Irish rig worker union representatives, but it was felt that this disturbing practice of deception was being ignored by the officials involved. Media organisations were also informed.

## Industry Lobby against Justin Keating's Terms

Amongst the oil companies operating in Irish water in the 1970s and into the 1980s, there was opposition to Keating's terms and conditions, particularly the half-share of any discovery that went to the State. The oil companies lobbied hard to amend the 1975 terms. In 1985, Dick Spring, as energy minister, introduced a sliding scale of royalties and state participation, where any discovery proved to be a marginal field. At the same time, Spring stuck to the Keating philosophy that Ireland should be the main beneficiary of any oil and gas found in Irish waters.

The oil companies in the early eighties claimed that the significant decrease in drilling activities and the decrease in licence applications was due to the Irish fiscal regime. There was some wild-cat exploratory drilling off the Waterford and south-west coasts, with rigs including the Diamond M. Hunter, the Ali Baba, the Chris Chenery and the Sedco 704, which made an oil discovery off Helvik Head in Waterford for a consortium that included Atlantic Resources. The reality was, however, that there was a major slump in oil/gas exploration and production worldwide. Crude oil was $7 a barrel, and along with the lack of proven deep-water production technology, exploration activities were being greatly curtailed in Irish waters by the oil companies during the 1980s.

In the early 1980s, there were drilling operations serviced out of Galway, Foynes, Fenit and Cork, although to a much lower extent. The Ocean Ranger rig was serviced out of Fenit in Kerry. The rig moved to Canadian waters and was drilling off Newfoundland. Tragically, the Ocean Ranger sank in a storm after the rig's ballast control room was damaged by salt water. All lives were lost. Many of the rig workers who died had previously worked with the Irish rig workers based around Fenit when the rig had drilled in Irish waters.

## DEPARTMENT OF ENERGY BECOMES INDUSTRY CAPTIVE

The civil servants in the Energy Department were blissfully unaware of the oil companies' game and some became 'persuaders' on behalf of the oil companies in trying to change the terms in Ireland so they were more favourable to the oil companies. There was a genuine belief amongst civil servants that special incentives were needed to attract the oil companies into Irish waters. This is exactly what the oil companies wanted them to think. This increased the subservient attitude of the State towards the oil companies and allowed the companies to plan for a long-term strategy in increasing their control over any further hydrocarbon discoveries in Irish waters or on land.

Ireland contains potentially thousands of oil- and gas-bearing zones in the 660,000 square kilometres of water that surrounds the island. This is ten times the size of the island of Ireland and nearly a quarter of the EU waters. The oil companies incrementally gained control of Ireland's hydrocarbon resources through a combination of exploration information control, hoodwinking of clueless civil servants, funding of political parties (mainly Fianna Fáil, but also Fine Gael) and intense lobbying of politicians and former ministers, two of whom were ultimately found to be corrupt. Because the oil industry have effectively dictated the terms under which they have operated in Ireland, this country stands to gain practically nothing from exploration, development and production of our natural hydrocarbon resources as legislation is presently constituted.

## THE 1980S, LOW OIL PRICES AND RAY BURKE

Into the late 1980s, drilling tapered off to just a few wells. The oil companies pressed home their advantage by pushing the myth that Ireland's hydrocarbon tax terms were the cause of this near-cessation of exploration activity in Irish waters. This was propaganda because, as mentioned above, the recession in the oil-exploration industry, coupled with the low price of crude oil and lack of effective deep-water production technology for the type of seas off Ireland's west coast, were the real reasons for the near-cessation.

The oil industry found a champion for their cause in Ray Burke TD, a senior Fianna Fáil politician. Burke, in opposition, lobbied hard in the Dáil for changes to Ireland's tax deal 'so as to encourage further drilling'. There were several alleged late-night visits to Taoiseach Charlie Haughey's Kerry island Inishvickillane by oil-company executives using a night-flying helicopter. Ray Burke, not long after becoming energy minister, at the end of September 1987, and after having met with the oil companies on his own and without any officials present, did away with Ireland's automatic right to *any* share of a hydrocarbon discovery. This was done without a Dáil vote, and against the advice of well-informed senior civil servants. The information concerning the island meeting between Haughey, Burke and the oil companies was relayed by staff at Cork Airport to rig workers who were flying out to south coast rigs.

Burke did away with royalties in their entirety. He introduced very generous tax write-offs. The balance swung completely in favour of the oil companies. But drilling didn't increase. Burke claimed that his changes would increase exploration in Irish waters. But this was not the case. He said that he had to 'incentivise' Ireland's oil and gas terms and conditions in favour of the oil companies. But all it did was open the path for the oil companies to control Ireland's hydrocarbon resources.

Worse was to come. In late 1992, Energy Minister Bobby Molloy and Finance Minister Bertie Ahern introduced even more favourable terms. The tax rate was halved to 25 percent – at that time the lowest rate in the world. This followed strong recommendations from government advisors, who themselves had been strongly lobbied by the oil industry to lower the rate to this level. Full 100 percent write-offs of *any* oil company costs going back twenty-five years, and long-term 'frontier licences', were introduced that could be held for fourteen years and could, with some minor works taking place, be extended to twenty years.

The capitulation to industry was complete: the 1992 terms had no commitment enshrined to use any Irish-based jobs, goods and services. The oil companies would become the owners of Irish oil and gas with the issuing of petroleum leases when a well was declared to be commercial. In 1993, frontier licences were issued; these included the licences for the Corrib Prospect off the north Mayo coast, issued to a consortium that included Enterprise Oil, Statoil and Saga.

Enterprise Oil was founded in 1983 in the UK after Margaret Thatcher de-nationalised British Gas. Her husband Denis was a significant shareholder. Enterprise arrived in Ireland in 1984, and even though they did not drill any exploration well until 1996, they were to the fore and at the centre of the plan to change Ireland's oil and gas terms in favour of the oil companies. They lobbied and networked with politicians, civil servants, editors, journalists, television and radio editors and producers, semi-state managers and local authority public servants and management throughout the State.

## The 1990s, Enterprise Oil, Corrib and Dublin Bay

Apart from some low-level drilling operations in 1994, there was little activity in Irish waters. At this stage, unionised Irish rig workers, now in the successor union to the ITGWU, SIPTU, organised for a National Offshore Committee to prepare for an increase in drilling in Irish waters. Many Irish rig workers worked on drilling operations worldwide when there was little activity in Irish waters. Those who worked in the UK North Sea sector often witnessed the standing joke on rigs and production platforms, and in the bars of Aberdeen in Scotland, that the oil companies had gained control of Ireland's oil and gas resources by paying off the debts of the ruling party, Fianna Fáil, in the early 1990s!

It was felt by the union that the plunder of Ireland's resources was about to begin, and it was vital to continue to have Irish-based rig workers aboard the rigs. Prior to Enterprise Oil's plan to drill at the Corrib Prospect, articles began to appear in Irish newspapers that Irish rig workers were demanding outrageous pay rates. The rates quoted were completely exaggerated and were challenged by SIPTU, who supplied the media with the correct pay rates agreed with the drilling companies who owned the rigs that were contracted to the oil companies. These agreements went right back to early 1970s for rigs operating in Irish waters. Enterprise threatened to service their operations out of Ayr on the west coast in Scotland instead of Foynes in Limerick.

To his credit, Energy Minister Emmet Stagg blocked this move, saying that Enterprise could not outsource service operations out of the State and write off the huge costs involved, which would be spent outside the jurisdiction. Enterprise Oil relented, and reluctantly agreed to allow a negotiated number of Irish rig workers on the Petrolia drilling rig. It was felt by Irish rig workers that the oil companies did not want a knowledgeable presence on rigs operating in Irish waters. Irish rig workers always challenged the description of so called 'dry holes' (i.e. no oil or gas shows) on many wells drilled in Irish waters. Their presence aboard rigs challenged this deception, put out by some oil companies.

Enterprise Oil 'spudded in' (sank drill pipes in specific locations to be drilled) and commenced drilling at Corrib in 1996, serviced out of Foynes. After a number of months of drilling on the Petrolia rig, and as the well reached target depth, Irish workers got word 'to beach' (oil company slang for 'ashore': if a rig worker is 'on the beach', he is ashore) that there had been a very strong gas 'kick' (a near-blowout) after hitting a massive reservoir of natural gas. The situation was tense aboard, but the kick was eventually contained. Drilling stopped, and Enterprise declared that operations would cease due to 'technical difficulties'. Operations finished, and the rig moved off location. Two years later, in 1998, Enterprise returned with the Sedco 711, a more suitable rig for a field as big as Corrib.

The year 1997 saw drilling activities in the Porcupine Basin, Connemara Field, west of Galway. Rigs included Transocean Sedco, Sovereign Explorer and the J. W. McLean rig, drilling for Norway's Statoil. The oil produced at this well was taken out of the jurisdiction to be refined: this fact seemed to be lost on the department and the minister's office. Media reports about the Connemara Field oil flow into the production tanker failed to grasp the significance of the scale involved, as did the PAD. Of course they had the detailed well reports from Statoil, but the fact that oil had been produced in Irish waters has never featured in subsequent Ministers' analysis (or lack thereof!) of the first commercial oil shipment from Irish waters. Presumably PAD examined the reports, but the significance of filling a tanker with crude oil to be refined outside the jurisdiction appeared to be lost on them.

The following year saw drilling off Dublin Bay by Enterprise Oil, who managed to operate without Irish-based rig workers aboard. The mistake SIPTU made was to fall for an assurance from Enterprise Oil that the drilling operation was only going to be a two-week token operation – to retain the exploration licence. Irish rig workers had warned senior SIPTU officials about the danger of the precedent of no Irish aboard being set. The rig was there for three months. This emboldened Enterprise Oil to challenge the union for their upcoming return to Corrib on the west coast.

Enterprise, who managed to gain a very significant number of licences in Irish waters, were encouraged when their favourite political party, Fianna Fáil, returned to power in 1997, and blocked the hiring of Irish rig workers on the Sedco 711, even though there was the legitimate agreed presence of Irish rig workers on rigs for many years, and Sedco had hired many Irish rig workers over the years. There were protests at Foynes Port, and at Shannon Airport, where the non-Irish-based rig workers were being flown in from Aberdeen to take the local jobs, at Enterprise Oil's Dublin offices, at the Leeson Street offices of the Department of the Marine and Natural Resources, and at Statoil's offices in Dublin.

Enterprise Oil, after engineering the situation they wanted, was allowed to move their service operations to Ayr in Scotland. Irish rig workers knew that they were in a 'catch 22' situation. The rig workers had to protest about the tearing up of twenty-seven years of written agreements and long-standing custom and practice arrangements. Enterprise Oil wanted to break the custom and practice of the drilling companies using highly experienced rig workers when they were operating in Irish waters. This practice was underwritten by written agreements on job-manning levels, pay rates, terms and conditions, and so on. Enterprise did not want the knowledgeable presence of Irish-based rig workers on any rigs they hired in Irish waters. They also instructed the drilling company Transocean Seco not to hire Irish-based unionised rig workers.

Enterprise engineered a confrontation at Foynes Harbour, where Irish-based rig workers had gathered to protest at the loading of a rig-supply boat with casing pipe. They were picketing the supply boat because of Enterprise blocking their agreed right to work. They also knew that they would be used as Enterprise's excuse to leave Irish waters. The particular diameter of the casing pipe that Enterprise was attempting to load onto the supply boat was to be used much later in the drilling operation and was only to be loaded onboard as a 'setup' to start a confrontation. This was the excuse for Enterprise to leave Foynes and set up their drilling operations in Ayr in Scotland – which was what they had wanted to do all along.

A TnaG (now TG4) camera crew established in 1998 that some senior Enterprise Oil personnel were involved in development work making Ayr a highly lucrative oil and gas service port, servicing the drilling operations on the western side of Scotland, where two hydrocarbon discoveries were made at the Schellion and Fonievan fields. Many established servicing operations were being expanded from Aberdeen on Scotland's east coast to Ayr for drilling activities on Scotland's west coast. The Irish State allowed for the precedent to be set that drilling operations in Irish waters were serviced from a port outside the jurisdiction.

Ayr is set to become the main base for the service industries and companies involved in drilling operations in the Atlantic Margin, stretching beyond the north-west of Scotland to below Ireland's south-west coast. The massive spend on the outsourced service operations could be written off against future Irish tax. The oil and gas service industry became a huge earner for Scotland, with spin-offs from drilling and production activities in the North Sea.

The economic lunacy of service operations being carried out in another country for drilling in Irish waters had begun. This was allowed by Fianna Fáil minister Michael Woods, who said he had no power to stop either Enterprise from using ports outside the jurisdiction or the non-hiring of Irish-based rig workers, because of EU law. However, the Dutch, French, UK, Spanish and other EU states that had drilling operations in their waters would *not* allow service operations for these operations from ports outside their waters.

Prior to returning with the Sedco 711 to drill so-called 'appraisal' wells in the Corrib field in 1998 (these wells eventually became production wells – their true purpose all along), Enterprise and the Corrib North consortium knew early on, from discovery in 1996, that this gas field was massive. Oil consultants Wood McKenzie, in a report brought out in 1998 ('Corrib North: The End of the Rainbow'), discussed the possibility of the size of Corrib and surrounding areas being up to 7 trillion cubic feet of gas (7 tcf). Later on, Enterprise claimed that Corrib contained less than 1 tcf of gas. The Department accepted these estimates, but Irish rig workers had no faith in the fairly limited information supplied to the State by the oil companies.

An Oil and Gas Economic Framework Group was set up by Minister Woods in the late 1990s (mainly due to media pressure from Irish-based rig workers) to see how Ireland could benefit more in terms of jobs, goods and services from hydrocarbon-related activities. The Framework Group consisted of PAD civil servants, Forbairt, IOOA (Irish Offshore Operators Association), ICTU, oil company reps, labour agencies and shipping companies, and representatives from SIPTU's national offshore committee. Enterprise Oil stayed away from the Framework Group because of SIPTU's presence. Enterprise eventually took part in the Framework Group. However, the Framework Group was abandoned when Frank Fahey became minister.

After much comment and media engagement by SIPTU's national offshore committee members about outsourcing jobs, goods and servicing operations out of the State, Enterprise began to use the harbour at Killybegs in Donegal in a limited basis. Their drilling at the Dooish Prospect off Donegal attracted a significant amount of interest due in part to very favourable speculation about a major hydrocarbon discovery at the location. The seismic surveys of this area indicated huge potential. The water was very deep but the technology was now available for extraction of any oil or gas found, and the field was declared to be commercial.

There was an off-the-cuff remark in Irish by Minister for the Marine Frank Fahey on

TG4 that if Dooish proved to be commercial, the State might revisit the terms. SIPTU welcomed this in an *Irish Times* article. There was uproar from the oil companies, who threatened that all offshore drilling activity would cease in Irish waters if there were any changes in Ireland's oil and gas terms. Top-level contacts were made from the Taoiseach's office to SIPTU in an effort to stop the challenges being made by the national offshore committee of the union about the free rein the oil companies had in Irish waters. Only the underdeveloped African state of Cameroon had a lower hydrocarbon tax rate.

The naivety still shown by successive ministers and their advisers to the tactics of the oil companies is remarkable, reinforcing perception of industry captivity. The oil companies have held back, and have given the impression that they are not too interested, safe in the knowledge that to date there has been no real effort to change Ireland's oil and gas terms and conditions by successive governments.

## Corrib Goes Commercial

Enterprise Oil took a number of years to declare Corrib commercial. Then the focus shifted to how the raw gas would be cleaned and processed. Various sites were investigated in the north Mayo area. At the start, this was seen by locals and some politicians as a great potential economic boost to the area. But less innocent local observers were under no illusions as to how transient this 'economic boost' would be, and were fully aware of the huge potential for danger and environmental hazard such an inland processing plant and production terminal would pose.

Enterprise was challenged at various PR events and conferences by local activists and Irish rig workers. Fianna Fáil minister Fahey gave various leases, authorisations, foreshore licences and other permissions over a period of time to enable the development strategy of the Corrib Consortium (consisting of Enterprise Oil, Statoil, Saga and Marathon). A six-hundred-acre forest at Bellanaboy in north Mayo was sold to the Corrib Consortium by Coillte, the State forestry agency, for an undisclosed nominal sum in 1999, and Enterprise applied for planning permission for a processing plant in November 2000. The location of this forest was crucial to the plans of Enterprise and her partners. The initial size of the processing plant was eighty acres; this could be expanded as more gas discoveries were made along Ireland's west coast, using the Corrib sub-sea manifold (an infrastructure hub on the seabed capable of connecting to a large number of raw gas upstream production pipelines) to connect to; this would then be added to the raw high-pressure gas coming ashore via one pipeline to start with, and then more upstream pipes as gas volumes increased.

The expanding production processing plant would give the Corrib Consortium monopoly status in the cleaning and processing of raw gas from west coast waters. Mayo County

Council had rapidly given permission for the project. This was subsequently appealed to An Bord Pleanála, who, after a long oral hearing, overturned the original Mayo County Council planning permission. Kevin Moore, the ABP Inspector, had said in his report to the board that this was 'the wrong project in the wrong place'. The oral hearings took place at the Downhill Hotel in Ballina in Mayo.

The way the cars were parked in the hotel car park, and the lunch arrangements, spoke volumes. The older cars, working jeeps, vans and the odd banger belonging to local inhabitants of Erris tended to be parked in one area of the car park while the nearly new Passats, Mondeos, Vectras and Avensises belonging to the middle management Mayo County Council officials were parked with the oil company 'big boys' and sharp-suited legal eagles with their top-of-the-range Mercs, BMWs and the odd Lexus! When the hearings used to break for lunch, the locals went to the bar for bar food, sandwiches, tea, coffee and the odd pint, while council officials went to dine in gourmet style with the oil company big boys and the legal eagles in a private dining room. Of course the oil companies could write off the cost of their lavish largesse because *all* 'costs', going back twenty-five years, can be written off under Ahern's 1992 tax deal, including entertainment costs, grants to Belmullet Golf Club, Belmullet GAA pitch development, scholarship grants, alcohol gifts, college bursaries to selected families in the Erris area, and so on.

## SHELL ARRIVES

Shell Oil had bought out the share capital of Enterprise Oil (renamed Enterprise Energy Ireland Ltd – very similar to the 'double Irish' company set up in the Bahamas in 1996 called Enterprise Energy Ireland Inc) in a hostile takeover bid in 2002. Enterprise had prospects in the UK North Sea, Norway, Newfoundland, Vietnam and Ireland. The favourable licensing options that Enterprise had acquired in Ireland were very attractive for Shell's Atlantic Margin strategy. Shell took over as operator of the Corrib project with 46 percent of the consortium. Pressure mounted on An Bord Pleanála (APB) from Taoiseach Bertie Ahern for ABP to reverse its decision following a meeting he had with top management of Shell, including Shell president Tom Botts, on 19 September 2003.

That same day, there was a devastating landslide from Dooncarton hill onto the village of Pullatomas near Bellanaboy. This massive landslide came tearing down the side of the hill and devastated large tracts of land along one of the original proposed routes for the ten kilometre land-based section of the raw-gas pipeline.

After a second ABP oral hearing in Ballina, permission was given to go ahead with the production processing plant at Bellanaboy. Compulsory Acquisition Orders (CAOs) were put in place by the Department to lay the raw-gas pipeline through lands of people who were not agreeable to it. This was the first time in Ireland that the State used CAOs on behalf of a private company. There was ongoing opposition to these forced measures against the local community of the Rossport area, through which a section of the high-pressure raw gas pipe was intended to be laid by Shell. The presence of soft bog as part of this route added to local fears. The weight of the heavy-wall twenty-inch pipe, along with the proposed 340 bar untreated gas pressure, potentially increasing the danger of sinking in the bog, terrified locals. Nearly two-ton-per-square-inch pressure in a pipeline buried little more than a metre under the soft bog! The dangers of gas under very high pressure escaping from a ruptured pipe are devastating, with explosion being the immediate danger.

In 2001, *Magill* magazine ran a cover story, written by investigative journalist Sandra Mara, entitled 'How the West Was Blown'. At this stage, it had become apparent to some thinking journalists just how a combination of possible corruption and definite stupidity had given the oil companies the best deal in the world.

Allied to a growing questioning of the earlier dodgy Corrib deals, there was awareness rising nationally as to just how bad the oil and gas terms were for the Irish people. The Department and politicians trotted out the same old line as to how the terms were needed to attract the oil companies into Irish waters. This minimalist approach has been the hallmark of the PAD over the years. The oil companies have effectively run rings around the civil servants, politicians and their PR advisers. State agencies, government departments, some semi-state companies, public bodies, planning authorities, local authorities, law enforcement agencies, the naval service, and so on have been ordered by successive administrations to fully enable the activities of the oil companies.

Shell's attitude to the protesters hardened, and in 2005, after delays and blockades, injunctions were served on five local men chosen by Shell as being principal protesters. When these men – Willie Corduff, Brendan Philbin, Philip McGrath, Vincent McGrath and Micheal O Seighin – refused to be bound by the injunctions, they were taken to the High Court in Dublin and were imprisoned in Cloverhill Prison in Dublin for contempt of court. The plant site at Bellanaboy was blocked by supporters of the imprisoned men, who became known as the 'Rossport 5'. There were large-scale protest marches around the country, with thousands of people from all walks of life angered by the way that the five were being treated by the State, which was seen to be serving the interests of a multinational giant which was getting Ireland's Corrib gas with very little in return for the country, and allowing the imposition of a potentially highly experimental production plant in the men's local area.

The 'Free the Rossport 5' campaign struck a chord with people. Shell did not realise the extent of the sense of outrage to the men's imprisonment and the folk memory of landlordism and evictions in the Mayo of Michael Davitt in the late nineteenth century. The issue of their imprisonment stayed in the media. Independent TD Jerry Cowley championed the cause of the Rossport 5, and Fine Gael TD Michael Ring spoke at rallies in support of them. The other Fine Gael TD (and subsequent Taoiseach) proposed that concerned citizens from the Rossport area be given the option to move en masse to a housing estate in Castlebar in Mayo. Many observers felt that this was a puzzling proposal, to say the least!

Shell held tight on the injunctions, in spite of massive public pressure. Since Statoil held 36 percent of Corrib, Jerry Cowley and relatives of the Rossport 5 flew to Norway to inform the Norwegian people and their political representatives as to what the real situation was in Mayo, and about the unjust imprisonment of the men. There was public outcry in Norway about Statoil's role in the debacle. The visit was very effective. Within a couple of days of the return of the Rossport delegation to Ireland, a Statoil vice president came to Dublin and convened a number of urgent meetings. After ninety-four days in prison, the Rossport 5 were released after Shell dropped their injunction. There were scenes of jubilation outside the Four Courts among supporters of the men.

In 2005, the Centre for Public Inquiry (CPI), a non-governmental organisation, chaired by retired Judge Fergus Flood (of the Flood Tribunal), which was established to investigate scandals in Irish public life, issued a report entitled 'The Great Corrib Gas Controversy'. The report gave the background to the oil companies' role in Ireland and outlined the main factors in how the Corrib gas controversy came about. The report examined the roles of Ray Burke, Bertie Ahern and others in giving special deals to the oil companies. The Corrib Report also had a thoroughly researched study from a leading international pipeline expert, Richard Kuprewicz of Accufacts Inc, which found that the consortium's pipeline plans were hazardous in the extreme. Official Ireland moved quickly. The CPI was becoming a threat to the controversial dealings at the top levels in Irish society. Extreme pressure was exerted on Atlantic Philanthropies, founded by altruistic billionaire Chuck Feeney, to cease its funding of CPI. The pressure finally worked; CPI could not survive without long-term financial support to do their essential work.

With a change of management in Shell, they increased the pressure on the State to remove the ongoing protests from Bellanaboy and reopen the plant site. Shell's construction contractor, Roadbridge, had brought a large number of workers into the area, but they were unable to get past the blockade. A large force of Gardaí arrived in the Bellanaboy/Glenamoy area, and the Roadbridge workers were forced through the protesters and into the plant site. The protests continued early every morning and throughout each day, with a constant presence of local people and some supporters from all over Ireland and abroad.

At first, the protesters, who each morning staged peaceful marches and occasional sit-down protests, were moved away from Roadbridge workers driving to the plant site entrance by a large force of Gardaí. However, as time went by, the level of force used by the Gardaí increased, with protesters being thrown into ditches, forcibly removed from the road, and in some cases arrested. Events finally culminated in 2006 in a baton charge on protesters who were staging a sit-down protest. Protests and arrests continued – and still continue – in the

Rossport, Bellanaboy, Pullathomas, Glengad and Aghoose areas, which cover the district around the production plant, various proposed pipeline routes, the shore gas reception depressurisation valves at the Broadhaven Bay beach at Glengad, and the construction site entrance for the eventual proposed five kilometre tunnel under Sruwaddacon estuary.

Television images of the 2006 baton charge were beamed around the world, and there was disquiet in Norway because of Statoil's participation in the Corrib project. Shell's image had been tarnished due to their involvement in the awful controversy in Nigeria concerning the executions by the military of human rights activist Ken Saro-Wiwa and eight others who had challenged Shell's activities, and the massive pollution associated with oil produced in the Ogoniland region of Nigeria.[1] Also, there had been a huge public environmental back-lash against Shell with the attempted scuppering of the decommissioned Brent Spar oil pro-duction platform in the Atlantic Ocean. It was felt in Norway that Statoil was disgracing itself due to their involvement in the Corrib project.

## THE LONG GAME

The long-term strategy of the oil industry and the European Union energy policymakers was predicated on a huge expansion of gas production in Irish waters. Other oil companies had intended to use the Corrib offshore infrastructure and the production plant to pump any commercial gas discovery ashore, for the consortium to clean and sell on the gas through the Bord Gáis lower-pressure gas pipeline that leaves the plant and connects to the gas ring main grid near Galway.

The Irish State has two gas interconnectors linked to Scotland from County Louth. Gas is pumped into the Irish gas grid from Moffatt in Scotland. A former board member of Bord Gáis, An Taisce solicitor Greg Casey, told a Ken Saro-Wiwa lecture in Erris organised by the Shell2Sea organisation in 2006 that the second interconnector was operating at a low capacity and that its eventual *real* purpose was to reverse the flow of gas *out* of Ireland into Scotland and the UK gas grid, and on into the EU gas grid, in order to cut EU dependen-cy on gas from non-EU countries, including Russia, Algeria and Norway. Ireland will buy the gas that it needs at full market price, and the rest will be exported out of the State, with min-imal benefit for the Irish people as things stand. The EU then has its security of supply from an EU source via the UK.

Another part of the long-term strategy of the oil companies in Ireland is the low uptake (and in some cases no uptake) by the major companies in the various licensing rounds that occurred throughout the 2000s. This, coupled with little drilling activity, creates a fear-based dependency within the Department and with ministerial advisors, and an obsession by the PAD about so-called 'security of supply' (a misnomer if ever there was one, due to the fact that the oil companies get to own the hydrocarbon resource when they are awarded a petroleum lease). Because the oil companies will own and control the product, it might as well be coming from Venezuela, even though the oil and gas will be produced in Irish waters.

The value-added, economic spin-offs from the jobs, goods and services that come from oil and gas exploration and production activities in Ireland has hardly featured in the light-touch approach of the PAD in their dealings with the oil companies operating in the Irish offshore. The companies can outsource as much of their spend outside the jurisdiction as they wish, and still write off 100 percent of their costs against their tax on profits under Bertie Ahern's 1992 tax deal. This is economic lunacy.

After a private members' Dáil motion in 2006 by Mayo TD Dr Jerry Cowley to change the rotten 1992 deal – a motion which was defeated – Energy Minister Noel Dempsey, under pressure from Opposition deputies, commissioned a study from research company Indecon. Indecon's findings startled some thinking politicians and were quietly shelved. However, financial journalist Colm Rapple broke the story with a leaked copy of the Indecon report. This had three effects.

Firstly, it stopped a proposed reduction of the lowest hydrocarbon tax rate of 25 percent down to an outrageous 12.5 percent rate under a callow commitment by the government to oil company representatives. When the contents of the Indecon Report were released, even Fianna Fáil knew that they couldn't go to the 12.5 percent rate. Secondly, the report gave some hint of what the oil companies knew themselves for years about the potential extent of what hydrocarbon potential there was in Irish waters. The Indecon report estimated that there was ten billion barrels of oil and gas equivalent off Ireland's west coast alone. It recommended an increase in Ireland's hydrocarbon tax rate to 45 percent and strongly recommended a reduction in the length of Frontier Licences, down from the fourteen years that was part of the 1992 terms and conditions. The report was conservative in its scope and recommendations, but it recognised the ludicrous nature of the way that Ireland dealt with the oil companies. In one respect, it was recognition of the colonial-style way in which the administration in Ireland engaged with multinational transnational companies.

In 2007, Eamon Ryan became minister in charge of natural resources. He made limited amendments to the 1992 deal based on Indecon's recommendations, with the introduction of a 'rent tax' of 15 percent on top of the 25 percent for very large discoveries. The problem is that the oil companies control the information, and only they will know the real extent of any oil or gas discovery in Irish waters or on land. Irish geologists, who now find it very hard to secure work in Irish waters, have drawn attention to how potentially false geological readings could be sent via closed so-called 'real-time' intranet connections to the Energy Department. Other changes included the minor reduction in the length of the term of Frontier Licences, down to ten years. Ryan's changes were disappointing but nevertheless were achieved in the face of strong opposition to significant changes to the terms from Fianna Fáil and some civil servants.

In 2008, the massive *Solitaire* pipe-laying ship arrived in the waters off Broadhaven Bay in Erris in north Mayo to lay the upstream production raw-gas pipeline from the beach reception valve pads to the Corrib sub-sea manifold seventy-five kilometres offshore. Local fishermen opposed the laying of the pipe directly in their lobster- and crab-fishing grounds. However, one by one they were induced to drop their protests, with payments being made to them. Only a handful remained determined to protect their livelihoods and businesses from the massive disruption that the laying of the pipe would cause.

## Attempt to Crush Local Resistance

The natural leader of the local fishermen was Pat 'The Chief' O'Donnell from Porturlin on the north Mayo coast. A lifelong fisherman from a local fishing family, he also ran a crab-meat processing plant that produced top-quality product for the Irish and international market, as well as providing much-needed employment in the area. Pat was a long-standing campaigner against the Corrib plant and raw-gas pipeline as it was presently constituted. He knew the potential dangers from the experimental system that the consortium were intending to put in place, both at sea and on land.

The pristine clean waters of the sea around Broadhaven Bay were in danger from potential pollutants from the processing of the raw gas at the production plant. The Chief took his half-decker fishing boat to keep the *Solitaire* from entering the area where there were up to eight hundred lobster and crab pots laid. He was boarded by Water Unit Gardaí from high-powered Garda and Naval Service rigid inflatable boats (RIBs). Again, all agencies of the State were being put at the disposal of the oil industry, above the interests of local inhabitants. The Chief was arrested many times at his place of work and appeared many times, with fellow Corrib protesters, in the District Court, the Circuit Court and the High Court. The *Solitaire* left Irish waters after failing to lay the upstream pipeline due to equipment failure. Maura Harrington, a local national school principal and long-time campaigner for the protection of the Erris area, ended her hunger strike when the *Solitaire* left Irish waters. The following year, the *Solitaire* returned. Environmental protesters from the Rossport Solidarity Camp and the Shell2Sea Campaign were roughed up on many occasions by security personnel working for Shell and the consortium, on land and on sea, as they protested against the laying of the pipe and the construction of the depressurising plant.

On 11 June 2009, while the Chief was in his boat with a fellow fisherman keeping a watch on where his pots had been laid, a number of armed masked men forcibly boarded his fishing boat from a large high-speed RIB and sank the boat. Pat and his colleague, both unable to swim, were left hanging on to a poorly inflated life raft. There was very little official investigation into the sinking.

The full weight of the law was being used to crush dissent, but the protests continue to the present day, with the Rossport Solidarity Camp, Shell2Sea, Pobal Chill Chomáin (a local community group) and Pobal Le Chéile (a group comprising concerned local businesses who protest against the negative impacts of the Corrib Project) being the main protest groups against the project as it is presently constituted.

Attempts, of sorts, to broker some kind of solution were made by then minister Eamon Ryan and Minister for the Gaeltacht and Community Affairs Eamon O Cuiv – without much success. After different routes being considered by the consortium for the raw-gas pipeline to the inland production plant, a plan for a five kilometre tunnel under the Sruwaddacon estuary was decided upon. This was the real agenda coming to fruition, as this tunnel would have the capacity for up to five upstream pipelines eventually, as more and more gas discoveries were connected to the unused connectors on the Corrib sub-sea manifold and pumped ashore to the expanding production-plant colossus.

As the Celtic Tiger crashed and the country started to plunge into recession, there was a small but growing awareness amongst free-thinking individuals of the inexplicable madness of Ireland going with the begging bowl to the IMF and the ECB while at the same time giving away potentially hundreds of billions of euro worth of oil and gas reserves to the oil companies.

## SIPTU's Report

In 2011, an Oil and Gas Research Group was set up under the auspices of SIPTU; the group was chaired by SIPTU president Jack O'Connor. The group comprised of economists, a sociologist, union officials, former oil-rig workers, environmentalists and a PhD candidate in oil and gas taxation regimes worldwide. Its report, launched in 2012, 'Optimising Ireland's Oil and Gas Resources', gave alternative taxation and development arrangements that could be used in Ireland, as well as showing how the oil companies were not giving the full picture in terms of past hydrocarbon discoveries and potential discoveries in Irish waters.[2]

Following on from the publication of the SIPTU report, Sinn Féin moved a Private Members Bill to change Ireland's hydrocarbon corporate tax rate to 51 percent and rebalance the terms and conditions back in Ireland's favour. This was defeated in the Dáil by the government parties. Minister Pat Rabbitte agreed to a proposal from Eamon O Cuiv to an examination of Ireland's oil and gas policies by the Oireachtas Joint Energy and Natural Resources Committee. After hearing submissions from the oil companies (represented by the Irish Offshore Operators Association, IOOA), SIPTU, civil servants, Pobal Chill Chomáin, Pobal Le Chéile, Mayo 'Pro Gas', Shell2Sea, the Norwegian Ambassador, the Norwegian Deputy Energy Minister, representatives from the Portuguese Energy Ministry and other individuals, the Oireachtas Committee recommended a tougher regime in Ireland in terms of rebalancing the massive benefits back in Ireland's favour.

The Committee suggested an 80 percent tax rate in the case of major hydrocarbon discoveries.[3] It recommended as vital more use of Irish-based jobs, goods and services in relation to the value-added economic spin-offs connected to hydrocarbon-based activities. The Committee also recommended much more involvement of local communities in decision-making where there was to be major oil- and gas-related infrastructural projects. The politicians on the Oireachtas Committee realised, much to the opposition of civil servants, and major protestations from the IOOA, that Ireland was poorly served by those who had made deals with the oil companies down through the years, with the notable exception of minister Justin Keating and his dedicated policy advisors.

In 2012, Dublin Shell2Sea published 'Liquid Assets', which gathered from many sources very significant information about oil and gas reserves in Ireland. The main sources of information in this well-researched document came from oil-industry analysis and their own private research into the undisclosed hydrocarbon prospects and potential discoveries in Irish waters and on land.

The tunnel-boring operation began tunnelling operations at Aghoose beside Sruwaddacon, opposite Rossport, in 2013. The German-built Tunnel Boring Machine (TBM) was called Finnoula, named after one of the Children of Lir. According to legend, the Children of Lir were turned into swans by a wicked stepmother, and the swans lived on Sruwaddacon for three hundred years. This is seen as mythological blasphemy by some, who see this estuary as a sacred place. Short-term construction jobs were created in the construction operations, associated with the Corrib project, scattered around Bellanaboy, Rossport, Glengad, Bangor and Aghoose.

The visionary idealists who established the First Dáil of the Irish Republic published the Democratic Programme of the First Dáil. That inspiring Programme declared the ownership of Ireland for the people of Ireland. They declared 'that the Nation's sovereignty extends not only to all men and women of the Nation, but to all its material possessions, the Nation's soil and all its resources, all the wealth and all the wealth-producing processes within the Nation'. They also affirmed in the Programme: 'It shall be our duty to promote the development of the Nation's resources, to increase the productivity of its soil, to exploit its mineral deposits, peat bogs and fisheries, its waterways and harbours, in the interests and for the benefit of the Irish people.'

In the 1937 Irish Constitution, Bunracht na hÉireann, Article 10 states that: 'All natural resources, including the air and all forms of potential energy, within the jurisdiction of the parliament and Government established by this Constitution, and all royalties and franchises within that jurisdiction, belong to the State subject to all estates and interests therein for the time being lawfully vested in any person or body.'

Look beyond the Constitution and ask, what has been the behaviour of the State? The giveaway of the birthright of future generations must surely be the biggest scandal of all, potentially dwarfing, many times over, the capitulation to the banks and the EU in 2010. In the whole history of Ireland's oil and gas story, isn't it fairly clear that the oil companies have set the agenda and dictated the terms for their activities in Ireland?

Drawing on the Norwegian experience outlined elsewhere in this book, it was only Labour minister Justin Keating TD and his advisors in 1975 who struck the right risk/reward balance between the Irish people and the oil companies. This was dismantled in 1988 by Energy Minister Ray Burke and was improved further in favour of the oil companies by Energy Minister Bobby Molloy and Finance Minister Bertie Ahern in 1992. Ray Burke's role as energy minister has never been investigated, even though he was found to be corrupt by various Tribunals of Inquiry into his role and activities in his other ministries.

What we are left with is merely a pricing policy – one of the world's most generous. There is clearly no detailed strategy to develop Ireland's hydrocarbon potential, nor a set of principles such as those that drove Norway's success from the early 1970s. The Irish people are at a huge loss from the present debacle – a series of disconnected, ad hoc decisions made across government administrations and dictated by a captive civil service elite from the Department of Finance to the PAD.

Future generations are to be robbed of the wealth of a nation in terms of the potential loss of benefits from Ireland's oil and gas resources. Other natural resources, including water, wind and hydro energy, and forestry, all appear assembled for the stocks, to be sold off to some large corporation for next to nothing. The same establishment mentality that gave away our fisheries rights prevails. Let's remember that even though Ireland has an off-shore economic zone of 660,000 square kilometres (nearly a quarter of EU waters), it gets only, at best, a quota of 4 percent of the fish catch. When it comes to our natural resources, Ireland has settled for the crumbs from the table.

This need not be so: there are many ways a new strategy could be designed. Our oil and gas would be better left in the ground than given away for nothing, or next to nothing, to industry. A straight 50/50 deal should be struck with Norway through its semi-state. They develop, train, invest in Irish-based business, employ local Irish-based workers, capital-fund drilling and production, develop and maintain infrastructure to the highest environmental and safety standards; they get half, tapering as volume rises, giving them a reasonable return. Norway has shown the way. Anything is better than giving away the hydrocarbon assets of this wonderful nation – without a shot being fired!

## ABOUT THE AUTHOR

Padhraig Campbell is originally from Mayo. During the 1970s, 1980s and 1990s he worked in London on gas pipe conversion work, and gas pipeline work in Cumbria in the north of England. He also worked on oil rigs in the North Sea off Scotland and Norway and oil platform construction work on the west coast of Scotland.

Padhraig has also worked on oil rigs all around the Irish offshore and done plumbing/heating and construction work in Canada. He has spent many years as a trade union activist, and has been a researcher and long-time campaigner on Ireland's oil and gas resources. He has a BA and Diploma in Social Studies. He now lives and works in Galway.

## NOTES

1. remembersarowiwa.com

2. www.siptu.ie/media/media_14689_en.pdf

3. www.oireachtas.ie/parliament/mediazone/pressreleases/name-7873-en.html

# 3.

# WHAT LIES BENEATH
## Paddy Fahy

Oil and gas (hydrocarbons) produced from oil and gas fields are valuable resources buried in the sedimentary basins of the Earth. Oil and gas come from organic-rich source rocks that have accumulated in porous and permeable reservoir rocks throughout the vast ages of geological time.

For oil and gas fields to form, the coincident occurrence of four types of geological features must be present:

1. A source rock

2. A porous and permeable reservoir rock

3. A seal (cap rock)

4. A trap

## SOURCE ROCK

Source rocks (usually dark shale/claystone or coal) were deposited in quiet water and are rich in organic matter such as algae, wood and plants. These were deposited on land in quiet waters, in swampy areas (like present-day peat bogs), in shallow marine bays and in deep submarine areas. When these organic-rich rocks, containing 4 to 20 percent by weight of total organic matter, are buried over millions of years, they are subjected to increasing burial pressure and temperatures typically 30 degrees Celsius per kilometre (see Figure 1). At about 60-120 degrees Celsius and at a burial depth of 2-4 kilometres oil forms in the source rock due to the thermogenic breakdown (cracking) of organic matter (kerogen). The corresponding gas window is found in the 100-200+ degree Celsius interval and at a burial depth of 3-6 kilometres. The hydrocarbons flow into porous reservoir rocks and can form commercial deposits of hydrocarbons.

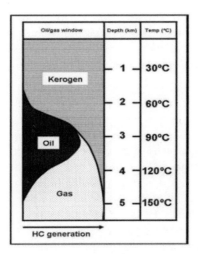

Figure 1

## RESERVOIR

After expulsion from the source rock the oil and gas migrate upward (or are forced downwards) into reservoir rocks. Reservoir rocks are both porous and permeable. They contain interconnected pores in which hydrocarbons are stored and can flow between the mineral grains of the rock. They are usually sandstone, limestone and dolomite. The oil collects usually in the pores within these rocks. Clean sandstone or a limestone can have excellent porosity (30 percent) and excellent permeability. Usually reservoirs are sandstones with varying clay percentage and have 10-20 percent porosity and somewhat lesser permeability. Open fractures within non-porous rocks (e.g. fractured granite) may also store hydrocarbons. In most reservoir rocks the pores are filled entirely with saline water called formation water, which has a density of 1.03 g/cm$^3$. Oil and gas have densities less than saline water. (Oil has a density of 0.82 to 0.93 g/cm$^3$ and gas has a density of 0.12 g/cm$^3$.) Because hydrocarbons are lighter, they move upwards along the pore spaces, displacing the saline water, until they meet an impermeable layer of rock.

## SEAL

This impermeable rock, known as a seal or cap rock, is a barrier and will prevent the hydrocarbons from migrating vertically or horizontally. Seals are generally fine-grained rocks with

39

little pore space such as shale/claystone, chalks and evaporites. Source rock can also be the sealing rock. In many reservoirs both hydrocarbons and formation water are present. Generally 40 percent or more of the pore fluids must be hydrocarbons (i.e. less than 60 percent water saturation) in order for the reservoir to be economic enough to produce.

## TRAP

The trap is a feature that ensures that with the combination of reservoir and seal the hydrocarbons remain trapped in the subsurface, rather than escaping (due to their natural buoyancy) and being lost. Oil and gas in the reservoir rock continue to move upward through the pore spaces until the movement is blocked at the highest point by the structure. If both gas and oil accumulate, the gas in the pores, because it is less dense, will rest above the oil, which in turn will rest above the water. Hydrocarbons traps can be structural traps, stratigraphic traps or combination structural-stratigraphic traps.

Structural traps (anticline) are formed when the reservoir rocks and seals have been deformed by folding and faulting caused by major geotectonic events. This can be an anticline type (arch). The rocks were folded during tectonic events into an arch-type structure called an anticline. Hydrocarbons accumulate on the top of the arch. The seal rock is impervious.

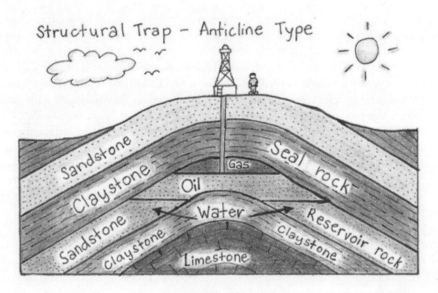

Figure 2

### Structural Traps (Fault)

Major tectonic events caused movement along the fault resulting in an impervious claystone seal being placed across the sandstone reservoir. In the hydrocarbon kitchen deeper the source rock is cooked from effects of increased temperature and pressure to generate oil or gas which moves into the reservoir rock and upwards until it is blocked by the claystone seal rock at the fault line.

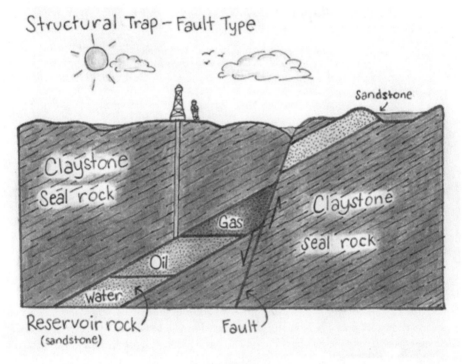

Figure 3

### Stratigraphic Traps

Stratigraphic traps are formed when the reservoir rock is formed as a discontinuous layer (pinchout) and the seal rock is deposited at the side and over the reservoir. The rock on the roof and sides is impervious. The sandstone reservoir is surrounded by claystone seal rocks, which may also be a source rock for hydrocarbons.

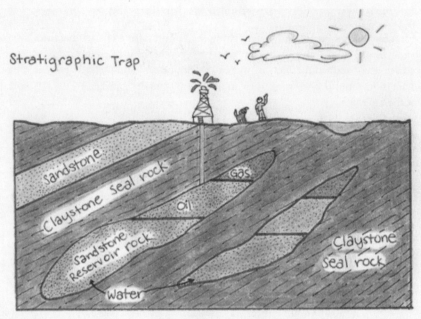

Figure 4

## BASINS

Sedimentary basins are regions of the earth of long-term subsidence associated with plate tectonic activity in which sediments were deposited. As the many kilometres of sediments are buried, they are subjected to increasing pressure and the process of lithification. They can range in age from Upper Paleozoic to Cenozoic (444 million to 2 million years ago). As the sediments that are organic-rich pass the oil and gas window (Figure 1), they are subjected to increasing burial pressure and temperatures that generate hydrocarbons from the source rock.

Ireland has a large offshore territory relative to other European countries. This territory contains Upper Palaeozoic to Cenozoic sedimentary basins containing up to 10 km of Upper Carboniferous to Tertiary sediments – the Irish Rockall basis, the Porcupine and Goban Spur basins, the Slyne, Erris and Donegal basins. These basins are geologically significant for hydrocarbons but are underexplored. The southern and eastern Irish offshore area is dominated by six sedimentary basins, the Kish Bank Basin, the Central Irish Sea Basin, the North Celtic Sea Basin, the South Celtic Sea Basin, the Fastnet Basin and the Cockburn Basin.

These basins developed due to extension and rifting relating to early opening of the North

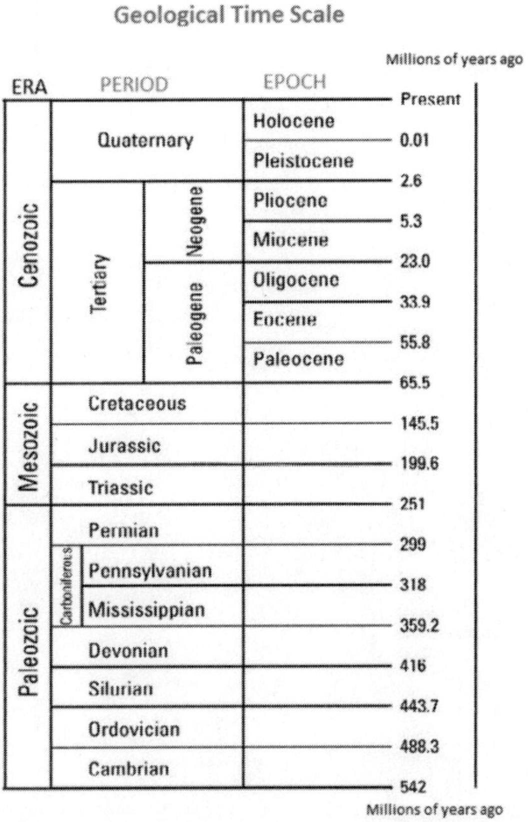

## Geological Time Scale

Millions of years ago

| ERA | PERIOD | | | EPOCH | Millions of years ago |
|---|---|---|---|---|---|
| | | | | | Present |
| Cenozoic | Quaternary | | | Holocene | |
| | | | | | 0.01 |
| | | | | Pleistocene | |
| | | | | | 2.6 |
| | Tertiary | Neogene | | Pliocene | |
| | | | | | 5.3 |
| | | | | Miocene | |
| | | | | | 23.0 |
| | | Paleogene | | Oligocene | |
| | | | | | 33.9 |
| | | | | Eocene | |
| | | | | | 55.8 |
| | | | | Paleocene | |
| | | | | | 65.5 |
| Mesozoic | Cretaceous | | | | |
| | | | | | 145.5 |
| | Jurassic | | | | |
| | | | | | 199.6 |
| | Triassic | | | | |
| | | | | | 251 |
| Paleozoic | Permian | | | | |
| | | | | | 299 |
| | Carboniferous | Pennsylvanian | | | |
| | | | | | 318 |
| | | Mississippian | | | |
| | | | | | 359.2 |
| | Devonian | | | | |
| | | | | | 416 |
| | Silurian | | | | |
| | | | | | 443.7 |
| | Ordovician | | | | |
| | | | | | 488.3 |
| | Cambrian | | | | |
| | | | | | 542 |

Millions of years ago

### Figure 5

Atlantic with the major rift phases occurring during the Permo-Triassic, Late Jurassic and Early Cretaceous.

The exploration results in Ireland's basins are encouraging, with the discovery of four commercial offshore gas fields, one oil and gas field and many proven or possible petroleum systems. Proven giant oil and gas fields in geologically similar basins to some of Ireland's basins have been found on all sides of Ireland's basins, in the sedimentary basins of the UK and Norway, and the Newfoundland and Labrador offshore and onshore areas of east Canada. Giant oil and gas fields have also been found on both sides of the south Atlantic, in West Africa and Brazil.

## IRELAND'S EXPLORATION HISTORY

Exploration for oil and gas in Ireland began in 1962 with the Ambassador Irish Oil Company, which drilled six wells to test carboniferous targets in onshore basins in Meath, Clare, Cavan, Kilkenny and Cork. The Dowra No. 1 well in carboniferous sandstones in the Lough Allen Basin was classified as a gas well. Since then four other wells were drilled, with two wells classified as gas wells drilled by Evergreen Resources Inc. in 2001, Dowra No. 2 well and Thur Mountain No. 1 well in the Cavan-Leitrim area.[1]

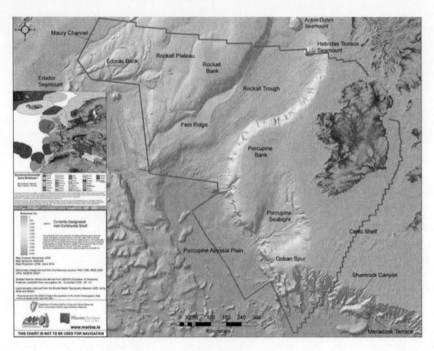

Figure 6
Map of Ireland with seabed territory of 220 million acres.[2]

Drilling started offshore in 1970 when the first well was spudded in the North Celtic Sea Basin by Marathon, who on their third offshore well discovered the Kinsale Head gas field in 1971. The field came on stream in 1978. Exploration moved to the Fastnet, Porcupine, Kish Bank, Irish Sea, Goban Spur, and Northwest Offshore Erris, Slyne, Donegal, and Rockall Basins. One hundred and eighty-eight wells of all types (exploration, appraisal and development) were drilled in Irish waters between 1970 and 2010 (most of the wells were drilled before 1990, after which the more advanced exploration technologies began to emerge). Fifty-four of these were classified as oil or gas wells (exploration, appraisal and development). Twenty-five were classified as oil or gas discovery wells, including five wells deemed commercial discoveries (Kinsale Head gas field, Ballycotton gas field, Seven Heads gas field, Corrib gas field and Barryroe oil and gas field).[3]

## New Technology

Many of the oil wells drilled earlier may not have been fully evaluated in light of the advanced technologies in use today in hydrocarbon exploration. These new technologies include 3D seismic data acquisition and processing, logging while drilling tools, magnetic resonance logs, managed pressure drilling, horizontal drilling and geosteering, floating production systems and sub-sea completions.

## Seismic Exploration

Seismic exploration is one of the most important tools available to the petroleum geologist, providing more detailed information about the licence that will be used to locate hydrocarbon accumulations. The principle is similar to sonar used by bats in locating objects and also to the ultrasound used by doctors for imaging. A seismic survey is done by sending and measuring the time taken for the return of sound waves. With computer-assisted processes to get a sound picture at depth, sedimentary structures are mapped to assist in planning drilling programs.

To carry out this survey, a ship at sea tows a seismic acoustic source behind it. The seismic source releases compressed air to create sound waves. The sound waves penetrate and are reflected by the sea floor. They then penetrate and are reflected by the rock layers, and are picked up by streamers of hydrophones (listening devices to hear the reflected sound) that are towed behind the ship (Figure 7).

Once all the data has been acquired the information is fed into supercomputers for processing. The result is that geoscientists can see the data translated to form sharp two- and three-dimensional images of underground formations, aiding in locating oil and gas deposits.

When seismic lines are two-dimensional they represent a cross-section. Nowadays, with technology pioneered by ExxonMobil, three-dimensional seismic imaging is standard throughout the hydrocarbon exploration industry. Three-dimensional data represents a volume, and four-dimensional data includes the dimension of time. Two three-dimensional surveys done at different times would represent four-dimensional data and it can be used to look at the effects of water injection into an oil field to measure the hydrocarbon depletion over time.

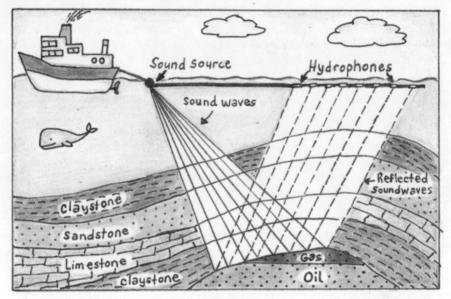

Figure 7

## DRILLING

After a target has been identified a well proposal is then prepared with the following objectives:

- To determine the presence of hydrocarbons.

- To obtain the geological and petrophysical data necessary to evaluate the formation, in the form of cores, logs and reservoir pressures data, to determine the formation fluid types, the depth of the oil-water contact and gas-oil contact, the reservoir porosity and permeability and to determine the thickness of the Net Pay.

- To flow-test the well to determine its production potential, and obtain fluid samples.

The life of an oil or gas field can be sub-divided into the following phases:

- Exploration phase, in which the initial exploration wells are drilled to find hydrocarbons. If hydrocarbons are not found, valuable geological information will still be obtained.

- Appraisal phase. When a significant hydrocarbon accumulation is found by an exploration well the appraisal stage starts by drilling appraisal wells to delineate the extent of the discovery. The reservoir properties, connectivity, hydrocarbon type and gas-oil and oil-water contacts are determined to calculate potential recoverable volumes.

- Development phase, in which producing wells will be drilled and completions installed to produce hydrocarbons. Production wells are drilled and completed in strategic positions based on 3D seismic imaging used to target wells precisely for optimal recovery. Later, as the production begins to decline, water injector wells can be drilled and completed to boost production.

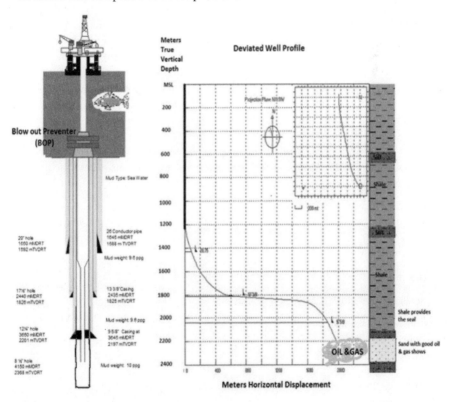

Figure 8
Deviated Well Profile

During the drilling of an exploration well it is steered directionally and the formations are evaluated by the various logging tools for the presence of hydrocarbons at the same time. When porous and permeable horizons confirmed by the various logs while drilling are encountered, formation pressure readings are taken and the fluid type (gas, oil or water) is determined.

## WELL LOGGING

Geophysical wells logs are recorded while drilling the well. These logging tools are incorporated in the bottom hole assembly (BHA) of the drill string above the drilling bit. As the well is being drilled the measurements from these geophysical tools are transmitted to the surface using pressure pulse telemetry transmitted through the drilling fluid. These geophysical measurements obtained while drilling in real time are used to evaluate the formations. The data are transmitted via satellite from the rig site to the operating centres of the oil company's office and displayed as a log in real time. The values of the parameter measured are plotted continuously against depth in the well (Figure 9). This allows early evaluation of the formation being drilled for timely decisions to be made regarding the operations.

The purpose of logging is to:

- identify potential reservoir intervals

- distinguish non-permeable, non-reservoir intervals from porous permeable potential intervals

- estimate thickness of the potential reservoirs

- determine rock type of the potential reservoirs

- calculate porosity

- determine resistivity of formation water

- calculate water saturations, using resistivity

- estimate in-place and movable hydrocarbons.

### Inclination and directional

Accurate measurements of inclination and azimuth (angular measurement) are obtained during the drilling. These measurements are an essential requirement to drill vertical, horizontal or extended-reach wells.

## Formation pressure

Formation pressures are taken to measure the formation pressures and the reservoir permeability at different depths and to determine the fluid type by establishing a gas, oil or water gradient. These formation pressure tests help in formation evaluation by:

- obtaining real-time formation fluid gradients and fluid mobility
- identifying the fluid contacts and determining the reservoir connectivity/compartmentalisation, and depletion
- increasing safety of the operations by determining optimal drilling fluid density to balance the formation pressure
- giving information of formation pressure changes when they occur, and helping to prevent an influx of formation fluid into the well that could cause a blowout
- continuously updating well-bore stability assessments
- helping to prevent the reservoir formation damage by allowing optimal drilling fluid density to be used and avoidance of too high a drilling fluid density that would cause the drilling fluid to enter the reservoir formation
- helping to increase drilling efficiency by determining the precise overbalance, thereby maximising the rate of penetration (ROP).

The hole-cleaning effectiveness is monitored with the pressure-while-drilling sensor, reducing formation damage due to surging.

## Gamma ray

Gamma ray logs measure the naturally occurring gamma radiation to characterise the rock in a borehole. Shales/claystones have high gamma ray readings because radioactive potassium is a common component in their clay content and their natural radioactivity emits more gamma radiation than other rock types like sandstone, limestone, dolomite and coal. Clean sandstones are mostly composed of non-radioactive quartz and normally have low gamma ray readings.

## Resistivity

Resistivity logs measure the ability of rocks to impede the flow of an electrical current. Most rock materials are insulators. Resistivity logs differentiate between formations filled with salty waters (good conductors of electricity) and those filled with hydrocarbons (poor conductors of electricity). When a porous rock contains salty water its resistivity will be low and when it contains hydrocarbons it will be higher. Resistivity and porosity measurements are used to obtain values of water saturation to help evaluate hydrocarbon content of the formation. Resistivity is measured in ohm-metre$^2$/metre.

## Density

This is one of three well logs that are commonly used to give good indications of lithology and to calculate porosity, the other two being sonic logging and neutron porosity logging. A density well logging tool's function is to determine porosity. It can measure and provide a continuous record of the formation bulk density including solid matrix and fluid in the pores. Porosity matrix and fluid densities can be determined.

A radioactive source emits gamma rays into the formation. These gamma rays interact with electrons in the formation and are scattered in an interaction known as Compton scattering. The number of scattered gamma rays that reach the detector, placed at a set distance from the emitter, is related to the formation's electron density, which is related to the formation density.

## Neutron porosity

Neutron logs, by measuring the hydrogen in the formation, can provide the formation fluid-filled porosity, where the porosity is filled with water or oil. (Both contain hydrogen.) Neutron porosity measurement employs a fast neutron source and two detectors to measure the hydrogen in a reservoir. The source bombards the formation with neutrons and the detectors measure their loss of energy as they pass through the formation to the detectors. The neutron has approximately the same mass as hydrogen nuclei. So the neutrons lose energy by elastic scattering more efficiently by interaction with hydrogen nuclei and much less efficiently by interaction with more massive nuclei such as silicon or oxygen. As hydrogen atoms are present in both water- and oil-filled reservoirs, measurement of the amount allows estimation of the amount of liquid-filled porosity.

## Sonic

The sonic log measures the rock formation's ability to transmit sound waves. The rock interval transit time, known as delta T, varies with lithology and rock properties, particularly decreasing with an increasing effective porosity. The logging tool consists of a transmitter and receiver, and the time taken for the sound wave to travel the fixed distance between the two is recorded as an interval transit time. Sound travels more slowly though fluid-filled rocks than through rocks with no porosity. A sonic log can be used to calculate the porosity of a formation if the seismic velocities of the rock matrix and pore fluid are known.

## Magnetic resonance

Magnetic resonance logs provide a continuous record along the borehole to measure porosity, give information on permeability and estimate pore size. Magnetic resonance responds exclusively to protons – hydrogen nuclei, which are abundant in rock's pore spaces in the form of water and hydrocarbon. A similar technique is used in medical scanning. Magnetic resonance, by imposing an external magnetic field, makes a measurement which is proportional to the quantity of hydrogen nuclei from water or hydrocarbons in the formation. This can be calibrated to give a value for porosity. This allows identification of the free- and bound-fluid volumes and the free-fluid type (gas, oil or water).

## Gas logging

During the drilling of wells through a hydrocarbon-bearing rock formation, hydrocarbons enter the drilling fluid and are carried to the surface. Gas is continually extracted from the drilling fluid and the gas obtained is analysed in fast chromatographs that perform an analysis cycle from C1 to C5. The quantity and chromatographic composition of the gas from the formation is fundamental in evaluating the hydrocarbon potential of the reservoir. The results of the analyses are plotted on logs that record gas quantity and composition for the well. The depths of these potential gas or oil zones can be determined from these gas chromatograph logs.

## Mud-logging

During the drilling of a well there will typically be a mud-logging unit on the rig. This unit will be manned by a crew of four mud-logging geologists. This unit has three main responsibilities:

1. To monitor the quantity and composition of the gas in the drilling fluid coming from the well using gas detectors and chromatographs (see gas logging above). This is essential for the safety of the rig. The gas values and composition are necessary in the evaluation of the hydrocarbon potential of the reservoir.

2. To monitor the drilling parameters, fluids and solids returns from the well to assist the drilling department in the safety and optimisation of the drilling process.

3. To provide real-time information on the drilling parameters and the gas to the geologist and petroleum engineering department that can be used for evaluation purposes.

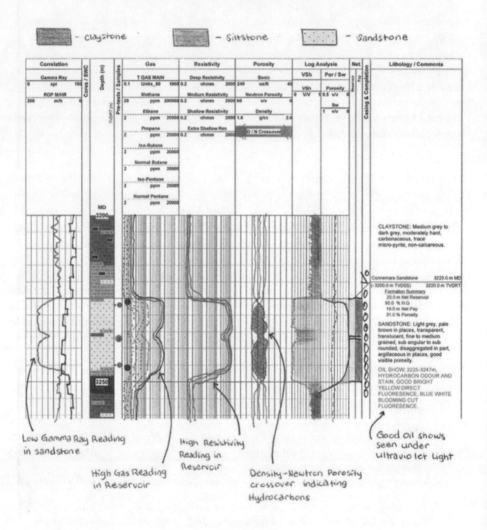

Figure 9

The mud-logging unit will produce a daily 'mud log', which is transmitted to the oil company office on a daily basis. Items that will be included are:

- gas readings and composition as measured by a gas detector/chromatograph
- a check for non-hydrocarbon gases ($H_2S$, $CO_2$)
- a report of cuttings received over the shale shakers, with full lithological descriptions and relative percentages
- rate of penetration (ROP) measurement of the drilling rate
- hydrocarbon indications in samples.

The mud log may be of great use to the petrophysicist and geologist in operational decision making and evaluation. Areas in which the mud log may be particularly important include:

- identification of the lithology and formation type being drilled
- identification of porous/permeable zones
- picking of coring, casing or final drilling depths
- confirmation of hydrocarbons being encountered and whether they are oil or gas.

## Lithology examination

The drill bit cuttings of the formation being drilled are carried to the surface by the circulation of the drilling fluid. At the surface these drill bit cuttings are removed from the drilling fluid by screens known as the 'shale shakers'. A sample of rock cuttings are prepared and examined by the geologist under a microscope to describe the type of lithology, porosity and any oil shows.

## Drilling Operations

Wells are drilled in sections, with the diameter of each section decreasing with increasing depth. Drilling fluids, also known as muds, are a fundamental part of the drilling process. The wells will be drilled using a combination the two main types of drilling fluids, which are water-based drilling fluid (usually called water-based mud (WBM)) and non-aqueous drilling fluid (usually called oil-based mud (OBM)).

The main functions of drilling fluids include:

1. Providing hydrostatic pressure to prevent formation fluids from entering into the well bore. If the formation pressure increases, drilling fluid density will also be increased mostly with the addition of ground barite (which has a specific

gravity of 4.2 or greater) to balance the formation pressure. If the drilling fluid density is not high enough to balance the formation pressure an unexpected influx of fluid into the well-bore (a kick) will occur. If this influx is not controlled it can lead to a blowout from the pressured formation fluids. High-accuracy flow meters are incorporated into the drilling fluids returns system to detect formation influx to the well-bore (and fluid loss) in time to prevent a blowout.

2. Keeping the drill bit lubricated, cool and carrying drill cutting out of the hole to prevent the drill pipe getting stuck.

3. Maintaining the stability of the well-bore. Drilling fluid density must be within the necessary range to balance the mechanical forces that cause collapse of the hole and to maintain its size and cylindrical shape.

4. Sealing the permeable reservoir formation with calcium carbonate flakes and preventing drill solids from invading the formation, thereby minimising reservoir formation damage.

5. The drilling fluid is also the medium by which the logging-while-drilling tools transmit formation evaluation information to surface in real time through mud pulse telemetry.

The first step in the drilling of a well is to drill a 36'-diameter top hole section into the sea bed using seawater. The drilled cuttings generated by the drilling process are returned to the seabed during this phase of the well, accumulating close to the wellhead. The 30'-diameter conductor pipe is run into the hole and cemented. The second hole section of the well, the 26'-diameter section, will be drilled using seawater with the drilled cuttings also returned to the seabed during the drilling of this section. Again, this section will be cased with 20'-pipe and cemented after drilling.

A blowout preventer (BOP) will then be installed on top of the subsea wellhead. The weight of the drilling fluid acts as the first line of well control by keeping underground pressures in check. If an influx of pressurised oil or gas does occur during drilling, well control is maintained through the rig's BOP. This is a set of hydraulically operated valves and other closure devices (rams) which seal off the well, and route the well-bore fluids to pressure controlling equipment. Trained personnel operating this highly reliable equipment minimise the possibility of a 'blowout', or an uncontrolled flow of fluids from a well.

Once the BOP is in place and a marine riser – a large-diameter pipe that connects the drilling rig and the BOP – is installed, the drilling fluid and drill cuttings will be returned to the drilling rig. The cuttings are separated from the drilling fluid and the clean fluid is pumped down the drill stem to the drill bit and then circulated back to the drilling rig via the annulus – the space between the drill string and the open hole or casing and riser.

The third section of the well, the 17 ½'-diameter section, and the fourth section, the 12 ¼'-diameter section, will be drilled using OBM with the drill cuttings returned to the drilling rig. The fifth section, the 8 ½'-diameter section, where the hydrocarbon-bearing formations are usually reached, will also be drilled using OBM and the drill cuttings returned to the rig.

The drilling rig will use solids control equipment to separate drill cuttings from the mud and the cleaned mud will be re-circulated. Where oil base drilling fluid is used, the drill cuttings will be passed through a drill cuttings dryer, which will remove as much oil base drilling fluid from cuttings as practicable. The target is to achieve an average of less than 5 percent residual oil-on-cuttings (OOC) levels. Monitoring of the average OOC will be carried out during operations involving oil base drilling fluid.

The drill cuttings must be disposed of, together with any adhering mud and chemicals not removed by the cleaning system.

Under the OSPAR (Convention for the Protection of the Marine Environment of the North-East Atlantic) Decision 2000/3, the discharge into the sea of cuttings contaminated with oil-base fluids at a concentration greater than 1 percent by weight on dry cuttings is prohibited. This option is therefore not available for oil-contaminated cuttings unless they can be cleaned offshore to meet these requirements. Although pilot projects are currently running in the North Sea, offshore cleaning of oil-contaminated cuttings is not yet considered to be achievable in general industry practice. A more common approach for oil-contaminated cuttings is to ship them to shore, where they can be cleaned and recycled, for example as road aggregate, or put into landfill. Cuttings re-injection (CRI) is another disposal option, useful for contaminated cuttings, where drill cuttings are mixed into slurry with water and pumped at high pressure down a separate injection well. CRI is slowly becoming more widespread in mature oil development areas where there are enough potential injection wells available.[4]

As each well section is drilled, the drill string will be pulled out of the hole and protective steel casing of appropriate diameter is inserted and cemented into place, to provide stability and a barrier between the well-bore and surrounding formations. The casing provides structural integrity for testing and possible future production operations.

While drilling each section of the hole, a combination of down-hole and surface equipment is used to monitor all possible parameters of the drilling operation and to collect and record all possible data that can be used to evaluate the down-hole geological and geophysical characteristics of the rocks being penetrated, and the fluids contained in the pore space within these rocks.

## Well Testing

When the well has penetrated the objective horizons, and has been fully evaluated and hydrocarbon zones outlined, well flow testing may be undertaken to obtain fluid samples from the reservoir and collect further information on reservoir pressure, permeability, production and fluid characteristics.

The well test method involves flowing or producing the reservoir fluids up to the drilling rig, where they are flared off. Whilst producing the well at different flow rates, a comprehensive evaluation of the well and certain reservoir characteristics can be made which will help in evaluating whether the reservoir could be developed commercially in the future.

## Well Abandonment/Suspension

Depending on operational programmes and the hydrocarbon reserves found, an exploration well can either be abandoned or suspended after completion of data acquisition, evaluation and flow testing. Plug and abandon (P&A) operations will involve placing a series of cement plugs within the well-bore. Cement plugs are placed across the reservoir, extending above the hydrocarbon bearing interval, at appropriate barrier points in the well and at the surface. The casing will be mechanically cut below the seabed and all well-head structures will be recovered prior to completion of the exploration drilling campaign.

If further development of the well will be done in the near future, the well may be suspended. If this is the case, the well will be left intact and a series of mechanical and/or cement plugs will be placed inside the well to prevent the escape of hydrocarbons. The conductor and casings will be sealed and left protruding approximately 2 metres above the seabed.

## Managed Pressure Drilling (MPD)

The International Association of Drilling Contractors (IADC) states that the objectives of MPD are 'to ascertain the down-hole pressure environment limits and to manage the annular hydraulic pressure profile accordingly'.

Wells drilled in the eighties and nineties may have suffered formation damage to the reservoirs due to maintaining hydrostatic overbalance to control formation pressure while drilling these wells. The high hydrostatic overbalance can flush the permeable hydrocarbon-bearing formations with water-based salt-saturated drilling fluid filtrate, and solids invade and are deposited in the pore spaces. This can cause an incorrect response on the logging tools and a subdued chromatograph gas reading. The formation may not be correctly evaluated. When solids invade and are deposited in the pores they can impair productivity during well tests.

Now, with the introduction of managed pressure drilling combined with logging while drilling (LWD), the formation is drilled and logged without disturbing the formation fluid equilibrium. This enables accurate formation evaluation. With the release of gas from the formation being drilled, the advanced gas detectors and chromatographic analysis will give accurate evaluation of the fluids in the reservoirs during drilling.

### Directional Drilling and Geosteering

Directional drilling is drilling wells at multiple angles to better reach and produce oil and gas reserves. This allows the drilling of multiple wells from the same vertical well-bore. Multiple wells can be drilled from a single location at many angles, tapping reserves over 10 km away.

Geosteering using real-time combined deep resistivity and directional tools while drilling can detect bed boundaries and oil water contacts at a distance from the drill bit and steer it along the productive sands 'sweet spot' in highly deviated wells and in wells with dipping or horizontal beds. Advanced petrophysical analysis can be done in real time. By identifying approaching beds and the fluid type, the operators can ensure precise well placement and maximise reservoir exposure for increased production and reduced costs by avoidance of drilling out the top or bottom of the reservoir, avoidance of drilling into problem zones and avoidance of drilling into the water zone.

### Directional Drilling and Geosteering

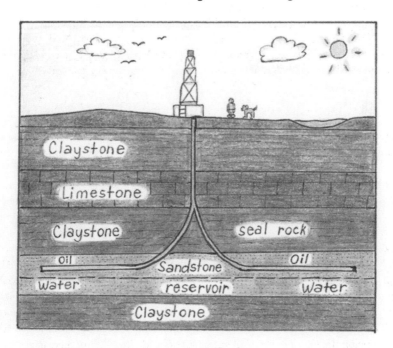

Figure 10

When the Troll field was discovered in 1979, the directional drilling and completion technologies available at that time made Troll's oil reserve uneconomic to produce because of its low accessibility and thin reservoirs. To recover the hydrocarbons, engineers had to overcome extreme challenges as new drilling technologies were required. The first horizontal wells were drilled on the Norwegian Continental Shelf in 1988 and represented a step-change for all of Norway's offshore field development. In the early 1990s, the Baker Hughes Company introduced the first complete reservoir navigation tool system. This technology enabled operators to precisely steer horizontal well-paths, staying within the reservoirs. The new drilling technologies turned one of the North Sea's largest offshore gas fields into one of Norway's largest oil fields. Using state-of-the-art technologies, Norway continues to make huge discoveries as they continue to drill more demanding and technically challenging wells.

### Semi-Submersible Drilling Rigs (Semi-Subs)

A semi-sub (Figure 11) is supported on two parallel submersible hulls (pontoons). Columns extend upward from the hulls above the sea and support the main deck, superstructure and drilling rig.

Figure 11
A modern self-propelled semi-sub drilling rig, *Eirik Raude,* owned by Ocean Rig.

These rigs were originally designed as submersible rigs, which are completely submerged, resting on the ocean floor in shallow water. Naval architects realised that these rigs would maintain their stabilisation if they were only partially submerged. They would then be able to drill in deep waters.

When the hulls are ballasted (flooded) they cause the rig to partially submerge. In this half-submerged state the rigs offer exceptional stability for deep-water drilling operations with rolling and pitching from waves and wind greatly diminished. They are chosen for harsh weather conditions because of their ability to withstand rough waters.

A moored semi-sub will have eight to twelve anchor lines set at various points around the rig to keep it in position. When working in deep water, instead of being anchored, the semi-sub rig may also be kept in position by a dynamic positioning (DP) system. Several thrusters (or propulsion units) are used in a dynamic positioning system. The thrusters are guided by a computer that determines the exact position of the drilling rig relative to the well from satellite positioning information and signals from beacons on the ocean floor. The thrusters are automatically actuated as necessary to maintain the rig precisely on station.

Modern semi-sub drilling rigs are self-propelled and are becoming more sophisticated, with advanced state-of-the-art drilling technology. Multiple concurrent drilling activities are possible. The newest rigs are capable of drilling 10,000 metres measured from the seabed and are capable of operating in water depths up to 3,500 metres. This makes the rigs particularly well-suited to drilling in deep and geologically complicated areas.

## Drill Ships

A drill ship (Figure 12) is a marine vessel that has been built to drill oil and gas wells. Drill ships are equipped with a drilling derrick and an opening in the hull (moon pool) through which the drill string, the riser and the BOP are run.

Drill ships are employed in deep and ultra-deep waters, in water depths ranging from 800 to more than 3,600 metres. In shallower waters drill ships are moored to the seafloor by six to twelve anchors. In deeper waters these drill ships are also positioned by dynamic positioning (DP) systems which use satellites orbiting the Earth to fix their position on the sea to within a tiny margin. DPS relies on several thrusters located on the fore, aft and mid sections of the ship, which are activated by an onboard computer that constantly adjusts the thrusters to maintain their position. Drill ships can operate at water depths that exceed 3,600 metres.

These modern semi-subs and drill ships can drill wells in ultra-deep waters (waters at least 1,500 metres deep), and often into several thousand metres of rock to the reservoir below. An increasing percentage of new offshore discoveries, up to 50 percent, are coming from deepwater and ultra-deep-water plays.

Figure 12
A Modern drill-ship owned by Maersk Drilling

## PEOPLE EMPLOYED AT THE WELLSITE ON AN OFFSHORE DRILLING RIG

A drilling rig operates all year round, around the clock, and therefore the crew works in two twelve-hour shifts. The work period on board the rig has a duration of between two and four weeks, followed by a number of days off.

### Offshore Installation Manager (OIM)

The Offshore Installation Manager (OIM) is the most senior manager of an offshore rig or platform. This position is equivalent to a Captain's position on board a ship. The OIM manages the drilling company's interest at the rig site in respect to the oil company, the well programme and all personnel onboard the rig, and is the person with overall responsibility for Quality Health Safety and Environment (QHSE), maintenance, drilling operations and personnel.

### Drill Site Supervisor (Company Rep)

A Drill Site Supervisor (DSV) is a representative of an operating/exploration company. Other terms that may be used are company man/representative. The DSV reports to the office-based Operations Superintendent. In oil and gas drilling, the oil companies rent or lease rigs from another company that owns the rigs, the drilling contractor. The majority of the personnel on the drilling rig are employees of the drilling contractor. The DSV is the on-site representative of the operating oil company and is in overall charge of the drilling and associated activities. Rig operations and maintenance and crew upkeep are attended to by the tool-pusher, who works for the drilling contractor.

The DSV is knowledgeable in the area of drilling operations and completion operations. He works with the onsite geologist and a team of office-based engineers and geologists and is the team member responsible for carrying out the written drilling program in an efficient and safe fashion.

## Well-Site Geologist

A well-site geologist tracks operations on the site of an oil or gas well. This person is responsible for obtaining the maximum amount of subsurface information possible during the drilling of the well. The geologist analyses samples of rock carried to the surface in the drilling fluid and evaluates all hydrocarbon shows found in these rock cuttings. This information is used to construct a composite profile log of the formation being drilled. The well-site geologist gives advice on geological hazards to the drilling supervisor on site in order to drill the well efficiently and safely. Reports are submitted to geologists at the company's headquarters. People working in this field usually have a degree in geology or petroleum engineering, along with substantial experience in the oil and gas industry.

The geologist's responsibilities include:

- ensuring compliance with all safety, health and environmental procedures and guidelines

- achieving the geological objectives set forth in the formation evaluation program

- supervising Geological Service Company personnel including data engineers, mud loggers and gas detection systems

- logging-while-drilling operation

- wire-line logging operation

- core-point selection and coring operations

- description of lithology and core samples

- hydrocarbon-show evaluation from the lithology samples

- interpretation of petrophysical logs

- casing-point selection (together with drilling supervisor)
- daily reports to main office and dispatch of data.

## Tool-Pusher

The tool-pusher is in charge of running the drilling operation. He supervises and co-ordinates the activities of drill rig crew members engaged in drilling for oil or gas, operating service rigs, or providing oil and gas well services. The tool-pusher is usually a senior experienced individual who has worked his way up through the ranks of the drilling crew positions. The tool-pusher ensures that the oil rig has sufficient materials, spare parts and skilled personnel to continue efficient operations. The tool-pusher reports to the OIM. The tool-pusher also serves as a trusted advisor to many personnel on the rig site, including the oil company's representative, the company man. Tool-pushers usually start at an entry-level position (i.e. a roustabout or roughneck) and work their way up to driller and then tool-pusher over many years.

## Driller

The driller is the person who carries out the actual drilling. He has his own workplace, from where he runs the entire drilling operation. He is also a team leader in charge of the crew and drilling operations during the process of well drilling. The driller operates the hoisting, circulatory and rotary machinery. He monitors critical parameters and is responsible for interpreting the signals the well gives regarding gas levels and fluids with high pressure. In an emergency, such as an influx of hydrocarbons into the well, he is responsible for taking the correct measures to control the well.

## Drilling Fluids Engineer (Mud Engineer)

The drilling fluids engineer, most often referred to as the mud engineer, works on the rig during the drilling of an oil and gas well. He is responsible for ensuring that the properties of the drilling fluid, also known as drilling mud, are within designed specifications.

The drilling fluids engineer may be a university, college or technical institute graduate, or may have come up having gained experience working on rigs and attending a special training course.

## Compliance Engineer

The major potential environmental effects from offshore drilling result from the discharge of wastes, including drilling fluids, drill cuttings and produced formation water. Emphasis must be placed on ensuring that there is no discharge of toxic wastes and that water returned to the ocean is as free as permissible by regulations from oil and chemicals.

The compliance engineers at the well-site are environmental inspectors from the appropriate government body. These department officials ensure maximum compliance by the operators to high environmental standards concerning the safe containment and handling of drilling fluid contaminated cuttings. No type of oil/synthetic-based drilling fluid or drilled cuttings contaminated with oil-based or synthetic-based drilling fluids may be dumped in European waters, and this is now becoming the standard worldwide. Contaminated mud and cuttings must either be shipped back to shore in skips or processed on the rigs and injected into appropriate rock formation at a specified depth below the seabed.

## Floating Production, Storage and Offloading (FPSO)

Floating production, storage and offloading (FPSO) (Figure 13) vessels are now a leading part of the offshore oil and gas industry. These are floating tank systems designed to receive hydrocarbons produced from subsea templates, and to process and store them. FPSO production equipment can be used for water separation, gas treatment, oil processing, water injection and gas compression. Hydrocarbons are then transferred to the vessel's double-hull for storage until they can be offloaded onto export tankers.

FPSOs are superior to fixed installations with their greater efficiency and cost effectiveness. They are preferred in deep-water and ultra-deep-water offshore regions. They are easy to install, and do not require a local pipeline infrastructure to export oil to markets around the world. By avoiding dredging and dock construction and the onshore construction of an LNG processing plant, the environmental footprint is reduced and the marine and coastal environments are better preserved. When the field is depleted, the FPSO can be moved to a new location.

A central mooring system allows the vessel to rotate free and unrestricted by 360 degrees to best respond to weather conditions. The FPSO will normally lay head-on to the prevailing wind and waves.

An FPSO is connected by flexible pipelines to multiple subsea wellheads on the seabed to gather hydrocarbons from subsea production wells.

Treated oil is transferred to cargo tanks in the FPSO ship's hull. Treated gas is used as fuel for on-board power generation and excess gas is either re-injected back into the subsea reservoirs or maybe exported via a pipeline to shore. Water that is produced during production is injected into the reservoirs via injector wells to boost production in depleted reservoirs.

The development of the floating liquefied natural gas (FLNG) market looks promising. An LNG FPSO works under the same principles an oil FPSO, taking the well stream and separating out the natural gas (primarily methane (C1) and ethane (C2)) and producing LNG, which is stored and offloaded. FLNG technology development is important for the LNG industry as it reduces both the project costs and environmental footprint of an LNG development onshore.

Shell is developing FLNG for its Prelude and Concerto fields in the Browse Basin, off Broome, Western Australia. After processing on the FLNG, liquefied natural gas (LNG) carriers will offload liquefied gas for delivery to markets worldwide. This will be the largest floating structure ever built. Safety of the FLNG facility and its operation has been paramount during its design, and the facility and its mooring system have been designed to withstand the most severe weather conditions.

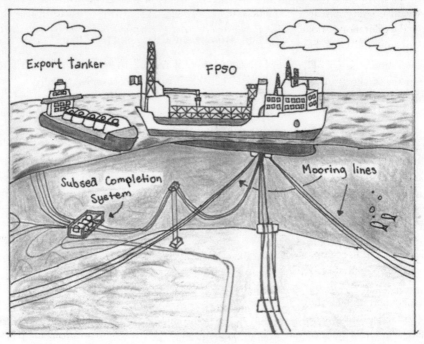

Figure 13
FPSO vessel

## Conclusion

In hydrocarbon exploration the study of source rocks and their geological history is important when it comes to understanding the petroleum systems in sedimentary basins. It takes skilled exploration geologists, geophysicists and reservoir engineers many years of dedicated work using numerous advanced techniques to find commercial accumulations of oil and gas. Information and the interpretation of that information is the key to success. When it is proven that there is a working petroleum system, surveys are carried out and exploration wells are drilled for information, which is processed and analysed. This will eventually lead to commercial discoveries.

Geology is not an exact science and geologists outline many risks that serve to point out what may go wrong in the hydrocarbon potential interpretation. This should not be taken in a negative sense. These risks are usually based on lack of studies and data on these basins and hydrocarbon systems. Some outstanding geological studies have been done by various geoscientists over the years on Ireland's offshore basins with a focus on the petroleum geology and exploration – notably *The Petroleum Exploration of Ireland's Offshore Basins*, edited by P. M. Shannon, P. D. W. Haughton and D. V. Corcoran, published by the Geological Society. There is much more work that needs to be done on petroleum source, reservoir and trapping potential for the full potential of Ireland's petroleum basins to be realised.

## ABOUT THE AUTHOR

Paddy Fahy earned a BSc from National University of Ireland, University College Galway, in 1974. He is a geoscientist with twenty-five years of international operational experience in the hydrocarbon exploration and development industry.

*Expertise in geological evaluation:* Writing and implementing the geological programmes for the acquisition of complete and accurate geological data. Supervision of geological evaluation acquisition operations, carrying out geological evaluation from log interpretation, reservoir engineering, coring operations and hydrocarbon detection and analysis during the well-drilling process. Predicting and detecting geopressure using logging while drilling analysis in real time. Production of geological logs and reports.

*Expertise in Well Construction and Engineering:* Drilling and petroleum engineering, hydraulics and drilling fluids rheology, well control and stuck pipe prevention. Drilling optimisation towards a safe, efficient, environmentally sound and cost-effective drilling operation. Experience in deep-water, high-pressure/high-temperature and managed-pressure drilling operations.

*Countries of Work Experience:* United Kingdom, Australia, Russian Federation, Brunei, Malaysia, Indonesia, Japan, China, Vietnam, Myanmar, Philippines, Thailand, Korea, Yemen, Angola, Qatar, Saudi Arabia and India.

Experience working worldwide on the Fica formations of the Qamar Gulf in Yemen, the Miocene Green Tuff formations of Japan, the Funning formations of the Yellow Sea in China, the Miocene Carbonate formations of Sarawak and the Philippines, the Miocene to

Pliocene deltaic formations of North Sakhalin, the Triassic and Jurassic formations of the North Sea, the late Permian to lower Triassic dolomitic shelf Khuff Carbonates of the Arabian Gulf, the Ordovician Clastics of Saudi Arabia, the early to middle Miocene turbidite formation of the Congo Basin, the Oligocene to Miocene sediments in the North Malay Basin in Malaysia, the Pliocene to Cretaceous formations of the Krishna Godavari Basin in the Bay of Bengal, the Gujarat Saurastra Carbonate reservoirs offshore Mumbai of Miocene and Oligocene age and the Mid-Eocene Sandstones of the Cambay Basin, India.

## NOTES

1.  Petroleum Affairs Division of the Department of Communications, Energy and Natural Resources. www.pad.ie

2.  The Marine Institute website

3.  Petroleum Affairs Division of the Department of Communications, Energy and Natural Resources. www.pad.ie

4.  Irish Offshore Strategic Environmental Assessment 1445 R002 s4 draft plan and alternatives

# 4.

# THE OIL INDUSTRY
# AND THE ENVIRONMENT:
# AN UNEASY RELATIONSHIP
## Jack O'Sullivan

### THE EARLY DAYS: BANTRY BAY HITS THE HEADLINES

It was the summer and autumn of 1968, and teams of marine biologists were surveying the intertidal and sub-tidal rocky shores of Bantry Bay in County Cork. Working between the tides, they identified and counted the relative abundance of living marine organisms from the high-water mark to low water, while other members of the team surveyed the underwater kelp beds which fringe the magnificent rocky coastline of the bay.

Just over a year earlier, two of these biologists had carried out a very similar survey of parts of the coast of Cornwall immediately following what was then the largest oil spillage from any source – the grounding of the tanker *Torrey Canyon* on the Seven Stones reef on 18 March 1967. What they found made headlines in the scientific press – the attempts to clean the rocky coast of Cornwall by using toxic dispersants had caused more ecological damage than the oil itself.[1]

The *Torrey Canyon* incident and its aftermath revealed clearly how we were unprepared to deal with a major spillage of oil. It was of course the first really large spillage, and therefore the knowledge of its effects and the means to prevent an ecological catastrophe were in their infancy. Nevertheless, some lessons were learned, one of which was that when oil is moved by sea, or is being extracted from offshore oil fields, spillages are inevitable.

Late one evening in February 1968, at a conference held at Orielton Field Studies Centre in South Wales on the effects of oil pollution on marine life,[2] the news was discussed that

Gulf Oil intended bringing the world's largest super-tankers to Bantry Bay. Five marine biologists, including the writer of this chapter, expressed concern and a strong desire to undertake an ecological survey of what was seen as a completely pristine area of the Atlantic coast, one of the most westerly parts of Europe, and an area of extreme bio-geographical interest. Discussions at the conference had highlighted the importance of obtaining pre-pollution data as a reference point for further studies.

We knew that Bantry Bay would be a completely new oil port, where deep water would allow these huge ships to berth alongside an offshore terminal, pump crude oil via undersea pipelines to a tank farm on shore, or transfer the oil to smaller tankers which would ship the oil to European ports. The Suez Canal was closed to shipping, and Gulf Oil hoped that by bringing crude oil to Europe from the Middle East around the Cape of Good Hope at the southern tip of Africa, the economy of scale offered by these ultra-large vessels would be very profitable.

The *Torrey Canyon* spillage and the number of relatively frequent minor oil spills at oil ports such as Milford Haven on the coast of Wales convinced the biologists that Bantry Bay would suffer the same fate. A series of expeditions was planned, funding was obtained from international sources including the World Wildlife Fund,[3] and the principal ecological surveys were completed before the first tanker – the *Universe Ireland* – entered the bay in October 1968 and berthed alongside the newly constructed oil terminal. Her arrival was greeted with much celebration by government officials, elected politicians and local dignitaries.[4] Cork County Council was very pleased, despite having no control over the new oil terminal, and government spokespersons proudly declared that the largest tankers in the world had begun shipping oil to Bantry Bay. But they never mentioned that because there was no harbour authority in Bantry Bay, the huge tankers paid no harbour dues!

What was remarkable was that, despite a great deal of lobbying by Cork County Council and local groups in Bantry,[5] the government many times refused to allow a harbour authority to be established.

In Dáil Éireann on 6 November 1968, two TDs (Mr Martin Corry (FF) and Mr Patrick Donegan (FG)) questioned the Minister for Transport and Power as to why he had refused Cork County Council's request to set up a harbour authority at Bantry, given that Gulf Oil apparently had no objection to its establishment.

Mr Patrick Lalor, Parliamentary Secretary to the Minister for Transport and Power, replied that 'Gulf Oil Company are the only commercial user of Bantry Bay and, therefore, there is no need for a harbour authority, whose main function would be to reconcile conflicting requirements of different users and to develop, maintain and operate the harbour in their common interest. While Gulf Oil are paying no harbour dues they are providing for themselves the expensive facilities which would normally be provided by a harbour authority.'[6]

This reply must have seemed like a gratuitous insult to the commercial fishermen who operated out of Bantry pier and other small harbours in the bay, and to the boatmen who ferried tourists daily between the town of Glengarriff and the well-known tourist attraction of Garnish Island. They felt that their needs were ignored, and the opportunity to improve the town pier and other facilities was being lost if Gulf paid no harbour dues.

Perhaps the Minister believed some of the headlines in the newspapers of that period, when *The Paper* reported that 'Liquid Gold May Make Bantry a Boom Town',[7] and that 'The Project Would Have 1,000 on the Pay-Roll'.[8] When the *Universe Ireland* arrived in Bantry on 29 October 1968, she was the world's largest vessel afloat at the time, and the *Cork Examiner* described her arrival as setting in motion 'a development which could lead to Bantry Bay becoming a big industrial centre'.[9]

Even the probability of oil pollution from the new terminal was seen as an unlikely possibility, despite the fact that there were six similar major oil spills around the world since the *Torrey Canyon* disaster a year earlier.[10] Gulf Oil's terminal manager, Captain Henry Downing, was reported as saying that 'we stand a good chance of avoiding any pollution whatsoever'.[11]

It is easy to see, especially with the benefit of hindsight, how wrong these predictions were. Exaggerating the benefit of the development and ignoring its potential adverse consequences seems to be a characteristic view shared by the oil industry and the Irish State! There were rumours of a 'secret deal' between Gulf and certain government ministers, but what was not foreseen was that the absence of a harbour authority seriously weakened any external control or supervision of Gulf's activities, especially at the offshore terminal, which could be reached only by boat.

## INTERLUDE: THE CONTRAST WITH SHETLAND

The seafaring community has always exchanged news quickly, and the Bantry Bay fishermen and other local people with a maritime background soon became aware of the very different situation in the Shetland Islands, shortly after the first oil fields had been discovered in the North Sea in 1969. When Sullom Voe, a remote harbour in the northern part of Shetland, was quickly identified as the prime location for a pipeline terminal and tank farm to service the oil installations in the northern North Sea, British Petroleum (BP), as the principal operator, had expected to buy land and operate its own marine terminal facility. But BP found a very tough negotiator in Shetland Islands Council!

The Islands Council obtained power (by means of the Zetland County Council Act, 1974) to purchase the land needed by the oil industry, leased it to BP and other companies, and established the Sullom Voe Harbour Authority (SVHA). The Council has complete control over all marine activities, all tankers and other vessels using the port pay harbour dues, the oil industry rents the land on which the onshore facilities are located, and the SVHA maintains a stock of pollution control equipment, carries out regular oil spill response training exercise, ensures that high safety standards are maintained by all companies operating in the harbour, cleans up oil spillages, and charges the oil companies the full cost of all clean-up operations.

In addition, the Zetland County Council Act has provided a lasting revenue stream for the benefit of the islands from the development of the Sullom Voe terminal. Money paid by the oil industry to Shetland County Council to compensate people for the inconvenience of having the terminal based in Shetland was used to establish a charitable trust to receive and distribute this money. The Shetland Charitable Trust started life as Shetland Islands Council Charitable Trust (SICCT) in 1976 when Sullom Voe Terminal began operating; and from 1975 to 2012 the trust's investment returns were £395 million, of which some £259 million (approximately €304 million) has been distributed for the benefit of people in Shetland over the same period.[12] This figure is over and above the funds contained in the Shetland Reserve Fund, administered by Shetland Islands Council.[13]

The result is that Shetland and its people have benefitted greatly from the oil industry, the worst environmental effects are controlled and minimised, and there is a constant flow of funds to the council for road improvement, for the upgrading of other smaller harbours, and for facilities such as better schools, indoor swimming pools and other public amenities.

At the present time, when it was feared that Sullom Voe might decline in importance as the major North Sea oilfields are reaching the end of their commercial lives, Shetland appears to be set for a new oil boom at Sullom Voe which could keep the terminal open another thirty years or more. A plan by BP to use the harbour for servicing oil fields in the Atlantic, west of Shetland, could result in Sullom Voe staying open until possibly 2050 or beyond. At one time it was expected to close by 2000. Shetland could also benefit substantially from the exploitation of offshore renewable energy (wind, wave and tidal) as a consequence of the foresight shown by Zetland County council in 1973 and 1974.[14]

Despite the commercial orientation of the Sullom Voe Terminal, the Sullom Voe Harbour Authority recognises the importance of tourism and welcomes cruising yachts. The Authority's website advertises the beauty of the islands:

> For a unique and unforgettable experience visit Shetland by sea – take the top of Britain tour. Over 100 small islands and 906 miles of coastline shaped from a beautiful combination of dramatic cliffs and sheltered, natural harbours make it an ideal place for sailing. The scenic inlets shelter dozens of high-quality piers and marinas each offering a unique perspective on Shetland. The charming coastal scenery forms a relaxing backdrop for excellent cruising waters. Or, if it is adventure you are looking for, your yacht allows you unrestricted access to all the islands – find one and explore!

The contrast with what has been happening in Ireland could not be more stark – Shetland proudly declaring its financial independence, facing up to the oil industry, taking control of and celebrating its natural resources, and providing a model which Ireland might have followed.

## THE BANTRY BAY SAGA CONTINUES:
## A SUCCESSION OF SPILLAGES

However, back to Bantry Bay! The arrival of the first tanker was soon followed by the first oil spillage on Christmas Day, 25 December 1968, confirming the biologists' fears that Bantry Bay would soon lose its pristine status.[15]

What was most interesting about that spillage was that it occurred at a time when the wind was north-easterly, driving the oil south-westwards towards the small harbour of Gearahies, south-west of the terminal. According to Gulf Oil, the spillage occurred in the tank farm, and the oil escaped through a bund designed to prevent such an occurrence. The quantity of oil lost was unknown, the spillage was cleaned up reasonably quickly and local fishermen were compensated.[16] Nevertheless, the *Irish Times* noted that the spillage followed 'close upon the most explicit assurances from Gulf Oil Corporation . . . that there was virtually no possibility of an oil leak'.[17] Gulf Oil Terminals (Ireland) Limited was fined £250 at Bantry Court in February 1969.[18]

During the next six years, there was a succession of small oil spillages from the Gulf Oil terminal, or from the ships discharging and loading oil. None of these were serious, but they indicated a lack of spill prevention and control, and general carelessness in the operation of the terminal.

Six years after the arrival of the first cargo of oil, Bantry Bay experienced the first major spillage.[19] During the night of 21 and 22 October 1974, the 93,000 tonne dwt Liberian tanker *Universe Leader* was loading a cargo of Kuwait crude oil, but an underwater valve had been left open, and several hours elapsed before the escape of oil was noticed. During that time, 2,600 tonnes of Kuwait crude was spilled into the bay. By an extraordinary coincidence, the wind was again in the north-east, and the oil was driven south-westwards towards the boat harbour at Gerahies.

One of the significant features of this incident was the failure by the terminal operator to detect the spillage in time; and, after it had been reported, to admit that the amount spilled was unknown and they seriously underestimated the quantity of oil spilled. During darkness, the spillage went undetected, despite a report by a fisherman at Gerahies that there was a smell of oil. By daylight, small amounts of oil were seen on the surface of the sea around the ship, and at 08:00 a fisherman telephoned Gulf Oil to say that oil had appeared in Gerahies Harbour. Gulf Oil's terminal manager first estimated the spillage at no more than 5 barrels, but on the following day he was forced to increase his estimate to 250 barrels or 36 tonnes.[20]

Oil was beginning to accumulate at Gerahies, and a continuous slick of oil some 50 metres wide was seen stretching south-westwards from the terminal as far as the shore, approximately 6.5 km distant. Gulf dispatched three tug boats to begin spraying this slick south-west of Whiddy Island with dispersant in an effort to stop some of the oil reaching the shore. By the following day a massive clean-up operation had begun; and on 24 October, when the *Universe Leader* had completed loading, a shortfall of some 2,304 tonnes was discovered. A rough calculation made by the writer of this chapter, based on the spill being Kuwait crude oil of a fairly high viscosity and a low spreading rate, suggested that a slick 50 metres wide and 6.5 km long could contain between 1,650 and 3,300 tonnes of oil. The final estimate by Gulf, when the ship unloaded her cargo in Spain, was that some 2,600 tonnes had been spilled.

As a clean-up operations continued on 25 October, an oil spill was discovered at Gort na Coille on the south shore of Bantry Bay, only 13 km from Sheep's Head, which marks the southern extremity of the bay. The clean-up operation was carried out by Gulf Oil, which at one time had approximately 200 local men employed. One hundred forty tonnes of dispersants were sprayed on the oil, and at Gerahies, 130 tonnes of oil were contained by booms and then pumped ashore. Changing wind directions moved the oil slicks so that over 30 km of coastline became polluted. Sorbents such as straw, peat and synthetic materials were used to soak up the oil; but in many places the shoreline was so inaccessible that oil slicks driven onto the coast could not be reached, and were left to degrade naturally.

Large amounts of oil-contaminated straw and seaweed were collected and sent to Cork County Council's landfill, where a combination of moisture, nutrients and micro-organisms resulted in the oil being biologically degraded within a year. Oil lingered on in a few places for several years, where lack of oxygen and energy slowed down the degradation process.

Where oily straw had been carried across the upper part of the shoreline, lichens were seriously damaged in a few places. The team of biologists who had surveyed the shoreline in 1968 (including the author of this chapter) returned to resurvey the same transects,[21] and their findings were that biological damage, particularly to fish, was relatively low.

This incident, and the way in which Gulf had been forced to increase its estimate of the amount of oil spilled for several days, aroused great concern.[22] An Taisce called for a public sworn inquiry,[23] and the members of Cork County Council decided unanimously to urge the government to establish a full Harbour Authority for Bantry Bay.[24]

But more was to come. A couple of months later, on 10 January 1975, the tanker *Afran Zodiac* was struck by one of the two tugs assisting her, causing the twenty-fourth spillage since the terminal operation began just over six years earlier.[25] As the damaged tanker departed from Bantry Bay, she continued to leak heavy fuel oil from the hole in her side. A few days later, oil had contaminated the northern coastline of Bantry Bay, including part of Glengariff Harbour, and stretching south-westwards almost as far as Castletownbere.[26] The amount spilled was estimated at just over 100,000 gallons.

The Minister for Transport and Power declared that he was pressing ahead with all speed to establish a Harbour Authority which would cover the entire bay, including the fishing port of Castletownbere, while the Cork County Manager urged the Minister and Gulf Oil to take interim measures and immediate action to prevent spillages.[27] Gulf Oil was also criticised by an international expert for excessive use of dispersant to deal with the most recent spillage, while the Irish Fishermen's Organisation warned that the continuous use of dispersant on recurring oil spills could wipe out the commercially important herring spawning grounds in the Bay.[28]

Later that month, the Minister for Transport and Power, Mr Peter Barry, stated that he considered Gulf to be 'grossly negligent' and warned the company that he might be forced to 'consider putting them out if they continue to spill oil'.[29] Despite these warnings, and a further spillage from the *Fina Canada* on 22 March 1975, Gulf continued to operate.

However, one beneficial consequence of these spillages was that Gulf Oil tightened up the management of their operation at Whiddy Island. Four pollution-control officers were appointed, ships were boarded and inspected before they were allowed to berth at the terminal, and a pollution-control officer was stationed on board a ship at all times. The master of every incoming vessel was instructed to provide a plan of the number and location of his vessel's sea suction and overboard discharge valves, and all of these valves were checked and sealed by Gulf Oil's pollution-control officers. Ship personnel were not permitted to break the seals or to open the valves unless permitted by a pollution-control officer. Most critically, in 1975 Gulf Oil established a new unit to supervise and control all anti-pollution and cargo transfer procedures and practices, and this unit was headed by a newly appointed professional seaman with practical tanker knowledge and possessing a Master's Foreign Going Certificate of Competency.[30]

For a number of years the frequency and size of oil spillages at Whiddy Island began to decline, with only three spillages during the remainder of 1975, two spillages in 1976 and one in 1978. For a while, it seemed that Gulf Oil and the ships which called weekly to the terminal could be reasonably trusted to prevent further oil spillages.

## EVENTS LEADING TO THE *BETELGEUSE* DISASTER

But other changes were taking place worldwide, and in Bantry Bay, which would lead to the largest oil spill, the greatest loss of life and the destruction of the terminal itself.

A substantial increase in the price of crude oil, an economic recession and a mild winter in 1975-76 led to a significant reduction in oil consumption in Europe. Reduced shipping charter rates and the reopening of the Suez Canal undermined the economic advantage of the very large tankers used by Gulf, and the company began diverting crude oil (which was formerly trans-shipped at Bantry) to a new deep-water port at Bilbao in northern Spain. In 1975, the throughput of oil at the Whiddy Island terminal fell to 9.1 million tonnes compared with 17.1 million tonnes in 1974, and the number of ships also declined. In 1974, the terminal handled 74 very large crude oil carriers and 309 smaller shuttle tankers taking oil to

European refineries, but in 1975 the numbers dropped to 40 and 171 respectively. To make matters worse, the operating costs of the terminal had increased, and Gulf had attempted to find a partner, or even a purchaser, but had failed to do so.[31]

Despite this gloomy reality and forecast, Gulf stated that there would be no reduction in the pollution-prevention staff. Nevertheless, Gulf implemented other cost-saving measures which came to light only after the *Betelgeuse* disaster in January 1979 and the subsequent tribunal of inquiry.

The tribunal's report, published in May 1980, was one of the most comprehensive and technically detailed investigations of any maritime incident which this writer has seen; and it identified serious failings by the ship owner (CNP, a French state-owned company), the terminal operator and the Irish public and State authorities. Before going on to examine these failures, we must first describe what happened in Bantry Bay on 8 January 1979.

Shortly after midnight, while the ship was taking on seawater ballast, she broke in three as the result of excessive stress caused by improper ballasting and a seriously weakened hull.[32] A small explosion and fire caused by the buckling and fracturing of the vessel's hull was followed half an hour later by a massive explosion and fire, which overwhelmed the after part of the ship, the accommodation and the off-shore jetty, the result of which was the loss of fifty lives. All the crew of the tanker, the wife of one member of the crew, two visitors on board the tanker, Gulf Oil personnel on the jetty, and the ship's pilot died. The *Betelgeuse* was rendered a complete wreck and extensive damage was caused to the offshore jetty and installations. The remains of the ship were eventually salvaged and removed (at the cost of yet another life), but the jetty remains a disfigured monument to this day.

Following the explosion, a fire raged on and around the ship for almost twenty-four hours, and the intense heat caused much of the crude oil to polymerise into a tarry residue denser than water. After the fire, oil continued to leak from the wreck for several weeks, while small oil spillages occurred intermittently during the eighteen-month salvage operation. Floating oil slicks initially contaminated the north shore of Whiddy Island, but within a few days patches of oil became spread more widely around the inner part of Bantry Bay and as far south-westwards as Berehaven. Oil which had sunk was partially cleared from the sea-bed by scallop-dredging boats employed by the insurers.

Commercial fishing was disrupted by the pollution and the clean-up process. Floating oil prevented fishing in some areas of the bay, while sunken oil fouled scallop dredges. The exploitation of shellfish, particularly periwinkles, scallops and clams, was most seriously affected.

## THE TRIBUNAL OF INQUIRY AND ITS FINDINGS

The tribunal's terms of reference required it to inquire into the cause of the explosion and fire on the *Betelgeuse* and the measures taken to prevent such accidents. At the tribunal 184 witnesses were heard, of whom 78 gave technical or expert testimony, 97 gave evidence relevant to the facts of the disaster, while others assisted the tribunal by the production of photographic and other evidence.

As part of its work, the tribunal obtained evidence from a very large number of people living around Bantry Bay who had witnessed the event. As the result, the tribunal was able to establish, with a considerable degree of accuracy, the time the disaster commenced, its nature and its development. In addition, the tribunal had available to it some seven experts who were able to give evidence based on their specialist knowledge.

One of the most important findings of the tribunal was that Gulf management and personnel took active steps to suppress the truth of what had happened. They attempted to hide the fact that there was no person in the control room on Whiddy Island when the disaster began, false entries were made in logs, incorrect times were knowingly given to the tribunal, efforts were made to avoid making statements to the Gardaí, and false accusations were made against Gardaí who were taking evidence from witnesses.

The tribunal also found that Gulf had carried out during the 1970s a number of modifications to the fire-fighting system at the terminal and offshore jetty. When first commissioned, it was of a good international standard, but a decision had been made not to keep the fire mains pressurised, and this resulted in the jetty crew being unable to activate the system without the intervention of the dispatcher at Gulf Control on Whiddy Island. A decision had also been taken by Gulf to decommission the remote-control button situated in the control room which was designed to start the fire-fighting foam production on the four fire monitors on the centre platform of the offshore jetty. The foam system on the jetty was also modified so that it ceased to be automatic. The original fire-fighting system was much superior to what was in place when the *Betelgeuse* caught fire. Some important items of fire-fighting equipment were allowed to remain unusable or out of action for much longer than was desirable, and standards of maintenance had been lessened for some time prior to the disaster.

Some of these changes resulted from economy measures, while others were made to reduce maintenance; but, as the tribunal stated, 'it would have been preferable to have improved maintenance techniques rather than to modify the system', 'not enough consideration was given to the redesign of the system' and there was an inadequate appreciation of the consequences of these decisions.

Changes were also made by Gulf during the 1970s to the way in which personnel on the offshore jetty could make their escape in an emergency. The original operational plan made adequate provisions for an emergency evacuation of personnel, but the personnel transfer facilities at Dolphin Number 1 (the most westerly part of the offshore structure) were removed, and there was only an inflatable life raft available at the centre platform. This was totally inadequate, given the risk of an oil spill catching fire, and the fact that there was no direct means of access from the jetty to Whiddy Island. According to the tribunal, proper rescue boats or escape capsules should have been provided at each end of the jetty:

> The structure of the jetty from the west breasting dolphin to Dolphin 22 was completely devastated in the disaster. There was, however, no fire or explosive damage westwards of the west breasting dolphin. Had any member of the ship's crew or the personnel on the jetty been able to reach Dolphin 1, he would, in all probability, have been saved.

The tribunal also identified major defects in the emergency procedures which had developed over the years. The first arose from the fact that the duty tug was permitted to moor out of sight of the jetty and at a considerable distance from it (4.5 km); the second from the fact that initiation of the procedures depended entirely on the constant presence of the dispatcher in the control room.

The position of the duty tugboat on the night of the disaster was not that contemplated in the original operational design of the terminal. Gulf altered the original position of the duty tug as a result of pressure from the company operating the tugs, and in the knowledge that the alteration was undesirable from the point of view of safety. Gulf's 'Policy and Procedures' manual, updated in 1976, gave a wholly misleading description of the role of the tugs in an emergency and was not complied with in practice. Had the duty tug been moored in sight of the *Betelgeuse* and in its vicinity, her crew would have observed the fire and it is probable that, notwithstanding the absence of the dispatcher from the control room, the lives of those on board the ship and the crew of the jetty would have been saved.

A general decline in safety standards had also taken place; 'temporary employees' got no formal training in fire-fighting techniques, no escape plan to evacuate the jetty had been prepared, and no training in evacuation had been given.

## THE *BETELGEUSE* – A SUBSTANDARD SHIP

Despite being owned by the French state oil company, Compagnie Navale des Pétroles, a subsidiary of the French and multinational petroleum company Total, the *Betelgeuse* was in very poor structural condition.

The tribunal of inquiry found that a conscious and deliberate decision had been taken by Total not to renew certain of the longitudinals and other parts of the permanent ballast tanks which were known to be seriously wasted by corrosion, and not to renew the tanks' cathodic protection. These decisions were taken by the ship owner at the time of ship's second special survey in Singapore in the summer of 1977; they were taken in the interests of economy and because it was then considered that the ship would be sold in the near future. Furthermore, the welding of certain of the longitudinals which were renewed in Singapore was improperly carried out, and contributed to the potentially dangerous condition of the ship. All of these matters had the most serious consequences, as they contributed to the fact that on 8 January 1979, the vessel was in a seriously corroded and wasted condition.

Following her arrival at the Whiddy Island terminal, the *Betelgeuse* was superficially inspected on 7 January 1979, by two surveyors on behalf of potential purchasers of the vessel. Neither surveyor inspected the permanent ballast tanks or the cargo tanks and neither was in a position to provide information about the internal condition of any of the tanks. However, the paint-work on the deck was in poor and rusted condition, the deck's steam line was in a poor condition near the cargo room, the electric cable ducting was in a poor condition, and considerable sections of the small-bore piping ducting required renewal.

It was widely known in Bantry at the time that Gulf Oil's pollution-control officers, who had inspected the ship when she arrived in Bantry Bay, were very critical of her condition, and had advised caution about allowing her to berth at the terminal. However, there was considerable pressure from Gulf management to allow the ship to discharge her cargo: if she had been sent away, the costs would have been serious.

On the night of the disaster the structure of the vessel was abnormally, seriously and significantly wasted due to corrosion, and the wastage was particularly marked in way of the permanent ballast tanks. An important cause of the excessive corrosion was Total's deliberate decision not to renew the cathodic protection in the permanent ballast tanks and/or its failure to have the tanks coated with a protective coating. Neither the master nor the chief officer could have been aware on the night of the disaster how much the vessel had been allowed to become seriously weakened.

Secondly, despite it being standard practice for large tankers to have a computer known as a 'loadicator' or other electronic or mechanical means to assist in calculating the stresses on the ship's structure, the *Betelgeuse* had no loadicator or any other similar type of equipment. In taking on intermediate ballast (as the ship did on the night of 7 and 8 January), the master and chief officer had available to them only a document known as the '*Conditions de Chargement*', which, had they consulted it, would have been of little or no assistance to them. Total was aware that the absence of a loadicator (an effective model of which would have cost only a few thousand pounds) caused problems for its chief officers. No adequate explanation for this omission was given to the tribunal and its absence had the most serious consequences. The ship's officers therefore did not know that the amount of ballast taken aboard, and its distribution in the permanent ballast tanks and the Nos. 2 to 5 centre tanks, created sagging conditions in the centre of the vessel and set up very large stresses amidships, where the first failure of the vessel's hull occurred.

The tribunal concluded that the stresses which were set up during ballasting were well above the critical buckling stress limits of some of the deck and side-shell longitudinals in the permanent ballast tanks. Some of these buckled and were torn from their welding, leading to a weakening of the deck and side-shell plating, which in turn buckled, and a progressive failure of the hull developed.

The buckling process caused gas from the No. 3 wing tanks or from the No. 4 centre tank to enter the permanent ballast tanks. An explosive mixture in these tanks was ignited by incendiary sparks created by the buckling of the longitudinals. Explosions in both permanent ballast tanks occurred in the very early stages of the disaster; and, combined with the tensile force which had been set up by the failure of the hull, resulted in fractures of the bottom plates of the vessel.

The initial break caused the centre part of ship to sink below sea-level at a point not far forward of the manifold, while her bow and stern became elevated; i.e. she broke her back. Flammable vapour from oil which escaped from the No. 3 wing tanks was ignited, and caused the fire which was seen amidships by the witnesses around the bay. Large quantities of oil escaped on either side of the vessel, and this became ignited, leading to the beginning of the second phase of the disaster as observed by the eye-witnesses.

When the vessel broke her back originally, it caused the fire-main on the deck of the ship to fracture; and, as a result, the crew were unable to fight the fire from the monitors on the main deck. The fire amidships caused large quantities of smoke to be blown across the centre platform of the jetty, leading to its evacuation by the jetty crew and preventing the use of the jetty's fire-fighting equipment at the centre platform.

A fire then developed on the sea and on the ship herself from oil which had leaked from the cargo tanks, resulting in a massive explosion, huge fire and loss of all lives on board.

The tribunal found that the major share of the responsibility for the loss of the ship lay with the management of Total; but Gulf must also share the blame.

## A Substandard and Unsafe Oil Terminal

The tribunal of inquiry also found that:

- Had the dispatcher in the control room observed the initiation of the disaster it is probable that the lives of the jetty crew and those on board the ship would have been saved.

- Had Gulf maintained the stand-by tug close to, and in sight of the jetty, it is probable that, notwithstanding the absence from the control room of the dispatcher on the night of the disaster, the lives of the jetty crew and those on board the vessel would have been saved.

- Had Gulf supplied suitable escape craft at the jetty it is probable that, notwithstanding the absence from the control room of the dispatcher and notwithstanding the absence of the stand-by tug from the vicinity of the jetty, the lives of the jetty crew and those on board the vessel would have been saved.

- Had access to the sea from Dolphin 1 been maintained and had the jetty crew been properly trained in emergency procedures so that they would run up-wind of a fire, it is possible – but no certain conclusions on this point can be arrived at – that the jetty crew on the centre platform would have been saved.

- Had the decision to discontinue the automatically pressurised fire-main not been taken, it is possible – but again no certain conclusions on this point can be arrived at – that the jetty crew might have been able to contain the fire from the eastern breasting dolphin so that it would not develop in the manner in which it did, and so as to permit the rescue of the jetty crew and those on board the tanker by one or more of the two workboats operated by Gulf. When the fire on the *Betelgeuse* began, these boats were at the 'Ascon Jetty' on the far side of Whiddy Island, out of sight and sound of the events unfolding at the offshore terminal; and, because of the absence of the dispatcher from his post in the control room, they were alerted too late, and reached the tanker only after the huge explosion and major fire had occurred.

- Had the alert been raised at the beginning of the disaster or had the stand-by tug been closer to the jetty, it is probable that the fire would have been contained and that the contents of No. 5 wing tanks (as well as those in No. 2 wing tanks which were saved) would have been saved.

- Had the tug been moored in sight of the jetty and close to it, it would have been able to contain the fire and probably extinguish it before it spread on either side of the ship, and it would then have been able to remove the ship from the jetty. The damage to the jetty would then have been minimal in comparison to that which it, in fact, suffered.

## THE WEAK ROLE OF THE PUBLIC AUTHORITIES

We have noted earlier in this chapter that the government had resisted the representations by local residents of Bantry and by Cork County Council to establish a harbour authority for the bay.

The tribunal found that this failure to establish a harbour authority with jurisdiction over Whiddy Island meant that Gulf itself was responsible for drafting by-laws under the Petroleum Act 1881, which would make provision for the safe handling of petroleum products and which would have to be approved by the Minister. This was a highly anomalous situation and contributed to the fact that no by-laws were ever made under the Act of 1881. After a government decision was announced in 1972 that safety regulations would be made under the Dangerous Substances Act 1972, the relevant department failed to act, and no regulations had been made under that act before the disaster in January 1979.

The failure to establish by-laws under the provisions of the Petroleum Act 1881, or to introduce regulations under the Dangerous Substances Act 1972, had serious consequences. The statutory obligations placed on Gulf to maintain proper safety measures and standards, and to provide effective fire-fighting systems (particularly in relation to the position of the duty tugboat as noted above) were wholly inadequate. There was a correspondingly inadequate obligation on the public authorities, both at government and local level, to supervise and inspect the safety measures and fire-fighting systems at the terminal.

Had the Dangerous Substances (Oil Jetties) Regulations 1979 been in force prior to the disaster it is very likely that at least some of these deficiencies would not have occurred, or, if they had, that they would have been observed by a departmental inspector and remedied.

The tribunal also found that a highly anomalous legal situation existed in that the jurisdiction of Cork County Council both as a planning authority and as a fire brigade authority did not extend to the offshore jetty at the terminal; its jurisdiction ended at low-water mark at Whiddy Island. Gulf did not seek any kind of permission for making alterations to the personnel building on the jetty, for altering the escape routes from the jetty, or for making changes in the fire-fighting systems because it did not occur to the company that permission would be necessary.

Furthermore, because Cork County Council had no jurisdiction over the offshore jetty, the Council did not know about the changes made to the personnel building, to the jetty itself, or to the position of the tugs' moorings. According to correspondence between the county council and Gulf, and from Gulf's 'Policy and Procedures' manual which was forwarded to the council, Cork County Council made the incorrect assumption that no changes had been made.

## Some Further Lessons

The tribunal of inquiry identified some extremely important lessons to be learned from the disaster, but there are other lessons which we feel are equally important, especially after the disaster, and at the present time.

If we consider the impact of the oil industry on the environment in terms of oil spillages – a relatively simplistic view to begin with – we can see that ship owners and governments are equally important participants in the field. Nearly all of the large oil spillages from shipping accidents – for example the *Torrey Canyon*, *Amoco Cadiz* and *Exxon Valdez* – were the result of actions (or inaction!) by the vessel's master or owner. Of course the oil company which chartered these vessels must also take part of the responsibility, but in nearly all cases it was the action of the ship which caused the disaster.

In the case of the *Betelgeuse* disaster, described in some detail earlier in this chapter, the failure by the State and its agencies to ensure proper control over the installation in Bantry Bay was a major factor. Protection of the marine and coastal environment relies not only on the work of organisations such as the International Maritime Organisation (IMO) and on international conventions such as MARPOL, but on the implementation and enforcement of legislation and environmental and safety standards. The failures to establish an effective Harbour Authority and to enact regulations giving the relevant government department power to inspect the offshore jetty and to enforce good operating standards and procedures were highlighted by the tribunal of inquiry into the disaster.

The second lesson to emerge from the series of oil-pollution incidents in Bantry, and especially from the *Betelgeuse* disaster, is that the oil industry cannot be trusted to police itself. The statement in 1968 by Gulf's terminal manager that 'we stand a good chance of avoiding any pollution whatsoever' was followed by a lowering of operational standards until the *Universe Leader* spill, followed in quick succession by oil spillages from the *Afran Zodiac* and the *Fina Canada*, provided a wake-up call. Despite these and other incidents, changes were made in the operation and staffing of the terminal which resulted in a serious reduction in standards of safety and environmental protection. Then, when faced with the reality of what had happened, Gulf management and certain personnel made deliberately false statements and attempted unsuccessfully to suppress the truth. If the tribunal of inquiry had not been so meticulous in its work, the complete range of causes and their consequences might never have been fully identified.

## AFTER THE *BETELGEUSE*:
## A HARBOUR AUTHORITY AT LAST, AND A NEW INDUSTRY

Even though the tribunal of inquiry deplored the absence of a harbour authority for Bantry Bay, steps had already been taken to establish such an authority. The promise by Mr Peter Barry, Minister for Transport and Power, in January 1975 was followed by the passing of the Harbours Act 1976, establishing the Bantry Bay Harbour Commissioners, in accordance with the Harbours Act 1946. Unfortunately, it was not until 1990 that the Minister for the Marine extended the function of the commissioners to give them the full powers of a harbour authority, with the exception of the power to levy harbour dues. That power was not given to the harbour commissioners until 1991 (Harbour Rates (Bantry Bay Harbour) Order 1991 (S.I. No. 36/1991)), some twelve years after the disaster and sixteen years after the minister made his promise.

The Bantry Bay Harbour Commissioners' jurisdiction includes the bay area inside a line between Dursey Island and Sheep's Head, but excludes the Castletownbere Fisheries Harbour. There are eleven Harbour Commissioners: Cork County Council, Bantry Town

Commissioners and Bantry Chamber of Commerce each appoint two members; two are elected by ship owners who have paid harbour dues; and a further three are appointed by the Minister of Marine and Natural Resources.

For most of that period, the Bantry Bay Harbour Commissioners had no power to make by-laws within the Bantry Bay area, and they operated under the 1946 Harbours Act and the Dangerous Substances (Oil Jetties) Regulations (1979). Nevertheless, the harbour-master developed one of the most advanced radio and radar tracking systems in Europe, allowing him to continuously monitor maritime traffic and receive automatic notification by mobile telephone if any ship approached the bay or moved from its allocated anchoring position. When the necessary legislation was passed allowing the commissioners to levy harbour dues, they became financially independent and self-funding.

In September 1979, the Dangerous Substances (Oil Jetties) Regulations 1979 (S.I. No. 312 of 1979) were implemented, giving wide-ranging power to determine what activities were permitted at jetties handling oil cargoes, and to impose safety standards.

Six years after the disaster, the government extended the boundary of County Cork to include a part of Bantry Bay inside a line from Muccurragh Point to League Point, giving Cork County Council jurisdiction over the offshore jetty (Local Government (Reorganisation) Act 1985; Section 28 (1) (a)) and the Local Government Reorganisation (Supplementary Provisions) (Cork) Order 1985 (S.I. No. 174 of 1985).

In the meantime, the Bantry Action Group (formed to bring employment and suitable developments to the area) began experimenting with suspended mussel culture in the inner part of Bantry: rafts and longlines were constructed, mussel spat collected, and the first mussels were harvested commercially in March 1983. In 1984, the first conference on mussel culture was held in Bantry, at which Irish and international speakers described how this new industry could revive the area.[33]

In December 1984, the Tánaiste, Dick Spring, announced that Gulf Oil would restore the damaged terminal at a cost of $60 million, and it would be upgraded to handle refined petroleum products as well as crude oil. The tank farm would store the State's strategic oil reserve, and two of the tanks on Whiddy Island would be placed at the disposal of the State free of charge indefinitely.[34] However, during that year, Gulf Oil Corporation had merged with Standard Oil of California, to form a new company, Chevron, which was now the ultimate owner of the Bantry Bay terminal and tank farm.

On 21 June 1985, Gulf Oil Terminals (Ireland) Ltd applied to Cork County Council for planning permission to reconstruct the offshore jetty at Whiddy Island.[35] Cork County Council granted planning permission on 22 August 1985, subject to thirty-five conditions. The decision was appealed to An Bord Pleanála by the newly established Bantry Mussel Farmers' Association, HOPE (a locally based environmental NGO), the West Cork Association of An Taisce, and by Comhdháil na nOileán (the Association of Irish Islands, representing the residents of Whiddy Island).

One of the principal grounds of appeal was the fact that the conditions attached to the decision to grant planning permission failed to recognise the importance of the mussel-growing industry, made no provision for its protection from oil spillages or any other form of pollution, and made no arrangements for compensation in the event of mussel harvesting having to be stopped because of pollution. The Bantry Mussel Farmers' Association pointed out in their appeal that an earlier oyster-farming venture in Bantry Bay had been wiped out in 1979 by oil from the *Betelgeuse* disaster, but no compensation was paid until April 1985, six and a half years later.

On 29 October 1985 An Bord Pleanála announced that it would hold an oral hearing of the appeals, on a date yet to be fixed, but probably in January 1986. Following this announcement, all of the above organisations came under considerable pressure from Cork County Council to withdraw their appeals. Gulf Oil (now renamed Chevron) had not initially expected to have to apply for planning permission to re-construct the offshore jetty, and were caught by the then recent extension of Cork County Council's jurisdiction over part of Bantry Bay. Gulf then complained that the new powers of the council, and especially the appeals to An Bord Pleanála, would have the effect of delaying the project and potentially damaging their plans for the re-construction; and the company threatened to withdraw its application.

The government had also issued its own ultimatum to Chevron – either rebuild and operate the offshore jetty, or remove the entire terminal and restore the site to agricultural land, in accordance with the original planning permission.

Following very detailed and intense discussions between Cork County Council, the Bantry Mussel Growers Association, Comhdháil na nOileán (the Association of Irish Islands, representing the residents of Whiddy Island), the Whiddy Island Residents themselves, and HOPE, all of the appeals were withdrawn on the basis of an agreement made between the parties. However, while these negotiations were going on, Chevron decided in January 1986 not to reopen the terminal but to hand over its entire assets on Whiddy Island to the Irish government, together with several million pounds. Gulf had taken successful legal proceedings in the United States against Total, the owner of the *Betelgeuse*, and had been awarded a much larger sum in compensation for the destruction of the oil terminal. In 1986, ownership of the terminal was transferred from Gulf Oil to the Irish National Petroleum Corporation (INPC), a State-owned company.

The people of Bantry felt that a significant proportion of the funds handed by Gulf to the Irish government should have been spent in Bantry for the improvement of the town's facilities and to help develop new and alternative commercial enterprises. However, Cork County Council made it clear that they had other uses for the money, and intended to spend all of it; though eventually some small grant aid was given to the newly developing mussel-culture industry.

Having learned earlier that the oil industry could not be trusted to police itself, or to be truthful in emergencies, the people of Bantry now learned a further lesson – that when the future of a natural resource such as Bantry Bay was being considered, the relevant public authorities will throw their weight behind the oil industry. During the negotiations which took place in November and December 1985 and in January 1986, it became clear that the mussel growers' concern about the environment and the water quality in Bantry Bay (a concern shared by HOPE and by An Taisce) was of far less importance to Cork County Council than ensuring the return of the oil industry. It did not matter at the time that the culture of mussels was a socially and environmentally sustainable industry, while the use of Whiddy Island for the storage and transhipment of oil had an uncertain future, largely determined by factors outside of the control of the people of Bantry or the people of Ireland.

This situation might be considered a prelude to what happened a decade later, when the State gave its full support to Shell Exploration and Production Ireland Ltd, despite widespread national and local protests and environmental problems resulting from the way in which Shell are being 'permitted' to exploit the Corrib gas field, under licensing terms which will bring no benefit to the people of Ireland.

## A Period under State Ownership

In 1982, the Irish National Petroleum Corporation (INPC) had already acquired Ireland's only oil refinery at Whitegate in Cork Harbour as a result of a decision made by the refinery's shareholders at that time (Esso, Texaco, Shell and BP) to permanently cease operating on the grounds that there was excess refining capacity in Europe. The government had challenged this decision, with the result that the refinery came free of charge into state ownership: it did not have to be purchased; only modernisation and upgrading were required. In addition, legislation was passed requiring all distributors and sellers of oil products throughout Ireland to source a proportion of their raw material from Whitegate.

INPC decided not to attempt to rebuild the damaged terminal but to install a single-buoy mooring (SBM), in deep water 1,600 metres north of Whiddy Island, linked to the onshore tank farm by an undersea pipeline. Two shipments of crude oil were imported to the terminal in April 1998 to commission the SBM. The SBM began operating with written consent from the Bantry Bay Harbour Commissioners, issued under the Dangerous Substances (Oil Jetties) Regulations 1979; and under an Integrated Pollution Prevention and Control (IPPC) licence issued by the Environmental Protection Agency. The oil terminal, including the SBM, is subject to other legislation, including the Dangerous Substances (Petroleum Bulk Storage) Regulations 1979 and the Safety, Health and Welfare at Work Acts (1981 to 1995).

Under INPC control and a fully functioning Harbour Authority, there were very few spillages of oil, and the mussel industry continued to expand. The number of ships calling to the terminal was much less than during the years when it was operated by Gulf, but the huge tanks provided convenient and cost-effective storage for Ireland's strategic oil reserve.

## LOSS OF CONTROL AGAIN

This situation could have continued reasonably successfully, if it were not for the uncritical adoption by the Irish government of a neoliberal economic doctrine which preached that such assets would function better in private hands. Not all countries took this view. Norway, for example, continued to keep all its oil-related resources and assets under the control and ownership of Statoil – a company in which the State holds a majority of shares.

In Ireland, the Whitegate refinery and the Whiddy Island tank farm and offshore SBM were put up for sale; and the State's involvement in oil industry operations ceased with the sale of these assets to the United States-based Tosco Corporation on 16 July 2001. Legal provision for this transaction was provided by the Irish National Petroleum Corporation Limited Act 2001. The INPC no longer operated as an oil company since the disposal of its business and commercial assets, and the company's current activities are limited to finalising residual issues arising from the 2001 transaction (primarily environmental claims lodged against INPC). The refinery and the Bantry Bay facility subsequently passed into the ownership of ConocoPhillips, another major oil company based in Texas.

ConocoPhillips, which subsequently changed its name to Phillips66, has operated the SBM since 2001, and remarkably has had no significant spillage of oil during that period. Of course the number of ships discharging and loading oil has been much less than during the time when Gulf Oil controlled the terminal, but it would be fair to say that this company's record is very much better than that of Gulf.

However, uncertainty once again dominates the situation in 2013, with rumours widely circulating in Bantry that Phillips66 are intending to sell both the Whitegate refinery and all of the facilities in Bantry Bay. Given the doubtful future of the oil industry worldwide, and the possibility that no purchaser may be found, the closure of the Bantry facility may be a distinct possibility.

It is interesting to compare the situations in 1982 and 2013: in the earlier period the Irish government acted with some degree of strength and national concern to prevent the closure and abandonment of the Whitegate refinery, with the result that it was given into State hands, while in the current situation the government appears to have offered no challenge to Phillips66's plan to sell the refinery, or even to close it down.

## REPORT RECOMMENDATIONS

In 2011, the Department of Communications, Energy and Natural Resources commissioned from Purvin & Gertz and Byrne Ó Cléirigh Consultants a strategic study of the need to have an oil refinery in Ireland. The report of the study, published in 2012, entitled 'A Strategic Case for Oil Refining on the Island of Ireland', concluded that:

- If Ireland did not have a refinery it would be the largest national market in the EU without a refinery. Currently, the largest EU country without a refinery is Slovenia which has a demand of about one quarter of the demand in all of Ireland.

- Among all EU member states, Ireland has the greatest dependence on oil for its primary energy supply.

- Ireland is the one country where refinery production is far short of domestic demand and has been for some time.

- Whitegate oil refinery is currently an efficient and reliable facility within its class, has a commendable safety record, and continues to operate within the conditions of its IPPC License and in compliance with the COMAH Directive under which it is regulated by the Health and Safety Authority.

- The refinery is capable of operating for the long term, provided the levels of expenditure on maintenance remain sufficient in real terms.

- Recent dredging works in Cork Harbour will, when completed, permit Whitegate to import crude oil cargoes of up to 105,000 tonnes, and this will reduce the cost of sourcing crude oil.

- Whitegate refinery is an important source of supply of oil products to the All-Ireland market, and it should be encouraged to continue operating, given its important contribution to employment and the local economy.

- If Whitegate were to cease operations as a refinery and to continue only as an oil terminal to hold some of Ireland's strategic stocks, there might be an opportunity to use some of the tanks on the refinery site; but, apart from the cost of acquiring a lease on the tankage and access to the jetties, the cost of upgrading this tankage alone would amount to approximately €10 million.

- A newly constructed modern refinery in Ireland would add value in the order of €29 billion to €35 billion over the 2017-to-2050 timeframe; equivalent to around $1 billion per year in constant 2011 money; and the report estimates around €140 million to €215 million per year in constant 2011 money would flow directly to the Irish economy via operating-cost expenditure and taxation, while other broader economic benefits could arise through supporting other industries.

- In the case of Whitegate, the value added would be closer to €3.5 billion over the same period, equating to around €110 million per year in constant 2011 money; and the report estimates that around €21 million to 29 million per year of this added value would contribute directly to the Irish economy through local taxation and local expenditure, plus additional benefits that would arise through the support of local industries. (Currently around 150 people are directly employed at the Whitegate refinery plus a further 30 or so regular contract staff.)

Given the above findings and conclusions, it is clear that the combination of Whitegate refinery and the Bantry Bay oil terminal should be kept operating; and if it were to revert to State ownership, as happened in 1982, the economic benefits would be substantial.

As if the above uncertainty was not enough, the government has also been attempting to extinguish the power of the Bantry Bay Harbour Authority by forcibly merging it with the Port of Cork Company. This merger is part of government policy to merge regional harbours that have significant commercial traffic with a port company, and to transfer smaller harbours to a local authority. This policy is based on a review of regional ports and harbours by KPMG, published in 1999. To date, eleven harbours have been transferred to local-authority control, leaving Bantry Harbour as the only regional harbour operating under the Harbours Act of 1946. Provision was included in the Harbours (Amendment) Act 2009 to allow the transfer of Bantry Bay Harbour to the Port of Cork to take place.

The proposed merger was greeted with horror by the people of Bantry, and the almost unanimous view of the Harbour Authority members was that the least acceptable option was to succumb to a takeover by the Port of Cork.

In a report in the *Southern Star* newspaper dated 15 March 2013, Senator Denis O'Donovan is quoted as saying that 'Bantry Harbour Board has been a success story and it should be left as it is. Although it is an unusual model the current structure is a low operating cost model and the members, by their own volition, get no payment whatsoever and all profits are retained and spent locally. The Board has local control, with many users' interest in the bay being properly looked after. Its key focus is improving the marine infrastructure deficit in the inner harbour, which is an historic problem going back decades, and it has a healthy bank balance somewhere in the region of €1.5 million.

'Its net worth and balance sheet has grown eight-fold in the past ten years, with €4.5 million having been spent in the past seven years on the development of Whiddy slipway, the Abbey Point slipway, commercial pontoons, pier raising at the main pier, land acquisition, derrick purchase and the surveys and planning costs required for the master plan for the development of the inner harbour. In my opinion, the best way forward is to continue operating the harbour as it is, and using the resources to improve local infrastructure.'

During a debate in Seanad Éireann on 21 February 2012, Senator Denis O'Donovan pointed out that Bantry Harbour has a viable Harbour Board, which is self-sufficient in that it costs the State little or no money. Furthermore, there has been a sizeable income to the

Bantry Bay Harbour Authority for the past fifteen or twenty years, primarily due to the input of funds from ConocoPhillips. Senator O'Donovan also stated that former and current members of Cork Port informed him that they do not want the merger to take place.

He pointed out that 'Apart from Whiddy Island, there are many intricacies in Bantry. It is designated as a tourist hub; there is inshore fishing and fish farming in the bay. Garnish Island is nearby and people are living on Whiddy Ireland. The Bantry Harbour Board area comprises 80 percent of Bantry Bay, from Bere Island to Ardnagashel and across the bay.'

He said that the harbour authority 'has been run successfully and much money has been spent within the harbour board area by the existing board. The board provided a slipway on Whiddy Ireland, with support from the council and the government, and a slipway on the mainland.' For the first time in his life, 'there is a roll-on roll-off service onto the island, which can be used by an ambulance or a fire brigade'.

The response by Leo Varadkar, Minister for Transport, Tourism and Sport, was merely to restate that the continued operation of regional harbours under the Harbours Act 1946 is unsustainable, according to the government's 2005 ports policy statement.

The Minister also restated that the core business of Bantry Harbour is the oil storage and transhipment terminal on Whiddy Island – almost echoing the words of Patrick Lalor, Parliamentary Secretary to the Minister for Transport and Power, in 1968. However, he added that 'aquaculture, fishing and tourism are prevalent in the harbour and a small number of cruise liners also visit the harbour each year'. No mention of the environment of course, and certainly no need to consider that a Harbour Authority should consider care or protection of the environment as one of its responsibilities! That would be far too logical.

The minister urged that 'amalgamation with Cork would provide access to port expertise, marketing, strategic development, planning and the skills required for the regulation of navigation, ship and port security requirements, pilotage, safety, emergency response and pollution, etc', and he also took care to point out that 'the operation of large oil tankers, bulk carriers and cruise liners in and out of the bay requires specific expertise' – as if that expertise did not already exist in Bantry Bay!

As a result of local pressure, the Department of Transport, Tourism and Sport issued a request for submissions or comments, to be submitted by 5 April 2013. The results of the public consultation are awaited at the time of writing.[36]

But, you might ask, what have these issues got to do with the relations between the oil industry and the environment?

In this chapter, we have shown that the oil industry cannot be fully trusted, especially in an emergency, or in difficult economic circumstances, when cost-saving measures are likely to lead to accidents, pollution and environmental damage. It also became clear from the recent history of Bantry Bay that not all oil companies behave similarly: Gulf had an appalling record of spillages, while ConocoPhillips and Phillips66 appear to be much more careful and safety-conscious.

It also appears that, when there is a question of ownership of natural resources, or who will benefit, the State agencies almost invariably take the side of the oil industry against the local people's interest. Rarely, if ever, are environmental issues seen as a priority.

A strong indication of the way in which the environment is perceived may be seen in the government's 'Ports Policy Statement 2005' which notes that 'Ports have encountered increased regulatory and operational burdens arising from environmental and security measures'. The environment is seen as a barrier to 'progress' instead of something valuable to be protected in its own right, in addition to whatever contribution it makes to human welfare. This is clearly an extremely retrograde attitude to the environment, showing that some Irish State agencies and government departments have learned very little or nothing since the time when the worldwide growth in environmental awareness began in the early 1970s.

For example, let us consider the following phases in environmental policy and attitudes within governments and industry, as first described by the Dutch Committee for Long-Term Environmental Policy in 1990:

- *Phase 1: Environmental pollution as a side-effect.* Industries regard the environmental problem as a minor irritation, with regulatory authorities making what are considered to be unnecessarily strict regulations; while legal measures are seen as cost-raising emission restrictions (the end-of-pipe approach).

- *Phase 2: Environmental pollution as a cost factor.* Governments and industrial policy-makers begin to see that it may be beneficial to reduce pollution levels (adaptations at process level).

- *Phase 3: The environment as a boundary condition.* Governments and industrial policy-makers incorporate environmental factors when planning new investments, and are thereby forced to produce or consume differently (adaptations at process and product levels).

- *Phase 4: The environment as a policy-determining factor.* Environmental factors play a significant role when policy-makers and industrial operators are optimising their activities, and this leads to different system designs (adaptations at system level).

- *Phase 5: The environment as a key objective.* Society and government incorporate the environment as an essential factor and vital goal in social and economic policy. As a result of this, there are far-reaching changes in the patterns of production and consumption as well as in mental attitudes accompanied by shifts in values (adaptations at structural level).

While the long-term aim is to achieve Phase 5, it is recognised that different sectors of the Irish economy and society are at different phases in the process, and will exhibit varying degrees of readiness to change. Port policy seems to be lagging far behind, and stuck at phase one, while some sectors of industry have moved ahead.

To some extent this almost complete lack of environmental awareness may be a legacy of the 1946 Harbours Act, in which the environment is not even mentioned, and the members of harbour boards are selected to represent local authorities, chambers of commerce, manufacturers, livestock traders and exporters, some ship owners, organised labour or trade unions, and of course members appointed by the relevant Minister.

The 1996 Harbours Act went a little bit further, in that Section 12 (1) (d) requires a harbour company 'to have due regard to the consequences of its activities on the environment, the heritage (whether natural or man-made) relating to its harbour and the amenities generally in the vicinity of its harbour'. It seems therefore that we have moved forward, to somewhere between phase two and phase three, but nowhere near phases four or five, but we still lag at least two decades behind Europe's environmental leaders.

Even though the Harbours (Amendment) Act 2009 does not specifically delete or revoke Section 12 (1) (d) of the 1996 Harbours Act, it fails to give any recognition to the environmental importance of the natural harbours and estuaries in which nearly all Irish ports are located. (We have no artificial or man-made harbours except Dun Laoghaire.) The environment is not even mentioned as a factor to be taken into consideration in port operations, and other environmentally sensitive activities in our harbours, such as mariculture, commercial fisheries, tourism and recreation are not recognised at all. The 2009 Act has also eliminated the concept of managing harbours as public utilities for the common good – instead they are to be operated as commercial entities, competing with each other, and permitted to participate in a range of commercial ventures with private enterprises outside of their harbour limits. Furthermore, the boards of the harbour companies are no longer required to include representatives of local authorities and port users, never mind the environmental interests!

Competition between harbours is senseless, leading to duplication of facilities and 'turf wars' such as that which emerged between Cork and Waterford when the Port of Cork lodged an application with An Bord Pleanála in 2007 to construct a very large container terminal at Ringaskiddy in Cork Harbour. At an oral hearing held by An Bord Pleanála in 2008 into the planning application by the Port of Cork, one of the strongest appellants was the Port of Waterford, whose expert witnesses argued that any increase in the number of containers being shipped through Cork would lead only to a reduction in the number of containers handled by other ports, including Waterford. The size of the 'cake' would not change, but each port fought to get a larger slice for itself!

The rights and responsibilities of port and harbour companies derive from the legislation that creates them and gives them their power, and each port company can operate only within its powers. Without a specific mandate under the legislation to consider the natural environment and the beneficial uses of the environment for the common good, it is clear that the profit motive and commercial objectives will override all other considerations.

In Britain, for example, port and harbour authorities have a statutory duty to balance nature conservation with their other duties. Section 48A of the Harbours Act 1964 (inserted by Schedule 3 of the Transport and Works Act 1992), states clearly that:

> It shall be the duty of a harbour authority in formulating or considering any proposals relating to its functions under any enactment to have regard to:
>
> (a) the conservation of the natural beauty of the countryside and of flora, fauna and geological or physiographical features of special interest;
>
> (b) the desirability of preserving for the public any freedom of access to places of natural beauty; and,
>
> (c) the desirability of maintaining the availability to the public of any facility for visiting or inspecting any building, site or object of archaeological, architectural or historic interest;
>
> and to take into account any effect which the proposals may have on the natural beauty of the countryside, flora, fauna or any such feature or facility.

The contrast with the Irish legislation could not be more dramatic. Thankfully, there is other legislation in force in Ireland that requires port companies (and oil companies operating within ports) to have regard to the environment when carrying out their functions. However, nearly all of this legislation is derived from our membership of the European Union, with some additions resulting from Ireland's ratification of international conventions. It is an unfortunate fact that almost none of our legislation to protect natural resources has been initiated by Irish governments: in nearly all cases we have been forced to act as a result of our membership of the European Union.

## A Slow Awakening of Environmental Awareness?

For example, the requirement to transpose the EU Habitats Directive and Birds Directive into Irish legislation has resulted in the prohibition of any damage to Special Areas of Conservation (SACs) and Special Protection Areas (SPAs) for birds, while the Water Framework Directive requires good water-quality status to be maintained or improved. There are at least thirty other EU Environmental Directives which must be complied with, and these have collectively brought Ireland's State agencies and other authorities into line with European practice.

Where shipping and ports are concerned, the MARPOL convention and its six annexes provide international rules for the prevention of oil spillages and to minimise their consequences. MARPOL also addresses the environmental threat caused by routine operations such

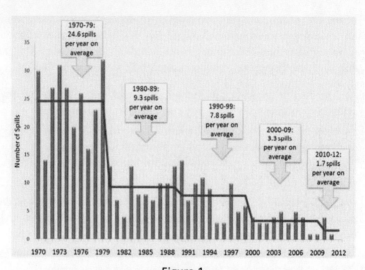

Figure 1

Number of large spills (>700 tonnes) from 1970 to 2012. Source: International Tanker Owners Pollution Federation (ITOPF)

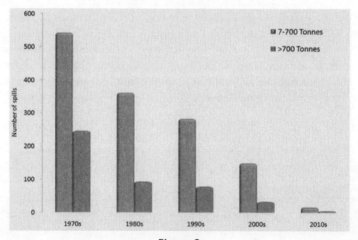

Figure 2

Number of medium sized (7 to 700 tonnes) and large (>700 tonnes) spills per decade from 1970 to 2012. Source: International Tanker Owners Pollution Federation (ITOPF)

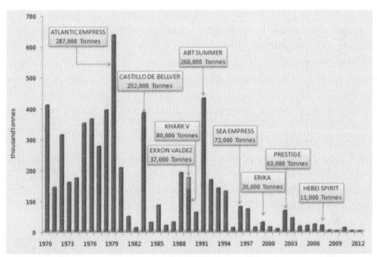

Figure 3
Quantities of oil spilt > 7 tonnes, from 1970 to 2012 (rounded to nearest thousand).
Source: International Tanker Owners Pollution Federation (ITOPF)

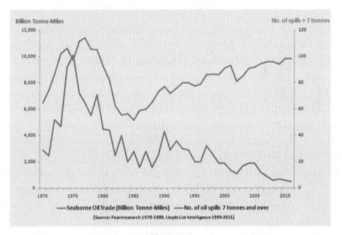

Figure 4
Seaborne oil trade and number of tanker spills >7 tonnes, 1970 to 2011, from crude oil
and product tankers of 60,000 tonnes DWT and above. Source: International Tanker
Owners Pollution Federation (ITOPF). The reduction in the quantity of oil transported
per year, from approximately 1977 to 1985, can be clearly seen.

as the cleaning of oil cargo tanks and the disposal of engine room wastes – in tonnage terms a bigger menace than accidental pollution – and also pollution of the sea by chemicals, goods in packaged form, sewage, garbage and air pollution. The number of large and medium-size spillages from oil tankers has been decreasing year on year since the 1970s (see Figures 1 and 2), while the total quantity of oil spilled each year has also been decreasing (see Figure 3).

More significantly, while the amount of oil transported has been increasing slowly year on year since around 1985, there has been a more or less continuous fall in the number of spillages each year (see Figure 4).

Updated figures for 2012 show that the tanker industry suffered zero large oil spills – defined as above 700 tonnes – for the first year since systematic records began in 1970. With only seven 'medium-sized' spills, defined as 7 to 700 tonnes, the International Tanker Owners Pollution Federation (ITOPF) concluded that the industry put around 1,000 tonnes of oil in the world's seas last year – the lowest figure on record.

We must point out, however, that the above statistics deal only with spillages from oil tankers whose owners are members of ITOPF. All ships carry bunker oil, and spillages from these vessels are not recorded in the ITOPF statistics. For example, the oil spillages from the *Kowloon Bridge* on the coast of County Cork,[37] and the two oil spillages in the Shannon Estuary during the last two decades (*Clipper Cheyenne* and *Crystal Water*), would not be included by ITOPF.

There are also other indicators that the situation is improving, and the absence of any significant reported oil spillages in Bantry Bay may be an indication of this. Eleven Irish ports are members of the European Sea Ports Organisation (ESPO), which has provided guidance to its members on the implementation of European environmental law for almost twenty years. In 1994 ESPO published the first Code of Environmental Practice, revised and adapted to changes in EU law in 2003, encouraging port managers to implement environmental plans and address environmental issues.

ESPO *recommends* that port authorities, especially those situated in estuaries, should actively participate in environmental management plans; that port authorities carry out active conservation management of ecologically valuable sites within port areas; and, in so doing, try to facilitate stakeholder engagement. ESPO has also been the main driving force behind the creation of the European ECOPORTS organisation and network, which has four member ports in Ireland: Shannon-Foynes, Dublin, Cork and Belfast.

Ports are encouraged to follow the 'Green Guide', which urges port authorities to be proactive and to commit to sustainable development and the continuous improvement of their environmental performance. The Green Guide points out that the environmental management of ports has progressed over the last decades from a 'point-focused' exercise to an integrated seaport area management concept. The overarching administrative role of the port authority in most European countries means that the port is the obvious point of contact, and is the most readily identifiable player for any environment-related issues in the whole port area.

Shannon-Foynes is possibly the leading port in Ireland which has embraced this concept most fully. Having established the Shannon Estuary Anti-Pollution Team (SEA-PT), which includes among its membership all of the local authorities and the principal marine-related commercial activities in the estuary, SEA-PT has invited environmental NGOs such as Birdwatch Ireland, Sea Alarm, and the Irish Whale and Dolphin Group to participate in the annual oil spill response training exercises, and has prepared a detailed atlas of all environmentally sensitive and vulnerable resources within the port's limits. In addition, the Shannon-Foynes Port Company commissioned the development of a location-specific oil spill tracking and spill trajectory prediction model for the Shannon Estuary and the adjacent sea area, linked with real-time data on weather and tides. The model contains regularly updated information on sensitive and ecologically vulnerable areas, clean-up guidelines, access points from which the shore may be reached, and other necessary information; all data is on a web-based GIS system, accessible 24/7 in the event of an incident.

The relationship between Shannon Foynes Port Company and environmental organisations has steadily improved, even though the Port Company has not yet clarified its role as including the protection of the environment and ecological resources of the estuary. The 'Port Information Guide to the Shannon Estuary', dated July 2013, contains no references to environmental resources and protected areas in the estuary, even though the Shannon Estuary is the largest complex of estuarine habitats in Ireland, with a resident population of bottlenose dolphins, greater numbers of wintering wildfowl and waders than any other site in the country, and a high number of priority habitats and species listed in Annexes I and II of the EU Habitats Directive. For these reasons almost all of the estuary has been designated an SAC and an SPA under the EU Habitats and Birds Directives.

But the question remains: who will ensure the protection of this unique and ecologically valuable area? Our National Parks and Wildlife Services is underfunded and understaffed, and the pressure to 'develop' large areas of land adjoining the estuary for industry is immense; and, of course, any incoming industry will be fully supported by the relevant government minister, and environmental concerns contemptuously brushed aside.

## LOOKING AHEAD:
## VESSEL TRAFFIC DENSITY AND PLACES OF
## REFUGE FOR SHIPS IN NEED OF ASSISTANCE

Given the increasingly tight control over shipping, and especially oil tankers, is it likely that we will experience further oil spillages on the Irish coast?

Unfortunately, the answer is yes. Ireland is surrounded by some of the busiest shipping lanes in Europe (see Figure 5), and oil spillages may result not only from tanker accidents but also from a shipping incident involving a vessel carrying significant quantities of bunker fuel. The Shannon Estuary and other inlets such as Bantry Bay may be used as places of refuge by ships in distress or in need of assistance, as happened previously.

In November 1986, the Italian tanker *Capo Emma*, 89,000 tonnes dwt and fully loaded with crude oil, sought shelter in Bantry Bay following damage sustained at sea. The ship was successfully off-loaded under the jurisdiction of the Marine Survey Office, despite continuing severe weather conditions.

While the *Capo Emma* was anchored in Bantry Bay, the Hong Kong-registered *Kowloon Bridge*, a 264-metre oil-bulk-ore carrier loaded with 160,000 tonnes of iron-ore pellets, got into difficulties during a stormy Atlantic crossing and also sought shelter in Bantry Bay. The vessel was permitted to enter Bantry Bay. She anchored for some four days during November 1986, lost one anchor and was unable to deploy her second anchor. Her master made the correct decision to head for the open sea, where he would be likely to be more safe than in an enclosed water such as Bantry Bay. Very soon afterwards, her crew were airlifted off and the ship eventually grounded on the Stag Rocks near Toe Head, causing extensive pollution of the coastline of County Cork during the first quarter of 1987.[38]

Less than four years later, in February 1990, the Isle of Man-registered bulk carrier *Tribulus*, owned by Shell Tankers (UK) Limited, and carrying 122,000 tonnes of iron ore from Canada to Rotterdam, was damaged at sea some 270 nautical miles south-west of Mizen Head. The ship had approximately 550 tonnes of heavy fuel oil on board, which was leaking slowly, and she was permitted to take refuge in Bantry Bay. Repairs were successfully carried out over a period of three months, and the ship left Bantry on 6 May 1990.

While these events were happening in Bantry Bay, the Singapore registered general cargo vessel *Toledo*, carrying a cargo of 14,000 tonnes of potash fertiliser from Canada to Denmark, sent out a distress message. Her entire crew were airlifted by helicopter, and the ship was abandoned 150 nautical miles south-west of Mizen Head. A request was made by the ship owner for a place of refuge on the Irish coast. The request was refused, and the damaged ship was towed to the south-west coast of England, was again refused a port of refuge, and was eventually towed out to sea and scuttled.

The most recent incident occurred in July 2012, when the container vessel *MSC Flaminia* caught fire and was abandoned in mid-Atlantic. There were a number of containers on board containing hazardous substances, and the Irish Coast Guard was notified that the ship's salvors might request a place of refuge at some stage in the future. No request was made, but the Coast Guard subsequently assisted in the search for containers lost overboard and reported to be adrift in the Irish EEZ.

Among all of these incidents, only the *Kowloon Bridge* shipwreck resulted in significant oil-pollution and environmental damage; and that was caused primarily by a failure to deal with the bunker oil in the ship's fuel tanks during a period of relatively calm weather and before it became obvious that she was beginning to break up and could not be salvaged.

## OFFSHORE OIL EXPLORATION AND PRODUCTION: A CAUSE FOR CONCERN

If exploration for offshore oil was to continue in Ireland's extensive EEZ, leading to the discovery of a commercially viable field, would the exploitation of this field give rise to a risk of oil spillages? Would such an incident be probable, and could the environment be adequately protected?

Perhaps the best-known recent incident is that which occurred in the Gulf of Mexico on 20 April 2010, when the BP Deepwater Horizon oil rig exploded and caught fire, causing the largest spill in offshore oil production history.[39] Eleven people died in the explosion, and it took eighty-seven days to cap the well. By then, almost 5 million barrels of oil had been spilled into the Gulf of Mexico, and the projected loss to Gulf tourism was estimated at more than $22 billion. Assessing the widespread ecological impacts of this spill in such deep water will be probably one of the most challenging tasks, as significant amounts of oil have sunk to the sea-bed. Several more years will be required before long-term studies determine the true costs to wildlife, fisheries and the ecosystem.[40]

As in the case of the cost-cutting by Gulf Oil Terminals Ireland which led to the *Betelgeuse* disaster in Bantry Bay, described earlier in this chapter, 'BP's push to maximize profits and cut costs at the Macondo well was a "root cause" of the explosion that led to the 2010 Gulf of Mexico oil spill,' a safety expert who studied the disaster said. Oil company executives pressured supervisors of the Deepwater Horizon rig to speed up drilling operations and hold down expenses as part of a corporate culture that put profit ahead of safety, University of California retired engineering professor Robert Bea told the judge who is hearing claims over the spill.[41]

And not only were costs cut by BP, it appears that Halliburton, the world's second-largest oil-field services company, has agreed to plead guilty to destroying evidence related to the 2010 Gulf of Mexico oil spill.[42] The company also agreed to pay a $200,000 fine and to donate $55 million to a wildlife group after the disaster.

Very soon after the disaster occurred, US President Barack Obama signed an executive order to establish a National Commission to investigate and report on the disaster.[43] Some conclusions of the commission's report are worth quoting here, as they indicate the failure of management and the regulatory agencies to control and reduce risk.[44] In the foreword to a lengthy and detailed report, the commission concluded that:

- The explosive loss of the *Macondo* well could have been prevented.

- The immediate causes of the *Macondo well blowout can be traced to a series of identifiable mistakes made by BP, Halliburton, and Transocean that reveal such systematic failures in risk management that they place in doubt the safety culture of the entire industry* [emphasis added].

- Deep-water energy exploration and production, particularly at the frontiers of experience, involve risks for which neither industry nor government has been adequately prepared, but for which they can and must be prepared in the future.

- To assure human safety and environmental protection, regulatory oversight of leasing, energy exploration, and production require reforms even beyond those significant reforms already initiated since the Deepwater Horizon disaster. Fundamental reform will be needed in both the structure of those in charge of regulatory oversight and their internal decision-making process to ensure their political autonomy, their technical expertise, and their full consideration of environmental protection concerns.

- Because regulatory oversight alone will not be sufficient to ensure adequate safety, the oil and gas industry will need to take its own, unilateral steps to increase dramatically safety throughout the industry, including self-policing mechanisms that supplement governmental enforcement.

- The technology, laws and regulations, and practices for containing, responding to, and cleaning up spills lag behind the real risks associated with deep-water drilling into large, high-pressure reservoirs of oil and gas located far offshore and thousands of feet below the ocean's surface. Government must close the existing gap and industry must support rather than resist that effort.

- Scientific understanding of environmental conditions in sensitive environments in deep Gulf waters, along the region's coastal habitats, and in areas proposed for more drilling, such as the Arctic, is inadequate. The same is true of the human and natural impacts of oil spills.

These conclusions are of direct relevance to the situation on the Irish continental shelf, where extremely challenging conditions of deep water and Atlantic storms increase the risk of accidents. The report refers to sensitive environments such as the Gulf of Mexico and the Arctic, but it must be stated that the west coast of Ireland – in fact the entire coast of Ireland – is equally sensitive because of the importance of our coastline for fisheries, aquaculture, tourism, recreation and the number of sensitive and vulnerable habitats and species.

In some ways similar to the tribunal of inquiry report on the *Betelgeuse* disaster in Bantry Bay, from which we quoted earlier in this chapter, the report by the National Commission on the BP Deepwater Horizon Oil Spill points to significant regulatory failure and poor oversight by the US Minerals Management Service (MMS), which had been given primary responsibility for regulating the offshore oil and gas industry prior to the Deepwater Horizon accident. Unfortunately, the MMS was not only responsible for offshore leasing and resource management; it also collected and disbursed revenues from offshore leasing, conducted environmental reviews, reviewed plans and issued permits, conducted audits and inspections, and enforced safety and environmental regulations. This mingling of distinct statutory responsibilities led inevitably to internal tensions and a confusion of goals that weakened the agency's effectiveness and made it more susceptible to outside pressures.

All of these problems were compounded by an outdated organisational structure, a chronic shortage of resources, a lack of sufficient technological expertise, and the inherent difficulty of coordinating effectively with all the other government agencies that had statutory responsibility for some aspect of offshore oil and gas activities.[45]

The power of the MMS was further weakened by the policies pursued under President Ronald Reagan from January 1981, when he made clear from the outset his view that *government regulation was a leading cause of the nation's problems – a drag on the nation's economy in general and the development of its rich natural resources* in particular.[46] It should be obvious to any Irish reader that this view has deeply pervaded Irish government policy on our offshore licensing regime, resulting in the appalling damage done to the communities and the environment in north Mayo, and the loss to the nation of any benefits from the Corrib gas field currently controlled by Shell, as briefly noted earlier in this chapter.

Because of the huge number of wells drilled in the Gulf of Mexico, this area appears to have suffered the largest number of accidents. Within a few months of the Deepwater Horizon explosion and fire, a fixed offshore platform – the Vermilion Block 380 A Platform – located approximately 180 km off the Louisiana coast, exploded and caught on fire on 2 September 2010. The quantity of oil spilled is understood to be relatively small.

## THE *IXTOC I* DISASTER

One of the first major oil-well blowouts, which resulted in the largest oil spill ever to take place from offshore operations at the time, also occurred in the Gulf of Mexico – the *Ixtoc I* disaster. *Ixtoc I* was an exploratory oil well being drilled by the semi-submersible drilling rig Sedco 135-F in the bay of Campeche, in relatively shallow water only 50 metres deep. On 3 June 1979, the well suffered a blowout, resulting in a huge oil spill of some 475,000 tonnes.

Approximately 30,000 tonnes of the oil landed on Mexican beaches, 4,000 tonnes were deposited along the Texas coast, and about 120,000 tonnes sank to the bottom of the Gulf. Oil from the *Ixtoc I* disaster had an extremely destructive impact on the littoral crab and mollusc fauna of the beaches which had become contaminated; crabs were almost totally eliminated over a wide area, and the crab populations on coral islands along the coast were also reduced to only a few percent of normal about nine months after the spill. The Mexican state oil company Pemex reportedly spent $100 million to clean up the spill and avoided most compensation claims by asserting sovereign immunity as a state-run company!

Between 2006 and 2010, nine major oil-rig fires have killed at least two people and seriously injured twelve in the Gulf of Mexico. Those fires are among 509 recorded on oil platforms in the Gulf since 2006, according to the US Mineral Management Services.

## BLOWOUT AND SPILL IN THE TIMOR SEA

Another relatively recent oil-well blowout and spill occurred in the Timor Sea off the northern coast of Western Australia on 21 August 2009, from the *West Atlas* drilling rig, owned by the Norwegian-Bermudan company Seadrill, and operated by PTTEP Australasia (PTTEPAA), a subsidiary of PTT Exploration and Production (PTTEP), which is in turn a subsidiary of PTT, the Thai state-owned oil and gas company. The rig was operating on the Montara field some 690 km west of Darwin, and the spillage of oil continued until 3 November 2009 (a total of seventy-four days).

Estimates of the quantity of oil spilled in this incident range from 1.2 million US gallons (4,500 cubic metres) to more than 9 million US gallons (34,000 cubic metres), or about 4,000 tonnes to 30,000 tonnes; and it is considered to be one of Australia's worst oil disasters. PTTEPAA estimated that it spent $170 million on the gas and oil leak up to 3 November 2009; and the environmental clean-up cost $5.3 million.

## LEAKS AND SPILLAGES FROM
## NORTH SEA OIL RIGS AND PLATFORMS

Closer to home, the exploitation of offshore oil fields in the North Sea has not been without incident. North Sea oil rigs and platforms operating in the British sector suffered major or significant leaks at a rate of almost one every week throughout 2009 and 2010. This data has emerged from an investigation by the *Guardian* newspaper of shortcomings in safety and oversight in British operations.[47] The data, obtained through the Freedom of Information Act, shows that more than 25,000 kg of oil and gas leaked from British oil platforms between January 2009 and December 2010, in 110 separate incidents. A further 6,000 kg of oil and gas leaked in incidents classed as 'minor'.

The register of incidents quoted by the *Guardian* includes all leaks voluntarily declared by operators to the Health and Safety Executive, as part of security measures set up in response to the Piper Alpha disaster in 1988, which killed 167 workers. The worst-performing rig on the register was *Brent Charlie*, owned by Shell, which leaked a total of 4,900 kg of material in seven separate incidents rated as significant or higher.

According to a more recent report, Shell and other major companies are spilling crude, diesel or other contaminants into the North Sea on a daily basis despite the oil industry's efforts to improve its safety record. On the day that Shell reported global annual profits of $27 billion (€20.25 billion), government statistics revealed that the Anglo-Dutch group has been responsible for over twenty pollution accidents in British waters over a six-month period.

Data released in January 2013 by the British Department of Energy and Climate Change reveal 429 oil and chemical spills in the UK North Sea in the ten months to 8 November 2012, compared with 464 for the same period the previous year (2011).[48]

Reliable statistics of oil spillages and environmental damage from well blow-outs, fires and other offshore exploration and production disasters worldwide are incomplete and difficult to obtain, since the quantities of oil lost are hard to estimate in many cases, and there is no single database of all spillages. Nevertheless, it is clear from the above examples that oil spillages will continue to occur from offshore rigs and platforms; and that some of these spills are extremely difficult to control, that they continue for relatively long periods before being stopped, and that the quantities of oil spilled may be very large, resulting in very significant environmental damage and huge clean-up costs. Furthermore, there is significant under-reporting of the size and frequency of spillages from offshore operations.

As offshore drilling moves into deeper waters, and into more hostile marine environments (e.g. greater wave heights, storm frequencies and strengths), it is likely that oil exploration and production accidents will continue to occur. The improved safety features, and the lessons learned from previous incidents, are counterbalanced by the increased risks being taken by offshore operators. One of these risks, which has been quietly hidden so far, is offshore fracking, to which we will refer later in this chapter.

## Risks in Irish Waters

So far, only relatively minor discoveries of oil have been made on the Irish continental shelf, and significant commercial production has not begun. But the risks remain, and we have seen no sign that any government department or agency in Ireland is willing to draw up and enforce stringent rules to prevent and control spillages of oil from exploration or production. The recent case taken successfully in the High Court by An Taisce against the decision by the Department of Environment, Community and Local Government to grant a foreshore licence to Providence Resources for surveying and drilling for oil in Dublin Bay reveals the low level of protection given by the State to the environment when granting such licences.

An Taisce pointed out that 'the heritage and ecological value of the Dublin Bay area is of critical importance, for a number of protected habitats and species including various bird species and cetaceans (e.g. whales, dolphins and porpoises). Not only does the bay provide an important and critical habitat but also a wonderful amenity for Dubliners and tourists, both national and international, to enjoy and respect'. Yet the decision to allow the oil exploration work to take place in an area about 6 km off Dalkey did not comply with the provisions of the Environmental Impact Assessment Directive!

An Taisce also stated that 'a failure in the national legislative framework, on which this decision was made, has implications for drilling both offshore and onshore'. However, the good news for the environment is that some or all of the area covered by the foreshore licence granted to Providence Resources has been proposed by National Parks and Wildlife Service for designation as a Special Area of Conservation (SAC). The proposed SAC is a large marine area (40 km by 7 km) between Rockbill and Dalkey Island, especially to protect the Harbour Porpoise, as the area holds one of the densest populations of this species in Ireland. The designation will have significant implications for a number of existing and possible uses such as fishing, dredge-spoil disposal, offshore wind generation, and oil and gas exploration.

## IS SAFE FRACKING AN ILLUSION?

As new oil and gas resources become harder to locate, and more difficult to extract, attention has turned to ways of increasing the quantities of gas and liquid hydrocarbons which can be removed from previously worked-out fields, or from fields where the gas is locked tightly in almost impermeable rock formations. A number of new techniques have been developed to exploit these possible resources, and one such technique is 'fracking', also referred to as 'unconventional gas' (UG) production.

While apparently offering economic and energy-security benefits (according to its promoters), UG production presents considerable environmental risks. These range from potential water and soil contamination from surface leaks or from badly designed or poorly cemented well-casing, to spills of partially treated or untreated wastewater, increased competition for water usage, and fugitive emissions of methane and other gases, with serious consequences for the global climate. A number of other issues, related to environmental degradation, can also occur, including air pollution from volatile contaminants, noise pollution, negative impacts on ecosystems, biodiversity losses and landscape disruption.

### Gas Fracking: What Happens?

Firstly, it is necessary to consider what 'fracking' is, and what happens during this activity. Hydraulic fracturing (usually shortened to 'fracking') is a process by which large amount of fluids (water with chemicals and sand) are injected at very high pressures into rock formations to fracture them,[49] enabling gaseous or liquid hydrocarbons that are held tightly inside to be released.[50]

Most unconventional gas is trapped deep inside shale formations at depths between 1,500 to 3,000 metres; and, to exploit this gas, large numbers of wells are drilled vertically and then deviated horizontally from a single well site. The rock is then hydraulically fractured multiple times at intervals of around 100 metres along the horizontal sections of the drilled well. The fractures produced can extend between 150 and 250 metres perpendicularly from the horizontal well and should, in theory, not propagate vertically more than the thickness of the gas-producing layer (see Figure 5 below).

Chemicals added to fracturing fluid include friction reducers, surfactants, gelling agents, scale inhibitors, acids, corrosion inhibitors, antibacterial agents, and clay stabilisers. The sand fills the pores and stops them collapsing; the gas is returned to the surface via the well, along with water contaminated with fracking chemicals and naturally occurring pollutants.

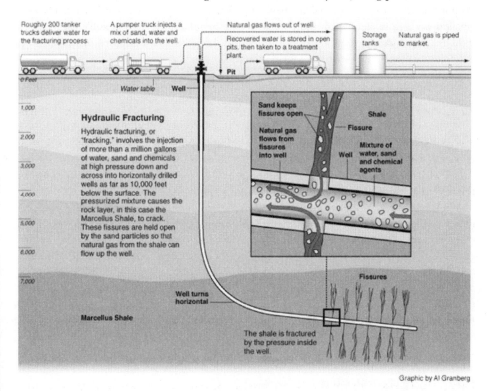

Figure 5
Schematic showing the fracking process. Source: ProPublica.

When hydraulic fracturing has been completed, and the well has been depressurised, some 25 to 75 percent of the initial fracturing fluid, now mixed with produced water from the fractured formation, returns to the surface, where it is usually placed in temporary storage ponds before being removed by road tanker trucks and sent for treatment or disposal. Water requirements can be very significant, as high-volume fracking needs between 7 million and 11 million litres of water for a single well. At the exploratory stage, gases produced may be flared or vented to atmosphere.

## Why Should We Be Concerned?

There are numerous concerns about fracking from an environmental and health perspective, with many uncertainties yet to be resolved. However, experience and research to date suggests that the process is significantly risky to the environment and human health. Some of these risks are the result of inappropriate use of the technology, or may be caused by human error, but others will occur despite proper use of the technology, i.e. they are inherent in the process.

### Contamination of surface and ground water

The most obvious risk associated with the use of fracking is contamination of both surface and ground water by chemicals contained in the fracking liquids utilised in the process, as well as potential contamination by chemicals contained in the underlying rock formations.

Another problem associated with fracking is the discharge of produced water to surface waters as a result of spills, accidents or intentional releases. Such discharges may occur at well-heads, collection ponds, pipelines, or other production facilities. If fracking is carried out off-shore (see below), the risk of contamination of the surrounding water could be even greater.

### Contamination of soil, and impacts on agriculture and land use

An unavoidable impact of fracking is the very significant amount of land occupied by drilling pads, parking and manoeuvring areas for trucks, heavy equipment, gas processing and transporting facilities as well as access roads.[51] Fracking disrupts the landscape, with particularly significant adverse impacts on rural areas and on landscapes of conservation value or interest. It also can lead to the industrialisation of a rural landscape, especially when multiple drilling pads are in relatively close proximity.

In the United States, where large numbers of farmers have leased their land to the gas industry, examples of the negative impacts of fracking on agriculture and food production have emerged. Water contamination from toxic fracking chemicals has sickened and killed livestock, while accidents and spills have contaminated croplands. A long-term risk of soil pollution from fracking due to the risk of leakages from polluted tailing ponds, wastewater and well blowouts has also been identified.

Given this experience, it is not surprising that there is widespread concern in Ireland that, if fracking were to be permitted, incidents that have occurred in other places could occur here and would adversely affect consumer confidence in the food produced in Ireland.

## Water use

Very large amounts of water are required to extract shale gas, putting severe pressure on water supplies in areas where drilling is being carried out. Even though Ireland is generally well supplied with water, the quantities of water required for fracking could cause local shortages.

## Air pollution

According to a recent study by the US EPA, the natural-gas industry in the US emitted in 2006 the equivalent of 261 million metric tonnes of $CO_2$ in the form of methane gas. This shows that approximately 3.25 percent of methane produced by natural gas wells in the US leaked into the atmosphere – much higher than the 'fraction of 1 percent' previously claimed by industry.[52]

## Noise

Noise from drilling equipment, trucks, earth-moving machinery and other heavy construction and processing equipment (including pumps) is very likely to be a major source of irritation and annoyance to local residents, and the noise may also affect agricultural livestock and wildlife.

## Seismic activity

Fracking increases the risks of earthquakes, which in turn increases the risk of damage to, and leakages from, gas wells. In April 2011, the town of Blackpool in Britain experienced a small earthquake (1.5 on the Richter scale), which was followed in June 2011 by a larger one (2.5 on the Richter scale). The company Cuadrilla Resources, which was conducting hydraulic fracturing operations in the earthquake area, had to stop its operations.

## Transport and infrastructure

Extensive fracking operations require the development of very significant infrastructure to support the drilling programmes. Transportation and treatment facilities must be built and maintained, including access roads, well-heads, pipelines and wastewater treatment ponds).

It has been estimated that up to 2,000 truck trips are needed per well developed.[53] In Ireland, the areas over which licensing options and a petroleum licence have been granted are served by rural roads which are not designed for such traffic. Road realignment and pavement strengthening would be needed, or, as would be more likely, road surfaces would be damaged by the increased heavy traffic, along with an increased risk of truck-traffic accidents.

## Risks to human health

Toxicological information about the chemicals used by the industry, and the amounts used, is very incomplete, and frequently held from public view because of commercial secrecy. It is estimated that a third of the chemicals in fracking fluid remain unknown to the public.

In the US, the natural gas industry uses a wide range of chemicals in fracking liquids; these substances include benzene, ethylbenzene, toluene, boric acid, monoethanolamine, xylene, diesel-range organics, formaldehyde, methanol, hydrochloric acid, ammonium bisulfite and others. A significant number of these substances are toxic, while many are carcinogens, neurotoxins, endocrine disruptors and mutagens.

## Community disruption

In addition to the above risks to individual human health, widespread or large-scale fracking activities have threatened mental health and community well-being as a result of people in local communities becoming aware that they have lost control in the face of these issues.

As we have seen earlier in this chapter, when natural resources are being opened for exploitation or development, the State has in most cases sided with the industry, against the wishes of local communities. As a result of the disruption, communities have been split, setting neighbour against neighbour. Wealth from this type of development (which is similar to mining in many ways) is invariably distributed very unequally, especially if the State leaves most of the decision-making to the licensed operator.

Another potentially disruptive effect occurs when a rapid change in population, industrialisation, economic prosperity and inequitable distribution of newly created wealth leads to a number of social ills, including increased rates of crime, drug and alcohol abuse; increased community dissatisfaction; increased hospital admissions; insufficient infrastructure; overstressed public services, and increased cost of living. Experience in other counties has shown that the positive effect of economic gains promised by the industry would be limited or offset by the inequitable distribution of risk and reward among local residents.

Whether fracking would ever be carried out in Ireland on such a large scale as to cause these problems is considered unlikely, but the risk exists. Small communities with a traditional way of life would be damaged, perhaps irreversibly; and the potential to create more sustainable agriculture- and tourism-based activities would be undermined.

## Delaying the transition to a low-carbon economy

Because natural gas is a relatively clean-burning fossil fuel compared to oil and coal, it has been promoted by the industry as a means of helping to make the transition to a future economy powered by low-carbon renewable energy resources. However, recent studies have demonstrated that increased development of shale gas may accelerate climate change because large amounts of methane, a potent greenhouse gas that makes up 90 percent of shale gas, will escape to the atmosphere during fracking.[54]

There is no currently no agreement that the greenhouse gas emissions from the exploitation and combustion of shale gas will be significantly lower compared to other conventional fossil fuels. The combustion stage of natural gas may be cleaner than that of coal, but a life-cycle analysis of shale gas production tells a different story and does not warrant the 'transition fuel' label. There is also a concern that shale gas production will lock Europe into fossil fuel use, jeopardising emissions reduction targets and retarding investment in renewable energy development.

## Offshore Fracking

Fracking is generally associated with onshore activities, but this year (2013) some new information has revealed that the practice has been quietly taking place off the coast of California for the past two decades. A recent report by the Associated Press documented at least a dozen instances of fracking since the late 1990s in the Santa Barbara Channel, the site of a disastrous 1969 oil-platform blowout that spurred the modern environmental movement.[55] Companies have used hydraulic fracturing at least a dozen times to 'force open cracks beneath the seabed'.

The largest offshore fracking event occurred in 2010 when Venoco Inc. targeted the Monterey Shale, a 1,750-square-mile area extending from the State's agricultural Central Valley to the Pacific Ocean; but it was reported that the effort only mildly boosted production. This is a huge area which US federal energy officials say could ultimately comprise two-thirds of the nation's shale-oil reserves.

The Coastal Commission, which is charged with protecting the shoreline and marine resources of California, was not aware until recently that fracking was occurring, mainly because of the complicated web of agencies involved. However, the commission has now promised to look into the extent of fracking beneath federal and state offshore waters and any potential risks, while a group of Californian legislators has called on the Department of the Interior and the Environmental Protection Agency to launch an investigation into off-shore hydraulic fracturing. Residents groups in California have expressed alarm and concern, and have urged the Coastal Commission and the legislators to do everything in their power to stop the practice offshore.

There are lessons here for Ireland, not only about the danger of offshore fracking and the risks to the marine environment, but also about the difficulty of identifying what the oil companies are actually doing offshore. Given that offshore rigs are operated by specialist companies located in other countries, and that the information obtained by offshore drilling is normally very confidential, it is difficult for any national regulator to keep a close eye on what is happening.

## The Situation in Ireland

In February 2010 the Minister for Communications, Energy and Natural Resources issued a competitive onshore licensing notice, inviting applications for 'Onshore Licensing Options' to be granted under the Petroleum and Other Minerals Development Act (1960) over the Northwest Carboniferous Basin and the Clare Basin.

In March 2011, three 'licensing options' were granted by the Department of Communications, Energy and Natural Resources to:

• Tamboran Resources and LANCO for the Lough Allen Basin, also known as the North West Carboniferous basin, covering an area of approximately 1,500 square kilometres in parts of counties Cavan, Donegal, Leitrim, Mayo, Monaghan, Roscommon and Sligo.

• Energi Oil for the Clare Basin, over an area of approximately 500 square kilometres in parts of counties Clare, Cork, Limerick and Kerry.

These 'licensing options' are essentially an undertaking by the State to grant an exploration licence to the applicant.

In the North of Ireland, the Department of Enterprise, Trade and Investment granted a petroleum licence to Tamboran Resources on 1 April 2011, also for the Lough Allen Basin, and covering a large part of County Fermanagh. The licence is valid for five years, and in years one to three, the licensee is required to carry out a work programme which includes acquiring and interpreting gravity, airborne magnetic and seismic data, drilling shallow cored boreholes and analysing the core material, carrying out a preliminary environmental review, making an assess-ment of the resources, and deciding whether to undertake more drilling or abandon the licence.

In years four and five, the licensee is required to select proposed exploratory drilling loca-tions and carry out an environmental impact assessment; drill two exploration wells, includ-ing a coring, fracturing and testing programme; process and interpret the data acquired;

review the economic potential of the resource; and either apply for a second stage of licensing, or relinquish the licence.

In the Republic of Ireland, no exploration licences for unconventional gas have been issued, and the government has stated that none will be issued until the Environmental Protection Agency (EPA) has completed a study of the technology of fracking and its potential effects. This detailed study will follow on from the preliminary research into the environmental aspects of shale-gas extraction, conducted by the University of Aberdeen, and published by the EPA in May 2012. The proposed terms of reference for the detailed study were the subject of a public consultation process which concluded in March 2013, and the EPA has issued a call for tenders to carry out the study.

## The Situation on the Mainland of Europe

In Europe, the development of fracking lags several decades behind the USA.[56] Tight gas formations have been developed with hydraulic fracturing in Germany for about fifteen years, though at a very low level. The total European production of unconventional gas is in the order of several million cubic metres per year, compared to several hundred billion cubic metres per year in the USA.[57] However, since late 2009 the activities have been increasing, with some concessions granted in Austria (Vienna Basin), France (Paris Basin and South East Basin), Germany and the Netherlands (North Sea-German Basin), Sweden (Scandinavia Region) and UK (Northern and Southern Petroleum System).

Triggered by information from the USA, public opposition against these projects has risen fast. For instance, in France the National Assembly set a moratorium for such drilling activities and has banned hydraulic fracturing. The proposed law passed the National Assembly in May, but was not adopted by the Senate. The French industry minister proposed a different bill which would allow hydraulic fracturing only for scientific reasons under strict control of a committee composed of lawmakers, government representatives, NGOs and local citizens.[58] This modified law was approved by the Senate in June 2011.

In the German state of North Rhine-Westphalia, affected citizens, local politicians from almost all parties and representatives from water-supply authorities and mineral-water companies raised their concerns opposing hydraulic fracturing. The State Parliament of North Rhine-Westphalia also demanded a moratorium on fracking until improved knowledge would be available. A first step was to ensure strict protection of water quality, to make fracking subject to the same level of strict control as mining, and to ensure that permits would not granted until prior agreement had been obtained from water authorities. The discussion process is not yet finalised, and the most strongly involved company, ExxonMobil, started an open-dialogue process to discuss the concerns of the citizens and to assess the possible impact of fracking.[59]

In Central Europe, the situation is different. As a region still generating a significant percentage of electricity from coal, Central Europe faces more serious air-quality issues in comparison to the rest of Europe. Furthermore, high-priced imported gas from Russia continues to play a role in Central European energy policy, and the region has suffered from politically motivated import-energy disruptions more than any other part of Europe.

Hydraulic fracturing is viewed positively by governments as a means of increasing energy security, and accelerating the competitiveness of energy-related industries such as steel, chemicals and other manufacturing industry. On the other hand, public demonstrations in Poland, Ukraine, Lithuania, Romania and Bulgaria over environmental risks from fracking have led to indecision by some Central European policy-makers; while, at the same time, American and West European companies are eager to use the same fracking methods in Poland, Lithuania, Romania and Ukraine as they have been using in the USA.

The largest number of exploration concessions have been granted in Poland, and the prime minister of Poland issued a strong statement supporting fracking operations by foreign energy firms. The UK and Polish secretaries of state for the environment called jointly for a fact-based discussion of the environmental and economic merits of fracking. The government of Ukraine is adopting positive changes to the law covering production sharing agreements dealing with natural-resource exploration and development.

Nevertheless, fracking and the implications for the future of Central European energy security and environmental protection has continued to spark an intense debate in the region.

## What Should We Do in Ireland?

The above summary of adverse impacts on the environment, on agriculture and other land uses, and on communities which have emerged as a result of fracking should serve as a warning to Irish policy-makers to avoid a decision to permit fracking. The possibility that these issues might be mitigated should be considered, however, and therefore the most appropriate approach would be to declare a moratorium on fracking until it can be clearly shown that all of these real and potential problems can be successfully addressed. In any decision-making, reliance should not be placed on the information provided by the promoters of the process, but independently gathered information should form the basis of any policy. Furthermore, if a local community agrees that fracking should not be permitted in a particular area, their wishes should be respected, and not ignored and trampled upon, as happened in County Mayo.

And of course the larger question should not be ignored: is this constant search for more and more underground and undersea hydrocarbons leading to an even greater reliance of fossil fuels as our major source of energy?

Human societies are already addicted to hydrocarbon fuels as a primary energy source; we have come to depend on them to such an extent that for several decades we have ignored the serious warnings by responsible scientists and organisations such as the Intergovernmental Panel on Climate Change that the burning of fossil fuels is causing irreversible climate change and disruption of the Earth's ocean-climate system.

In May of this year, 'the concentration of climate-warming carbon dioxide in the atmosphere has passed the milestone level of 400 parts per million (ppm). The last time so much greenhouse gas was in the air was several million years ago, when the Arctic was ice-free, savannah spread across the Sahara Desert and sea levels were up to 40 metres higher than today.

'These conditions are expected to return in time, with devastating consequences for civilisation, unless emissions of $CO_2$ from the burning of coal, gas and oil are rapidly curtailed. But despite increasingly severe warnings from scientists and a major economic recession, global emissions have continued to soar unchecked.'[60]

Professor James Hansen, one of the world's best-known and respected climate scientists, who drew attention to the reality of climate change in 1988, has stated that our understanding of the sensitivity of the Earth's climate system is based on the Earth's history, not on climate models, and on good data on how the Earth responded in the past when carbon dioxide levels changed. Most importantly, he stated that there was no reason to change the long-term forecast of what will happen to the Earth's climate if we continue to emit enormous volumes of greenhouse gases each year.[61]

Prof Hansen has caused controversy by stating that the 'CEOs of fossil fuel companies should be tried for high crimes against humanity and nature'; his views echo those of Professor Donald Brown of Penn State University, who declared that climate-change sceptics and deniers may be guilty of a 'new crime against humanity' for causing a twenty-five-year delay in acting to stop climate change.

In recent years there has been a growing awareness among academics and international-law experts that countries which continue to pursue climate-damaging policies, and companies or individuals who deny human-induced climate disruption or who deliberately promulgate false information that this type of climate change is not occurring, should be held accountable for criminal acts under international law. Under national law, legal cases related to the effects of climate change have been filed against public and private entities in a number of jurisdictions, and this trend is likely to continue.

So where does that leave us in relation to our central question of oil and the environment? Clearly, the issues of concern go well beyond controlling or reducing oil spillages, even though the history of such events gives us a very significant insight into the way in which the petroleum industry has operated in the past, and is likely to continue, though with some modifications. Fewer oil spillages are occurring, major disasters are less frequent (but still occur), but the ongoing and desperately pursued search for underground and undersea hydrocarbon sources in more difficult environments is an indication that human societies, facilitated and led by the oil industry, are heading on a path to irreversible climate disruption.

Our only way out of this situation is to become much less dependent on oil and natural gas as our principal energy sources (along with coal, which is even more polluting), and move rapidly towards a human society based on renewable and sustainable energy resources. Making the transition to such a society is one of the most challenging tasks facing humanity, and will require a degree of change of about the same order of magnitude as the change from hunting-gathering to settled agriculture several thousand years ago, or from preindustrial agriculture to today's highly technical society.

### ABOUT THE AUTHOR

Jack O'Sullivan graduated in 1964 from University College Cork in zoology and biochemistry, and he was initially employed as a sea-fishery officer, biologist and pollution-control officer in northwest England and Wales, where he was responsible for coastal-pollution control and sea-fisheries management on 720 km of highly varied coastline.

In 1967, Jack was one of the first biologists to investigate and report on the ecological effects of the *Torrey Canyon* oil spillage and subsequent clean-up, following which he organised a series of expeditions to Bantry Bay to record pre-pollution data and the effects of major oil spillages; he also studied the ecological effects of the massive spillage of crude oil from the tanker *Amoco Cadiz* on the coast of Brittany. He returned to Ireland in 1975 to fulfil a contract as a science-policy analyst with the National Science Council (NSC), where (as an Irish delegate to the EU) he participated in negotiations between government departments, the European Commission, environmental NGOs and other organisations.

Jack has represented Ireland as delegate and technical adviser at the Paris Convention on Marine Pollution from Land Based Sources, and assisted in the drafting of the Convention on Civil Liability for Oil Pollution Damage from Offshore Exploration and Exploitation. He has also provided advice to government on technical and legal aspects of the MARPOL Convention and Annexes, the International Oil Pollution Compensation Fund Convention, and the UN Convention on the Law of the Sea.

Jack has represented environmental NGOs on the Advisory Committee of Ireland's Environmental Protection Agency, and he is a member of the Council of An Taisce (Ireland's longest-established environmental NGO). He is a founder-member of Zero Waste Alliance Ireland, an environmental NGO promoting the concept and practice of zero waste as an internationally recognised approach to dealing with discarded materials and objects.

For the European Commission, Jack worked on a comprehensive 'impact reference system' aimed at providing advice on the effects of oil in the marine environment and on the impact of hydrocarbons on fauna and flora, so as to enable the authorities in charge of spill clean-up to assess quickly and accurately an oil spill event in terms of its actual or potential damage to marine life and biological resources.

## NOTES

1.  O'Sullivan, A.J., and Richardson, A.J. 'The *Torrey Canyon* disaster and intertidal marine life.' *Nature*, 214, pp 448, 541-542, London, 1967

2.  'The Biological Effects of Oil Pollution on Littoral Communities.' Proceedings of a Symposium held at the Orielton Field Centre, Pembroke, Wales, on 17th, 18th and 19th February 1968. Edited by J.D. Carthy and Don R. Arthur. London, Field Studies Council, 1968; pp 198

3.  Crapp, G. 1970. 'The biological effects of marine oil pollution and shore cleansing.' Ph.D. thesis, University of Wales

4.  'Largest Vessel Afloat at Whiddy.' *Irish Times*, 31 October 1968

5.  'Port Authority to Control Bantry Bay Advocated.' *Irish Times*, 22 March 1968

6.  Dáil Éireann Debate; Vol. 236 No. 13; Wednesday, 6 November 1968: Questions and Oral Answers – Bantry Bay Harbour Authority. historical-debates.oireachtas.ie/D/0236/D.0236.196811060013.html

7.  *Cork Examiner*, 23 December 1966

8.  *Irish Times*, 1 October 1968

9.  *Cork Examiner*, 31 October 1968

10. *Irish Times*, 2 October 1968

11. 'Bantry will keep Vigilant Eye on Oil Pollution Risk'. *Irish Times*, 2 October 1968

12. www.shetlandcharitabletrust.co.uk

13. 'Securing the Benefits of Scotland's Next Energy Revolution.' Riaghaltas na h-Alba (The Scottish Government), November 2010

14. 'Shetland: a model for the future.' *Shetland Times*, 5 April 2013

15. 'Freak Oil leak at Whiddy.' *Cork Weekly Examiner*, Thursday 2 January 1969

16. 'Bantry Oil Firm Pays for Damage.' *Irish Times*, 30 December 1968

17. 'Leak,' *Irish Times*, Editorial, 7 January 1969

18. 'Oil Company Fined £250 for Sea Pollution.' *Irish Times*, 1 March 1969

19. O'Sullivan, A.J. 'Massive Oil Spillage in Bantry Bay.' *Marine Pollution Bulletin*, Vol 6 (1), pg 304, January 1975

20. 'Oil Spillage put at over 8,850 gallons.' *Irish Times*, Thursday 24 October 1974

21. 'The Rocky Shore Biology of Bantry Bay: A Re-Survey.' Unpublished report dated 1976 by J.M. Baker, S. Hainsworth, D. Levell, G. Bishop, M. Willis, R. Collinson, R. Kitchen and A.J. O'Sullivan. Later published as Irish Fisheries Investigations, Series B (Marine), No. 23 (1981)

22. 'Gulf Shuts Whiddy to Mop up Huge Slick – 800-ton Oil Spill Now Estimated; 6 Tankers Queue in Bantry Bay.' *Irish Times*, 26 October 1974

23. 'An Taisce Seeks Public Inquiry into Oil Spills.' *Cork Examiner*, 29 October 1974

24. 'Oil Spill May be above 1,000 tons; Experts Start Inquiries; Preparations Begin for Inquiry into Bantry Oil Spillage.' *Irish Times*, 29 October 1974

25. 'Another Bantry Oil Spill: Tanker is Holed by Tug.' *Cork Examiner*, 11 January 1975

26. O'Sullivan, A. J. (1975). '*Afran Zodiac* oil spill, Bantry Bay,' 10 January 1975. Unpublished report

27. 'Call to Act Now on Bantry Bay Control.' *The Cork Examiner*, 13 January 1975

28. 'Gulf Criticised on Use of Dispersant.' *Irish Times*, 15 January 1975

29. 'Barry Lays it on the Line for Gulf.' *The Irish Times*, 25 January, 1975

30. 'Oil Terminal Spill at Bantry Bay.' *Pollution Monitor*, No. 23, February/March 1975, pp 13–16

31. 'Loss-making Gulf Oil will keep Whiddy Terminal Going.' *Irish Times*, 16 January 1976

32. See 'Three In One – The Salvage of the *MT Betelgeuse*' on *YouTube*

33. 'Mussel Bound: Proceedings of an International Shellfish Seminar' held at the West Lodge Hotel, Bantry, Co. Cork, Ireland; 6-7 March 1984. Edited by A. J. O'Sullivan. Dublin, Environmental Management Services. Copies may still be obtained from Environmental Management Services, Outer Courtyard, Tullynally, Castlepollard, County Westmeath, Ireland

34. Press release, Department of Energy, 11 December 1984

35. Planning reference W/1425/85

36. www.southernstar.ie/News/Public-views-sought-on-future-of-Bantry-Bay-Harbour-07032013.htm and www.kildarestreet.com/wrans/?id=2013-03-27a.119

37. 'Cargo of Uncertainty: The Kowloon Bridge Experience – Choices and Lessons,' pre-

sented at a seminar held at University College Dublin, 23-24 March 1987 organised by Frank Convery, Jack O'Sullivan and John Wilde-Crosbie, Maritime Institute of Ireland and the Resource and Environmental Policy Centre, University College Dublin

38. O'Sullivan, A.J. 'Clean-up of the Coastline – Strategies and Options for Dealing with Oil from the Kowloon Bridge Spill.' In *A Cargo of Uncertainty: The Kowloon Bridge Experience – Choices and Lessons*, proceedings of a seminar organised by the Maritime Institute of Ireland and the Resource and Environmental Policy Centre, University College Dublin, 23 and 24 March 1987

39. 'BP oil spill timeline.' *Guardian* online, 22 July 2010. www.theguardian.com/environment/2010/jun/29/bp-oil-spill-timeline-deepwater-horizon

40. 'Oil spill: Deep wounds – The Gulf of Mexico oil spill set records for its size and depth. A year on, the biggest impacts seem to be where they are hardest to spot.' *Nature* 472, 152-154 (2011), 13 April 2011

41. 'Cost cutting led to Deepwater spill.' *The Irish Times*, Wed, Feb 27, 2013

42. 'Halliburton pleads guilty to destroying Gulf spill evidence.' *The Irish Times*, 26 July 2013

43. Executive Order – National Commission on the BP Deepwater Horizon Oil Spill and Offshore Drilling, 21 May, 2010

44. 'Deep Water: The Gulf Oil Disaster and the Future of Offshore Drilling.' report to the president by the National Commission on the BP Deepwater Horizon Oil Spill and Offshore Drilling, January 2011

45. *Ibid*, pp 254-255

46. *Ibid*, pg 63

47. 'Oil and gas spills in North Sea every week, papers reveal.' *The Guardian*, 5 July 2011

48. 'Shell continues spilling oil in North Sea despite efforts to improve.' *The Guardian*, 31 January 2013

49. 'Gas fracking: can we safely squeeze the rocks.' United Nations Environment Programme – Global Environmental Alert Service (GEAS), November 2012

50. IEA. 2012. 'Golden rules of a golden age of gas,' World Energy Outlook, Special Report on Unconventional Gas, International Energy Agency, pp 143, Paris, France, 2012

51. European Parliament, Directorate General for Internal Policies, Policy Department A:

Economic And Scientific Policy, June 2011. 'Impacts of shale gas and shale oil extraction on the environment and on human health.' Report Ref. IP/A/ENVI/ST

52. 'Greenhouse Gas Emissions Reporting from the Petroleum and Natural Gas Industry – Background Technical Support Document.' U.S. Environmental Protection Agency, Climate Change Division, Washington DC

53. European Parliament, Directorate General for Internal Policies, Policy Department A: Economic and Scientific Policy, June 2011. 'Impacts of shale gas and shale oil extraction on the environment and on human health.' Report Ref. IP/A/ENVI/ST

54. Wigley, Tom. 'Coal to gas: the influence of methane leakage,' *Climatic Change*, Vol. 108, August 2011. Howarth, Robert W., et al. 'Methane and the greenhouse-gas footprint of natural gas from shale formations.' *Climatic Change*, Vol. 106, June 2011. Jackson, Robert B., et al. 'Research and Policy Recommendations for Hydraulic Fracturing and Shale-Gas Extraction.' Center on Global Change, Duke University, Durham, North Carolina

55. 'California Panel Launches Probe into Offshore Fracking.' Alicia Chang, Associated Press, 15 August 2013. 'Fracking Offshore California? Lawmakers Call for Investigation.' *Offshore Energy Today*, 9 August 2013. www.offshoreenergytoday.com

56. European Parliament, Directorate General for Internal Policies, Policy Department A: Economic and Scientific Policy, June 2011. 'Impacts of shale gas and shale oil extraction on the environment and on human health.' Report Ref. IP/A/ENVI/ST

57. Korn, Andreas (2010). 'Prospects for unconventional gas in Europe.' www.eon.com/de/downloads/ir/20100205_Unconventional_gas_in_Europe.pdf

58. 'French Minister Says "Scientific" Fracking Needs Strict Control.' Tara Patel, Bloomberg News, 1 June 2011. www.bloomberg.com/news/2011-0601/french-minister-says-scientific-fracking-needs-strict-control.html

59. European Parliament, Directorate General for Internal Policies, Policy Department A: Economic and Scientific Policy, June 2011. 'Impacts of shale gas and shale oil extraction on the environment and on human health.' Report Ref. IP/A/ENVI/ST

60. 'Global carbon dioxide in atmosphere passes milestone level.' Damian Carrington, *The Guardian*, 10 May 2013

61. 'Global warming has not stalled, insists world's best-known climate scientist.' Damian Carrington, *The Guardian*, 17 May 2013

# 5.

## VOICE OF YOUTH: OWN OUR OIL
### Patrician Secondary School Students

When I first heard of the Own Our Oil campaign, I was surprised at how much oil and gas Ireland had off its shoreline. It has potentially 10 billion barrels worth of oil and gas, and they also represent nine times the size of Ireland. I was also surprised at the fact that Ireland was practically giving away the oil and gas to big multinational companies and getting next to nothing for it. Before the 1980s, Ireland had a good strategy for any oil or gas drilled off the coast of Ireland: it said that for any oil or gas extracted, Ireland got a 12.5 percent royalty, which is money given to Ireland for every barrel of oil or gas extracted, and the State also had a 50 percent share in the oil and gas resources. In the 1980s, a government minister called Raphael 'Ray' Burke went into meetings with big multinational oil companies and practically handed the oil companies the licensing terms – which are like permits to let the companies drill for oil – for nothing. He changed the law so that Ireland's share in offshore oil or gas was reduced from 50 percent to 0, and he also got rid of royalties. Ray Burke was later sent to jail for corruption.

If Ireland were to benefit from the oil and gas, we would be able to get rid of the national debt and become a very rich country. A good example of this is Norway. Norway was once a poor fishing country; an oil company approached the Norwegian government and offered them some money to explore for oil and gas which they thought was not very profitable. The Norwegians refused and decided to get a better deal, and now they are the world's largest producers of oil and gas outside the Middle East, and the fourth-richest country in the world, according to their GDP (Gross Domestic Product).

People need to realise that by campaigning for change in these licensing terms, Ireland would become a completely different country – a country without a national debt, a country without high unemployment, and a more prosperous country. Ireland does not want to go back into another Celtic Tiger period. In the situation Ireland is in now, any young person leaving secondary school has basically no other option but to hop on a plane and go to

Australia or Canada – places where there are actually opportunities to work and earn a living for themselves. If as many people as possible can get involved, whether it be teenagers or old-age pensioners, it tells the government that we aren't happy with staying the way we are, and that we want change. The government has not completely ignored the actions of previous governments; in 2012, the Joint Oireachtas Committee on Communications, Natural Resources and Agriculture, made up of fifteen TDs and six senators, published a report on off-shore oil and gas exploration. When they were writing this report, they didn't ask any geologist, economist or anyone relating to oil and gas exploration, except an assistant director of the Ministry for Oil and Energy in Norway, for any of their opinions or advice. In their report they recommended that the government do nothing about the licensing terms, as they did not want to anger or upset the big oil companies. It is completely wrong for the government to say that we aren't going to do anything about offshore oil and gas exploration, which could be very profitable to the Irish economy, which is in a terrible state.

The Irish government is still inviting oil companies to buy licensing terms and drill for oil and gas, and again Ireland gets absolutely nothing. There is nothing stopping the government from renegotiating the licensing terms, but they remain reluctant to do so. They won't renegotiate the licensing terms in case they damage Ireland's reputation. Ireland's reputation for what? For giving oil companies what they want?

—Sean Doran

\*

My name is Ryan Keane. I am fourteen years of age and attend the Patrician Secondary School in Newbridge, County Kildare. The reason I was motivated to write this, and the reason I am motivated to take action, is plain and simple, to improve the quality of life for Irish people such as myself now and in the future. The future is important to me – I intend to live in it.

As of 2012, the Irish national debt is at 117.2 percent, as published by Eurostat, well above the likes of Canada (84.1 percent) and the UK (88.7 percent) and a distant memory of the 25 percent we enjoyed in 2007/08. Further showing our extremely vast debts, which are mainly due to the mismanagement of banks, assisted by our government's high rate of borrowing.

Ireland's national debt is still on the rise, due to our government's policy of austerity. This is further echoed by Christine Lagarde, head of the IMF. This policy is killing any chance of substantial economic growth. This stance has been foolishly followed by the British government, who also have been recommended by Ms Lagarde to review their plan of austerity as their national debt fast approaches 100 percent.

The austerity I am talking about can be recognised by every person in this country: it is the cutting back of such things as child benefit, which some people depend on. This government has shown, and is showing, its lack of initiative, and lack of ability to take risks, by sticking to the age-old plan of cutting benefits and hiking taxes, as I'm sure anyone will tell you. The government are also cutting vital public services, such as the Gardaí and the already badly funded HSE. This approach is diminishing both public confidence in the government and the economic state of the country, and further shows how our current government, particularly Minister Noonan, are grossly mismanaging our nation.

As stated before, ask anyone and they will tell you that all we see in budgets is services being cut and taxes being hiked, but still people such as Enda Kenny and Michael Noonan continue to try and persuade us things are getting better, when they are clearly getting worse. I am sure if you ask President Obama if austerity is the answer, he would say no, and he would also add that a government needs the people behind it – something our government lacks. The fact is that economic stagnation means that money needs to be pumped into the economy, not taken out of it.

You just have to look at the Own Our Oil campaign website to see that our nation has a pension fund of €5 billion, but if you look at Norway, for example, who own their oil, it is €650 billion. Ireland's oil was mismanaged from when Sean Lemass sold a £700 million oil field for £500 in 1958. In 1975, Justin Keating brought in laws to regulate the Irish oil industry, but this work was foolishly undone by Ray Burke and Bertie Ahern. (Ray Burke was found guilty of corruption in relation to separate allegations and was the only Irish politician ever to spend time in jail due to corruption charges.) Under severe pressure from oil companies lobbying for deregulation, they unravelled the terms Justin Keating had put in place. Ireland now has the second-lowest tax rate in the world out of 142 countries.

The Department of Communications, Energy and Natural Resources is responsible for awarding and maintaining oil-licensing agreements, and these can be renegotiated at any time. As stated by the Oireachtas report on oil and gas licensing terms in 2012, there is no law against it. It was also stated, however, that no politician would risk renegotiating the terms in case of reputational damage to Ireland – which is basically politicians avoiding risking their careers. The only politician that can do this is the Minister for Energy and Communications.

I feel that this report was a waste of taxpayers' money because they found the solution to our problem (renegotiate the terms of the licences) but basically said that no politician has the courage to stand up and do so.

For the reasons I have outlined above, I feel compelled to bring this issue to wider attention. Getting a fair deal from the oil resources that exist off our shoreline is too important to our collective future to conveniently ignore. The revenue that could be generated from this national resource could be the difference between prosperity and employment for a generation of young people like me, or a continuation of a recession that brings misery to so many. Turning a blind eye is simply not an option. Get involved in the Own Our Oil campaign? Can we afford not to?

—Ryan Keane

# 6.

# CAN THE STATE SELL THE NATION?

## Diarmuid Rossa Phelan, SC

Own Our Oil inform me that the first question asked of their team is whether or not the Constitution protects Irish natural resources from exploitation, including by the State, and preserves their benefit for the nation, and whether existing licences can, through legally sound means, be unpicked.

Own Our Oil requested a contribution to address constitutional limits on the State's disposal of natural resources, and on legal restrictions on the increase of fees for successful natural resources licensees.

The short answer is that there is almost no straightforward constitutional control on the State's disposal of natural resources, and that the increase of license fee is primarily a matter of contract.

## THE NATURE OF THE INQUIRY

There may be nuanced constitutional and contractual arguments not arising on the face of the Constitution and statutory provisions which ground some constraint on State disposal, and some flexibility to increase fees beyond the flexibility, if any, in the contract. There is also the possibility of raising taxes.

However, setting out such arguments as may in the future be advanced by Own Our Oil or others to constrain the State's disposal of natural resources will alert the exploiters of natural resources to head off that possibility in the statutory and contractual framework, rather than dissuading them from their intended actions. Furthermore, the prospect of success of anything other than a certain, clear and reasonably simple legal challenge to the State is slim, though not nil.

The State, and the oil exploration notice parties, may pay lawyers limited only by the tax pool, and oil-company turnover. The civil servants may instruct forever as part of their permanent pensionable employment; the oil companies' executives as part of their employment and direct commercial interest. The individual plaintiffs or groups will be either unemployed or trying to minimise the disruption to their employment and the performance of their tax and debt obligations.

Cases involving oil licences will be transferred by the State and oil companies to the Commercial Court, where the well-resourced have both tactical and strategic advantage and a communality of interest with the Commercial Court's institutional policies and procedures. Litigation against the State and oil companies combined is liable to be crushed in the early stages of interlocutory pressures before it progresses near a trial on substance. Even if the litigation got to trial in any sort of proper shape, which is doubtful, the Courts are disinclined, with justification, to read the Constitution as controlling the State in economic matters.

## THE NATURE OF THE PROBLEM

A constitution does not preserve a people or a nation, nor save them from themselves. A constitution draws limits on competences in the sense of powers, but not on competency (in the sense of skill and efficiency) in the exercise of those competences. Disparate groups and individuals in recent times have looked to the Constitution to preserve what they consider to be the core of the nation from government intrusion or incompetence. The State, that is the government, the Oireachtas and the civil service, have a history in Ireland of separation of interest from People and Nation.

The State has a form of limited democratic legitimacy from elections based partly on vote, partly on inheritance of seats, partly on clientelism and state favours, which maintains in legislature and cabinet political parties, families and public servants (primarily school teachers) since the Civil War. The State expels its People and sells its Nationhood to preserve itself. Regime change, not legal challenge, is the solution.

## THE CONSTITUTIONAL POSITION IN OVERVIEW

The Constitution of 1937 provides, in one of the articles under the heading of 'The State', as follows:

### Article 10

1. All natural resources, including the air and all forms of potential energy, within the jurisdiction of the Parliament and Government established by this Constitution and all royalties and franchises within that jurisdiction belong to

the State subject to all estates and interests therein for the time being lawfully vested in any person or body.

2. All land and all mines, minerals and waters which belonged to Saorstát Éireann immediately before the coming into operation of this Constitution belong to the State to the same extent as they then belonged to Saorstát Éireann.

3. Provision may be made by law for the management of the property which belongs to the State by virtue of this Article and for the control of the alienation, whether temporary or permanent, of that property.

4. Provision may also be made by law for the management of land, mines, minerals and waters acquired by the State after the coming into operation of this Constitution and for the control of the alienation, whether temporary or permanent, of the land, mines, minerals and waters so acquired.

The Article applies to all natural resources within the jurisdiction of the Parliament and Government established by the Constitution (Article 10(1)). If the exploited natural resources are outside the jurisdiction, then this Article does not apply. In such a case, the constitutional position of activists may be weaker, because the resources lie outside the jurisdiction. Although State activity outside the jurisdiction may be the subject of constitutional control, the State's assertion of ownership or control of resources outside the jurisdiction would not give rise *ipso facto* to any constitutional control.

The Article expressly allows for permanent disposal by the State of the property which belongs to the State by virtue of Article 10, although such disposal may be only pursuant to law (Article 10(3) and (4)). The apparent meaning of 'law' in sub-articles 3 and 4 is statute law. Consequently the government, for example, could not dispose of the property without statutory authority, but could with statutory authority.

There are several acts, such as the Petroleum and Other Minerals Development Act, the Continental Shelf Act, the Minerals Development Act and amending legislation, the State Property Act, the Strategic Infrastructure Act, and associated amending legislation, which give the State the authority.

The constitutional power of the State to permanently alienate the natural resources extends to lesser action, such as leasing or licensing.

The Constitution of 1922 provided in Article 11:

All the lands and waters, mines and minerals, within the territory of the Irish Free State (Saorstát Éireann) hitherto vested in the State, or any department thereof, or held for the public use or benefit, and also all the natural resources of the same territory (including the air and all forms of potential energy), and also all royalties and franchises within that territory shall, from and after the date of the coming into operation of this Constitution, belong to the Irish Free State (Saorstát Éireann), subject to any trusts, grants, leases or concessions then existing in respect thereof, or any valid private interest therein, and shall be controlled and administered by the Oireachtas, in accordance with such regulations and provisions as shall be from time to time approved by legislation, but the same shall not, nor shall any part thereof, be alienated, but may in the public interest be from time to time granted by way of lease or licence to be worked or enjoyed under the authority and subject to the control of the Oireachtas: Provided that no such lease or licence may be made for a term exceeding ninety-nine years, beginning from the date thereof, and no such lease or licence may be renewable by the terms thereof.

This provision was more limited than the current Article 10. For example, it prohibited alienation. So far as leases and licences were permitted, these were permissible only (a) in the public interest, and (b) under the control of the Oireachtas. In the Constitution of 1937, there is no mention of the public interest. So the Constitution of 1922 was more restrictive in (a) prohibiting alienation, and (b) making leases or licences expressly subject to the public interest. Furthermore, whereas the Constitution of 1937 requires legislation to be in place, and the Oireachtas can certainly repeal or enact legislation, the Constitution does not provide a requirement for any 'control of the Oireachtas' as such.

The change in articles between Constitutions was deliberate, the contrast intended, and the control relaxed.

## THE CONTRACTUAL POSITION IN OVERVIEW

If the lease or licence specifies that the State can increase the fees, then the State can. If the lease or licence does not, then the State cannot. To do so would breach contract and be remedied by injunction and/or damages. An increase contrary to contract would contravene (arguably also breach) the right to private property protected by the Constitution.

For example, the Licensing Terms for Offshore Oil and Gas Exploration, Development and Production 2007 provides for fees in Appendix 1. These fees are set in advance. They are on the website of the Department of Communications, Energy and Natural Resources.

The terms provide expressly in Article 45, entitled 'Increase of Money Terms', as follows:

The Minister shall have the right, from time to time, to increase all money amounts mentioned herein having regard to relevant economic factors and shall notify the authorisation holder accordingly. The increases shall have effect from the date of such notice.

This is an unusual provision as it appears to allow unilateral increases in consideration restrained only by the preposition-unspecific and metric-unspecific clause 'having regard to relevant economic factors'.

Article 19(4) provides for an increase of the licensee's contribution to research fund to be in line with the consumer price index.

The terms also provide for the right of a licensee to surrender its licence or part of its licence, and impose obligations to surrender over time percentages of areas (of licensee's choosing) covered by the licence.

The terms also provide for the alienation (e.g. sale) of the licence for a nominal fee, subject to Ministerial consent. So there will be a trade in licences. This has a long history in Ireland, where the accord of a licence (e.g. a mobile phone licence), or a permission (e.g. a planning permission), the effect of which is to remove a State prohibition on activity, has been sold on, with the State gaining the minimal return of the licence or permission fee, and the trader increasing the cost (which the operator will recover from the people) and taking the profit, of the sell-on.

The terms provide for the licensers' right to compel a grant of a lease. The terms specify in Section 36 that the licensee or lessee is liable to tax in Ireland for profits and gains (except Petroleum Prospecting licensees).

Furthermore, Section 67 provides that all petroleum sold must be sold to a person in Ireland, and paid for in Ireland. This should have tax benefits to the State.

Section 39 provides:

### Exclusive jurisdiction of Irish Courts

All claims and all disagreements and disputes whatsoever and howsoever arising in regard to any contract or authorisation entered into by the Minister in pursuance of the Petroleum and Other Minerals Development Act, 1960 or in anywise related thereto shall be subject to Irish Law and all disputes requiring arbitration shall be subject to the Arbitration Act, 1954 as amended. All such disputes, claims or arbitrations shall be justiciable in Irish Courts.

However, Section 51 provides:

### Arbitration

(1) Any dispute between the parties hereto arising out of or in connection with the authorisation unless otherwise resolved shall be settled by arbitration proceedings between the Minister as one party and the authorisation holder as the other party and such proceedings shall determine the measures to be taken by the parties including, if appropriate, payment of compensation, to put an end to or remedy the damage caused by any breach of the provisions of the authorisation.

Disputes arising under authorisations are to be arbitrated. Under the current Arbitration Act of 2010, arbitral awards are effectively unreviewable by the Courts. This was a policy choice by the Oireachtas to reduce, where contracting parties consent, the role of the courts (a policy choice not without support of courts). Consequently, disputes under these authorisations/licences have been removed from the jurisdiction of the Courts. Therefore Section 39 is of less consequence than otherwise appears. The Section remains important for choice of law (Irish law), for removing court supervision of contract (because an Irish court will apply the Arbitration Act 2010, whereas a foreign court may review disputes referred to arbitration), and residual issues outside of arbitration.

## The Constitution of a State, People, and Nation

The Constitution contains provisions referring to State, People and Nation. These concepts are distinct legally. The extent of the difference is contestable. The concepts are also distinct politically. This is not unusual in constitutions.

What constitutes the People, and the Nation, is indeterminate. It is easier to say who would constitute part of the People (for example, a citizen of voting age) than who would not. It is not easy to state with authority what the concept as a whole embraces, or the effect of time on its identity. This also is not unusual in other constitutions.

The State is not the People, nor the Nation, constitutionally or politically. Citizens in this State-declared republic (by The Republic of Ireland Act 1948) may assume that the State, and the State's interest, is identical with that of the People. This is erroneous. This is unusual in western States. This may explain why interest groups have difficulty believing that the Constitution does not protect the People or the Nation from the State, for example from the State disposing of natural resources for what they estimate to be low value. This is not primarily a legal deficiency, but a regime failure.

## A State Subverting the Nation and Its People

Subvert may be the wrong verb, since the Nation and the People never fully established themselves in Ireland, whereas the State did. The focus on provisions misses overarching constitutional issues, and leaves groups such as Own Our Oil thin legal ground on which to find support (such as Article 10), and court space only to fail.

Own Our Oil's concerns bring an overarching and very real constitutional problem into relief, which is not single-issue (e.g. oil) dependent. For example, the following State actions, in the areas of (1) taxation/bank interest rates, (2) population exchange, (3) growth of State apparatus and decrease of State sovereignty, are not unconstitutional in the current legal understanding. Yet they are of constitutional significance, in the sense of the identity and future of the Nation and its People.

- The State continues to grow, although the powers of the State have shrunk beyond recognition with the transfers to the European Union. The size of the State in cost burden, personnel and presence is detached from its *raison d'être* and incommensurate with the scope of its powers.

- The State exercised some of its remaining competences so incompetently that the State volunteered to partly cede these, for a time period, to a Troika comprising the European Central Bank, European Commission and International Monetary Fund, in return for money.

- The State, in the European Union referendums, proceeded on its decided course contrary to the referendum result, and thus contrary to the People, the point of popular control, the purpose of the referendum provisions, and the Constitution. However the State did not ratify the Treaty without a subsequent referendum, thus observing those provisions. This is not primarily a deficiency in the wording of the Constitution, but in the composition, ethos and regime in the State.

- The State, having transferred powers to the EU, having placed some remaining freedom of movement under the Troika, having not reduced its burden footprint on the people, plans to seek a part-solution to its ills by selling the nation's national resources. To be clear, the State which does not want competences, and exercised competences incompetently, will now sell the national resources to sustain itself.

- The State's direct income taxation and aggregates on its resident citizens is more than 50 percent, that is, over half citizens' income. More than half of a citizen's working life is now unpaid servitude to the State. ('It was the wish of Tokugawa Leyasu, venerated now as the deity who shines over the East, that rural peasants be taxed not so heavily that they die, nor yet so lightly that they live.'[1])

- Of the remainder of a citizen's working life, much is now controlled by paying for the banks. The citizen is paying for banks' failure through unilateral interest rate hikes, which now charge in the region of ten times Euribor, on the basis that this represents their costs (over which the debtor has no control) in addition to their subventions sustained through taxation and State borrowing.

- The State charges 23 percent VAT or sales tax on most transactions in the private sector.

- The State's corporation tax is 12.5 percent, with lesser rates applied in practice to international companies, and higher rates applied in practice to small domestic companies (such as 'service' companies).

- The State in practice is more efficient in collection of taxes from citizens than from non-citizens.

126

- This system of differential taxation between individuals and companies, and nationals and non-nationals, is one of the cornerstones of the State's economic and EU policy.

- The State dominates the economy to an unprecedented degree.

- The State has severed the natural, and arguably moral, connection between production and reward.

- The economic oppression of productive citizens, in particular private sector citizens, excludes them in practice from political participation. They have no spare resource.

- The State has a *de facto* policy of exile of citizens and immigration of foreign citizens. (The CSO reports that net emigration of Irish nationals for the year ending April went up from 25,900 in 2012 to 35,200 in 2013. Immigration rose from 52,700 to 55,900 in the same period – some immigrants being returning Irish nationals and shows a 3 percent turnover in population through migration alone in 2013.) This helps preserve the State by removing the most natural opposition – those pushed to the point of exile, the young, the productive and the educated.

- The State-owned broadcasting network Radio Teilifís Éireann is by far the most important former of public opinion. The State sustains RTÉ both by State funding and by maintaining a system of licence levies on residents for any equipment capable of receiving broadcast transmissions, backed by criminal prosecutions and sanctions including imprisonment.

These perverse State actions are normal in Ireland.

The Constitution does not control the State in its oppression and expulsion of its productive citizenry. On its current (questionable) reading, the Constitution allows the State to dispose of the income and property of its citizens. The natural resources which are vested in the State are vested in the State, not the People, and may be disposed of by the State. This State is not the People's guardian. The electoral system perpetuates the regime, but appears not to allow for its reform. The referendum system is subverted. If the People believe that they should protect the natural resources of the Nation from the State, the law of the State will not help them.

The Preamble to the Constitution professes that the People gave themselves the Constitution. Legally, the State is a creature of the Constitution. Article 6.1 of the Constitution provides:

> All powers of government, legislative, executive and judicial, derive, under God, from the people, whose right it is to designate the rulers of the State and, in final

appeal, to decide all questions of national policy, according to the requirements of the common good.

The People may have to appeal to themselves, outside of the State and its unreformed electoral system, to their law, given by them: the Constitution. This may be viewed as subversion of the State, or as saving the Nation, or as freeing the People. It may be constitutional, just as the State selling the country to cover the incompetence and corruption of its regime may also be constitutional. This deliberation may need to be taken outside the State institutions – the courts and the unreformed electoral system.

It is in the overarching constitutional structure that the People may seek to prevent the State selling the Nation, and in the State's *de facto* control and *de iure* Article 10 that the State may seek to sell it.

## ABOUT THE AUTHOR

Diarmuid Rossa Phelan, BCL (NUI - UCD), LLM (UC Berkeley), BL (King's Inns), DALF (Paris), PhD (EUI - Florence), MA (Dub), Senior Counsel at the Bar of Ireland, Attorney/Counsel at the bars of New York, England and Wales, and Northern Ireland. Assistant Professor, Trinity College Dublin. D. R. Phelan has been in practice in Ireland since 1994, and in other employments has worked in the Court of Justice of the European Union and for a US law firm. He has acted in a number of pro bono constitutional and administrative law cases, and is widely published.

## NOTES

1.  Takano Jodo (1796) in R. Overy, *The Times Complete History of the World* (8th ed. 2010), pg 196.

# 7.

# RESOURCE NATIONALISM AND THE PUBLIC TRUST DOCTRINE: A CONSTITUTIONAL SOLUTION TO IRELAND'S INEQUITABLE OIL AND GAS REGIME

Vincent Salafia, BA, JD, LLM

## INTRODUCTION: MINISTER'S REVIEW OF THE OIL AND GAS REGIME

The 'Report on Offshore Oil and Gas Exploration', published in 2012 by the Joint Committee on Communications, Natural Resources and Agriculture (JCCNRA), recommended an approximate doubling of the tax take from development of Ireland's oil and gas reserves.[1] In response, the Minister for Communications, Energy and Natural Resources, Pat Rabbitte, in June 2013 announced that he was seeking 'independent expert advice on the "fitness-for-purpose" of Ireland's fiscal terms.'[2] He said, 'Such expert advice would focus on what level of fiscal gain is achievable for the State and its citizens and, equally important, on the mechanisms best suited to produce such a gain.'[3]

On 24 September 2013, the Department of Communications, Energy and Natural Resources (DCENR) commenced a public procurement process, seeking the provision of expert advice.[4] The terms of reference (TOR) stated:

> Having regard to the fact that *Ireland's indigenous oil and gas resources belong to the people and to the policy goal of maximising the benefits to the State,* from exploration for and extraction of those resources, the Minister for Communications, Energy and Natural Resources seeks expert advice as to:
>
> (i) the 'fitness for purpose' of Ireland's current fiscal regime for oil and gas exploration, development and production having regard to:

- the petroleum prospectivity of the Irish offshore

- Ireland's relative attractiveness as a location for mobile international exploration investment

- the findings of the May 2012 report of the former Joint Oireachtas Committee on Communications, Natural Resources and Agriculture, together with the debate of that report by Dáil Éireann

- other relevant reports

- comparative international experience

> (ii) Supported by analysis, whether revisions should be made to the fiscal licensing regime, in particular having regard to:
>
> - the level at which the terms are set
>
> - the nature of the instruments used
>
> - the tax reliefs available.[5]

This chapter addresses all of the issues raised in the TOR, and concludes that the current petroleum regime, including fiscal terms, is not 'fit for purpose' and that some recommendations of the JCCNRA report should be followed. Critically, the tax rates should be raised to much higher levels. Based on the clear evidence that Ireland has substantial oil and gas reserves, it is clear that a much higher level of fiscal gain is achievable for the State and its citizens, in dealings with multinational oil companies (MOCs).

The main focus of this chapter relates to the issue of ownership, raised in the TOR, and examines whether or not it is indeed a 'fact' that 'Ireland's indigenous oil and gas resources belong to the people', in light of the fact that Article 10 of the Constitution places ownership in the hands of the State. It concludes that the Irish people do not have enforceable rights under the Constitution, on its face, due to the wording of Article 10, granting ownership of natural resources to the State, as well as the declaration of nonjusticiability of public rights to natural resources, in Article 45. However, it also concludes that there are grounds for a constitutional challenge to assert that the people do indeed have implied beneficial ownership of their natural resources, and that the ownership by the State, contained in Article 10, is merely nominal ownership, under the Public Trust Doctrine (PTD). However, unless the Constitution is amended by referendum to clearly reflect this fact, the only way to have the PTD recognised is to go to court and seek to have it enforced. Various grounds for such an action are advanced.

Two 'mechanisms' are proposed in this chapter which will result in an equitable oil and gas regime for the Irish people that is 'fit for purpose':

1. The PTD is an internationally recognised legal principle that can be traced back to early Roman and English law, which vested ownership of natural resources in the public. It applies private trust law principles to modern State 'ownership' and management of natural resources, and places the highest duty of care possible on the State, in the form of a fiduciary duty.

2. 'Resource nationalism' is an internationally recognised economic policy strategy, containing certain measures, such as increased taxes, that is designed to maximise the return to the State from MOCs, in order to directly benefit the people of the State.

Ironically, the elements of both of these mechanisms are already contained in the TOR themselves. Firstly, the TOR refer to 'the fact that Ireland's indigenous oil and gas resources belong to the people'. This means that the State's ownership of natural resources, based on Article 10 of the Constitution, is only nominal ownership, in the form of a trusteeship, and that the State must always act in the best interests of the real owners and beneficiaries – the public. This is the PTD in a nutshell.

Secondly, and following on from this, the TOR advocate 'the policy goal of maximising the benefits to the State from exploration for and extraction of those resources'. This is resource nationalism in a nutshell. The only problem is that the benefits should accrue to the people (or the 'nation'), not 'the State', exposing a basic contradiction in state policy and the TOR themselves. However, the range of measures envisioned by resource nationalism and the PTD, which are needed to achieve the gain in revenue (at the expense of MOCs), is the same.

Reading the TOR, a reasonable person would assume that Ireland's natural resources are in safe hands, due to its policy of resource nationalism and its implementation of the PTD. However, nothing could be further from the truth. Ireland is engaged in 'resource privatism', and the PTD does not exist in Ireland, where the public right to ownership over natural resources was eviscerated in the 1937 Constitution, when the State was effectively granted full ownership and control of them. That means that the current rights of the public are actually less than existed under absolute monarchy, since the time of Magna Carta.

Constitutionalising the PTD in Ireland, either through referendum or court action, and adopting of a policy of resource nationalism are essential to ensuring that the fiscal terms for oil and gas deliver the maximum benefit possible to the Irish people.

## RESOURCE NATIONALISM:
### THE 'RISING PHENOMENON' WORLDWIDE

One of the biggest financial risks facing oil and gas companies worldwide is 'resource nationalism'. It is defined as 'the tendency for states to take (or seek to take) direct and increasing control of economic activity in natural resource sectors'.[6] While often discussed in terms of the oil and gas industry, resource nationalism applies to government policy over all natural resources, and has been ranked the number one risk to mining companies world-wide for the past two years by Ernst and Young.[7] According to Helena Ward:

> Resource nationalism can be found in a variety of natural resource sectors, includ-ing food and agriculture, fisheries, mining and minerals and oil and gas. However, the current visibility of energy security and climate change considerations on the global stage has meant that it is the oil and gas sector that dominates much contem-porary analysis of resource nationalism.[8]

According to risk analytics experts Maplecroft, in the introduction to their Resource Nationalism Index 2012, 'resource nationalism is a rising phenomenon where governments of countries hosting large reserves of natural resources try to secure greater economic ben-efit from their exploitation'.[9] Unlike outright nationalisation, the new policy adopted by the State still results in some form of public private partnership (PPP), or concession agree-ment, but under radically altered terms, in favour of its citizens and local communities.

Governments use a number of devices to increase state revenue from multinational exploitation of their natural resources, such as increased licence fees, royalties, corporate taxes and customs duties which are based on the amount of oil and gas produced. In addi-tion, according to one expert, 'a growing trend has emerged whereby governments in natu-ral-resource-rich countries are now seeking to impose a capital gains tax on gains realised by international (non-resident) companies from non-resident or overseas transactions where the value is derived from assets based within their jurisdiction'.[10]

In 2012 Maplecroft published a report entitled 'Maplecroft Resource Nationalism Index', which rates 197 countries under various economic, social and political risk factors. Two-thirds of the twelve member nations of OPEC feature at the top of the index. Ireland is rated 'low risk', along with all other EU member states.[11]

## RESOURCE NATIONALISM:
### SOCIAL JUSTICE AND SOCIETAL TRANSFORMATION

Resource nationalism is not simply a financial trend or economic strategy. According to Maplecroft Associate Director James Smither, 'Resource nationalism not only encompasses economic factors and the control of production, in many nations it has now come to sym-bolise social justice and a milestone on the road to societal transformation.'[12] In practice, the term 'resource nationalism' usually implies an active citizens' movement within the state that hosts the multinationals. As one commentator recently noted:

Resource nationalism explains the situation where there is a certain sense that a country deserves a lot more from its natural resource endowments. There is therefore a citizen movement that makes a conscious attempt to get government to participate fully in natural resource extraction.[13]

Maplecroft predicts an increase in resource nationalism over the next two years, threatening profits for multinationals:

Potential challenges include the global trend toward resource nationalism, which is resulting in less favorable terms for international companies and greater local content or local partnering requirements.[14]

One effect of this trend is multinationals looking to different countries for alternative sources of cheap natural resources: 'The combination of resource nationalism and the continuing depletion of existing fields is driving companies, particularly oil and gas majors, to new frontiers.'[15] Ireland is clearly one of those new frontiers.

## New Petroleum Licensing Terms 2007: 'A resource of the people'

The 1992 fiscal terms were finally changed in 2007. Then Minister for Communications, Energy and Natural Resources Eamon Ryan said:

Ireland's oil and gas is a resource of the people. The Government acts as caretakers/owners of these resources on their behalf. It has a duty to ensure appropriate return and to ensure that they are adequately and properly explored.[16]

This is a concise statement of the PTD, where the people own their own oil and gas, with the government acting as trustees 'on behalf' of the people. The minister even described the fiduciary 'duty' that lies at the heart of this trustee/beneficiary relationship under Irish trust law.

The new licensing terms included a profit resource rent tax. This new tax was in addition to the 25 percent corporate tax rate then employed. This new tax ranged from 5 to 15 percent, depending on the profitability of the field, bringing the maximum possible tax to 40 percent. Minister Ryan claimed:

All changes, both fiscal and non-fiscal, alter the way Ireland deals with oil and gas exploration companies. They bring us into line with other comparable countries.[17]

However, these apparent improvements were largely illusory, according to the Services Industrial Professional and Technical Union (SIPTU), in a 2011 report called 'Optimising Ireland's Oil and Gas Resources'[18]:

if an exploration licence was granted between 1992 and 2007 and the petroleum lease was granted after 2007, the petroleum lease holding company will be subject to the 1992 Licensing Terms.[19]

SIPTU concluded:

Except in the case of very profitable fields, Ireland will see little additional revenue from the 2007 terms.[20]

In terms of international standards, SIPTU quoted some telling US reports, which show that Ireland's take, even at 40 percent, is less than half of that of many other countries:

A 2007 report by the US Government Accountability Office (GAO) examined 142 fiscal systems and confirmed that Ireland had the second lowest rate of government take of all the countries studied (Cameroon had the lowest). Of these 142 fiscal systems, only 34 resulted in government take of less than 50 percent (50 percent being twice the rate of Ireland).[21]

While the 2007 fiscal terms were a slight improvement on the 1992 terms, they are among the friendliest in the world to MOCs. However, the Fine Gael/Labour government elected in 2011 seemed to want to change that.

## PROGRAMME FOR GOVERNMENT 2011:
### 'TO MAXIMISE THE RETURN FOR THE IRISH PEOPLE'

Public concern over the flawed public consultation and the inequitable terms of the Corrib gas project began in 2000 and escalated over subsequent years,[22] making the fiscal terms of oil and gas development an election issue in both 2007 and 2011. In 2011 both Labour and Fine Gael promised a better deal for the Irish people during the election, and their programme for government proclaimed:

We will incentivise and promote off-shore drilling and streamline planning and regulatory process for bringing ashore these reserves and seek to maximise the return to the Irish people.[23]

Seeking to 'maximise the return to the Irish people' is a promise of resource nationalism, as it indicates an intention to 'fundamentally reposition' Ireland's economic policy and to make a 'major' improvement on the existing return from MOCs. It also confirms the existence of the PTD, as it recognises that beneficial ownership of natural resources lies with the people.

## JCCNRA: Recommendations for Improved Fiscal Terms for Oil and Gas

JCCNRA published its report 'Offshore Oil and Gas Exploration' on 9 May 2012.[24] It contained eleven key recommendations, the key one being:

> The overall tax take should, in the case of future licences, be increased to a minimum of 40 percent, with a sliding scale up to 80 percent for very large commercial discoveries.[25]

The Minister responded in the Seanad, on 27 June 2012, saying,[26]

> The changes in that tax regime that are now proposed are not minor or modest in nature. What is proposed is a fundamental repositioning which would raise our tax to a similar level to that of the UK and, in the case of very profitable fields, would result in a higher tax here than applies in Norway. It may be the case that the committee was signalling where Ireland should seek to reposition the tax regime over time. However, I struggle to understand how anyone could expect Ireland to have Norwegian-style tax rates without first having Norwegian levels of commercial discoveries.[27]

The Minister then concluded:

> I do not wish to be negative or to undersell Ireland as a location for exploration investment, quite the contrary, but one must deal in realities. The reality is that the Irish offshore is underexplored and its *petroleum potential is largely unproven*, particularly when compared with other petroleum regions such as Norway and the United Kingdom.[28]

A 2006 report by the Petroleum Affairs Division of that department stated that there is potential of at least 10 billion barrels of oil lying off the west coast of Ireland – which had a current value of €450 billion (at just €50 a barrel).[29] It was estimated in 2011 that the total oil and gas reserve, at current prices, had a potential value of around €750 billion.[30]

## International Comparisons: Norway and Uganda

Both ministers Rabbitte and O'Dowd have suggested looking at countries like France, Portugal and Spain, none of which are particularly notable when it comes to their people benefitting from oil and gas exploration. For that, it is necessary to compare Ireland with more inspiring examples, to show what is possible if the right legal and financial mechanisms are put in place.

JCCNRA and others have argued that Ireland should model itself on Norway and the UK, but the government consistently rejects these proposals. However, since Norway represents the ideal long-term model for Irish development, it is important to make the comparison and analyse the underlying legal and policy framework that are the recipe for its success; in particular, resource nationalism and the PTD.

In terms of countries that are at a comparable early stage in their petroleum development to Ireland, Uganda offers a very progressive approach. Ironically, the Irish government has given financial assistance to Uganda to develop its petroleum policy and legal framework, which is based on both resource nationalism and the PTD.

## NORWAY: RESOURCE NATIONALISM AND THE PTD

While the Irish government consistently downplays comparisons with Norway, it remains the international model for 'best practice' in natural resource revenue management.[31] Norway's tax model is drastically different from Ireland, where it receives up to 80 percent tax from oil companies. Behind this fiscal and tax regime, however, lie deeply embedded ideologies that can be defined in policy terms as 'resource nationalism', and in legal terms as 'the PTD'. This is as close to the opposite of the Irish way of thinking as you could get. And while the Irish government would criticise these mechanisms, and predict doom for Ireland if they were adopted, the multinational oil companies are still lining up to do business in Norway.

## CLASSIFIED US CABLE: 'RESOURCE NATIONALISM AND NORWAY'

On 29 November 2007, a classified cable, now available on Wikileaks,[32] was sent from the US Embassy in Oslo, Norway, to the Secretary of State in Washington DC, addressed to the Department of Commerce. The subject was 'Resource Nationalism and Norway'.[33] It describes Norway's 'resource nationalism', in part, as 'energy resource policies, which work to maximise governmental financial returns while ensuring its strict stewardship of natural resources'. It concludes that despite 'some criticism' of anti-competitive practices, 'major American energy companies operating locally...generally praise the Norwegian energy regime'.[34] It also concludes that 'The country's strong resource protections (motivated in no small part by the cultural sense of environmental stewardship) are reaping huge dividends.'[35] Norway is having its cake, and eating it too, with strong multinational investment and strong national returns.

So, what is the key to Norway's form of 'resource nationalism'? According to the communiqué:

> Understanding Norwegian resource policy necessarily involves recognising the Norwegian dedication to safeguarding, and sharing, public resources. The country's

strident commitment to a strong *public trust doctrine*, which aims to protect the environment for generations, evidences the core value of resource protection that affects all facets of Norwegian society. The commitment to *the greater public good, and sense of communal ownership*, is also clearly shown in the country's energy policy.[36]

The policy of resource nationalism and the legally entrenched PTD in Norway provide a high level of public services and a high degree of social welfare, while at the same time creating wealth and opportunity. Yet Norway remains an attractive investment environment for multinational corporations.[37] The wire goes on to say:

> While mindful of environmental concerns, the underlying motivation behind Norwegian energy policy remains wealth accumulation. The state sees vast NCS resources as Norwegian property, and private companies need explicit GON licence approvals to develop the shelf.[38]

The US also noted that:

> The Norwegian tax structure encourages private industry to maximise field development, while ensuring protection of energy resources. Although taxes are high, Norwegian Petroleum Ministry officials point out that no taxes are assessed until a company is profitable. Given that, GON officials believe Norway is 'one of the least expensive countries to do (energy) business in'. The state itself is burdened with early development costs through tax absorption.[39]

Ireland also gives tax breaks for exploration on the front end, but fails to recoup it on the back end, when production and profitability begins. But the bigger picture for Ireland is that there is no resource nationalism, and no PTD. There is no sense of communal ownership, scant protection for the environment, and the tax regime does not secure a strong return for the Irish people.

## UGANDA: COMPARABLE TO IRELAND IN ITS PETROLEUM DEVELOPMENT

While Norway is clearly the 'best practice' model to strive towards, the government is correct in saying that Ireland is not as advanced as Norway. In that regard, the government should look to another country that is very similar to Ireland in many key respects: Uganda. Both Ireland and Uganda are energy-dependent, and import most of their oil. Minister O'Dowd said: 'Over 95 percent of Ireland's total primary energy requirement is derived from fossil fuels and we have an 88 percent import dependency.'[40] Both have proven oil reserves that they are seeking to develop, and have signed a small number of contracts with multinational oil companies. However, Uganda has almost ten times the population of Ireland, with approximately 33 million people.[41]

In 2000, Uganda began seeking domestic oil reserves in response to rising oil prices and, in 2006, it struck oil.[42] Uganda has an estimated crude reserve of 3.5 billion barrels, compared to Ireland's 10 billion, and aims for commercial output of the resource by 2016 at the earliest. Ireland is at a very similar stage of petroleum development.

## UGANDA: IRISH GOVERNMENT'S CRITICAL ROLE IN UGANDA'S PROGRESSIVE OIL AND GAS POLICY

The Irish government had an important role in developing Uganda's progressive oil and gas regime. In 2007, it funded a comprehensive study on how to develop an effective and equitable model for oil and gas development.[43] The extensive study was produced by Advocates Coalition for Development and Environment (ACODE). The introduction states:

> The authors of this paper are indebted to the Government of Ireland through the World Resources Institute (WRI) for providing the financial resources that facilitated the research, production and publication of this work.[44]

ACODE has taken successful lawsuits asserting the people's constitutional rights, regarding land and natural resources, based on the PTD.[45] Its report focused largely on the constitutional framework as a mechanism for implementing of resource nationalism, and securing a long-term, equitable regime. The Irish government should fund similar research in Ireland.

## UGANDA: CONSTITUTIONAL IMPLEMENTATION OF THE PTD

Uganda's constitution provides for beneficial ownership, in that it has adopted the PTD. According to ACODE, 'The Constitution provides that "the entire property in, and the control of, all . . . petroleum" are vested in Government *on behalf of the Republic of Uganda*.'[46] The Ugandan PTD has both constitutional as well as statutory foundations, and has been enforced in the High Court, such as in the ACODE case.[47]

The Ugandan oil and gas fiscal regime, including taxation rates, flows directly from the constitutional mechanism of the PTD. Uganda's fiscal terms provide that the following rates apply: Royalty – 5 to 12.5 percent (production rate-related); Cost Recovery (Taxes) Cap – 50 percent; Profit Oil Government Share – 50 to 80 percent (production-level related). These rates are very similar to Norway, due to the fact that Uganda based its regime on that of Norway.[48] In other words, Uganda, despite the financial assistance it was given from Ireland, and the similarity of its stage in petroleum development, clearly chose not to model its fiscal regime on Ireland's.

## Uganda: Production-Sharing Agreements (PSAs)

The constitutional and legislative mechanisms adopted by Uganda directly influence the form and content of Uganda's agreements with oil and gas companies. Effective legal agreements are another essential mechanism for successful petroleum development. Uganda uses production-sharing agreements (PSAs), while Ireland does not. The ACODE report states, 'Uganda, like many other oil-producing countries, entered PSA because governments most frequently choose not to be directly involved in the actual process of discovering, extracting, refining and marketing such commodities.'[49]

Despite Ireland's policy of non-involvement in exploration, it does not use the PSA mechanism. This was strongly criticised in a position paper submitted by SIPTU to JCCN-RA during its review of the oil and gas regime. The paper states:

> The Department of Communications, Energy and Natural Resources (DCENR)'s use of a licensing system, as opposed to production-sharing contracts or service agreements, means that once Irish oil and gas is produced, ownership of these resources is transferred to the petroleum lease-holding companies with the State essentially conceding control over its resources to these corporations.[50]

The use of PSAs, in the context of the PTD legal regime, is a reflection of international law in relation to these matters, which is why ACODE states:

> Production-sharing agreements for Uganda represent a development in the petroleum industry which recognises the permanent sovereignty of states over their natural resources.[51]

Ireland's use of a licensing system, as opposed to use of PSA mechanisms, calls into question Ireland's behaviour in relation to international human rights norms, regarding 'permanent sovereignty' of the people over their natural resources. In addition, Ireland's terms are so low that they appear to breach other international agreements. The effective transfer of ownership to MOCs, combined with over-friendly fiscal terms, lead to knock-on effects on other human rights, due to the resulting low level of investment in social welfare and public services.

## The Public Trust Doctrine: The rising international trend

In addition to deglobalisation and resource nationalism, the PTD is another rising international trend that Ireland is out of step with. Should Ireland wish to amend the Constitution, and adopt international best practice and the PTD, there are numerous examples around the world to choose as models. Since the PTD became prominent in the US, in the 1980s, it has been formally adopted in many diverse countries on four continents: India, Pakistan, the Philippines, Uganda, Kenya, Nigeria, South Africa, Sri Lanka, Brazil, Ecuador and Canada.[52] Many of these countries have British common law legal systems, similar to Ireland, making Ireland an ideal candidate for its adoption. The adoption of the PTD in these diverse countries 'evidences an evolution of the doctrine towards becoming a general principle of international law'.[53] An examination of these countries also shows that most are members of the British Commonwealth. The exceptions are the Philippines, Brazil and Ecuador, which are former Spanish colonies. The PTD in all other countries came about as a direct result of the operation of the British common law system within those nations. Ireland's post-colonial status, along with its continued use of British common law, makes Ireland an obvious candidate for its formal adoption in the courts.

## ROMAN LAW: THE 'INSTITUTES' OF JUSTINIAN

The pubic trust doctrine is part of the common law and dates back to the Roman Empire, and the fifth-century jurist Justinian.[54] According to Professor Joseph L. Sax, the modern American exponent of the doctrine: 'At a superficial level, the shape of the PTD is easy enough to discern. It draws upon the Roman law idea of common properties (*res communis*) and on certain provisions of Magna Carta.'[55] The Roman *Institutes* of Justinian,[56] Chapter 2, 'The Book of Things', Section 1, 'The Division of Things', paragraph one states:

> By the law of nature these things are common to mankind – the air, running water, the sea, and consequently the shores of the sea. No one, therefore, is forbidden to approach the seashore, provided that he respects *habitations*, monuments, and buildings which are not, like the sea, subject only to the law of nations.[57]

Sax explained that 'Roman jurisprudence, developed in a society with heavy commerce, with important urban concentrations, and with a legal heritage from the sea-dependent Greeks, held that by the most basic "natural law" the "air, running water, the sea, and consequently the seashore" were "common to all".'[58] Essentially, the Roman law of Justinian provided that the state, as designated sovereign, holds title to certain lands and waters in trust for the people, the ultimate sovereign.[59]

## ENGLISH LAW: MAGNA CARTA

In *Arnold v. Mundy* in 1821,[60] where the Supreme Court of New Jersey invalidated the transfer into private hands of an oyster bed in state waters, the court recalled the effect of Magna Carta:

> By the usurpation of the Norman kings on the principles of Saxon liberty, prior to

the reign of Henry II, the king might grant a fishery; but since then he is restrained by Magna Carta, which simply restored the principles of the ancient law.[61]

The court also stated the basic rule of Magna Carta, which is, 'The king may grant his private property, his ordinary revenue, lands vested in him upon feudal principles, but not the public property.'[62]

Henry of Bracton (ca. 1210–68), an English jurist, wrote *De Legibus et Consuetudinibus Angliae* (*On the Laws and Customs of England*), which quoted Justinian, stating, 'By natural law itself, these things are common to all running water, air, and the sea, and the shores of the sea, as the sea's accessories.'[63]

The *Mundy* decision also described how the common law rights and the PTD came to exist in the US:

> That the people brought over to this country the same rights which they possessed in England. They had the same rights in navigable rivers here as in England; and the king had no greater rights over the people of this country than over the people of England. Magna Carta applied here in full force. This was declared by the Declaration of Independence, and asserted by all our writers of the day; and was one of the great principles upon which our revolutionary patriots founded their opposition to the acts of parliament.

How ironic it is then to realise that the rights enjoyed by citizens in independent Ireland to natural resources are not as strong as they were when the Irish were British subjects.

## MARTIN V. WADDELL (1842):
## RECOGNITION OF THE PTD BY THE US SUPREME COURT

The term 'public trust' itself first appeared in American jurisprudence in an 1842 US Supreme Court decision of *Martin v. Waddell* (1842).[64] The facts and issues of the case were similar to that of *Arnold v. Mundy*. It was an action for ejectment concerning oyster fisheries located in the public rivers and bays of East New Jersey. The claim was made under the charters of Charles the Second to his brother the Duke of York in 1664 and 1674 for the purpose of enabling him to plant a colony on the continent of America. The court concluded:

> And I must again repeat, if the King held such lands as trustee for the common benefit of all his subjects, and inalienable as private property, I am unable to discover on what ground the State of New Jersey can hold the land discharged of such trust and can assume to dispose of it to the private and exclusive use of individuals.[65]

## BROADENING THE US PTD: CASES 1842-PRESENT

After the *Martin* case, a long series of cases in the US asserting the PTD culminated in the landmark US Supreme Court case of *Illinois Central Railroad v. Illinois* (1892), which involved a grant by the State of Illinois of a large section of the land beneath Lake Michigan in the Chicago Harbour to the railroad company. Allegations of corruption abounded. Justice Stephen Johnson Field, in the US Supreme Court decision, declared that the state held the title to the submerged land, but the state held it 'in trust for the people of the State'.[66] Field said:

> There can be no irrepealable contract in a conveyance of property by a grantor in disregard of a public trust, under which he was bound to hold and manage it.[67]

The contractual terms of the conveyance of Ireland's oil and gas, by the State, to private hands, must be viewed in these terms. The 1955 case of *Mallon v. City of Long Beach* involved revenues from oil and gas leasing on tidelands of California. In reaching its conclusion that the revenue could not lawfully be freed from the public trust by a municipal grantee without producing a reversion to the state, the court said:

> It was held in *Trickey v. City of Long Beach*, 101 Cal.App.2d 871 [226 P.2d 694], that the income derived from the production of 'dry gas' from the tide and submerged lands granted to the city was subject to the public trust for commerce, navigation, and fisheries, and that the expenditure of that income for general municipal purposes was unlawful. It follows from the conclusion reached above that as a result of the 1951 statute the city holds all of the funds 'heretofore derived, or to be derived' from the production of 'dry gas' from the lands in question subject to a resulting trust in favor of the state.[68]

The PTD would be asserted in many later cases both in the US and around the world, with ever-increasing success, particularly after the doctrine was famously reasserted by Professor Joe Sax 1970.[69] Since then, 'the doctrine has evolved over the years to address generation of energy conservation, minerals/oil and gas contracts, scenic resources, open space, and preservation of ecosystems and historical sites'.[70] It is now also being used to tackle climate change[71] and even wind-farm developments.[72] In the most recent US Supreme Court case on the matter, *Philips Petroleum Co. v. Mississippi*,[73] the court 'extended the reach of the PTD to include inland non-navigable tidelands'.[74]

## THE PTD: AFFIRMATIVE DUTIES ON THE STATE

Later US cases interpreted the State's duty of care as being 'an affirmative duty'.

In *National Audubon Society v. Superior Court* (Mono Lake, 1983)[75], the California Supreme Court expanded the scope of the PTD and held that the State has an '*affirmative duty* to take the public trust into account' in making decisions affecting public trust resources, and also the duty of 'continuing supervision' over these resources which allows and may require modification of such decisions.[76] In *Shokal v. Dunn* (1985)[77], the Idaho Supreme Court placed the burden of proof on the developer who was seeking to convert public property to private use. The decision also required a set of criteria to be examined, reported and weighed by the administrator acting as the public trustee, mandating consideration of formal cost-benefit analysis.[78]

## HUMAN RIGHTS AND THE PTD: DECLARATION ON PERMANENT SOVEREIGNTY OVER NATURAL RESOURCES (1962)

While the PTD has reverberated down through centuries of common law since Magna Carta and gained a strong foothold in modern jurisprudence, in the US and other common law jurisdictions, there has been a parallel rise in human rights law governing natural resources, particularly since the 1960s. This itself has been largely incorporated into the modern principle of sustainable development.

As noted above, Uganda's use of PSAs 'recognises the permanent sovereignty of States over their natural resources'. The concept of 'permanent sovereignty' first came to wide attention with the 1962 UN Declaration on Permanent Sovereignty Over Natural Resources.[79] The Declaration came about after the 1952 landmark case of *UK v. Iran*,[80] in the International Court of Justice (ICJ). Iran nationalised its oil reserves, as well as oil company assets, and the ICJ refused to intervene, reaffirming Iran's sovereign right to ownership of its resources: permanent sovereignty.

The UN Declaration on Permanent Sovereignty Over Natural Resources states, in Article 1:

The right of people and nations to permanent sovereignty over their natural wealth and resources *must be exercised in the interest of their national development and of the well-being of the people of the State concerned.*[81]

The Declaration also provides in Article 2 that the nation and people must consent to the terms under which natural resources are traded:

The exploration, development and disposition of such resources, as well as the import of the foreign capital required for these purposes, should be in conformity with *the rules and conditions which the peoples and nations freely consider to be necessary or desirable* with regard to the authorisation, restriction or prohibition of such activities.[82]

It is highly doubtful that the Irish people 'freely consider the regime necessary or desirable'. In fact, Articles 10 and 45 of Ireland's Constitution may be in breach of the International Bill of Rights, which consists of the 1944 Universal Declaration of Human Rights (UDHR),[83] the International Covenants on Civil and Political Rights (ICCPR)[84] and its optional protocols, and the International Covenant on Economic, Social and Cultural Rights (ICESCR).[85]

## UN: THE INTERNATIONAL BILL OF RIGHTS AND SOVEREIGNTY OVER NATURAL RESOURCES

Articles 1 (1) of the ICCPR and the ICESCR) are identical, and begin by positing the right to self-determination:

> All peoples have the right of self-determination. By virtue of that right they freely determine their political status and freely pursue their economic, social and cultural development.[86, 87]

Articles 1 (2) of each covenant then links the right to self-determination to permanent sovereignty:

> All peoples may, for their own ends, freely dispose of their natural wealth and resources without prejudice to any obligations arising out of international economic co-operation, *based upon the principle of mutual benefit, and international law.* In no case may a people be deprived of its own means of subsistence.[88, 89]

## STOCKHOLM DECLARATION: 'FOR THE BENEFIT OF PRESENT AND FUTURE GENERATIONS'

The 1972 Declaration of the United Nations Conference on the Human Environment ('The Stockholm Declaration'), which is generally recognised as a founding document for the modern legal principle of sustainable development, links human rights and the environment, stating:

> Both aspects of man's environment, the natural and the man-made, are essential to his well-being and to the enjoyment of basic human rights the right to life itself.

Principle 2 of the Declaration states:

> The natural resources of the earth, including the air, water, land, flora and fauna

and especially representative samples of natural ecosystems, must be safeguarded *for the benefit of* present and future generations through careful planning or management, as appropriate.[90]

The duty that states must 'safeguard' natural resources 'for the benefit of' the people is trust-type language, and mimics the PTD. Furthermore, this highlights how trusts are intergenerational instruments, used for delivering intergenerational rights and justice, which fits perfectly with the principle of sustainable development.

## EU LAW AND THE PTD: ADVANCING THE OBJECTIVES OF SUSTAINABLE DEVELOPMENT

Finally, the PTD fulfils many of the goals, and performs many of the functions of the law of sustainable development, which has itself been constitutionalised, and made a primary objective in the Lisbon Treaty. Article 3.3 of the Treaty of the European Union (TEU), amended by the Lisbon Treaty, states that the Union:

> shall work for the sustainable development of Europe based on balanced economic growth and price stability, a highly competitive social market economy, aiming at full employment and social progress, and a high level of protection and improvement of the quality of the environment.[91]

The TEU now requires that the Union will strive towards the adoption of 'international measures to preserve and improve the quality of the environment and the sustainable management of global natural resources'.[92] In fact, the PTD legally implements sustainable measures where the law of sustainable development itself has hitherto failed.

Countries that have implemented the PTD generally grant the public certain procedural rights, in addition to substantive rights, which result in a participatory regime for decision-making on natural resources. For instance, the public has a right to have an independent, cost/benefit analysis performed on the proposed decision. These procedural rights are reinforced by complementary, affirmative duties on the state, to ensure that the public are fully educated and informed and have a right to participate in decision-making.

The human and procedural rights contained in the United Nations Economic Commission for Europe (UNECE) Convention on Access to Information, Public Participation in Decision-Making and Access to Justice in Environmental Matters ('The AARHUS Convention')[93], are now fully incorporated into EU and Irish law, and are complementary to those that would exist under the PTD. Rights of access to information, rights to participate in decision-making and rights of access to justice are rights that Irish citizens should have with regards to the fiscal regime for oil and gas, and all decisions concerning alienation of their valuable natural resources. Comparable rights also exist in EU directives such as the the EU Environmental Impact Assessment (EIA)[94] and the Strategic Assessment (SEA)[95] directives, and are already embedded in numerous Irish planning and environmental statutes and regulations. All these EU and Irish laws have the stated aim of achieving sustainable development.

Thus, there is no question of adoption of the PTD being in violation of EU law. In fact, it would be an effective tool for advancing it here in Ireland, and across the EU. The PTD goes beyond the law of sustainable development and environmental rights to place an affirmative, fiduciary duty on the State. The PTD is one of the few legal mechanisms capable of delivering sustainable management and rational use of natural resources in Ireland, by giving a greater share of the revenue to the people of Ireland, which will lead to employment, social progress and greater protection for the environment, the three main aims of the TEU, that collectively constitute sustainable development.

## CONSTITUTIONALISING THE PTD IN IRELAND: AMENDMENT OR LITIGATION

While government ministers and departments have issued statements describing the PTD as attaching to oil and gas reserves, there is no express provision enforcing it in the Constitution. Article 10 of the Irish Constitution gives ownership to the State, not the nation or the people.[96] Article 45 and certain parts of Article 10 contain the essential elements, but Article 45 is not justiciable. There are only two ways of having the PTD recognised in the Constitution. The first is by constitutional referendum and amendment, and the second is through the courts, which could agree that the PTD is already contained in the Constitution, if such an argument were advanced.

## PUBLIC TRUST AND PUBLIC INTEREST: SEEKING THE COMMON GOOD

The term 'PTD' has at its heart 'the public interest', also known as the 'common good', in relation to publicly owned natural resources. In fact, the expression itself, 'public interest', was first coined in relation to the law of shorelines and ports. Around 1670, Sir Matthew Hale, then Lord Chief Justice of the King's Bench of England, concluded an essay on the ports of the sea, called 'De Portibus Maris', wherein he famously referred to certain wharves as 'affected with a publick interest'.[97]

Lord Hale compared the king's property in the sea and tide-rivers to the ownership of lords of manors in the common or waste lands of the manor:

> The soil and freehold of the waste belong to the lord, but subject to certain rights

of the manorial tenants; such as common of pasture, piscary, turbary, ways, &c., claimed and enjoyed by them, by the custom of the manor, in and out of such waste lands.[98]

Hale described the 'common right to use these public trust lands and their resources for certain traditional purposes necessary to individual survival and livelihood, including navigation, commerce, and fishing'.[99] These are the exact issues on which (R) Moore v. Attorney General was decided and traditional fishing rights were granted to the public using the Magna Carta and Early Irish (Brehon) law.

Thus, seeking to enforce the PTD in Ireland is seeking to redefine the very nature of the 'public interest' and the 'common good', in constitutional terms.

## IRISH CONSTITUTIONAL FRAMEWORK: FRAMING THE PETROLEUM REGIME

The petroleum regime in any country is based on the constitution. Oil Contracts – How to Read and Understand Them, a 2012 book by transparency advocates Open Oil, states:

> The petroleum regime can be best thought of as a hierarchy, starting with the constitution of the relevant country and ending with the petroleum contract.[100]

Changing the petroleum regime, in order to implement the PTD in Ireland, will require changes to Irish law, ranging from the constitutional and legislative provisions to specific clauses placed in petroleum contracts. With regards to the Constitution, the Open Oil book states:

> The constitution will establish the authority for a government to make and enforce laws. It may also address the ownership of the country's natural resources and, in this case, will typically state that resources are owned by citizens of the nation, or held for their benefit by the current government.[101]

This is another clear expression of the PTD, which Open Oil shows to be commonplace throughout the world, in relation to national oil and gas policy. ACODE's research paper, concerning Uganda's oil and gas regime, discusses the need for constitutional entrenchment of principles relating to the development of oil and gas:

> Many questions on how the oil industry should be organised are better answered through legislation. However, certain basic principles should be secured in a Constitution to provide the basis for protecting against later abuses. Issues surrounding oil should be provided for in the Constitution to provide some constitutional safeguards to protect oil revenues and give constitutional recognition of host communities' and local governments' entitlements to benefits. Therefore, the first

avenue is through a constitutional provision. Once drafted and agreed to at the national level, a law should be backed by the constitution. Any amendment to the law must then require a constitutional amendment.[102]

Ireland's oil and gas regime must also be redesigned from the Constitution on up.

## THE DEMOCRATIC PROGRAMME (1919): SOVEREIGNTY AND RESOURCES

Natural resources have always been central to the constitutional history of Ireland, particularly in relation to the Revolution and the achievement of independence from Great Britain and the Commonwealth. Much of the PTD legal history is wrapped up in the legalities of post-colonialism. For Irish, American and other revolutionaries against the Crown, ownership and control over natural resources was a defining aspect of independence, and republicanism.

Since the foundation of the Irish State, natural resources have been officially recognised as a central part of the national sovereignty of the people of Ireland. The 'Democratic Programme', issued at the inaugural meeting of the first (All-Ireland) Dáil Éireann, 21 January 1919, opened with the following statement:

> We declare in the words of the Irish Republican Proclamation the right of the people of Ireland to the ownership of Ireland, and to the unfettered control of Irish destinies to be indefeasible, and in the language of our first President, Pádraig Mac Piarais, we declare that the nation's sovereignty extends not only to all men and women of the nation, but to all its material possessions, the Nation's soil and all its resources, all the wealth and all the wealth-producing processes within the Nation, and with him we reaffirm that *all right to private property must be subordinated to the public right and welfare.*[103]

This document clearly describes natural resources in terms of a state policy of resource nationalism, as well as a constitutional equation that links sovereignty and natural resources, providing a basis for the PTD, with ownership squarely vested in the people.

The Democratic Programme was recanted by Sinn Féin, in Dáil debate on their private members' motion on energy resources, 19 April 2011.[104] During debate, Minister Rabbitte responded:

> I do not have to remind the Deputies in whose names the Private Members' motion was submitted that the 1919 democratic programme also provided that, '*It shall be our duty to promote the development of the Nation's resources, in the interests and for the benefit of the Irish people.*'[105]

The minister, while seeking to rebut Sinn Féin, actually admitted that the State is subject to the PTD, and is under an affirmative duty to develop those resources 'in the interests and for the benefit of the people', which is the language of a trusteeship. The PTD was also present in the programme for government and in statements by ministers, seeking to take action on natural resources, 'on behalf of the people'.

Since the government repeatedly touts the idea in official statements, it should not object to it being clearly expressed in the current Constitution, especially since it was present in Ireland's first Constitution, the Constitution of the Irish Free State, which was directly influenced by the Democratic Programme, as can be seen from the drafting history.

## CONSTITUTION OF THE IRISH FREE STATE (1922): OWNERSHIP OF NATURAL RESOURCES

The ideals expressed in the Democratic Programme featured strongly in the drafting and adoption of the 1922 Constitution of the Irish Free State, which was the pivotal, founding document of the modern state of Ireland, in the wake of the Revolution. The Constitution dealt with natural resources in Article 11, which stated:

> All the lands and waters, mines and minerals, within the territory of the Irish Free State (Saorstát Eireann) hitherto vested in the State, or any department thereof, or held for the public use or benefit, and also all the natural resources of the same territory (including the air and all forms of potential energy), and also all royalties and franchises within that territory shall, from and after the date of the coming into operation of this Constitution, belong to the Irish Free State (Saorstát Eireann), subject to any trusts, grants, leases or concessions then existing in respect thereof, or any valid private interest therein, and shall be controlled and administered by the Oireachtas, in accordance with such regulations and provisions as shall be from time to time approved by legislation, but the same shall not, nor shall any part thereof, be alienated, but may in the public interest be from time to time granted by way of lease or licence to be worked or enjoyed under the authority and subject to the control of the Oireachtas: Provided that no such lease or licence may be made for a term exceeding ninety-nine years, beginning from the date thereof, and no such lease or licence may be renewable by the terms thereof.

While 'ownership' of natural resources vested with the State, the powers and duties to control and administer them rested with the Oireachtas. However, this 'ownership' by the State was severely limited, and 'subject to any trusts, grants, leases or concessions'. Critically, the Oireachtas was not granted the power to 'alienate' or sell them outright, and could only license or lease them for a limited time. Even those powers were constitutionally limited and could only be exercised in furtherance of 'the public interest'. A similar limitation is present in the Article 45(2)(i) of the 1937 Constitution, on Directive Principles of Social Policy, which states 'That the ownership and control of the material resources of the community may be so distributed amongst private individuals and the various classes as best to subserve the common good.' However, that entire article is, by its own terms, nonjusticiable and 'shall not be cognisable by any Court'.[106]

The most telling aspect of Article 11 of the Constitution of the Irish Free State is that it is contained in the first section of the Constitution, entitled 'Fundamental Rights', alongside the rights to liberty, education and citizenship, and freedom of expression, assembly and religion. However, *natural resources were moved from the 'fundamental rights' section in the 1922 Constitution to the section entitled 'The State' in the 1937 Constitution, thereby diminishing the public's rights, and increasing State powers over them.* Article 11 forbade the State from alienating or selling the people's natural resources. This makes sense, since people's rights to them are fundamental and inalienable. Therefore, there is a good argument to say that the 1937 Constitution cannot have abrogated the people's rights to their resources, since such rights were already recognised by the State as being inalienable.

## First Draft: 'Dáil Éireann shall regulate and control the same as trustees of the people of Ireland'

The Constitutional Committee was appointed by Dáil Éireann in January 1922, and nominally chaired by Michael Collins. It included: Arthur Griffith; Darrell Figgis; Hugh Kennedy, KC; James McNeill; C. J. France; James Douglas; James Murnaghan; and John O'Byrne.[107] A first draft of the Constitution agreed by the Committee was produced in mid-February 1922 and dealt with natural resources in Articles 81-84. Article 81 stated:

1. The sovereignty of the people extends over the natural resources of Saorstát Éireann.

2. None of these resources may be so used as to impair the welfare of the citizens of Saorstát Eireann, or to prejudice the provisions of this Constitution.

This reiterated the link between the sovereignty of the people over natural resources, found in the Democratic Programme. Article 82 stated, in part:

1. All right, title and interest heretofore vested in the Sovereign of Great Britain, to all or any of the lands, waters and natural resources of Ireland, *vested in the people of Ireland,* and

2. *Dáil Éireann shall regulate and control the same as trustees of the people of Ireland.*[108]

This was a clear and emphatic statement of the PTD. While nominal ownership was later changed to rest with the State and this specific trusteeship language was taken out of the final drafts, the principle itself is still clearly present in all versions, including the final, official version.

Article 83 went on to elaborate on mineral rights, and to limit the compulsory purchase powers of the State of private property:

1. All wealth below the surface of the soil which has hitherto been undeveloped or which is not the subject of a mineral or development lease agreement for purchase, is vested in the people of Ireland.

Committee members Kennedy, Douglas and France placed 'special emphasis' on natural resources in their final draft. They stated in a letter to Michael Collins:

> The four Sections [sic] taken together prevent the alienation of any of these resources in perpetuity or a leasing beyond 99 years, and in addition confer control over all water power in Ireland. We regard these four sections as among the most important in the Constitution. It has been demonstrated in other countries, notably in America, that when private individuals acquire for individual exploitation these great Natural Resources, they get a stranglehold on the Country. The result has been in America that notwithstanding a Republican and Democratic Government, an economic autocracy has developed which controls the Government of the Country and the personal liberties of the people almost as effectively as was ever done by an absolute monarchy.[109]

In summary, the first working draft of the Free State Constitution, agreed by the Constitution Committee, was clearly founded on the PTD, and a policy of resource nationalism. These articles, and the principles therein, were later altered by the Committee and Provisional Government, in reaching Article 11 of the Free State Constitution. But even Article 11 can be said to contain the PTD, as it is clear that the state did not have complete ownership of natural resources, could not alienate them, and had to act in the public interest with regards to their development.

## NATURAL RESOURCES IN THE 1937 CONSTITUTION: ARTICLE 10

Bunreacht na hÉireann, the 1937 Constitution of Ireland placed ownership and control of all natural resources in the hands of the State, with very few checks and balances, in favour of the people or the Nation. For instance, Article 10.1 states:

All natural resources, including the air and all forms of potential energy, within the jurisdiction of the Parliament and Government established by this Constitution and all royalties and franchises within that jurisdiction belong to the State, subject to all estates and interests therein for the time being lawfully vested in any person or body.[110]

Article 10.2 also states that all land and all mines, minerals and waters belong to the State.[111] During the secretive drafting of the 1937 Constitution, when Article 10 was being considered, opinions were sought by de Valera from a small number of sources. He formed the Constitution Committee of 1934, consisting of a small body of civil servants along with figures from within the Catholic Church.[112]

Some of these participants vigorously lobbied de Valera on the constitutional provisions relating to natural resources. Submissions of draft articles by the Irish province of the Jesuits were initially made through Fr Edward Cahill, who on 4 September 1936 sent a draft of a proposed amendment to the Committee:

> Since the natural resources of the country such as the land, mineral wealth, the fisheries, the waterways, etc, are the ultimate source from which the citizens of the State have to be maintained, it is a duty of the Government to prevent their being unjustly or unduly held up by private individuals or syndicates; and so to adjust property rights in regard to them as to secure that they be developed and utilised for the public good.[113]

The Jesuits linked the ownership of natural resources with private property in a separate draft Article V, section (c) of which stated:

> The State shall prevent by suitable laws the natural resources of the country, such as land, mines, fisheries, waterways, etc from being unduly held up by private individuals or syndicates, and shall so adjust property rights as to secure that these are duly developed and utilised in the interests of the common good.[114]

The parliamentary draftsman at the time, Mr Arthur Matheson, BL,[115] submitted a memorandum to de Valera, which stated, in part:

> The Theory underlying the old Article 11 [of the 1922 Free State Constitution] and the new Article 10 is that all natural resources should belong to the State and should be exploited for the benefit of the people and not for the private profit of individuals.[116]

None of the substance of the recommendations regarding public ownership of natural resources made it into the final draft of Article 10 or what would become Article 43 on private property. This must finally be changed.

## Adoption of the PTD by Irish Courts: Possible Grounds

Should the government fail to propose the PTD in a constitutional amendment, it is still possible for the courts to constitutionally implement PTD, if it is argued as grounds for a legal action against the State by a citizen, or group of citizens.

Certain government decisions or actions, such as changes to the petroleum regime, the issuance of a licence, or the rewarding of a contract, are normally subject to judicial review, which empowers the courts to nullify the State decision or action.

*Murdoch's Dictionary of Irish Law* defines a trust as 'An equitable obligation binding a person (or body) to deal with property over which he has control, for the benefit of persons (beneficiaries) ... and any one of whom may enforce the obligation.'[117] The duty of the trustee, called the 'fiduciary duty', is also defined in *Murdoch's Dictionary*:

> A person who has been entrusted with powers for the benefit of others but who in the exercise of those powers is not subject to the direct and immediate control of those others, e.g. company directors, trustees, liquidators, executors and court-appointed receivers. The general rule is that a person in a fiduciary is not entitled to make a profit and he is not allowed to put himself in a position where his interest and duty conflict.[118]

There are numerous different grounds that are sufficient for the Irish courts to find that there is in fact an 'implied public trust' in the Constitution, as it stands. This could be supported by Irish case law and English common law, as well as decisions from other English common law jurisdictions, such as the US, Canada, India and Australia.

## Historical Grounds for the PTD in Ireland: The Fisheries Cases

While the Irish courts have yet to decide on whether the PTD is implied in the Constitution of Ireland, there are a number of cases that bear a remarkable similarity to cases in other PTD jurisdictions, which assert the PTD. In particular, there is a series of cases, called 'The Fisheries Cases', which recognised public rights, similar to those under the PTD.

Indeed, one of these early Irish fisheries cases is quoted in the landmark New Jersey Supreme Court case of *Arnold v. Mundy* (1821),[119] which recognised the PTD in oyster beds along the New Jersey shoreline. Chief Justice of the New Jersey Supreme Court Andrew Kirkpatrick cited a leading sixteenth-century Irish case entitled 'The Case of the Royal Fishery of the Banne'[120] in support of his arguments on 'common property':

> Of this latter kind (of property), according to the writers upon the law of nature and of nations, and upon the civil law, are the air, the running water, the sea, the fish, and

the wild beasts. Vattel lib. i, 20. 2 Black. Com. 14. But inasmuch as the things which constitute this common property are things in which a sort of transient usufructuary possession, only, can be had; and inasmuch as the title to them and to the soil by which they are supported, and to which they are appurtenant, cannot well, according to the common law notion of title, be vested in all the people; therefore, the wisdom of that law has placed it in the hands of the sovereign power, to be held, protected, and regulated for the common use and benefit. But still, though this title, strictly speaking, is in the sovereign, yet the use is common to all the people. *This principle, with respect to rivers and arms of the sea, is clearly maintained in the case of the royal fishery upon the Banne, in Ireland, in Sir John Davies' report of that case* . . .[121]

The case of the Royal Fishery of the Banne was also precedent for landmark Irish case of *(R) Moore v. Attorney General* (1934),[122] known as 'The Erne Fisheries Case'. That majority decision was written, in part, by Chief Justice Hugh Kennedy, who had been a leading member of the Constitution Committee that drafted the Constitution of the Irish Free State. However, the Irish case did not view the public fishing rights in terms of a public trust, as the defendant fishermen, who focused instead on the chain of title, did not raise trust arguments.

In Ireland, in the *Moore* case some local fishermen intentionally trespassed on private fishing ground owned by a private estate. The estate owners brought an action claiming a declaration that they were entitled to a several fishery for salmon and all other fish in the entire tidal portion of the River Erne, in the County of Donegal: The defendants relied on Chap. 16 of Magna Charta as requiring that a several fishery in tidal waters must have been put 'in defence' prior to the death of Henry II, and they contend that such a fishery did not exist and was not historically possible in the *locus in quo*; they also denied the conclusive effect claimed by the plaintiffs for the Landed Estates Court conveyance; and they also denied that the statutes of Charles I validated the plaintiffs' title.[123]

The Supreme Court agreed and it was held by this court that:

neither of the statutes relied on by the plaintiffs, 10 Car. I, sess, 3, c. 3, or 15 Car. I, c. 6, gave to the Letters Patent of 1639 (granted by Charles I to one of the plaintiffs' predecessors in title) any statutory authority to override the provisions of Magna Charta in respect of the fishery, and that grant did not, therefore, bind the public.[124]

It can be argued that since the arguments, precedents and outcomes of the US *Martin* case and the Irish *Moore* case are almost identical, then the PTD was in fact recognised in Ireland by *Moore*, just as it was in the US by *Martin*.

## Constitutional Restraints on the State: Article 10

There are restraints on State power, in relation to natural resources, that are explicit in the Constitution. Article 10.1, above, states that the State's ownership is 'subject to all estates and interests therein for the time being lawfully vested in any person or body'. Therefore, the State's ownership cannot be assumed to be absolute. These estates or interests could include public trust rights.

While Article 10 does not explicitly impose an active duty on the State to always act in the best interests of the people with regards to natural resources, that duty is explicit in Article 45. While reference to the common good in Article 45 is nonjusticiable, the common good has been used by the courts in a number of cases relating to natural heritage, public property and state assets. The preamble of the 1937 Constitution proclaims that one of its principal aims is to seek 'the common good'. The preamble too has been deemed largely nonjusticable.

However, Article 6 forms the constitutional footing of the State, with Article 6.1 stating:

> All powers of government, legislative, executive and judicial, derive, under God, from the people, whose right it is to designate the rulers of the State and, in final appeal, to decide all questions of national policy, according to the requirements of the common good.[125]

Natural resources are essentially part of, or a manifestation of, the common good, and as such, the State is under a constitutional duty to protect it. A similar argument was adopted in the Supreme Court judgment of O'Higgins CJ in the 1985 Supreme Court case of *O'Callaghan v. Commissioners of Public Works*:

> It cannot be doubted that the common good requires that national monuments which are prized relics of the past should be preserved as part of the history of our people.[126]

The duty on the State to preserve the national heritage, for purposes of the common good, can serve as a precedent for imposing a similar duty on the State with regards to the natural heritage.

## The State's Duty of Care: 'Constitutional Imperative'

While courts do not often find constitutional rights that have been hitherto unenumerated in the Constitution, they do, on occasion, find unenumerated constitutional duties on the State. This occurred with regards to heritage, in the Carrickmines Castle case in the 2005 high court case *Dunne v. Minister for the Environment*.[127] While the Constitution is largely silent on the constitutional duties of the State, the courts have recognised that it has a constitutional duty to protect certain national assets, corresponding to its constitutional powers to 'own' them.

*Dunne* entailed a constitutional challenge to Section 8 of the National Monuments (Amendment) Act 2004, which gave the State the power to demolish the national monument at Carrickmines Castle.[128] Judge Laffoy relied on *O'Callaghan*, in part, to support the claim that the State is under a constitutional duty to protect Ireland's heritage, based on the State's claim of ownership over it. She said:

> The principal source of the constitutionally protected right for which he contends suggested by the Plaintiff is the decision of the Supreme Court in *Webb v. Ireland* [1988] IR 353, in which the State's entitlement to possession and ownership of the Derrynaflan Hoard was at issue. Expressing the majority view of the Court, Finlay CJ stated as follows (at p 383):
>
>> It would, I think, now be universally accepted, certainly by the People of Ireland, and by the people of most modern states, that one of the most important national assets belonging to the people is their heritage and knowledge of its true origins and the buildings and objects which constitute keys to their ancient history. If this be so, then it would appear to me to follow that a necessary ingredient of sovereignty in a modern state and certainly in this State, having regard to the terms of the Constitution, with an emphasis on its historical origins and a constant concern for the common good, should be an ownership by the State of objects which constitute antiquities of importance which are discovered and which have no known owner. It would appear to me to be inconsistent with the framework of the society sought to be created and sought to be protected by the Constitution that such objects should become the exclusive property of those who by chance may find them.[129]

Judge Laffoy noted that the State has invoked its constitutional ownership on many occasions. She noted:

> Finlay CJ invoked both Article 5 and Art 10, which provides that, inter alia, 'all royalties' within the jurisdiction belong to the State, when construed in the light of Art 5, to support his conclusion that there exists in the State a right or prerogative of treasure trove having the characteristics of treasure trove as known at common law.[130]

But with rights, often come corresponding duties. Judge Laffoy found foundation for the duty in the concurring opinion of Walsh J. in *Webb*:

I am satisfied that the People as the sovereign authority having by the Constitution created the State, and by Article 5 declared it to be a sovereign state, *have the right and duty*, acting by the State which is the juristic person capable of holding property by virtue of the Constitution, to exercise dominion over all objects forming part of the national heritage.[131]

Judge Laffoy then recognised, for the first time in Irish legal history, that there is an unenumerated, but clear, constitutional duty on the State to protect the national heritage:

It is beyond doubt that it is a *constitutional imperative* that the State safeguard the national assets, including monuments of cultural and historical significance.[132]

Such a constitutional imperative could also be said to lie with the State with regard to safeguarding the national assets, including natural resources, under the existing Constitution.

## ARTICLE 45: DIRECTIVE PRINCIPLES OF SOCIAL POLICY

Article 45 of the Irish Constitution basically expresses the PTD, saying natural resources belong to the people, and must be developed so that:

the ownership and control of the material resources of the community may be so distributed amongst private individuals and the various classes as best to subserve the common good.[133]

Like the PTD, Article 45 does not place a complete bar on privatisation or alienation of natural resources, but does place a clear requirement that there must be a general, social benefit to the people, in order to justify the transfer of assets. However, this is unenforceable, as Article 45 is nonjusticiable, by its own terms, and 'shall not be cognisable by any Court under any of the provisions of this Constitution'.[134]

However, this is not impossible to overcome, as is shown by the Supreme Court of India, which adopted the PTD. It has been well documented that the Directive Principles on Social Policy in the Irish Constitution were 'the inspiration for Part IV18 of the Indian Constitution', which was drafted in 1950.[135]

According to Takacs:

Article 21 of India's constitution declares: 'No person shall be deprived of his life or personal liberty except according to procedure established by law.' Laws that conflict with or abridge fundamental rights named in the constitution are voided. Citizens are allowed to challenge violations of these rights directly, and in fact citizen suits are the most rapid means to challenge actions that threaten fundamental rights. In India, Judges have taken these substantive and procedural rights seriously and have buttressed them by establishing the PTD to secure powerful protections for citizens' Environmental Human Rights.[136]

This is consistent with the UN Declaration on Permanent Sovereignty, and other human rights instruments mentioned above, which protect people's rights to their natural resources.

## VOIDING OIL AND GAS CONTRACTS: POSSIBLE COURT INTERVENTION

In the 2010 Supreme Court case of *Reliance Natural Resources Ltd v. Reliance Industries Ltd*[137] the Supreme Court intervened in private oil and gas contracts, for violations of the PTD. The Court rescinded a natural gas pricing agreement and required the contracting parties to renegotiate the contract, with governmental participation, to ensure equitable revenue sharing. In doing so, the Court stated:

> It must be noted that the constitutional mandate is that the natural resources belong to the people of this country. The nature of the word 'vest' must be seen in the context of the public trust doctrine. Even though this doctrine has been applied in cases dealing with environmental jurisprudence, it has its broader application.[138]

Application of the PTD to oil and gas agreements, not just between public and private parties, but between two private parties, represents an even wider scope for the doctrine than has been found elsewhere.

In summary, there are many possible grounds for a high court case alleging the PTD in Ireland, including human rights. One question that is sure to arise in any such case is whether the PTD would violate, not just the Constitution of Ireland, but the EU Constitution or other EU or international law. It is clear that it would not, and in fact it would advance EU, international and human rights law.

## CONCLUSION

This chapter has attempted to show that since the birth of the State we have seen a complete devolution or reversal in ideology – a retreat from revolution. The ideals of the drafters of the first Constitution of the State, our equivalent of the American 'founding fathers', which saw the State as the 'trustee' of the people's resources, ceased to have any clear basis in policy or law. With all of the nation's resources – such as wind, water, sea, fisheries, forest, oil and gas – being routinely alienated, a strong citizens' campaign must demand true resource nationalism, and a fair deal that benefits the true beneficiaries: the people, as opposed to the self-interested political parties that have commandeered the State. Natural resources were seen as part and parcel of the sovereignty of the people. Unfairly taking away the people's resources is an unconstitutional attack on their sovereignty, and a breach of human rights. So extreme has been the loss of public rights in natural resources that it can be safely said that the Irish had much better rights over them under British rule than they do today, due to the English common law recognition that the king's sovereign ownership over certain resources was subject to a public trust or interest.

Government ministers keep talking about the 'fitness for purpose' of the fiscal regime. Fitness for what purpose? For whose purpose? The purpose of the petroleum should be to ensure a fair benefit to the people and the nation first, and the State second.

When launching his 2013 review of the oil and gas regime, Minister Rabbitte said: 'I do not wish to be negative or to undersell Ireland as a location for exploration investment, quite the contrary, but one must deal in realities.'[139] The reality is that the Ministers are indeed 'underselling Ireland', to the point of giving it away. At current terms, these non-renewable resources would be better left alone, where they would remain an appreciating asset for present and future generations.

Minister O'Dowd, while announcing to the Oil and Gas Summit that the government was seeking independent expert advice on the fiscal regime, said, 'Ireland continues to remain an open and attractive location for oil and gas exploration.'[140] If Ireland adopts a regime like Norway's and Uganda's, incorporating resource nationalism and the PTD, it will still remain open and attractive, because two things are certain: we have proven resources, and there is an ever-increasing demand for them.

The government must either change its policy or offer the people a chance to vote on a referendum that will clearly constitutionalise the PTD. *Failing that, there is no option but for the public to go to court, on some of the grounds offered here.* For it is worth recalling the defining words of the Chief Justice of the New Jersey Supreme Court, Andrew Kirkpatrick, in 1821, when he recognised the PTD in New Jersey:

> The sovereign power itself, therefore, cannot, consistently with the principles of the law of nature and the constitution of a well-ordered society, make a direct and absolute grant of the waters of the state, divesting all the citizens of their common right. It would be a grievance which never could be long borne by a free people.[141]

## ABOUT THE AUTHOR

Vincent Salafia, BA, JD, LLM (TCD) has a good deal of experience in running large, public campaigns, as well as a strong professional background in environmental law. He is a member of the Irish Association of Law Teachers (IALT) and was a lecturer in Planning & Risk Management and Environmental Legislation at the Management School of Queen's University Belfast for four years. He is currently working on a PhD at Trinity College Dublin Law School in sustainable development issues.

Vincent handled media and legal affairs for the Carrickmines group that won two Supreme Court injunctions against the M50 in 2002-3. He was a founder of TaraWatch, which campaigned against the M3 motorway at the Hill of Tara. He also took a High Court action against the Minister for the Environment over the M3 and the Hill of Tara, and settled his Supreme Court action. In addition to lecturing, Vincent is a legal consultant.

## NOTES

1. Joint Committee on Communications, Natural Resources and Agriculture, *Report on Offshore Oil and Gas Exploration* (CNRA 010, May 2012)

2. Labour Party. 'Rabbitte announces review of fiscal terms for oil and gas production' (Press Release, 14 June 2013). Accessed 13 September 2013

3. *Ibid.*

4. Department of Communications, Energy and Natural Resources, 'Tenders sought for expert advice on oil and gas exploration tax terms' (Press Release, 24 September 2013). Accessed 28 December 2013

5. *Ibid.* (emphasis added)

6. Helena Ward, 'Resource nationalism and sustainable development' (2009) IIED 5/2009, 5. Accessed 20 September 2013. pubs.iied.org/G02507.html

7. Ernst and Young, 'Business risks facing mining and metals 2012-2013' Accessed 23 September 2013

8. Helena Ward, 'Resource nationalism and sustainable development' (2009) IIED 5/2009, 5. Accessed 20 September 2013. pubs.iied.org/G02507.html

9. Maplecroft, 'Two thirds of OPEC members among countries posing the most risk' (2012). Accessed 13 September 2013. maplecroft.com/about/news/resource_nationalism_index_2012.html

10. John Skoulding, 'Capital Gains Tax – The New Resource Nationalism?' Accessed 11 September 2013

11. Maplecroft, 'Two thirds of OPEC members'

12. *Ibid.*

13. Ellimah, Richard. 'A Case for Resource Nationalism in Ghana!' (GhanaWeb, 18 October 2012). Accessed 11 September 2013

14. Maplecroft, 'Two thirds of OPEC members'

15. Ernst & Young, 'Exploring dual perspectives on the top 10 risks and opportunities in 2013 and beyond' (2008) 21. Accessed 20 September 2012

16. Ryan, Eamon. 'New regime is in greatest public good' (DCENR, Press Release, 1 Aug 2007). Accessed 21 December 2013

17. *Ibid.*

18. Services Industrial Professional and Technical Union, 'Optimising Ireland's Oil and Gas Resources' (SIPTU Oil and Gas Review Group, 2007) 12. Accessed 22 September 2013

19. SIPTU

20. *Ibid.* at 10

21. *Ibid.* at 11

22. Vulliamy, Ed. 'Shell's battle for the heart of Ireland,' *The Observer* (London, 29 May 2011). Accessed 23 September 2011

23. Department of Public Expenditure and Reform, 'Statement of Common Purpose' (25 February 2011. Accessed 12 September 2013. per.gov.ie/wp-content/uploads/ProgrammeforGovernmentFinal.pdf

24. *Ibid.*

25. Joint Committee on Communications, Natural Resources and Agriculture, 'Natural Resources Committee calls for new fiscal licencing regime in Offshore Oil and Gas exploration' (Press Release, 9 May 2012). Accessed 13 September 2013

26. Seanad Deb., 27 June 2012, Vol. 216, Col. 5

27. *Ibid.*

28. *Ibid.* (emphasis added)

29. 'Ireland on the verge of an oil and gas bonanza' *The Irish Independent* (Dublin, 20 May 2007)

30. SIPTU at 9

31. Muhwezi at al, 'Crafting an Oil Revenue-sharing Mechanism for Uganda' (ACODE Policy Research Series No. 30, 2009) 20. Accessed 13 September 2013.

32. US Embassy, 'Resource Nationalism and Norway' (Oslo, 29 November 2007). Accessed 22 September 2013. wikileaks.org/cable/2007/11/07OSLO1134.html

33. *Ibid.*

34. *Ibid.*

35. *Ibid.*

36. *Ibid.* (emphasis added)

37. *Ibid.*

38. *Ibid.*

39. *Ibid.*

40. O'Dowd, Fergus. 'A Promising Future for Irish Oil and Gas Exploration' (Ireland Oil and Gas 2013 Summit, Dublin, 10 September 2013). Accessed 12 September 2013

41. Mundi, Alex. 'Uganda Demographics Profile 2013.' Accessed 22 September 2013

42. 'Uganda: Oil, Gas Discoveries Boost FDIS to Dar, Kampala' *Tanzania Daily News* (Dar es Salaam, 16 July 2013). Accessed 22 September 2013. allafrica.com/stories/2013 07160073.html

43. Muhwezi, et al. 'Crafting an Oil Revenue-sharing Mechanism,' vii

44. *Ibid.*

45. *Advocates Coalition for Development and Environment (ACODE) v. Attorney General Misc. Cause No. 0100* (Uganda 2004). Accessed 22 September 2013

46. Muhwezi, et al. 'Crafting an Oil Revenue-sharing Mechanism,' vii

47. *Advocates Coalition for Development and Environment (ACODE) v. Attorney General*

48. Muhwezi, et al. 'Crafting an Oil Revenue-sharing Mechanism,' 36

49. *Ibid.*

50. *Ibid.*

51. Muhwezi, et al. 'Crafting an Oil Revenue-sharing Mechanism,' x

52. Blumm, Michael C. and Rachel D. Guthrie. 'Internationalizing the PTD: Natural Law

and Constitutional and Statutory Approaches to Fulfilling the Saxion Vision' (20 April 2011) *University of California–Davis Law Review*, Vol. 44, 2012, 750

53.  *Ibid.*

54.  Justinian, 'Institutes,' 2.1.1-2.1.6. Accessed 22 September 2013

55.  Sax, Joseph L. 'Liberating the PTD from Its Historical Shackles' 14 *University of California–Davis Law Review* 185. Accessed 22 September 2013

56.  Justinian, 'Institutes,' 2.1.1

57.  Sax, Joseph L. Sax, 'The Public Trust in Tidal Areas: A Sometimes Submerged Traditional Doctrine, *The Yale Law Journal* Vol. 79, No. 4 (March 1970), pp 762, 765-68

58.  Sax, Joseph L. 'The Public Trust in Tidal Areas,' pp 762-789

59.  Salkin, Patricia E. 'The Use of the PTD as a Management Tool over Public and Private Lands,' 4 Alb. L.J. Sci. & Tech. 7 1994, at 1

60.  *Robert Arnold v. Benajah Mundy* 6 N.J.L. 1 (Supreme Court of New Jersey, 2 November 1821). Accessed 22 September 2013. fas-history.rutgers.edu/clemens/NJLaw/arnold1821.html

61.  *Ibid.*

62.  *Ibid.* at 62, citing 'Magna Charta, with Lord Coke's commentary upon it'

63.  Bracton, Henry. *On the Laws and Customs of England,* 39-40 (S. Thorne trans. 1968) (citing J. INST. 2.1.1-2.1.5)

64.  *Martin v. Waddell* 41 U.S. 367 (1842)

65.  *Ibid.*

66.  *Illinois Central R. Co. v. Illinois*, 146 U.S. 387 (1892)

67.  *Ibid.*

68.  *Mallon v. City of Long Beach*, 44 Cal. 2d 199, 282 P.2d 481 (1955). Accessed 22 September 2013. scocal.stanford.edu/opinion/mallon-v-city-long-beach-26631

69.  Sax, Joseph L. 'The PTD in Natural Resource Law: Effective Judicial Intervention,' 68 MICH. L. Rev. 471, 475 (1970)

70.  Salkin, Patricia E. 'The Use of the PTD as a. Management Tool'

71.  See, for example, Eichenberg, Tim, Sean Bothwell, and Darcy Vaughn, 'Climate

Change and the PTD: Using an Ancient Doctrine to Adapt to Rising Sea Levels in San Francisco Bay,' 3 Golden Gate U. Envtl. L.J. (2001). Accessed 23 September 2013. digitalcommons.law.ggu.edu/gguelj/vol3/iss2/2

72. See, for example, Klass, Alexandra B., 'Renewable Energy and the PTD' (March 17, 2011). 45 U.C. Davis L. Rev. 1021 (2012); Minnesota Legal Studies Research Paper No. 11-12. Accessed 23 September 2013. ssrn.com/abstract=1789027

73. 108 S. Ct. 791 (1988)

74. Golem, Donna A. 'The PTD Unprecedentedly Gains New Ground in *Phillips Petroleum Co. v. Mississippi*' 22 Loy. L.A. L. Rev. 1319 (1989), 1320

75. *Nat'l Audubon Soc'y v. Superior Court* (Mono Lake), 33 Cal. 3d 419 (1983)

76. *Ibid.* (emphasis added)

77. *Shokal v. Dunn*, 707 P. 2d 441 (1985)

78. *Ibid.*

79. 'Permanent Sovereignty over Natural Resources,' GA. Res. 1803 (XVII), 17 U.N. GAOR Supp. (No. 17) at 15, U.N. Doc. A/5217 (1962)

80. *Anglo-Iranian Oil Co., UK v. Iran*, 1952 I.C.J. 93

81. 'Permanent Sovereignty over Natural Resources'

82. *Ibid.* (emphasis added)

83. Universal Declaration of Human Rights (adopted 10 December 1948 UNGA Res 217 A(III)

84. International Covenant on Civil and Political Rights (adopted 16 December 1966, entered into force 23 March 1976) 999 UNTS 171

85. International Covenant on Economic, Social and Cultural Rights (adopted 16 December 1966, entered into force 3 January 1976) 993 UNTS 3.

86. See n. 92

87. See n. 93

88. See n. 92

89. See n. 93

90. UN Doc. A/Conf.48/14/Rev. 1(1973); 11 ILM 1416 (1972)

91. Art. 21.2 TEU

92. Art. 3.3 TEU

93. Convention on Access to Information, Public Decision-making and Access to Justice in Environmental Matters, June 25, 1998, 2161 UNTS 447, 38 ILM 517 (1999)

94. Council Directive (EC) 2011/92 on the assessment of the effects of certain public and private projects on the environment [2012] OJ L26/1 (EIA Directive)

95. Council Directive (EC) 2001/42 on the assessment of the effects of certain plans and programmes on the environment [2001] OJ L197/30 (SEA Directive)

96. Article 10.1 (on natural resources)

97. Hale, William. 'De Portibus Maris,' in 'Hall's essay on the rights of the Crown and the privileges of the subject in the sea shores of the realm' (1875). Accessed 1 December 2013. archive.org/details/hallsessayonrigh00halluoft

98. Hale, 'De Jure Maris,' in *A Collection of Tracts Relative the Law of England* 84, 89 (F. Hargrave 1st ed. 1787)

99. *Ibid.*

100. Open Oil, 'Understanding Oil Contracts' (2012) 23. Accessed 22 September 2013. openoil.net/understanding-oil-contracts

101. *Ibid.* (emphasis added)

102. Muhwezi, et al. 'Crafting an Oil Revenue-sharing Mechanism'

103. Dáil Deb. 21 January 1919 Vol. 1 (emphasis added)

104. Dáil Deb 19 April 2011, Vol. 730, Col. 22 (emphasis added)

105. *Ibid.*

106. Constitution of Ireland, 1937, Article 45 on Directive Principles on Social Policy

107. Farrell, Brian. 'The Drafting of the Constitution of the Irish Free State: I,' *The Irish Jurist* 1970, 1, 115-140 at 116

108. *Ibid.*

109. Farrell, Brian. 'The Drafting of the Free State Constitution: IV' 2 *The Irish Jurist* (1971) 345, 345

110. Article 10.1 (on natural resources)

111. Articles 10.2, 10.4

112. Keogh, Dermot. 'The Catholic Church and the writing of the 1937 constitution,' *History Ireland* Issue 3 Volume 13 (May/June 2005). Accessed 22 September 2013

113. Cahill, Fr Edward. 'Suggestions for drafting a new Constitution' (Lisdoonvarna, 4 Sept 1936) Memorandum, Section XVII. No. 49: UCDA, P150/2393 in Gerard Hogan, *The Origins of the Irish Constitution, 1928-1941* (Dublin: Royal Irish Academy, 2012) 238

114. Jesuit Constitution Committee, 'Suggestions for a Catholic Constitution', (Dublin, 18 October 1936) in Hogan (2012) 249-250, citing 90 – Pius, *Quadragesimo Anno*, (CSG, 18-20; CTS, On the Social Order, 19-20); CSP, nn 77-8. No. 58: UCDA, P150/2393

115. Keogh, Dermot. 'The Catholic Church'

116. Matheson, Arthur. 'Memorandum from Arthur Matheson to Eamon de Valera' (Parliamentary Draftsman's Office, 1 March 1937) No. 80: UCDA. P150/2397 in Hogan (2013) 313

117. Hunt, Brian and Henry Murdoch. *Murdoch's Dictionary of Irish Law*, 5th Ed (Bloomsbury 2009)

118. *Ibid.*

119. 6 NJL 1; 1821 NJ

120. The Case of the Royal Fishery of Banne, Davis 56, 80 Eng. Rep. 540 (KB 1611)

121. *Ibid.* at 147-148

122. *Robert Lyon Moore and Others v. The Attorney-General for Saorstát Éireann, William Goan and Others* (1934) I. R. 44

123. *Ibid.*

124. *Ibid.*

125. Article 6.1 (on the State)

126. *O'Callaghan v Commissioners of Public Works* (1985) *ILRM* 364, at 367-368

127. *Dunne v. Minister for Environment Heritage & Local Government* (2005) IEHC 79

128. *Ibid.*

129. *Ibid.*

130. *Ibid.*

131. *Ibid.*, quoting Walsh at 393 (emphasis added)

132. *Ibid.* (emphasis added)

133. Article 45 (on directive principles of social policy)

134. *Ibid.*

135. Lawlor, Ciaran. 'The Conscience of the nation: socio-economic rights in the Constitution,' 5 U. C. Dublin L. Rev. 34 2005, at 38. See also Keane, David, 'The Irish Influence on the Indian Constitution: 60 Years On,' 26 September 2010. Accessed 25 November 2013. humanrights.ie/constitution-of-ireland/the-irish-influence-on-the-indian-constitution-60-years-on

136. Takacs, David. 'The PTD, Environmental Human Rights, and the Future of Private Property,' 16 *New York University Law Journal* 711 (2008) citing Indian Const. Art 21, Art. 13(2)

137. *Reliance Natural Resources Ltd v. Reliance Industries Ltd.* (2010) INSC 374 (7 May 2010) at 199-209. Accessed 22 September 2013. indiankanoon.org/doc/1070490

138. *Ibid.*

139. Seanad Deb. 27 June 2012, Vol. 216, Col 5

140. O'Dowd, Fergus. 'A Promising Future for Irish Oil and Gas'

141. 6 NJL 1 at 25

# 8.

## A HISTORY OF IRISH SERVITUDE

### Bill McSweeney

Our version of history has tended to make us think of freedom as an end in itself and of independent government – like marriage in a fairy story – as the solution of all ills.

—Bishop of Clonfert (1957)[1]

The apparently ambivalent attitude of the Irish establishment towards our offshore territory and its natural resources is perhaps best first understood by examining our history, particularly how it has been intertwined with our natural resources, from land to sea. The question of the State's role in providing for, and indeed creating, infrastructural and employment opportunities for the nation, and more precisely, how responsibly it administers its constitutional obligation to, and its jurisdiction over, the resources of the nation, comes under scrutiny in the exercise of tendering oil and gas exploration to private commercial interests for extraordinarily low returns.

In the midst of a traditionally rhetoric-heavy understanding of Irish history, some of the most useful and perpetual lessons have been crowded out by the 'nationalistic narrative' and tone of a nation-state seeking recognition, often conservatively and at the expense of long-term economic development. Understandable initially in the context of a partitioned and economically weak State, it is nonetheless vital to examine the nature of the relationship between our official State and its role as the nation's social and economic driver.

Entering the ninth decade of this State, it would seem that some lessons still evade the ambition of the political class and the attention of state policymakers. Oil and gas exploration, and more importantly the vast amount of potential revenue from these reserves within the territorial jurisdiction of this State, would seem to have been irresponsibly 'outsourced' to private commercial interests, with only a paltry return to the Exchequer. Notwithstanding the pre-eminence of neo-liberal economic ideology in today's world, this trend to sell off potential natural resources, quickly and cheaply, displays a lack of ambition, duty and responsibility on the part of many governments.

The following are historical examples of socio-economic struggles, developments and shifts which provide a timely insight into what may have seemed, in retrospect, inevitable socio-economic progress, whereas it was generally viewed at the time as intractable realities of either our association within the British Empire or inescapable costs of a new-found sovereignty. The culture of locating responsibility for our situation on external forces, understandable as it may have been previously, has been overwhelmingly damaging. It also includes examinations of the persistence of outdated politics, intransigence by the State to the development of more decentralised and inclusive economic planning, one which would have been better able to bring the nation's talents, capitalist and socialist, to bear on a uniquely unresponsive industrial sector.

These examples also include precedents of state-sponsored infrastructural development, especially at times of very limited capital expenditure. They serve as a comparative lesson for Ireland in the twenty-first century, particularly in the tight grip of austerity and recession. Politics in its purest form – the 'art of the possible' – has emerged in times of great national importance when the need was greatest. From the pre-independence 'Land Question' to the Land Annuities Payments of the 1930s, through the development of Irish Shipping Ltd during the 'Emergency' of the Second World War, Irish economic development has staggered from laissez-faire economics, with little accompanying capital investment, to protectionism as a political ideology, rather than as an economic tool.

The sea-change of the 1960s, opening Ireland up to foreign direct investment and engaging with more liberal economic structures of the EU, has helped to modernise Ireland's agricultural sector, albeit employing a much smaller number, while providing oscillating degrees of industrial and service-based employment. Renewable and non-renewable energy remains a largely underdeveloped sector, lacking leadership, understanding and clear long-term planning.

Long before the Irish Free State was founded in 1922, the economic framework of an independent Ireland was created, or at least facilitated in its eventual development. This was done at first through agrarian and political pressure, later through constitutional means, even involving the Conservative Party of Britain. Parnell, the Irish National Land League and the Home Rule Party, succeeded in defining the existence of a separate State through the articulation of real socio-economic demands and claims to local ownership. The pursuit of independence between 1912 and 1922 founded a separate State, but much of the genesis of this State was shaped by these national movements forty years previously.

## THE LAND QUESTION AND HOME RULE: AN HISTORIC PARALLEL?

'You must not allow yourself to be dispossessed as you were dispossessed in 1847.'[2]

While it may be difficult to imagine from our present time, it wasn't until the emergence of land agitator Michael Davitt and his involvement with Charles Stewart Parnell, a Home Rule

MP, in the Irish National Land League that independence for Ireland was more seriously advanced than in previous generations. The connection between agrarian and constitutional politics forged the broad nationalist identity in the 1880s; the 'Land War' of 1879-1882 helped to focus many strands of separatist and socialist demands into one generally coherent, connected movement. The voice of this movement would be Parnell; the demand would be improved legislation, ultimately ownership, for the tenant-farmers of Ireland. It did not happen precisely by design: in fact, the Land League itself emerged only in Mayo as conditions during the terrible year of 1879 drove many to support any platform for improvements in the tenant-farmers' lot. What started as a local initiative to address a local concern in County Mayo became the engine of a national movement to address summary evictions, while simultaneously creating a blueprint for the first truly national organisation of party politics in Ireland. The 'Land Question' emerged as one of the most vexatious and incendiary of issues. It would also be the defining issue in exploiting the real potential for a separate State. How that local initiative became a national movement deserves our attention today, with the Corrib Gas Field and other locations around Ireland seemingly portrayed by the national media as isolated incidents rather than repeated symptoms of an emerging broader struggle over environmental impacts and state financial returns.

British control of Ireland had been based for centuries on economic control, with the tenant-farmers of Ireland largely subject to the fortunes of British economic well-being. The relationship between Irish tenant farmers and their landlords, many of whom resided in England, came under greater pressure after the famines of the 1840s. The foundation of a Home Government Association in 1870 pointed to an emergent desire for local control of industry and commerce, initially being backed by even moderate Unionists. What it would become, however, primarily under the leadership of Charles Stewart Parnell, was an experiment in nation-building. The 'Land Question' would be central to this new struggle between Empire and 'colony'. The Gladstonian government of the 1870s sought to 'pacify' Ireland, not empower her,[3] ensuring a conflict of interests between the British government and Irish interests.

### Parnell, Fenianism and the National Land League: The 'New Departure'

Parnell became leader of the Irish Home Rule Party in 1880. Realising that he needed broader, greater support than that offered by mostly Protestant Ascendancy members of the party, he had worked since 1875 on increasing his support base and creating connections with all parties concerned with the Irish issue. The Land League, formulated and tested in Mayo in 1879 by Michael Davitt to assert tenant-farmers' rights and resist rack-renting and evictions,[4] offered him the perfect constituency. His predecessor, Isaac Butt, had represented tenant-farmers in court, but the essence of tenant-farmers' dismay and disenfranchisement was palpable even after the 1870 Land Act. No real rights were conferred on the tenant-farmer (except the legalisation of the 'Ulster Custom') and the means by which that Land Act afforded tenant-farmers the right to buy out their holdings were wholly, and probably deliberately, unrealistic and economically impossible for all but a few tenant-farmers.[5]

Parnell gambled on association with Fenianism – bent on Irish independence and the overthrow of the landlord system[6] – and determined to combine the efforts of parliamentarians and non-parliamentarians together in one movement, popularly referred to by historians as the 'New Departure'.[7] Controversial as it was for constitutional Home Rulers, it provided a wide base of support in Ireland and in the USA for land reform. It was from this convergence of parliamentarians and socialists, democrats and militants, that Parnell would ultimately draw his support for the 1886 Home Rule Bill. Davitt's Land League went national: the Irish National Land League, founded in October 1879, seemed to point to a new beginning, a sense of direction and 'nationalisation' of a tragically persistent local economic reality.

Parnell developed a cornerstone of future Irish Catholic nationalism by involving the Catholic Church more closely in the efforts of the National League from 1882 onwards. With the backing of the Catholic Church, Parnell's new National League, which effectively replaced the outlawed National Land League, focused its efforts on creating a grass-roots organisation for the election of Home Rule MPs, with Parnell as its unassailable leader.

## All Politics is Local

One of the most important lessons learned from this period was that local disputes struggling to articulate a demand for legislative reform, existing purely in a local context, had little or no chance of succeeding. Only when the Mayo Land League went nationwide, later in 1879, did it begin to effect real pressure, social and political, on the landlord system, which had, up to this point, been restricted only by custom. The tenant farmer had never been afforded legislative protection; landlords were free to operate their estates as they saw fit, increasing rents, evicting and/or changing tenants based purely on their own economic concerns. When it was organised into a national platform, with widespread resistance through methods such as the 'Plan of Campaign', organising tenant farmers into effective pressure groups with regard to their own landlord, it became an issue that required parliamentary attention. In today's Ireland, the Corrib Gas protests are not connected strategically to other grass-roots movements concerned with or questioning the legality or financial impacts on Ireland's laissez-faire attitude to oil and gas exploration, such as Dun Laoghaire, Cork Harbour and many more untapped potential reservoirs on the Atlantic Shelf. Just as land was the defining socio-economic driver of the nineteenth century, resources such as oil and gas have the potential to define this country's progress in the twenty-first.

## THE BESSBOROUGH COMMISSION

The Bessborough Commission (1880-81) heavily criticised the 1870 Land Act as affording the tenant-farmer no real protection or legal status; following on from which, the 1881 Land Act was passed,[8] and so began a long and ultimately fruitful journey from economic servitude, through 'dual ownership' to tenant proprietorship. The subsequent Acts of 1885, 1887 and 1903 pointed to a realisation within the British government of the need to fundamentally cater for, if not change, the demands for land ownership in Ireland. The Land Acts of 1881, 1885 and 1887, and the 'Wyndham Land (Purchase) Act' of 1903, gradually altered the British government policy of 'provision' for change in land ownership to the 'abolition' of landlordism in principle. Of all the socio-economic changes that Ireland experienced from the Act of Union (1801) to the present day, this relatively short period represents the most radical change – and the retreat of a socio-economic order that had existed for well over three hundred years. All this took place, moreover, during the Victorian era, at the height of Britain's development as a world power.

## PUSHING THE PRINCIPLE

Parnell showed his innate political craft and ambition by refusing to endorse the 1881 Land Act – obstensibly introduced as a progression of tenant-farmers' rights, but more realistically designed to break the combined interests of larger and smaller farmers within the Land League. He feigned 'outrage',[9] speaking against the Act on a number of occasions, leading to his arrest and imprisonment. As rural crime escalated, the British government made a deal with Parnell, the 'Kilmainham Treaty', including small farmers and tenants in arrears under the 1881 Land Act in return for the pacification of the Irish countryside. In this, Parnell made sure that land reform could not be approached in a piecemeal fashion; the clear signal to the British government was that it was all or nothing. Once the principle had been established, controversially or not, Parnell ensured both the protection of the tenant-farmers and his position in dictating the tempo of reform, political and agrarian, in Ireland's relationship with Britain.

## THE LEGACY OF PARNELL:
## CONSTRUCTIVE UNIONISM AND THE LAND CONFERENCE OF 1902

Failure has a uniquely ambiguous meaning in politics. C. S. Parnell died long before any Irish State emerged, and twenty-three years before his elusive goal of Home Rule was achieved, but only after he had helped create the emergence of a national momentum, in particular placing the land issue to the very front of British and Irish politics. The work of the National League, the grass-roots organisation that chose candidates and organised the Irish

Home Rule MPs in almost every constituency, gave Parnell and his MPs a mandate that eventually achieved success in 1914. Rather than attempting to grasp abstract notions of nationality or independence, Parnell used the Land League to drive the nationalist agenda. The focus and intensity placed on the land system, its laws (or lack thereof) and the culture of entitlement often displayed by landowners and parliamentarians alike was progressively eroded. Once the 'status quo' had effectively been shaken to its core, British and Irish parliamentarians busied themselves with the framework for a changed socio-economic order.

## LAND CONFERENCE 1902

As a reflection of this changed order, even the Conservative governments of the 1890s invested significantly in Ireland with the development of the Congested Districts Board, investment in agriculture, light railways and road-building,[10] and most importantly the Local Government (Ireland) Act 1898, under Lord Salisbury, ending the domination of local politics by landlords. Whatever the motives of Conservative politicians at this time, whether it was an effort to 'kill Home Rule by kindness' or not, the British government provided the initial structures by which an independent Ireland could develop locally its economy of agriculture. The question of land ownership was solved through a more inclusive mechanism, particularly that of the Land Conference of 1902, where landlords and tenants were brought together to find mutually beneficial means to further their own interests. (This groundbreaking procedure would be echoed in a later proposal to an independent Irish government in the form of a National Assembly for Economic Planning, but would regrettably be ignored.) The Wyndham Land (Purchase) Act 1903 quickly followed, bringing a seemingly eternal conflict to a rapid conclusion and effecting the transfer of 9 million acres to tenant ownership by 1914.[11] The Land Purchase (Ireland) Act 1909 increased the transfer of lands to 11.5 million acres. In just forty years, the centuries-old domination of a country's socioeconomic order was almost entirely changed through consultation, compromise and an evolution of British attitudes. Similarily, it would be worth remembering the initial agreement by Justin Keating of the Fine Gael/Labour coalition government of 1975, which enshrined the 50 percent stake and royalties due to the State from any viable oil or gas field. The economic spine of a country can be altered drastically with just a few pieces of legislation, which we will examine again later in this chapter.

In retrospect, landlordism, which had been an integral framework of British hegemony in Ireland, was quickly swept away by a group of ambitious Irish parliamentarians, socialists and far-sighted British politicians. Economic needs served to shape the destiny of many political fortunes, British and Irish, and greatly evened the political and economic imbalance between Irish nationalism and British unionism. Even in the last generation of British control of Ireland, initiatives were introduced to foster economic and, in particular, rural-agricultural development. Though the coming radicalisation of both nationalism and union-ism in the early twentieth century took precedence over economic concerns, it is worth not-ing that independent Ireland owes much of its initial economic footing to this period of political and economic reform. Whatever the motives for such a turnaround of British administration in Ireland, independence less than twenty years later would prove to be a far more predictable handover, with the establishment of land ownership and the emergence of a small, but significant, Catholic middle class.

This is not a unique occurrence in history. Once the principle of tenant ownership had been established and successfully articulated by the majority, with a parallel policy-shift in Westminster, it became an issue of time and pressure. In effect, the British government paid a large political price for ignoring socio-economic disasters, such as the Famine and the increasing resistance of individual tenant-farmers to evictions and rack-renting. Political independence for Ireland was borne of frustration with economic strangulation and starva-tion, as much as cultural assertion. What parallels could be drawn today with an almost iden-tical State 'absenteeism' with regard to ownership and revenue from all State resources? Laissez-faire government regulation in times of economic hardship has always tended to spark radical movements. The concept of universal tenant onwership was far more alien then to the British government than this State's present duty to maximise returns for the people from national resources. When a State ignores its nation, or part of the nation, it tends to de-legitimise itself permanently.

## REVOLUTIONARY IRELAND: LOST IN TRANSITION, 1913-19

> A disillusioned and embittered Ireland turned away from parliamentary politics; an event was conceived and the race began, as I think, to be troubled by that event's long gestation.
>
> —W.B. Yeats, 1923

The radicalisation of both the nationalist and unionist population of the island of Ireland between 1913 and 1919 owes its initial origin to the successful passage of the Third Home Rule Bill, introduced in 1912. What this seminal period in Irish history does not often recall is the transformation and, indeed, assimilation of disparate forces, social and political, into one movement within nationalist and, later, republican Ireland. When Yeats accepted his Nobel Prize in 1923 with the above insightful explanation of the previous tumultuous years in his home country, he pointed to the failure of Parnell's parliamentary mission as the ori-gin of this radical generation.

Within this short period, three events occurred which justify examination in relation to the economic foundation and, more particularly, the ethos of independent Ireland. The

Strike and Lockout of 1913, the Easter Rising of 1916 and the First Dáil Éireann in 1919: the common thread through all three events is the consistent articulation of socialist ideology, alongside nationalist affirmation, in proclaiming an independent Ireland. James Larkin's struggle to establish a broader, stronger union of skilled and unskilled labourers in the ITGWU brought Ireland face to face with its first truly civil 'war'. William Martin Murphy, a Home Rule MP between 1885 and 1892, led the Employers' Federation in combating Larkin's attempt at unionisation in Dublin during the bitter feud. Murphy's *Independent* newspaper would later call for the execution of rebels following the Easter Rising. Powerful private interests utilised the need for 'law and order' on the streets of Dublin in 1913, effectively placing the Dublin Metropolitan Police between them and the determination of the striking workers. The spectre of an unusually overbearing Garda presence in Corrib during recent protests warrants much deeper media investigation, but sadly the fourth estate seems content with sporadic coverage and minimal investigation.

## A Party Out of Step

What was clear from the aftermath of the Lockout, and the emergence of an Irish Citizen Army to protect the striking workers from police baton charges, was the parallel evolution of the socialist cause alongside that of nationalist Ireland. This evolution had taken a decisively confrontational turn. Larkin and his trade union would give birth to the unofficial militia, themselves central participants in the Easter Rising three years later under the leadership of James Connolly. What was more clear was the ultimately outdated demand for Home Rule, bereft of the romanticised leadership of Parnell and the heady events of its early years, particularly the Land War and the initial Home Rule Bill of 1886. While the land question continued to be settled agreeably for Irish tenant-farmers, the Irish worker, particularly in cities such as Dublin, faced enormous challenges and restrictions to their demands, with John Redmond's Home Rule Party unwilling to criticise a prominent former Home Rule MP and his Employers' Confederation, a group of powerful and influential men. In this moment, with the benefit of hindsight, we can identify the beginning of the end for Redmond's Home Rule Party, conspicuously silent against the backdrop of outright civil war on the streets of Dublin. Larkin hoped to alter the protection of the unskilled labourers by uniting them with skilled labourers in one union. The iconic banner of the Irish Citizen Army, declaring 'We Serve Neither King nor Kaiser', had an obviously overt separatist tone, but the aim of this group remained proto-socialist to the core. James Connolly's leadership of this militia in the Easter Rising of 1916 served to underline the influence of events in 1913 on the radicalism that emerged onto its streets in 1916. Certainly, Connolly saw the Easter Rising as a transitory stage and not an end in itself, nationalism being a flawed, 'flag-swapping', superficial exercise in his mind. He believed that independence would be the first step to creating a Marxist republic for the workers[12] and was almost certainly responsible for the more 'socialistic clauses' of the Proclamation.[13] How much the other leaders of the Rising, the Military Council of the IRB, believed in this is open to question. Nonetheless, the IRB desperately needed Connolly and his men. And so an uneasy alliance between social-ists and extreme nationalists was formed, but never truly tested in its aftermath. In fact, whatever the initial intentions of Connolly and his followers, rather than the Rising being a necessary step towards a socialist republic, it was in fact consumed and abandoned by Yeats's 'event': political independence.[14]

> We declare the right of the people of Ireland to the ownership of Ireland. . . . The Republic guarantees religious and civil liberty, equal rights and equal opportunities to all its citizens, and declares its resolve to pursue the happiness and prosperity of the whole nation and all of its parts . . . by the readiness of its children to sacrifice themselves for the common good.[15]

Within the Proclamation of the Republic (1916), we see elements of socialism and econom-ic ambition, rhetorically yet repeatedly, alongside affirmations of Christian fidelity and 'nationhood', clearly attempting to address the religious, social and political demographics both among the rebels and their sympathisers and, more broadly, throughout Ireland. Connolly's ambitions for a socialist Republic would indeed echo in the eventual Declaration of Independence issued by the First Dáil Éireann in 1919:

> And whereas the Irish People is resolved to secure and maintain its complete inde-pendence in order to promote the common weal.[16]

The use of the phrase 'common weal' is indeed a persistent and historic claim, echoing the need for 'readiness of its children to sacrifice themselves for the common good' declared in the Easter Proclamation of 1916. The distracting political fallout from the split in Sinn Féin over the Anglo-Irish Treaty of 1921, none of which was predicated on economic differ-ences, ultimately leading to the formation of the two dominant political parties in Ireland, served to de-emphasise economics in favour of political and rhetorical differences for at least a generation.

The common good would again find its place in Bunreacht na hÉireann, underlining a persistent claim that an independent Ireland would have at least a socialist character, if not an explicitly socialist organisation. Successive Irish governments paid lip-service to this core mandate, introducing piecemeal legislation in Ireland, while continuing to cling to an agri-cultural obsession based on the previous limited industrial development since independence. In effect, the economic planning of Ireland for some periods was used to underpin and sup-port the ideological obsession with a rural-based, agricultural economy and society. All of this created a disproportionate imbalance in the national psyche; independence was seen as an end in itself, rather than being the vehicle to deliver socio-economic equality and industrial development that both the Proclamation of 1916 and older movements had proclaimed as one of their core revolutionary mandates.

## COSGRAVE, DE VALERA AND THE IRISH FREE STATE: THE ECONOMICS OF INDEPENDENCE, 1922-39

In this arena exalted leaders first fought out a brutal duel over a form of words, and then constructed a new state around preoccupations that resolutely ignored even the vague social and economic desiderata once outlined for Pearse's visionary republic.[17]

The heady idealism and bitter divisions of 1913–23, social and political, were brought firmly to earth by the economic realities facing W. T. Cosgrave and the Cumann na nGaedhael government of 1922–23. Whatever the disputes over the Treaty of 1921, no one could argue about the tenuous nature of the Irish Free State's fiscal constraints, limited initially to just a £20 million Exchequer per year. With an overwhelmingly agricultural dependency, and up to 90 percent of the Free State's export trade being with her historic nemesis, Britain, it was entirely natural that the Cumann na nGaedhael government approached her diplomatic relations with cautious ambition, with a longer-term view of industrial development. Again, issues of political and cultural identity dominated the national discourse, with questions of economic development only slowly beginning to emerge significantly *after* the variables of political connection with Britain had been debated. In contrast to this, the political desire, most persistently developed by de Valera, to use economic constructs to both justify and guarantee Irish independence and attempt to develop Irish industry between 1932 and 1948 would leave indelible marks on the Irish economy, namely protectionism, stagnation, emigration and an over-dependence on agriculture. All of this would be part of de Valera's unique approach, sometimes intransigent, sometimes belligerent, to secure the political and economic independence of the State. While Cosgrave's administration viewed economic development as a parallel to the consolidation of the State *internally*, its institutions and stability, de Valera's government from 1932 on would take a more belligerent approach, establishing the principle of increased sovereignty externally as a necessary precursor to economic development. Either way, the socio-economic idealism of 1913–19 was lost on the macroeconomic scale of difficulties that faced, for the first time, the added complexity of party politics. One could argue that this was inevitable and, indeed, healthy for the development of democracy in Ireland. Were it not for the fractured and divisive nature of Ireland's emergence as an independent nation in 1922, greater energies could have been focused on internal economic development.

## The Ardnacrusha Precedent

From 1922, Cumann na nGaedhael worked to establish the political and legal institutions of the Irish Free State alongside modest infrastructural development. Agriculture was already beginning to 'plateau': realising the need for modernisation, Cumann na nGaedhael put in place the first and probably most significant infrastructural development in independent Ireland – Ardnacrusha Hydro-Electric Power Station, built between 1925 and 1929. This station, and equally importantly, the statement it delivered, set the precedent of Irish economic survival: a small population, with few existing industries for export, must use all readily available power resources to compensate for late development. An argument concerning the relative cost of Ardnacrusha is also important, considering recent government dismissals of a nationalised Irish oil and gas infrastructure. Costing 20 percent of total government expenditure, Cosgrave and his administration realised the urgency required to modernise Irish dwellings, but more importantly the primary importance of delivering predictable, abundant and cost-effective power to small Irish businesses and factories. This revenue could easily have been used in other areas to ingratiate the population, albeit temporarily, with their first experience of national government. The construction project, by Siemens, employed a workforce of roughly 5,000, 80 percent of which was Irish. When it was finished in 1929, Ardnacrusha provided almost the entire electricity needs of the Irish Free State and was considered to be a landmark industrial-development project of its time. Nevertheless, it was a calculated risk to divert so much finance to one single project in a State which was so poorly financed and so politically unstable. From this project, the ESB was born, and one of the most successful semi-state bodies of post-independence Ireland emerged. Even in 2002, the relevance of this historic ambition in a small, poorly funded State is still recognised, receiving two international heritage awards: the 'International Milestone' presented by the IEEE (Institute of Electrical & Electronic Engineers) and 'International Landmark' awards presented by ASCE (American Society of Civil Engineers).[18]

Cosgrave was a conservative, more interested in the political stability of the nation, yet knew the dangers that lurked for a small, economically stunted state, particularly with an aggrieved and extremist minority brooding in the country. What is less-remembered is the entrenched opposition to this hydro-electric scheme by commercial interests throughout Ireland before the construction project came on stream.

## Opposition to Infrastructure: 'Creeping Socialism by the Back Door'[19]

The tendency to view Irish history, as with most histories, as a self-fulfilling prophecy, is a constant detriment to understanding our present position. Ardnacrusha in Irish economic history is an example of this. In post-primary education, the development of Ardnacrusha is somewhat portrayed as a natural, albeit significant, development of early modern Ireland. What receives very little commentary is the concerted opposition that attended the announcement of this national scheme. Paul Duffy describes, in the October 2004 edition of *History Ireland*, how 'the coal-importers and merchants orchestrated a campaign of opposition through various chambers of commerce'. Sir John Pursar Griffith and Laurence J. Kettle, two engineers with proposals for rival hydroelectric projects on the River Liffey, condemned the Shannon Hydroelectric Scheme. 'Acrimonious debate' followed in the Dáil with the introduction of the Shannon Electricity Bill on 1 May 1925. Opinions were offered, often veiled pseudo-warnings of the reluctance of the banking institutions to finance such a large-scale project. Duffy offers the opinion that vested interests protested, and attempted to block this scheme, namely the 'Irish Centre for Electrical Engineers did, as its membership was drawn from those engineers working for the many local electricity concerns around the country'.[20] It would be a useful instruction to both politicians and the national media if this historic example of misleading and disingenuous scaremongering was connected to proposals of a national oil and gas infrastructure today.

The opposition of these 'local electricity concerns' throughout Ireland must be viewed both in terms of Ireland's new-found independence at that time and also as a reminder of how 'vested interests' will always paint national schemes as a form of government control, 'socialism' and/or intrusion. W. T. Cosgrave, the president of the Executive Council, faced many dangers on many fronts. A new State, emerging only recently from a bitter civil war, was struggling to find its feet, while simultaneously attempting to project its sovereignty beyond the overbearing might of inclusion within the British Commonwealth of Nations. Before independence, these 'local electricity concerns' would have enjoyed the economic and infrastructural non-interference of the British administration. Post-independence, however, Cosgrave's Pro-Treaty administration had to deal with both harsh realities and unfair perceptions: the reality that the Irish Free State was infrastructurally deficient as a new, independent economic entity, alongside the perception of pro-Treaty Cumann na nGaedhael as not being 'true' to the socio-economic aspirations of either the Proclamation of the Irish Republic (1916) or the ambitious 'Declaration of Independence' (1919). In one fell swoop, Cosgrave delivered one of the most, if not the most, significant socio-economic drivers for modern Ireland. The success of both the Ardnacrusha Scheme and the ESB which emerged from it in 1927, points to the neccessity of investing in breakthrough technology and harnessing natural resources for the 'common good' of the State. With the foresight to give the government control over a vital technological commodity, the Irish Free State secured one of the cornerstone lifelines that propelled an often stagnant economy in the decades ahead. For a man and party often overlooked as a conservative, middle-class or laissez-faire administrator, the legacy of Ardnacrusha is still relevant today.

Considering the overwhelming political work that had to be completed to stabilise the new State, both internal and external, and the Wall Street Crash of 1929, it is understand-able that Cosgrave handed over a declining Exchequer to Fianna Fáil in 1932. The appear-ance of Seán Lemass, a dynamic and open-minded pragmatist at the Department of Industry & Commerce, was at odds with his direct superior, de Valera, a man convinced of a utopian ideal of self-sufficiency along nationalistic lines. The Economic War of 1932–38 did much to stymie economic development, albeit with the significant diplomatic victories of the end to Land Annuities Payments and the return of the 'Treaty Ports' in 1938. However, it was in the writing of a new constitution, ratified in 1937, that de Valera left an indelible mark on this State, socially and politically. We must also look closely at Article 10, not as a legalistic examination, but rather to understand why de Valera inserted the telling proviso that allowed for 'temporary or permanent alienation' of these national resources.

## Bunreacht na hÉireann (1937): De Valera's Design and 'The Common Good'[21]

> Article 10: 1. All natural resources, including the air and all forms of potential ener-gy, within the jurisdiction of the Parliament and Government established by this Constitution and all royalties and franchises within that jurisdiction belong to the State subject to all estates and interests therein for the time being lawfully vested in any person or body.[22]

De Valera's obsession with enlarging Irish independence is often the mainstay of many works on this period, with everything from 'dismantling' the Anglo-Irish Treaty of 1921 and his presidency of the League of Nations Council and Assembly dominating. Moreover, the formulation of the new constitution – Bunreacht na hÉireann – ratified in 1937, contains all the hallmarks of State-building, with the national flag, official language, education and the 'special position' of the Church all catered for and brought under the banner of a 'new' Ireland – one moving away from, yet building upon, the none-too-modest achievements of the previous fifteen years.

Articles 2 and 3, for so long the thorn in the side of unionist identity in Northern Ireland, received wide analysis between the 1960s and the 1990s. Within this constitution, de Valera laid the foundations of the primacy of the State's ownership of all resources – controver-sially, on a thirty-two-county basis. An interesting and somewhat ambiguous phrase occurs more than once throughout the constitution: the 'common good'. Taken in the broader con-text of de Valera's pursuit of self-sufficiency, realistic or not, this phrase underpins some of the key articles of the constitution. However, within Article 10, the claim to state ownership of all natural resources is made, but with the telling proviso:

Provision may be made by law for the management of the property which belongs to the State by virtue of this Article and for the control of the alienation, whether temporary or permanent, of that property.[23]

## THE LETTER OF THE LAW OR THE SPIRIT OF THE LAW?

What this proviso does is give options to the government to outsource management of these resources, for whatever reason. In effect, the State may retain ownership of the resources, while outsourcing the 'management' of same, or indeed, the permanent alienation or sale of these resources. These provisos are the basis, but not the whole story, of all past and current private commercial interests in the extraction of resources. The argument for a better financial return to the State based on the potential proceeds of these resources is not based on legal impropriety in principle; clearly the Constitution allows for the State to tender these resources to outside interests. However, the natural obligation enshrined in this constitution would be to *maximise* those returns, not diminish them due to structural deficiencies of the State. What it also shows is the explicitly repeated ethos of this constitution. Realising the vital need for private companies to help develop these natural resources, de Valera inserted the far-sighted provision of 'temporarily or permanently' outsourcing the management of these resources, depending on the needs of any future time.

### The 'Common Good'

When looked at in the broader context of de Valera's utopian rural Gaelic society, built along nationalistic lines and conservative structures – dominance of education by the Catholic Church and an emphasis on the primacy of rural life – one can see a general design for the nation in de Valera's mind – one which is underpinned in the Preamble of the Constitution ('seeking to promote the common good'[24]) and by Article 6 of the Constitution:

> 1. All powers of government, legislative, executive and judicial, derive, under God, from the people, whose right it is to designate the rulers of the State and, in final appeal, to decide all questions of national policy, according to the requirements of the common good.[25]

In this context, de Valera's democracy, though theocratic in culture and education, retained and emphasised the primacy of the 'common good'. While subsequent subsections in Article 10 allow for the 'temporary and/or permanent alienation' of natural resources, it can be reasonably argued that the 'common good' referred to in Article 6 remains the legislative and political aim of State management and/or 'alienation'. De Valera was no doubt 'ring-fencing' the territory, followed quickly by the return of the Treaty Ports in 1938,[26] to bolster and define the national territory and pre-empt any exploitation, political or economic, by foreign countries or private commercial bodies at the expense of the State and, by extension, the 'common good'. By ending the Land Annuities payments to Britain and returning the Treaty Ports in 1938, de Valera had achieved Irish control of all its territory and could now realistically claim to be a sovereign state in all but name. De Valera's refusal to continue handing over these payments to the British government, under the terms of the Anglo-Irish Treaty (1921), is a pertinent example of an evolving State, intervening on behalf of its citizens – the 'nation' – to end a financial arrangement that was incongruous with the farmers' position as citizens of that State.

## ARTICLE 45

De Valera harboured a persistent desire for self-sufficiency, certainly socially and, to a large degree, economically. Looked at in contemporary terms – the Great Depression, political unrest in Europe and a lingering uneasiness at the failure to 'complete' the revolutionary spirit of 1913-21 – it is easy to understand why de Valera, who contributed more than most to the outbreak of the Civil War over abstract terms, would want to maximise Ireland's economic independence. Again, the persistence of the phrase 'common good' is seen in one of the more intriguing articles of the Constitution, Article 45:

> 1. The principles of social policy set forth in this Article are intended for the general guidance of the Oireachtas. The application of those principles in the making of laws shall be the care of the Oireachtas exclusively, and shall not be cognisable by any Court under any of the provisions of this Constitution.[27]

This article, wide in scope, instructs as a 'Directive Principle of Social Policy' that:

> 2. The State shall, in particular, direct its policy towards securing:
> (i) That the ownership and control of the material resources of the community may be so distributed amongst private individuals and the various classes as best to subserve the common good.[28]
> (ii) That, especially, the operation of free competition shall not be allowed so to develop as to result in the concentration of the ownership or control of essential commodities in a few individuals to the common detriment.[29]

This Article lays the responsibility for 'management of material resources' squarely and explicitly at the feet of the Oireachtas, namely, the President, Dáil Éireann and Seanad Éireann. The caveat that the application of these principles should be the 'care of the Oireachtas exclusively' is curious, but understandable. A democracy, by definition, should naturally preserve and protect the rights and welfare of its core constituency: the people. These principles are meant to instruct and guide behaviours, discussions and proposals within the national parliament and the Office of the President. All deputies of the Dáil, in particular those in government at any given time, are clearly instructed to manage legal and contractual affairs governing 'material resources' in such a manner that best 'subserves the common good'. The fact that the application of these articles would not be 'cognizable by any Court' would surely reflect de Valera's desire for allowing greater scope of manipulation, as well as removing the threat of judicial review and possible censure of government action in these areas.

## THE AMBIGUOUS STATE

Repeated protestations of the present government and previous incarnations that Ireland does not have the ability nor the infrastructure to develop our potential oil and gas industry on a national basis, thereby necessitating the offer of lucrative enticements to private companies to exploit these potential resources, seems to be at odds with the repeated, explicit guidance of Article 45. These misguided 'explanations' are, in fact, irrelevant when one considers the moral and administrative guidelines explicit in this Article. One can never know for sure what the reasoning behind the seeming ambiguity of some key articles were, such as the initial article confirming the 'special position' of the Catholic Church.[30] One can only surmise that de Valera, much like his desire to keep the Catholic Church close to the positive development of the State, preferred to recognise this internal powerful ally, both as a reflection of Ireland's unique cultural identity and as a reflection of their dominating presence in education, without granting them exclusive status as a 'State Religion'. In all de Valera's dealings, from the Treaty guidelines offered to Collins and Griffith in 1921, to neutrality from 1939 to 1945, ambiguity was the hallmark of de Valera's stewardship. It is this ambiguity which has sparked debate and division from Articles 2 and 3 to Article 45 for decades since.

## A NATIONAL ASSEMBLY FOR A NATIONAL ECONOMY?

Whatever the success of de Valera's political and diplomatic gamesmanship with Britain during the 1930s, albeit delivering real political returns and an end to the universally unpalatable Land Annuities payments, the limits of de Valera as a politician can also be found in this period. Understandably, embarking on this belligerent path would require a strong and dependable politician in the Ministry of External Affairs. De Valera chose the one individual he trusted most for this position: himself. This decision has been debated for decades afterwards, but in true de Valera style, he was vindicated by the return of the Treaty Ports and Ireland's successful avoidance of the largest and most destructive war in history.

Buried in the footnotes of history, however, we can again see de Valera's tendency towards control: sometimes understandable, given the timing and nature of work to be done, sometimes damaging and limiting to the good of the nation overall. As Foster states: 'Fianna Fáil economic planning in the 1930s stressed the national duty to set up native industries.'[31] That being said, it would appear that de Valera was reluctant to hand over too much control to employers and workers in the suggested 'National Assembly' for economic planning and management, contained in the report of the Commission on Vocational Organisation (1939–43), which suggested precisely that. This National Assembly, comprised of employers and workers, elected as representative non-party members, would dedicate their expertise and knowledge to economic planning and development. As Foster states, it was met with 'resounding silence'.[32]

It would be unfair to paint de Valera as the only politician reluctant to cede such enormous control to another governing body, especially so soon after independence. It would also have a great deal to do with de Valera's reluctance to decentralise, as Ferriter explains: 'the opponents of bureaucracy had more than met their match in the administrators and politicians who were determined to develop a strong central state at a time of international economic and political instability'.[33] Both he and the Civil Service were entirely against the idea. The culture of political control, particularly in the Civil Service, played a significant part in burying this potential apparatus.[34] The primacy of the Dáil was ensured, and an opportunity to extricate economic planning from under the shadow of political culture was lost.

In a sense, while Fianna Fáil dedicated themselves to economic development, they made sure that economic planning was still subservient to party-political control in a centralised state. The idea of employers and workers sitting side by side in an economic assembly would surely have intrigued the likes of Connolly and Larkin. At the very least, it would have proposed different strategies, ones not overly dependent on or affected by conservative centralisation.

## SEÁN LEMASS: 'UNEMPLOYMENT IS MAINLY A SYMPTOM OF DEFECTIVE INDUSTRIAL ORGANISATION'

The extreme shortages and isolation, political and economic, of the wartime 'Emergency' period would serve to underline Ireland's strategic weaknesses and exposure to international events and conflicts. A common theme in Irish economic policy was the tendency to go to extremes, from the laissez-faire conservatism of the 1920s to the all-out economic warfare and protectionism of the 1930s, reflecting the evolving political needs of changed administrations. By 1940, it would fall to Seán Lemass to engineer a survival mechanism for an isolated state in a time of international peril.

Lemass's tenure at the Department of Industry and Commerce, and his role as Minister for Supplies during the 'Emergency', did, however, give rise to an important period of State innovation and strategic planning. Lemass set about exploiting the natural resources of the nation and, where necessary, creating new infrastructures aimed at alleviating the shortages of necessary commodities experienced during wartime. The creation of Irish Shipping Ltd in March 1941 was one of the most significant achievements of that time, given the extremely dangerous arena in which they operated, often alone, supplying the nation with vital commodities and delivering more than a superficial credence to Irish independence and self-sufficiency.[35]

It is important to note that Lemass was operating this fleet purely on the grounds of necessity, with far more pragmatism in mind than de Valera's preoccupation with abstract 'independent neutrality'. When the war ended, Irish Shipping Ltd emerged with a surplus of £3,000,000 and only two ships lost.[36] Ireland's territory, when including its territorial waters, is roughly 900,000 square kilometres, roughly ten times the size of our land territory.[37] Any independent nation, especially one such as the Irish Free State in the 1930s, seeking greater recognition and an expansion of its political sovereignty, should have looked to one of its greatest assets: its waters, their approaches, strategic and economic, as well as its fisheries, all of which suffered at the feet of political and agrarian obsessions. The failure to create an independent Irish Mercantile Marine service earlier on was, in hindsight, a failure of organisation and evolution of priorities. Reliance on British shipping proved to be an almost fatal weakness, notwithstanding Lemass's late, but ultimately successful, development of Irish Shipping Ltd.

Lemass's goal throughout the 'Emergency' was to create an infrastructure to offset the trade isolation that accompanied neutrality. In this, the exploitation of the peat resources of Ireland became a necessity for the State's survival in lieu of dwindling and inconsistent fuel supplies. The Turf Development Board, founded in 1934,[38] created state-sponsored schemes for the exploitation of a vast natural resource; authority was given to the county councils for the exploitation of turf while the State handled publicity and marketing for private turf production. One of the most significant results was the highly successful 'Kildare Scheme', resulting in over 600,000 tonnes of peat being produced by 1947.[39] The State showed its willingness to promote and carry, through its local county councils, both the infrastructural costs and national organisation needed to prioritise the exploitation of a vital commodity in an economically uncertain period. Bórd na Móna grew from this experience: it was largely a reactionary measure to counteract international events. What the period of the 'Emergency' proved is that, once again, Ireland's lack of resource awareness and infrastructural planning necessitated a reactionary and hurried response to a nationwide necessity. These hurried responses created the illusion of State planning, which in reality were disguises for too much political rhetoric and not enough industrial planning. The limitations of the Fianna Fáil administration, ideologically and economically, would emerge over the fifteen years following the end of World War II, with increased emigration, unresponsive employ-ment figures and Ireland's position in the Western World becoming ever more marginalised. Protectionism was an ideological facet of de Valera's new 'Éire' and helped to define the State's ability to extricate itself from the Commonwealth, but at a significant cost to the new Ireland it sought to create. The mistake was in attempting to prolong this concept, resulting in the 'lost' decade of the 1950s.

## T. K. Whitaker's Programme for Economic Expansion: The Legacy of Foreign Direct Investment and Decline in Agriculture, 1960-2004

The short-lived First Inter-Party Government (1948–51) brought new energy to a political-ly isolated and economically depressed nation following World War II. The foundation of the IDA (Industrial Development Authority) would usher in a new strategy of attempting to attract foreign companies to set up in Ireland, in return for grants and factories already built. That this occurred within a political culture of protectionism was indeed challenging, no matter how apparent the failure of protectionism was becoming. However, progressive socialist policies, particularly those of Dr Noel Browne, would bring an end to this first coalition government. By the 1950s, it was clear that de Valera's rural utopia was faltering, and indeed, preventing a necessary transition to a more 'internationalised' Ireland. Emigration increased, and protectionism had definitively failed to deliver the home-grown industries that a declining agricultural sector clearly demanded.

Seán Lemass, on becoming Taoiseach in 1959, inherited a flawed politico-economic model: the concept of a 'protectionist' Ireland, operating within its own ideological needs while somehow, simultaneously, connecting successfully with far more liberal and open international trade mechanisms. The narrative by which Lemass successfully brought Ireland forward into a more open economic model, relying on exports and industrial development to drive annual growth to 4 percent per annum between 1959 and 1973, rather than a dom-inant agricultural sector allied with protectionist industries, is still debated today. What is cer-tain, however, is that the realignment of Ireland's economic planning, including the intro-duction of 'programming' (strategic economic planning), and attracting foreign direct investment, drove an evolution of planning and development which, at the very least, final-ly removed the concept of protectionism and economic insularity from any serious debate concerning economic planning. This was ushered in with the passing of the Industrial Development Manufactures Act (1958). The Industrial Development Authority would become the manifestation of this dramatic policy change. Ireland's entry to the EEC would copper-fasten the complete abandonment of the policy of protectionism.

## GDP v. GNP

A new and more subtle threat to the relationship between the State and the people also emerged in this era, however. Concerns were expressed about government reliance on 'professional committees and advisory bodies; the complaint that interest-groups and bureaucrats were usurping the powers of TDs was increasingly articulated.'[40] The IDA's role became ever more concentrated on attracting foreign direct investment, and a deficiency in Ireland's economic performance between the late 1960s and the early 1990s was the failure to deliver consistent home-grown industrial development. This failure would be addressed by the division of the IDA into three distinct agencies in 1994: Forfás, IDA Ireland and Forbairt (Enterprise Ireland). Nonetheless, forty years of practice had decisively unbalanced the scales between foreign companies operating in Ireland and the development of home-grown industries, properly and competitively operating out of Ireland. The governments of the late 1980s and 1990s would be charged with addressing this imbalance, but as ever, subtle warnings inherent in the differences between GDP and GNP would not sufficiently alert the political administration into taking action, save that of the reorganisation and subdivision of the IDA. How then could the erroneous move be taken in 1989 to drastically reduce Ireland's take on any potential oil and gas from 50 to 25 percent, with the added loss of royalties, not to mention the 100 percent tax write-off to private companies for exploration costs? In a way, the shortcomings and strategic imbalance within the IDA for decades would be reflected by the political administration's lack of foresight, or even hindsight, regarding GNP.

Employment figures became the natural benchmark for every government, and with increasingly good news to report, the details of a significantly diminished and diminishing Gross National Product from the 1990s onwards (the more accurate estimation of a nation's real wealth and economic stability) were lost in the flawed stability of the Celtic Tiger and, subsequently, the 'boom' years. Ireland's economic future continues to depend hugely on the fortunes of multinationals. While we have successfully positioned ourselves as a very favourable location for these multinationals, the continuous discontent among our European partners with our low corporation tax rate is a warning of possible future tax harmonisations. If this was to happen, a severe blow would occur to our employment figures, as Ireland would lose its trump card in attracting these companies to shore up our inconsistent home-grown industry sector. More so than ever, serious efforts must be brought to bear on developing our GNP; its levels properly forecast our ability to assert control over our own fortunes.

Between 1960 and 2004, the shortcomings of foreign direct investment have proven to be of continuous concern. As workforce numbers in agriculture fell from just under 300,000 to under 100,000, both the industry and services sectors failed to compensate for this enormous fall, with industrial employment improving from roughly 50,000 to just over 100,000, and services increasing from 40,000 to 110,000 in the same period. One must also take into account that the terminal date of comparison was at the height of the 'Celtic Tiger', which has drastically worsened since 2008.

## AN 'EXPANSIONARY FISCAL CONTRACTION'
## LEGACY OF CRISIS: 1987

While I am at this stage satisfied that our licensing terms are competitive with those prevailing in western Europe, I am also keeping them under close review to ensure that they do not represent an obstacle to exploration in our offshore.'

—Ray Burke, Minister for Energy, 8 April 1987

The reason for revising our offshore licensing terms was that I was gravely concerned about exploration prospects. . . . Our existing licensing terms were unattractive to the exploration industry and there was the distinct possibility that our drilling programme would dwindle away to nothing over the next few years, unless we made the changes which I have announced. I decided to abolish royalties because such a measure was essential in order to make our terms competitive with the best currently available in Europe – that is, in the UK and Spain, both of which have abolished royalties in recent years. Even the Norwegians, who traditionally apply the severest terms of all, have also abolished royalties. . . . While as a method of taxing developments, royalties may be attractive to the State, I am convinced that if royalties were not abolished, drilling would quickly come to an end with little hope of a discovery being made, and the collection of royalty and any other form of income from a development would become academic. . . . I believe that the Irish people would prefer to have the prospect of an income from developments through the corporation tax system than to have no developments at all. The yield from any particular commercial field that may be discovered will, as under any fiscal regime, vary considerably depending on the circumstances of that field.[41]

—Ray Burke, Minister for Energy, 15 October 1987

The legacy of the fiscal crisis of the 1980s has left more than a mark on Irish socio-economic life. Once Alan Dukes opened the door to Opposition complicity in drastic public spending cuts, the effects were more substantial than many could have appreciated at the time. However much it was a necessary move to bring order to the nation's Exchequer, the political 'detente' signified by this move, which cost Alan Dukes his leadership of the Fine

Gael Party, can only now be assessed. In the heat of the controversy, there was naturally more focus on the impact of parliamentary politics and the role of the Opposition, crowded out by the public backlash to extraordinary cuts to public services and it is only much later that we begin to see the significantly negative trade-off that this fiscal correction created. Buried in the details of our income tax and corporate tax adjustments, as described by Minister Ray Burke in the Dáil on 15 October 1987, our cut in any oil and gas profits, explored and mined within the jurisdiction of Ireland, was reduced enormously.

Understanding how and why tax on profits was reduced from nearly 50 to 25 percent, and the loss of royalties, not to mention the 100 percent write-off of costs by the Irish Exchequer, has created a legacy which most policymakers must regret. Why this deal was done must be understood in the time that it was carried out: the desperation of Irish politicians to get spiralling deficits under control meant that not enough foresight was invested in the broad brushstroke that emaciated any future returns for the Irish Exchequer in relation to these finds. The subsequent improvement in drilling technology and engineering now places Irish oil and gas in a much more potentially lucrative situation. Simply put, in an effort to escape a horrendous fiscal trap, the State engineered an attractive and extremely cost-efficient mechanism to attract any foreign direct investment, and in particular, making resource exploration a lucrative deal for any private commercial interests. While the State recovered slowly into the 1990s, and the emergence of the 'Celtic Tiger' later infused certainty into state policymakers, Ireland's oil and gas resources became, albeit somewhat naturally, irrelevant to the economic thinking of the day. Minister Burke's modus operandi, to make Ireland 'competitive' with other drilling nations such as Spain, the UK and even Norway, does not stand up to any scrutiny whatsoever.

> I believe that the Irish people would prefer to have the prospect of an income from developments through the corporation tax system than to have no developments at all.

Minister Burke's rationale that any profit to the State (at that time) would meet the approval of the people, even at the cost of later and possibly far greater development, is fundamentally flawed on every count: constitutional, moral and ethical. In effect, he declared that changes were made to licences, tax and royalties because our 'existing licensing terms were unattractive to the exploration industry'.

In this statement, we see the negative evolution of governmental politics from constitutional safeguards to transitory opportunism. Whatever the rationale behind this thinking, it must surely have been apparent to both the Minister and his colleagues in government that, in effect, they were granting open season on Irish territorial waters. Every government minister, acting in his official capacity, must take the future, not just immediate, pressures into consideration before creating precedents. In line with this, the leader of the Labour Party, Deputy Dick Spring, countered on 15 October 1987:

Given those factors and the write-off that the oil companies are now entitled to claim, will the Minister accept that the abolition of royalties which guaranteed a direct income to the State, and to the people who are entitled to a return from oil, has meant that that was a complete mistake?'[42]

Tomás MacGiolla was then invited by the Ceann Comhairle to take part in this debate:

Will the Minister not agree that he has been hopelessly outmaneuvered by the oil companies? His announcement came after quite a long concerted campaign by the oil barons, some of whom have newspaper interests, to persuade him and the public to surrender to their demands. They were saying 'The State wants money from us. We will do this work if the State takes nothing.' The Minister has told them to do the job, that nothing is wanted. Those are the facts on the tax issue as well as the royalties issue.[43]

Certainly, Ray Burke's statement that he was possessed of a fear of Irish oil drilling dwindling away to 'nothing' is at best disingenuous and at worst damaging. Considering that the government of the day is charged with the maintenance, legal and otherwise, of the State's property, and therefore, its inherent value to the nation, these defeatist and openly pessimistic statements in the Dáil sealed any possible licence negotiations before (as Minister Burke claimed) they could begin. A fait accompli was delivered on vague comparative terms: the State was a beggar, and the matter was closed. One day in the Dáil which has received precious little scrutiny by national broadcasters and/or newspaper journalists saw Ireland surrender most of any possible future wealth dividends based on a broad comparative perception, a 'worry' that Ireland was falling behind in her drilling activities and a 'fear' that oil exploration companies would not stay unless they received extraordinary write-offs and tax breaks.

## THE BLINDING MIRACLE: PARLIAMENTARY POLITICS AND ECONOMIC HUBRIS

The OECD commented on the Irish economy's performance in 1999 as follows:

It is astonishing that a nation could have moved all the way from the back of the pack to a leading position within such a short period, not much more than a decade, in fact.[44]

In one sense, it is easy to admire that extraordinary change in Irish fiscal performance between 1987 and 2000. Unemployment dropped from 17 percent in the 1980s to roughly 4.4 percent by 2000.[45] As Patterson succinctly points out in his watering down of the 'economic miracle', the real warnings lay in the imbalance between GNP and GDP figures for this period. The issue of overstated profits by multinationals, themselves part of the 'economic miracle' of Ireland, at least in employment terms, created a false impression of Irish economic performance, eagerly seized on by governments of the day, but curiously unexamined by many opposition parties. This in itself could be somewhat explained by the legacy of Alan Dukes's 'Tallaght Strategy' in 1987: with Fianna Fáil moving in a more centre-right direction fiscally, while still holding claim to such electoral anachronisms as 'the Republican Party' and its enduring popularity as 'the people's party', criticisms and competition between economic policies all but disappeared during the boom years. Successive elections were fought between 1995 and 2007 based on the idea of holding and maintaining the economic performance that existed up to this point. The general election of 2002 saw the emergence of superficial marketing slogans, bereft of any real substance (which is not unheard of in politics) by Fine Gael, 'Vision, With Purpose', matched by the alarmingly vague Fianna Fáil slogan of 2007: 'A Lot Done, More to Do'. What these elections reflected, more than anything, was the sense that Irish economics had been definitively *solved*. Precious little scrutiny emerged between Opposition and government during the boom years, a situation which lent itself to hubris in economic planning and critique. What remained was purely politicking: a competition between two overly dominating historically anachronistic parties, who sought power on the premise of generous fiscal expenditure, rather than examining and strengthening the basis for Ireland's growth. Coupled with the recent EU Structural and Cohesion Funds, there existed a feeling of invulnerability as long as growth kept proceeding. Much was made of Ireland outstripping all other EU states with regard to employment, GDP and budget surpluses. There simply existed no expedient *political* need within the democratic framework for strategic shifts, analysis or examination.

The Tallaght Strategy of 1987 broadly reflects another area of Fianna Fáil/Fine Gael 'co-operation': Northern Ireland. Ever since the promising moves by Gerry Adams and John Hume in the early 1990s, allied with the Downing Street Declaration of 1993, there had emerged a 'non-confrontation' between Ireland's two biggest political parties in relation to the Peace Process. In effect, party politics was abandoned in the Republic of Ireland in the hope of creating stability and predictability in the pursuit of peace in Northern Ireland. This is one legacy that will undoubtedly live on as an extraordinary attribute of single-mindedness in Irish politics: maturity and a sense of a 'greater good' rose to prominence above all other considerations. However, in one sense it merely underlined a democratically disturbing similarity and lack of differentiation between major Irish political parties, albeit, it could be argued, for the greater good of creating a stable Anglo-Irish partnership in relation to the resolution of the 'Troubles' in Northern Ireland.

## IRELAND & THE EU: THE 'ILLUSION OF DELIVERANCE'

Apart from the initial 'surge' in the 1960s following the Programme for Economic Expansion, Ireland's stagnation in terms of development can often be masked by the favourable returns of European Union membership. From 1973 on, even with increasing funding from Europe, the Irish economy stagnated and the public sector became a burden on the Exchequer. Our national debt ballooned as it slowly became apparent that Brussels could not deliver Irish economic well-being, but could merely facilitate (temporarily) a transformation from an agricultural economy to a mixed economy. It would seem that our reliance on EU structural funding may have worsened our real competitiveness, the slash-and-burn Tallaght Strategy of 1987 only bringing the economic disaster to a standstill. However, the relative success of the Tallaght Strategy must be seen in its real economic effects: education and, in particular, health services were severely affected. Only by 1995 did Ireland begin to recover. The extraordinary expense of reinvesting in the Irish health care system from the late 1990s to 2007 bears testament to how much damage was done.

## Education as a Reflection of Political Culture

Even in education, our inability to realise multiple goals or a more balanced outcome has led to 'polarised educational outcomes', with academic progress far outstripping vocational skills and the need, as McDowell put it, to 'complement the academic stream with a vocational stream'. In this, we might look to our German counterparts, who provide a multi-stream infrastructure of education for the academically minded, vocational and otherwise. Our graduates are often left with little option but to emigrate. The connection between educational investment priorities and industry and employment has never been sufficiently strategic, all the more so as employment can sometimes be heavily dependent on multinationals.

Our reliance on low taxation as a means of attracting foreign direct investment and promoting employment has revealed its full limitations, particularly now in the catch-22 situation of enormous nationalised debt and unresponsive employment initiatives. The need to investigate all and any industrial and employment initiatives is vital. More so, it is vital that we secure resilient economic options, particularly home-grown industry.

Our historical tendency, albeit a natural one, to allow external forces to shape our social and economic policies throughout the nineteenth and twentieth centuries, pre- and post-independence, has clearly been a significant weakness, even allowing for inclusion within the EU. More so, the repeated behaviour of a 'dominant' economic policy, be it protectionism or foreign direct investment, one that delivers short-term improvements for the immediate future rather than building and investing in contingencies for a long-term future development, continues to put a stranglehold on economic development. The future of Irish oil exploration no doubt will yield economic dividends, as well as failures, missed opportunities and miscalculations. The lessons of the past are clear: inaction due to 'inability' will leave this country seeking marginal returns with no control and no predictability with regard to revenue. On the other hand, as the past has borne out, once a socio-economic aim is identified and prioritised, the returns can often exceed initial projections.

Such is the persistent common thread of Irish economic development since the 1960s, and apart from de Valera's unrealistic and insular protectionist policies, useful in the political and economic storms of the 1930s, but outdated and socially malignant by the 1950s, this servitude and supplicancy of subsequent Irish governments, ministers and semi-state bodies has given rise to the emergence of 'open-door' opportunities for multinationals. The question is where to draw the line: offering factories, services and communications to foreign companies or their local partners in exchange for employment is certainly a mutually beneficial deal, but what of resources?

Ireland's resources have traditionally been agriculture and fisheries, the former which has been propped up by CAP and the EU, the latter which has been traded, somewhat irresponsibly, in return for capital investment by the EU in Ireland. The ultimate tradable resource, however, is oil and gas, and in this debate over the proceeds of Ireland's resources many ideas and sectors must be equally treated: constitutionality, government regulation, political practice and protocols. What are the protocols that govern the State's investment in our natural resources? How do the courts decide which companies should be allowed drilling rights? What is the process between exploration rights and mining rights?

## THE FUTURE PRESENT: MORE THAN AN ECONOMIC CLAIM

The questions posed by Ireland's recent economic turmoil focus collective minds on realities and immediacies rather than aspirations or rhetoric based on national sovereignty and 'moral' ownership or duty. Throughout the previous 150 years, we have seen the extraordinary changes in land ownership, electoral reform, economic planning (or lack thereof) and gradual shifts towards more innovative approaches to employment and industrial development. The Tallaght Strategy of 1987 left an indelible mark on the socio-economic life of this country, on the one hand fostering fiscal stability and an eventual return to growth, but at the price of a seismic shock to public services, not to mention the country's tax base. It is in this area of taxation that the State holds a trump card.

The argument for privatised exploration of oil and gas within Ireland's jurisdiction is a structurally preferable one: the government and the State assume little or no risk in the costs of these explorations and drilling. However, the real cost to the State, and more precisely, the nation, are hard to assess fully at this time. One certainty is that private exploitation, and ultimately profit, of any natural resources in this State will leave very little benefit to this country. The future hindsight of historians will no doubt decry the lack of ambition and guile on the part of state agencies for selling off such potential revenue as an act of national self-betrayal and mismanagement. Many will wonder whether the crash of 2008 spooked politicians and policymakers into maintaining the cheapest possible revenue margin, with an almost zero margin of risk, at the expense of a more steadfast and self-determining economic plan.

## A History of Impossibilities

One thing is for certain: in a country that obsesses about 'what-ifs', a place where history always seems to invade the present and remind us of the impossibility of peasant land ownership in the nineteenth century, the improbability of British Conservative Party investment in rural Ireland, a country where forty years of steadfast support for modest Home Rule was cast aside for romanticism and idealism in a few short years, the element of risk and willingness is not bemoaned nationally. Considering the partial failure of a reunified Ireland along historical lines and the continued lack of a genuine renaissance of the national language, the national consciousness does not seem to assess progress in terms of outright victories and defeats. We celebrate historical courage and individuality as a national characteristic and cherish those who fail simply because they tried, for the common good, advancing our mindset as much as our actual gains, liberating us from servitude, first externally and more recently internally, and see it as a progress that is natural and beneficial to all, regardless of the immediate outcome.

We are at the business end of a recession that has brought emigration to significant highs. A close look at specific data concerning migration from Ireland with regard to key demographics shows a marked increase in emigration, particularly within the age range of 25-44-year-olds (from 14,100 in 2006 to 39,500 in 2012) and also in the age range of 15-24-year-olds (from 15,900 in 2006 to 35,800 in 2012) who would ostensibly be seen as forming the bulk of the next generation of the Irish workforce: public and private sector employees, entrepreneurs, and so on.[46] The flawed concept of any gain, no matter how minuscule, for no loss, clearly adopted by successive governments, including the present one, does not fit our national temperament nor our fiscal needs. In times of great political and economic hardship, the hard road has always been chosen as the right road. Neutrality during the Second World War defined our sovereignty; it made us very few friends and left us outside the vast amount of Marshall Aid reconstruction. It also began the development of some of our most successful semi-states, as well as enlarging and differentiating our ability to survive, economically and politically. It may very well have saved us from becoming a scorched battlefield. The advocacy of 'open-door' exploration of natural resources in this country is akin to handing the inheritance and value-added benefits of Ireland's future generations away in one fell swoop. This is the moral prerequisite that lies at the feet of the government; if Ireland controls, owns and oversees her territory, as is her duty, her obligation should be to maximise returns as much as possible. If this cannot be achieved through renegotiation and brokering, her duty should be clear. Leave it in the ground and develop a national infrastructure, over time, until the State can guarantee at least a substantial share of the proceeds. Our involvement in, and exposure to, a European-wide market and currency, as well as a much-vaunted global economy, has left us bereft of control, possibly to the detriment of our political class.

We have very little left which we control outright. As our co-dependence with and, indeed, dependence on these larger entities increase, it goes without saying that any potential returns, advocated locally and negotiated responsibly, should be of paramount national concern and focus. Yet we are assaulted daily with news of catch-up economics: how our bailout progresses, how we are meeting our repayments, and who, or what, is to blame for our present economic predicament. The only certainty is that it did happen, and our focus, while we are performing modestly well in not collapsing entirely, should be on broadening our horizons and reviewing all existing state policies that may hold benefits for now and the future.

## The Constitution: The Magnificent Myth

While the popular notion exists that the relationship between nation and state should always be linear – the State existing and operating to serve the needs and purposes of the nation – it would seem that this is not *constitutionally* the case. The harsh reality that the State may do what it will, within the confines of popular consent and the Articles of Bunreacht na hÉireann, and as a natural product of its own unique history, becomes ever more apparent with fiascos such as a 'referendum' on the Nice Treaty, brought before the people twice to secure a 'Yes' vote. While it has been proven that the government acted legally, the spirit of the law has certainly been tarnished. The spirit of the Constitution itself has been undermined. Our involvement with the EU, and the subsequent repeat referendums, all suggest that the State, as a political entity, is progressing away from popular consent to over-arching constitutional and legislative force. Much of what the Bishop of Clonfert said in 1957 alludes to this popular delusion of the State being an end in itself. If people want a fundamental change in the status quo, it is here in the legislative spine of the State that they must begin to effect change.

Furthermore, the reality is that our State, which is almost one hundred years old, has inadequately explained the virtues and responsibilities of deeper membership of the EU. Again, this is partly due to the nature of our own history. It could also be said that the State has acted improperly on these occasions, with repeated referendums on the same issue seeking a predetermined response, thereby perverting the constitutional control of the people over the State's actions. While the government may say it acted legally, the consent of the people was manipulated deliberately and openly. Does the State know better than its people? Surely the litmus test for any democracy is that the State does not have to resort to force, physical or abstract, in pursuit of what it feels is necessary for itself and the people.

## CONFLICT OF STATE AND NATION: AMBIGUITY OF THE 'COMMON GOOD'

The State, by virtue of its position, is the official face and representative of its people, no matter how complicated the legal framework. The 'nation', on the other hand, is a far more ambiguous entity, albeit defined broadly in the Constitution. How the general population is affected by the State, specifically in relation to key issues such as the oil and gas exploration within the State's jurisdiction, and therefore affecting the general well-being of the population with regard to debt burdens and high taxes, *is* estimable. The government's decision to enter a bailout programme has in many ways sharpened Irish society's interest in the nature of state control and executive authority. What constitutes the State's responsibility to the people? How does this responsibility reflect popular consent and continued support for the State since independence in 1922? Again, it must be that the government is responsible for both the temporary *and* the permanent betterment of its taxpayers and voters, without whom they would cease to have position or relevance. Ultimately, it must be remembered that the State itself can act in ways that are detrimental to the nation. The nature of our bureaucracy, itself a permanent government that more often than not knows what is best for the country, must still be examined in much greater detail. What limitations does the Civil Service inherently bring to the table of economic development? Are there conflicts of interest?

Previous to the ratification of Bunreacht na hÉireann in 1937, as previously examined, de Valera set a precedent regarding the relationship between state and nation. However much it can be argued that de Valera's administration ended the Land Annuities payments in 1932 as part of a larger, wider strategy of enlarging Irish independence, it must be remembered that the beneficiaries were *both* the individual farmers and the State. In removing the contractual obligations of the farmers, the State intervened, committing itself to a six-year economic struggle with Britain on the principle that its citizens could not be held financially liable to a foreign government for land within its own territorial jurisdiction. With the abrupt ending of these payments, fifty-two years of struggle for the economic liberation of small farmers was complete. The cost was significant, especially in terms of the tariff war with Britain, which severely affected Irish exports. However, with the Anglo-Irish (Trade) Agreement of 1938, these restrictions ended.

Democracy is based on checks and balances, responsibility and accountability. The era of authoritarianism, patriarchal or otherwise, is thankfully dead. Still, habitual cultures of control exist. Elected office in Ireland has been characterised by too many instances of irresponsibility and arrogance, especially at the highest levels of public service. The debate on Ireland's future as an oil and gas producer and exporter must become a national debate, properly furnished by public consultation and a completely transparent process of development. 'Taskforces' and 'sustainability reports', employed by successive governments in the past, have proven to be erroneous on some key issues. Even more so, the closed-door nature of these professional services, advising politicians within the establishment framework, reduces the citizens to spectator status and their representatives in the Dáil grasping with the details of a fait accompli. The electorate are left with only popular protest as their remedial weapon. The citizenry must be involved at the outset; anything less is a perversion of our 'Republic', its values and its historical origins.

## The Fourth Green Field

We collapsed into recession and overwhelming debt due to lack of oversight, hubris and a belief that continuity without questions heralded no storm. Our economy became dependent on continuing a short-term trick: mainly speculation, a construction bubble, a consumerist economy and an internationally credit-flooded banking sector. All of these had no long-term viability, or even a semblance of sustainability, to those in the know. We invested hugely in our infrastructure during the 'Tiger Years', flooded our health service with cash, yet ignored the one area of our national economy that held a promise of sustainability.

The multinationals that straddle our societies and nations have become the true superpowers of the twenty-first century. Their place is privileged: no national leader in his or her right mind would oppose or threaten these companies, which provide employment, and research and development, and act as a magnet to many down-stream services and industries. The issue is seemingly beyond politicians in that their hands are effectively tied to brokering deals and creating opportunities for these companies to offer employment and skills to people. Moreover, it is becoming increasingly obvious that the issue of depleting resources in a growing world population is becoming the revolutionary spark for the twenty-first century. Peoples are asserting their right to the proceeds of these natural resources, and without undue clichés, it is true, as ever, that power and control never concede easily.

It would seem that we have returned to the era of 'tenant-farmers' – our population and workforce dependent on their skills to serve the almost unchallenged omnipotence of multinationals and private commercial concerns. Our standard of living has changed immeasurably, but our economic future is still largely dependent on external forces. Oil, and all other natural resources, are our 'land' in twenty-first-century Ireland. The Constitution, the legal basis for our 'State' representing our nation, declares it so. Air, land and sea all form part of the national territory. Furthermore, the Constitution stipulates the behaviour of members of the Oireachtas, their duty especially in relation to material resources and the administration and control of these resources, to best 'subserve the common good'. This leaves Ray Burke's arguments of 'necessary' wholesale changes to the previous tax regime installed by Justin Keating in 1975 in grave ethical doubt. While we have ongoing tribunals about the rezoning of land around urban centres throughout Ireland, the desire to explore how oil exploration licences are granted, to whom and under what conditions, seems antecedent to many of our senior politicians and, more alarmingly, our media. The present government seem wholly uninterested, for one reason or another, in exploring the possibilities for a better deal between this State's resources and private commercial interests, yet increases indirect taxes at an alarming rate.

## About the Author

A native of Dromtarriffee, County Cork, Billy has worked as a History and English teacher in Post-Primary Schools in Dublin over the last ten years, most recently St Paul's College, Clontarf from 2009 to 2013. A member of the HTAI (History Teachers' Association of Ireland), he has also designed and published a website on post-primary history: www.stpaulscollege.ie/history. He has a BA in European Studies (Public Affairs), 2001, from the University of Limerick and a PGDE (Post Graduate Diploma in Education), 2007, from the University College Dublin.

## Notes

1. *Modern Ireland: 1600-1972*, pg 569

2. *Charles Stewart Parnell*, pg 84

3. *Ibid.*, pg 29

4. *Modern Ireland: 1600-1972'* pg 354

5. *A New Dictionary of Irish History from 1800*, pg 259

6. *Charles Stewart Parnell*, pg 71

7. *Ibid.*, pg 72

8. *Modern Ireland: 1600-1972*, pg 412

9. Parnell was in danger of losing ground to the British Government as the combination of a seemingly benign Land Act and oppressive Coercion Acts sought to dilute and divide the 'New Departure'. He couldn't argue against it without losing face with moderates such as the Catholic Church and public opinion in Britain, but neither could he accept it as it favoured tenants *not* in arrears, but discriminated against tenants who were in arrears. He had to do something to put the pressure back on the Government

10. *Modern Ireland: 1600-1972*, pg 425

11. *Charles Stewart Parnell*, pg 637

12. *Modern Ireland: 1600-1972*, pg 443

13. *Ibid.*, pg 443

14. *Ibid.*

15. *Ibid.*

16. historical-debates.oireachtas.ie/D/DT/D.F.O.191901210008.html

17. *Modern Ireland: 1600-1972*, pg 515

18. www.merrionstreet.ie/index.php/2012/07/an-taoiseach-marks-85-years-of-esb-ard-nacrusha-power-station-co-clare

19. *History Ireland*, Issue 4, Volume 12:'The Pre-History of the Shannon Scheme'

20. *Ibid.*

21. Our purpose here is not to make legal arguments, which are necessarily complex, but to examine again the nature of the relationship between State and Nation and its evolution in this Constitution. For an entirely accurate legal interpretation of these articles of the Constitution, please refer to the section 'Can the State Sell the Nation?' by Diarmuid Rossa Phelan, SC

22. Bunreacht na hÉireann (Constitution of Ireland), 1937

23. *Ibid.*, Article 10, Section 3

24. *Ibid.*, Preamble

25. *Ibid.*, Article 6, Section 1

26. *Modern Ireland: 1600-1972*, pg 554

27. Bunreacht na hÉireann, Article 45, Preamble

28. *Ibid.*, Article 45, Section 2 (i)

29. *Ibid.*, Article 45, Section 2 (ii)

30. *Ibid.*, Amending Acts, Article 44.1.2

31. *Modern Ireland: 1600-1972*, pg 540

32. *Ibid.*

33. *Judging Dev*, pg 202

34. *Modern Ireland: 1600-1972*, pg 540-541

35. *Seán Lemass: A Biography*, pg 99

36. *Seán Lemass: A Biography*, pg 100

37. www.gsi.ie/Programmes/INFOMAR+Marine+Survey

38. *Modern Ireland: 1600-1972*, pg 547

39.   www.heartland.ie/articles/brief-history-peat-industry-ireland

40.   *Modern Ireland: 1600-1972*, pg 571

41.   debates.oireachtas.ie/dail/1987/10/15/00022.asp#N12

42.   *Ibid.*

43.   *Ibid.*

44.   *Ireland Since 1939: The Persistence of Conflict*, pg 287

45.   *Ibid.*

46.   *The Changing Landscape of Irish Migration, 2000-2012*, pg 11, Table 7

# 9.

## THE NORWEGIAN EXPERIENCE: A CASE STUDY FOR IRELAND?

Helge Ryggvik and Aileen Canning

### INTRODUCTION BY AILEEN CANNING

In talking about oil and gas resource management, Norway is often referenced as the 'poster boy', an illustration of how collective interests can be maximised over pure profit and a model from which other countries can learn.

Dr Helge Ryggvik's seminal report is as powerful now as it was in 2010, when it was produced as a background document for those dealing with multinational energy companies who want to replicate the success that Norway harvested from its oil and gas.

This is of course immediately relevant to Ireland, as we face economic crises coupled with a situation where oil and gas extraction is now recognised as a potential way to address this.

Like Ireland, Norway's 1970s entry into the world of oil and gas extraction started from scratch, but the country has managed over the past forty years to develop one of the world's largest sovereign wealth funds, and to transform Norwegian society on this basis. In Ireland, by contrast, the argument of dependence on multinational companies has been used at every turn to divest the state (and Irish society) of these same resources and their economic benefits.

So why not read this fascinating case study and make up your own minds? Then you can truly answer the question, 'If not me, then who?'

### INTRODUCTION BY HELGE RYGGVIK

It was December 2004. In Caracas, Hugo Chavez called for a round of applause for Norwegian oil. Even in Latin America, Norwegian oil policy and Statoil were perceived as the only successful examples of a country which secured national direction of oil resources to ensure that profits were channelled to its citizens.

People's interest is piqued in two ways:

- Norway has developed an industry which can master all the challenges

- Norway has managed to find oil but nevertheless remains an egalitarian state. How can others learn from the respect it has garnered?

The first thing to be said must be that Norway started with luck. The discovery of the Ekofisk North Sea field in 1969 could not have come at a better time for Norway. The developments in Third World countries (Mexico, Iran) and the development of OPEC in 1951 had paved the way.

In 2010, oil is easily Norway's most important industry. Norway now has an economy whose main players have the same underlying interests as those companies that early Norwegian oil policy sought to protect the country from. Social groups, individuals and politics converge to mobilise, intervene, and so change the course of the economy and life.

## Oil: The state's property, the people's property

In 1962, one of the largest prospectors met with the Norwegian Minister Lied and Arve Johnsen, Minister Lied's permanent secretary. Lied's aim was to entice foreign companies to establish themselves there. In neighbouring Denmark, Gulf and Shell had secured monopoly rights. Instead of going this way, he took time to think about it and assigned expert civil servants to the task, and secured an agreement that gave Norway sovereignty. At that point few people, either in the public or in politics, knew how vital this time would be.

Foreign oil companies (mainly US) thought that Norway would set strict labour conditions as a socialist state. However, the advising government lawyer, Everson, made it possible for them to meet both sets of interests. At the outset there was no domestic know-how in the area so the committee sought to exploit the companies' expertise whilst protecting national interests. This led to a 1965 cabinet decree that all firms had to sign in order to be allocated concessions, but also protected the State's sovereign right of intervention and regulation of these firms. The overall goal was to get international companies to commit fully – to increase the probability of actually finding oil. First-round measures included:

- Health and safety of workers

- Extraction rights to gigantic tracts for six years, with rolling optional 'giving-up' of rights at three-year intervals (up to a maximum of forty-six years) and extension to guarantee Norway its rights

- Royalties set at 10 percent (the State taking a percentage of wealth) rather than taxation of profits

Norway was in a weak negotiating position – but had no alternative. It did, however, take a huge risk by opening a large proportion of its assets at what seemed like good terms for other countries. However, we must bear in mind that Norway was competing with the UK in a game where the tactic of multinationals was 'we will take our business elsewhere'. When the large Ekofisk field was found by Phillips, the State could have benefited from greater returns were there better terms. It is fair to say that in this first round of concessions, Norway oil policy would hardly have proven the model it has become. Luckily, most oil was to be found north of the area advertised in the first round. The message for others is:

- Don't give too much away in the first round

- Take the time to set up a legal framework

- Make sure this framework is flexible enough so that the State can tighten rules when conditions change.

The energy of Norwegian waterfalls had been given by nature. Its value should not go to any individual. The new waterfall laws determined that the energy, and hence the value, which could be collected from the big waterfalls belonged to the state, and hence the public. This was, of course, a radical encroachment on forest owners and large farmers, who often owned the wood and land on both sides of the river banks.

Conservative politicians protested loudly. But since the Norwegian state lacked both technology and capital, it depended initially on others to exploit this water power. In the first instance, therefore, major waterfalls were exploited by foreign-owned industrial companies. German and French capital and technology predominated. It was emphasised, however, that companies such as the large fertiliser producer Norsk Hydro should not own the energy. The provisional nature and lease character of these allocations was made clear through the so-called *escheat (hjemfallsrett)*, which was a central, if contested, part of the concession regime. Under the new law, all exploitation rights which were allocated were to return to the state, without compensation, after sixty years. With the help of this concessions law, the State subsequently managed to acquire the know-how needed to exploit hydro power.

When the oil companies came to Norway in the 1960s, the vast majority of hydro power production was thus publicly owned and operated. It was therefore entirely natural that the allocation of rights for prospecting for and potential extraction of oil and gas conformed to the legal approach and ideology which were already built into the existing Norwegian concessions regime. Norway had the experience of hydro power. Denmark – flat and dominated by agriculture – did not.

Thus it was not a particularly radical moment when the Norwegian government agreed on a cabinet decree on 31 May 1963 determining that 'The ocean floor and the underground of the underwater areas off the coast of the Kingdom of Norway are under Norwegian sovereignty as regards the exploitation and research of natural deposits.' Since there were no previous private owners, it was a straightforward matter for the state to declare itself the proprietor.

## A Radical, National Oil Policy

All of this coincided in the late 1960s/1970s with growing nationalism (the 1968 rebellion), and they took a hard and uncompromising approach, rather than the previous 'softly-softly' regime in negotiating with the skilled Americans.

And so began a new State company – Statoil – a completely new 100 percent state-owned company, to give the nation as much governance and control as possible.

The history of oil is full of examples of how controlling the transport network has been of decisive importance as to who secures the greatest possible share of oil rents. Being non-renewable, and given that 95 percent of the world's total oil production happens in 1,500 fields (with 40,000 registered), in the long-term controlling this 'economic rent' is nearly as important as the oil itself.

In Norway, the Ekofisk deal didn't state this explicitly. Were Phillips to have full control of transport, the company could have used this to secure rent from other oil fields using ownership rights. Civil servants had already signalled their agreement to this, but Johnsen sought a Statoil-owned and controlled entity to do so. The Americans were shocked – and are said to have shouted 'this is immoral' – but civil servants and, indeed, Johnsen (who was now outside government) had no authority to make demands. Phillips believed it was the rightful owner of everything to do with Ekofisk, without a formal agreement.

In the end, Phillips had to give in, but Norway had experienced for the first time how foreign companies could use lobbying and power to establish unshakeable positions in the absence of an opposing power.

## Strategic Ownership and Control

The next battle was over the role that the state and Statoil might play in future concession rounds. Johnsen wanted Statoil to have a 50 percent ownership share, which was granted in 1973. It was argued that too large a share might scare foreign companies away. The remainder of this field – Statfjord – was split among Mobil, Esso, Shell and Conoco. They were far from dismayed when the size of the find was revealed.

At that point, oil prices had risen four times in a year. Statoil's dominant position was entirely decisive, not just for Statoil but for Norway. Never was a field as large found again.

Again, Norway discovered that it was only by challenging foreign firms that real gains were to be made. A general rule for nations is that early agreements and decisions have massive implications.

## GOVERNANCE AND CONTROL

Johnsen was able to win so many battles for Statoil because he had solid political support and didn't operate in a vacuum. The state authorised a large number of reports studying all aspects of the industry, and all ministries and industry committees drew on the general expertise available, which was followed by debate. This led to a steep learning curve, but a great body of knowledge. They were also far-seeing: including socio-economic concerns, such as $CO_2$ concerns in an era before awareness of global warming, but also recognising that short-sighted self-interest might lead companies to cherry-pick and, hence, were Norway to benefit, it would not be enough to simply tax. Instead, Norway should develop its own national capacity. This meant not only securing the greatest share of wealth-creation, but also developing technological know-how.

## A MODERATE PACE AND A 'QUALITATIVELY BETTER SOCIETY'

The most far-reaching of all the reports from this period is White Paper Number 25 on 'The role of petroleum activities in Norwegian Society' (1974), which stated that the wealth from oil should be used to develop a 'qualitatively better society,' taking account of environmental concerns. The paper underlines how important it is for elected bodies to control all aspects of policy and, especially, the pace of development. It states:

> Wishing for a long-term perspective on the exploitation of resources, and after a comprehensive review of its social aspects, the Government has concluded that Norway should take a moderate pace in the extraction of petroleum resources.

This meant that oil and gas could be extracted in a defensible way, the conversion costs of adaptation to a new industry would not become too large, and the resources would last for longer. The paper assumed that the oil crisis – then at its height – would end with falling prices, rather than the oil running out. Rather than giving in to external pressures for maximum extraction, Norway should enter the oil industry with good intentions for a better society.

## MAXIMISING OIL RENTS

An oil-producing nation must do what it can to secure the greatest possible share of oil rent. If it needs foreign technology and capital to gain access to oil, it is reasonable to believe that companies involved should not earn more than the average profits for other purely capital-ist industries. Classical economists – Smith, Ricardo, George – would agree. Distributing economic rent in its entirety should fall to society via the state in question. And precisely because limited natural resources are unequally distributed, oil-producing countries have a moral responsibility – knowing what we know now about oil contributing to climate change – globally, to countries that do not have access to reserves of their own. Where production is allowed, both morally and economically, Norway's approach of moderate extraction is borne out.

## National Governance and Control

The pillars of the Norwegian approach were:

1. securing the greatest possible share of the rent from oil for the State, which would distribute it in an egalitarian way across Norwegian society

2. establishment of a state oil company

3. establishment of a petroleum directorate with national responsibility for both socially responsible resource administration and safety

4. support for the establishment of a strong national contractor industry

5. a political guarantee that the pace of extraction and investment would be a mod-erate one, so that other sectors would not be marginalised and resources would last

6. an emphasis on extraction taking place in an environmentally justifiable way.

## A Holding Company or a State Company with Operative Capacity?

Norwegian leaders were aware that the establishment of state oil companies was prevalent throughout the Middle East and Latin America, but also in Europe. In fact, Norway was one of the few countries not to have taken this route, with BP in Great Britain, ENI in Italy and Elf/Total in France. Even Sweden ran a co-operative for petrol stations and refineries (OK).

But there were major differences between BP, which had been created to secure oil sup-plies for a colonial power and the OPEC state companies, which were created to ensure that oil rent went to the nation. So on the political right, there was a view that Statoil would be limited to a holding company managing state ownership. Johnsen, however, was determined that the State should not only become an operator, but should – in the same way as the very largest oil companies – secure positions at each stage, from upstream prospecting/production down to refining and even the chemical industry and the sale of oil products. His mantra, 'We must conquer the strategic heights,' sums up the strategy behind Statoil. At the same time, Norwegian universities started training students for the new industry's needs.

## TECHNOLOGICAL POWER AND PIPELINES

Statoil first developed its knowledge of laying pipelines. This coincided with the technological and political role that it needed to challenge the power of foreign companies. For Phillips, the choice was simple. The markets for Ekofisk oil and gas were in Europe and the UK. The rugged terrain meant that it made more economic sense to build pipelines directly from the field than to bring the oil and gas onshore in Norway and then send it back out again. Also, Norway didn't need much oil because it had hydro power. Norway felt it was being dictated to by Phillips but at this stage couldn't challenge their technological expertise. The same situation happened in Frigg in 1974.

In contrast with this, when the Statfjord field was developed in 1979, Statoil set up its own engineering department to develop a pipeline ashore, paying 100 million kroner to various subcontractors for exploration. When Johnsen was asked which decision had been the most important in the company's early years, he said it was the 1981 parliamentary decision to construct the Statpipe, which was to bring the Statfjord gas ashore just north of Stavanger, to be processed and then shipped back across the Norwegian Trench. Johnsen was probably right. The Statpipe and the conquest of the Norwegian Trench at last was probably the single moment where Statoil most clearly realised what had been a central goal at its foundation. Statoil had done what was politically desirable – and technologically feasible. None of the many petroleum-related projects along the Norwegian coast could have been realised if the Statpipe project had not succeeded. By 1985, gas from Statfjord could be transported underwater to Germany via an onshore processing terminal in Norway.

## 'STRATEGIC HEIGHTS'

Statoil took over the operation in Statjford from Mobil in 1986, an important year for Norway. Statoil also took over production on the Gullfaks field the same year. With Statoil holding a majority share (91 percent) and Norsk Hydro the remainder, it was 100 percent Norwegian-owned field. This meant that the development of Gullfaks took place in parallel with the takeover of Statfjord, giving Statoil two different strategic bases. The control that came from owning and operating two of the North Sea's largest fields was without doubt the most important 'height' gained in Statoil's position under Johnsen.

They were not the only ones though, as the company established a solid position in the downstream aspect of the oil industry. Socio-economically it is very important – both for oil-producing countries and those who import – to ensure the greatest possible ripple effects associated with processing oil and gas.

It is hard for oil-reserve-rich countries to understand the political economy of the downstream side of activities, because companies are playing a strategic game where the goal is primarily to secure access to large oil fields. In Norway, Johnsen and Statoil had the strategic aim of establishing a fully integrated oil company with independent positions at all stages of the production chain. Establishing downstream activities was shaped by tactical positioning to secure their more important goal – lucrative allocations in future concession rounds.

## TAX AND NEGOTIATING POWER

The wave of nationalisations and attempts at establishing local oil capacity that took place in oil-producing countries during the 1970s was replaced by a neo-liberal counter-wave in the 1980s. Proponents believed that oil-producing states should leave the oil industry to established oil companies that had mastered the technology. This meant that tax was to be the vehicle for competitive advantage, but did not take into account the concept of economic rent. No country was to place barriers in international investment and all forms of protectionism to support local industry had to be combated because they disrupted competition. Direct state involvement in industrial activity was condemned.

This kind of thinking has on occasion led to the proposition that Norway should also have relied on the services offered by foreign companies, and that all attempts at localising the industry entailed large additional costs which reduced profits and, in turn, reduced the possibilities for taxing the companies. This would have done little for Norway in socio-economic terms. This was clear to the ministries and it would not have been possible to secure a correspondingly high tax-take for the Norwegian state if it had not held a technologically skilled Statoil in reserve, which could take over everything if the companies held back.

All the companies protested, saying that they would rethink their futures in Norway. The Ministry of Industry was sympathetic, but the Finance Ministry held its ground. Its underlying understanding was the same as in the Norwegian power regime – the State had to aim for the greatest possible share of fields like Ekofisk to go to the community. They believed that as long as profits were comparable to other industries, the companies would stay in Norway. And if they did, a Norwegian company which was in train could be an alternative. Even Phillips chose to conform rather than risking losing Ekofisk. Norway's negotiating strength was based on the fact that it had an alternative.

The first major strategic oil policy conflict in Norway was about bringing pipelines ashore. This has been echoed through history – ownership of pipes and choice of routes have always been significant both for who secured the oil rent and the economic side benefits. In Bolivia, the international oil industry wanted to build a pipeline over the Andes to the

Pacific coast in order to export oil to American consumers rather than building a distribution network that could contribute to economic development in the area.

## EMPLOYING A LOCAL WORKFORCE

Early on in Norway, the American company Odeco brought in workers from Mexico who owned the rigs and drills. However they also employed Norwegian workers – at lower wages, and for logistical reasons (e.g. the caterers were simply nearer). Despite providing ripple effects locally, it was difficult for Norwegian workers to break into strategic areas. Statoil's 50 percent ownership of the Statfjord field was to prove decisive once again. Johnsen had discovered that it was easy to get foreign companies to accept Norwegian contractors in ancillary services (such as catering) but not in core activities. He saw that this had to be addressed, and persuaded Mobil to give the engineering tasks to Norwegian engineering firm NPC. Learning from an American firm on one platform, they then led on other platforms.

Norway's experience would have looked very different without the many strategic interventions of Johnsen. Historical timing was key. In the first wave, foreign companies dominated – in the second wave, Norwegian. Norway established protectionism in line with other OPEC nations, which was still possible in the 1970s/1980s. However, later, the IMF/World Bank/GATT and the creation of the internal market led to pressure for Norway to conform. In the 1990s, with globalisation, it was argued that national ownership and control was no longer the key issue but rather holding on to the workforce and know-how. This is certainly important, but strategic ownership and control – whether for a company or a contractor – is decisive. Private owners, as the Transocean example shows, have little loyalty to national interests when foreign buyers can offer enough money.

Norway joined the EU's internal market with the European Economic Area (EEA) in 1993, and indirect protectionist measures in the contractors' market had to be removed. However, the know-how was by then in Norway, and legal adherence to Norwegian safety standards remained. In addition, Norwegian pay rates applied. This was decisive.

## FROM A MODERATE PACE TO THE LEADERS IN QUICK EXTRACTION

A large percentage of global oil lies in economically poorer regions, whereas consumption takes places in richer parts. These nations are therefore engaged in modern-day imperialism. However, international conditions mean that these economies are based on collecting rent, not on productive work. In an oil economy, however, the elite, in alliance with foreign oil firms, can manage without its own population – simply managing civil unrest where it needs to.

The fact that so many oil-producing countries look to Norway that means there is awareness of this. Interest in Norway is particularly great in countries where initial advantages seem large, and where the fields are in environmentally vulnerable areas. This may mean that an overall social evaluation may conclude that resources should remain underground. Hence, the Norwegian experience has to be seen in the context of not being hit by the curse of oil – instead, most Norwegians have already received a share of economic rent from the North Sea reserves, which is injected into the Norwegian economy.

However, that might change. Even in Norway, companies are aggressively seeking access to one of the country's most naturally beautiful and environmentally vulnerable areas. BP stated in 2009[1] that the reserves/production (RP) ratio show that Norway only had 8.3 years of oil production left, at current levels. Venezuela, Iran and Saudi Arabia had 91.3, 86.2 and 69.5 years left, respectively. Norway started late, but even the US, which started 150 years ago, has 11.7 years. This proves that Norway has been extracting its oil very quickly. The only countries worse placed than Norway are Thailand, Colombia and Great Britain (six years), but the first two may have undetected reserves in rainforest.

The Petroleum Directorate was created as a neutral instrument to ensure that the most socially appropriate extraction of oil reserves was achieved, and whilst it has played this role, it is now more closely allied to the interests of the industry in the withdrawal phase and presenting this optimistically, with future finds.

What the authorities highlight is the level of the petroleum fund – the Government Pension Fund – which stands in excess of $820 billion at the time of writing.[2] This fund is a direct result of the intensive pace of extraction. If Norway had used the oil money in the ordinary economy as it flowed in, there would have been negative consequences. Given the accelerated pace of extraction, saving the profit was entirely logical. But the alternative – slower extraction – may well have given Norway far higher profits. In the 2000s the price of oil has risen far more than the investments the petroleum industry has made.

To those who argue about keeping the oil income outside public finances, it is worth noting that it was not until the 2000s that the fund really expanded. Before this, in thirty years of extraction, the fund was as low as less than 200 bn kroner in 1998. Indeed, during the 1970s–1990s, money was pumped into welfare and public services. The money placed in the fund in the 2000s follows on from expenditure, so from that thesis, Norway has a very oil-dependent economy.

## THE CLIMATE DILEMMA

Since 1991, Norway has introduced a tax on $CO_2$ emissions – both petrol and linked to oil production. This was different from other countries, which often subsidised petrol for their own citizens. This tax was so high that petrol prices were higher than in neighbouring Sweden, which didn't have its own production. Norway's climate policy debate has strong actors: the oil industry on one side and environmentalists on the other. The former argue that since their emissions are lower than others', raising production is not destructive (and remains cleaner than coal), but the latter point out that emissions from Norwegian oil occur elsewhere in the world and, hence, Norway can massage its calculations.

## A Ruined Model?

Norwegian society's struggle to secure national governance and control of the oil meant limiting the power of foreign oil companies. But there is a danger that these national institutions simply became interest groups themselves – a concept described by Eisenhower as the 'oil-industrial complex', whereby an industrial/political network was opposed to society's needs. Rapid growth in Norway had that potential. The Petroleum Directorate's safety regulation function, started as an independent branch of the ministry and now the Petroleum Safety Authority, provided an institutional counter-balance to Statoil's dominance as a source of expertise.

In 1990, there was a comprehensive review of Statoil's goal. It was to conquer the international oil world, and establish it as a key player alongside others with ownership, production and operations on every continent. This coincided with the breakup of the Soviet Bloc and, hence, the opening of new regions to the international oil industry overnight. Since production in Norway peaked in 2001, and Statoil had such a central position, it couldn't maintain profitability without creating projects abroad – and, moreover, these had to be at a level that it could collect within its period as a protected company in Norway.

It is somewhat ironic that the company that had been created to ensure that the greatest possible oil rent went to Norwegian society was now to seek access not just to normal profits but to oil rent from other countries' reserves.

## Concluding Remarks

The Norwegian oil experience appears to be a success overall. Through Statoil, strategic state ownership, the strong, professional Petroleum Directorate and, above all, the continual build-up of technological knowhow, Norway has managed to ensure that most of the economic rent from its oil has gone to the State – and, hence, to society.

Although, in recent decades, Norway has followed developments in many other countries, and the income differences between a rich elite and the majority of the population have grown, the core of the Norwegian welfare state model is still intact. A significant portion of the oil fortune has gone to expand and improve it.

When oil income exceeded what was needed to strengthen the Norwegian welfare state model, the rest was placed in a fund for future use. In this way, Norway avoided being hit by the most extreme form of the curse of oil.

The international oil industry prefers to regulate itself. Yet, even if Norway has had its accidents and environmental emissions, it has developed an advanced regulation system that has demonstrably reduced the risk of operating advanced petroleum installations at sea.

However, the final judgement on the Norwegian experience belongs to the future. As a small country on the periphery of Europe, what happens now will depend on developments in the rest of the world, just as it has in the past.

There is no single Norwegian oil experience. The Norwegian oil experience has come about through constant conflict among interest groups. Norwegian oil experiences, therefore, are the product of an active democracy – a democracy which has not only expressed itself through formal parliamentary representation, but equally through direct popular mobilisation.

Therefore, the greater the degree of openness and general popular oversight of political priorities and decisive technological choices, the better a society will be able to manage a strategic energy resource in a way that benefits society as a whole.

## ABOUT THE AUTHORS

This 2010 report was originally produced by Dr Helge Ryggvik at the Centre for Technology, Innovation and Culture (TIK-Centre) at the University of Oslo, who holds a DPhil in history. As a researcher and economic historian, Helge's methodological approaches are comprehensive, from a broad political economy approach to more specific analyses of humans' relations to technology. A common empirical starting point for many of his studies is the oil industry. Recently, Helge has worked for the Norwegian Petroleum Museum on a project initiated by the Norwegian Parliament about Norwegian offshore oil divers.

This is a condensed version of the original report, which has been edited by Aileen Canning. Aileen is an Irish regulatory professional who has worked in the postal, telecoms and energy sectors at senior level in both semi-states and regulators, and holds degrees from Dublin City University (BBS) and ILM (Graduate Diploma in Strategic Leadership). She is skilled in translating academic concepts into presentations and easy-to-access documents for those interested in infrastructure issues and, in particular, has an interest in relating this to Ireland.

## NOTES

1. BP Statistical Review of World Energy 2009,' pg 6. BP's annual statistics give a good overview of the development of the world's energy production. www.BP.com

2. business.financialpost.com/2014/01/08/how-all-norwegians-became-crown-millionaires-theoretically-from-an-oil-saving-landmark

# 10.

# THE PLANNING AND ENVIRONMENTAL REGULATORY SYSTEM
## Dermot Flanagan

## SUMMARY

There are numerous administrative bodies including government departments whose functions, powers and duties touch upon the prevention and/or control of environmental risk as that relates to onshore and offshore activities for oil and gas exploration, drilling and extraction.

This chapter reviews the current regulatory framework for environmental compliance and considers changes to the existing framework. This is viewed in the context of obligations primarily at the EU level in relation to the planning- and emissions-based regulatory processes.

It considers the need to separate political, economic and environmental interests associated with oil and gas exploration, drilling and extraction, together with the need to ensure that best technical expertise and practice is brought to the assessment of environmental risk by appropriate expert bodies taking into account public health and safety in the human and natural environments.

## OVERVIEW OF EXISTING SUPERVISION

The Department of Communications, Energy and Natural Resources/Petroleum Affairs Division (DCENR/PAD) is primarily responsible for oil and gas exploration in Ireland. This includes the promotion, regulation and monitoring of exploration and development of oil and gas both onshore and offshore.

Ireland's foreshore extends from the low-water mark to 12 nautical miles (nm), the vast majority of which is state-owned. Ireland's exclusive economic zone is the area stretching from the outer boundary of the foreshore to 200 nm, except where we share boundaries with other countries within this limit. From 200 nm to 350 nm out to sea or to the end of the topographical continental shelf is known as the continental shelf.

The high seas are governed by the United Nations Convention on the Law of the Sea. The foreshore, under Irish legislation, comprises Ireland's territorial sea. Within the exclusive economic zone (EEZ), Ireland is entitled to exercise sovereign rights over natural resources, and has full jurisdiction over marine scientific research and the protection of the marine environment. The EEZ covers the water column, seabed and subsoil. In the continental shelf, Ireland exercises a limited form of jurisdiction over marine protection and has sovereign rights to natural resources in, on or under the seabed but these rights do not extend to the water above, which is part of the high seas. In summary, within the areas of the foreshore, EEZ and continental shelf, Ireland may implement a development-consent process for projects.

Legislation associated with environmental control of petroleum activities includes the Petroleum and Minerals Development Act 1960 as amended by subsequent acts and regulations including the Continental Shelf Act 1968, the Gas Act 1976, the Energy Miscellaneous Provisions Acts 1995 and 2006, the Sea Pollution Act 1991, the Dumping at Sea Act 1996, and legislation giving effect to EU Directives such as the Strategic Environmental Assessment (SEA) Directive, the Environmental Impact Assessment (EIA) Directive, and the Habitats and Birds Directive.

Historically, under the department's licensing terms, the holder of a petroleum lease is required to submit a detailed plan of development and the minister has discretion to require the submission of an environmental impact statement under the EIA Directive.

There are five different types of authorisations:

1. petroleum prospecting conferring on the licensee a right to search for petroleum in any part of the Irish offshore which is not subject to an exploration reserved area licence or petroleum lease granted to another party;

2. a licence option conferring a right to an exploration licence;

3. an exploration licence giving an exclusive right to search for petroleum including a standard exploration licence, deep-water exploration licence and frontier exploration licence;

4. a lease undertaking to grant a petroleum lease in relation to that part of the licensed area which contains a discovery;

5. a petroleum lease where there is a commercial discovery.

There have been a number of strategic environmental assessments (SEAs) of the offshore areas carried out by or on behalf of the DCENR.

## INTER-RELATIONSHIPS AT THE LEGISLATIVE LEVEL

### Dumping at Sea

The Dumping at Sea Act 1996 prohibits the dumping within the maritime area of any substance or material unless specifically permitted. The 1996 Act describes 'the maritime area' as comprising the territorial seas of the State, the seabed and the subsoil beneath the seas. Among matters described as 'dumping' are the disposal in the maritime area of offshore installations and the deliberate disposal in the maritime area of a substance or material from an offshore installation. The 1996 Act refers to 'offshore activities' as being activities carried out in the sea for the purpose of the exploration, appraisal or exploitation of liquid or gaseous hydrocarbons. 'Offshore installations' means any man-made structure, plant or vessel or parts thereof, whether floating or fixed to the said seabed, placed for the purpose of offshore activities. The 1996 Act also contains a prohibition on the incineration of substances or material in the maritime area but excludes the thermal destruction of substances derived from the normal operation of an offshore installation. It is an offence to deliberately dispose of or to permit the disposal in the maritime area of an offshore installation or any substance or material from any such installation.

Section 5 of the 1996 Act conferred on the Minister the right to grant a permit authorising the dumping of an offshore installation. Among the considerations and conditions to apply to the granting of such a permit is its interference with shipping, fishing, areas of scientific importance and the practical availability of alternative land-based methods of treatment disposal or elimination. The Act further provides for exceptions to the prohibition on dumping where permits have been issued by the competent authority of a contracting party, and this also relates to disused offshore installations. The contracting parties are, under that Act, obliged to refuse to issue a permit if the disused offshore installation contains substances which are hazardous to human health, living resources or the marine ecosystems.

Subsequent amendments granted these functions to the EPA. The Act also amended Section 5 of the Act of 1996 (permits in relation to dumping) by giving the EPA the power to grant a permit to any person authorising the dumping of an offshore installation. In making such an application, a person must provide information that will satisfy the EPA that there is no suitable alternative means of disposal of the offshore installation or substance or other material concerned. This Act also provides for a power of authorised officers to carry out an inspection of any offshore installations.

### Foreshore

Under the Foreshore Acts 1933-2009, an environmental impact statement in respect of cer-

tain projects carried out within the foreshore is assessed by the Minister, including the imposition of conditions in respect of any activities on the foreshore. The 2009 Foreshore
Amendment Act transferred functions previously exercised by the Minister for Agriculture
to the Minister for the Environment in relation to the foreshore. This includes the extraction of a natural resource from the foreshore – Section 6(1) of the 2009 Act.

## Commission for Energy Regulation (CER)

The Petroleum (Exploration and Extraction) Safety Act 2010 gave the Commission for
Energy Regulation (CER) new functions in the area of exploration and extraction. Since
April 2010, the CER has had responsibility for regulating petroleum undertakings with
respect to safety.

The term 'licensed area' means any part of the State, including the internal waters of the
State, the territorial seas of the State and a designated area under the Continental Shelf Act
1968. The areas of offshore include the foreshore. The term 'petroleum authorisation'
includes exploration licences, petroleum prospecting licences, reserved area licences and various petroleum and other lease and consents granted under various acts relating to both
onshore and offshore areas. The term 'petroleum infrastructure' includes facilities, structures and installations including onshore and offshore facilities or a combination of such
facilities, installations or structures and includes offshore processing. The term 'petroleum'
includes mineral oil and natural gas or other liquid or gaseous hydrocarbons and their deriv-
atives that are ordinarily produced from oil and gas wells and other substances contained in
oil and natural gas brought to the surface in the normal process of extraction, but does not
include coal or bituminous shales or other stratified deposits from which oil can be extracted by distillation.

The activities connected with a petroleum authorisation or petroleum infrastructure carried out in a licensed area include petroleum exploration in the seabed or subsoil, including
petroleum infrastructure for the drilling of wells and subsequent extraction and processing
including offshore storage and loading of petroleum. It also includes activities relating to the
conveyance of unprocessed, partially processed or fully processed petroleum by subsea
pipelines or vessels and petroleum infrastructure including the onshore section of any sub-
sea pipeline. It also includes activities relating to the processing of petroleum at a processing plant or terminal or offshore installation or other similar facility and activities relating to
the decommissioning of petroleum infrastructure.

Under that Act there is a prohibition against the carrying on of designated petroleum
activities without a safety permit. The principal objective of the CER in exercising its functions is to protect the public in respect of safety matters in the carrying on of designated
petroleum activities. It is a statutory duty of any petroleum undertaking to carry on its activ-

ities in such a manner as to reduce any risk to safety, and that any petroleum infrastructure is designed, constructed, installed, maintained and operated in a manner so as to reduce any risk to safety. The test is 'as low as is reasonably practicable'.

The CER has the power to refuse or revoke a safety permit in certain circumstances, including non-compliance with conditions attached to a permit.

### An Bord Pleanála

An Bord Pleanála is an independent statutory body conferred with specialist administrative decision-making powers in relation to the physical planning process for land-based (and some foreshore-based) infrastructure projects established in 1976.

### Environmental Protection Agency (EPA)

The EPA is an independent statutory body conferred with specialist administrative decision-making powers in relation to emissions-based activities, established in 1992. The functions generally of the EPA are provided for in Section 52 of the 1992 Act, and include the licensing, regulation and control of activities for the purpose of environmental protection. The First Schedule to the Environmental Protection Agency Act 1992 provides for integrated pollution control, and Article 9.1 of the First Schedule provides for integrated pollution control for 'the extraction, other than offshore extraction, of petroleum, natural gas, coal or shale'.[1]

### PRECEDENT: CORRIB GAS DEVELOPMENT PROJECT – CURRENT DECISION-MAKING

An analysis of the Corrib Gas Development Project establishes the regulatory cross-referenced decision-making for oil and gas exploration. In 2001, the Corrib developers sought a petroleum lease pursuant to the 1960 Act. This included a draft development plan.

- In November 2001 the Minister granted a petroleum lease and an application was submitted to the Minister for approval of a draft development plan, which was granted in April 2002.

- An application for consent to construct a pipeline pursuant to the 1976 Gas Act (Pipeline Authorisation) was also made in November 2001, accompanied by an environmental impact statement. The minister granted the pipeline authorisation in April 2002.

- An application to the Minister for consent under Section 5 of the Continental Shelf Act 1968 was submitted in April 2001 and was consent granted in April 2002.

- An application to the Minister for a foreshore licence under Section 3 of the Foreshore Act 1933, accompanied by an Environmental Impact Statement, was granted in May 2002.

Planning permission for the onshore terminal accompanied by an environmental impact statement was sought in April 2001, appealed to An Bord Pleanála and refused. In October 2004, planning permission was granted by An Bord Pleanála for a gas terminal and an associated peat deposition site. In 2011 An Bord Pleanála granted approval for an onshore pipeline by way of amendment.

An application was made to the Environmental Protection Agency for an integrated pollution prevention and control (IPPC) licence for a gas terminal and was granted in November 2007 pursuant to Section 83 of the EPA Acts 1992-2003. On 5 June 2013 the EPA granted an IPPC licence in respect of the operation of a refinery for the gas terminal.

## Environmental Impact Assessment – Independent Accountability?

The European Union, Environmental Impact Assessment (Gas) Regulations 2012, the European Union Environmental Impact Assessment (Petroleum) Regulations 2012 and the European Union Environmental Impact Assessment (Petroleum Exploration) Regulations 2013 transpose EIA directives into domestic law. In both the gas and petroleum regulations of 2012, it is the Minister for Energy who is responsible for the environmental impact assessment.

An example of a situation in which environmental issues remain attached, in the legal sense, to political structures is found in Statutory Instrument 134 of 2013, the European Union (Environmental Impact Assessment) (Petroleum Exploration) Regulations 2013. In summary, these regulations envisage environmental impact assessment in relation to exploration and prospecting licences, whether in the case of onshore or offshore prospection or exploration activities. Article 3 provides that, where the holder of a licence proposes to undertake activities under the licence, the holder shall apply to the Minister for Communications, Energy and Natural Resources for permission to undertake the activities and it is for the Minister to consider whether or not environmental impact assessment in respect of the activities which are the subject of the application is appropriate.

Environmental impact assessment under Article 4 envisages the production at first instance of an environmental statement and the making of submissions and/or observations and appropriate consultation with relevant bodies. In carrying out the environmental impact assessment, the minister has to have regard to all the submissions made and any reports prepared by officers of that department or by any consultants, experts or other advisers.

## Comment/Analysis

Under these regulations it is for the Minister and the Minister alone to decide on the application. This contrasts with the form of external consent envisaged before An Bord Pleanála in relation to many public infrastructure and private infrastructure projects in the nature of strategic infrastructure, whereby application for approval/consent is made to An Bord Pleanála and where An Bord Pleanála conducts an environmental impact assessment. While this relates to the physical planning process, the inter-relationship between that and emissions is reflected in the legislation requiring such activities to be the subject of separate licensing by the Environmental Protection Agency in circumstances where environmental impact assessment is carried out in parallel by the EPA. In this way, both the physical works and the emissions arising from the activity are subject to external scrutiny and consent by An Bord Pleanála and the Environmental Protection Agency respectively.

## KEY ISSUE – PHYSICAL PLANNING AND EMISSIONS – ENVIRONMENTAL CONTROL

The key question moving forward can be described as the inter-relationship between the Department (DCENR/PAD), the Commission for Energy Regulation (CER) and An Bord Pleanála in relation to the physical planning process and the EPA in relation to emissions-based environmental pollution control.

## Comment/Analysis

The current regulatory regime accords to ministers of government key decision-making for environmental risk. There remains a significant fault line or separation line between petroleum extraction and drilling activities as they relate to onshore and offshore activities. At the level of principle, there is no reason why there should be such a distinction made, other than for 'political' considerations.

Such an approach fails to recognise the existing expertise within An Bord Pleanála and the EPA, both of which have proven track records in environmental risk assessment. The extension of this role to the offshore industry is perhaps the most unexplained aspect of the current regulatory regime. These bodies with significant technical expertise in the areas of environmental and planning risk are excluded from granting consent and/or approval.

At the level of principle, the question is why An Bord Pleanála and the EPA should not be conferred with jurisdiction insofar as it relates to offshore activities including foreshore. For example, the EPA legislation excluded integrated pollution control for offshore extraction. When one looks at the activities identified under the heading 'fossil fuels' in Paragraph 9 of the first schedule to the Act, the agency has clearly been conferred with the specialist administrative responsibilities for dealing with all onshore activities relating to fossil fuel extraction, storage, refining and related processing installations. Apart from political considerations, it is inexplicable that the EPA be excluded from exercising appropriate regulatory control of offshore activities.

This also begs the question as to how and in what manner specialist bodies such as An Bord Pleanála and/or the EPA can apply their technical administrative decision-making to matters which are currently within the control of the minister, PAD and/or the CER.

## MARITIME SPATIAL PLANNING AND INTEGRATED COASTAL MANAGEMENT

In May 2013, the European Commission published proposals for a directive of the European Parliament and of the European Council establishing a framework for maritime spatial planning and integrated coastal management.[2]

The aim of this is to draw up plans to identify the utilisation of maritime space for different sea uses. It is clear that this proposal envisages spatial planning in the context of strategic environmental assessment under Directive 2001/42/EC. Thereafter it envisages environmental impact assessments for individual projects. Article 7 of the draft proposal envisages maritime spatial plans taking into consideration, inter alia, oil and gas extraction sites and infrastructure, energy extraction installations and pipeline routes. Article 9 of the draft proposal envisages public participation of relevant stakeholders and authorities. Article 11 provides that such spatial plans or integrated coastal management strategies be subject to strategic environmental assessment.

There is provision for the designation of a competent authority for the implementation of the proposed directive.

## EIA AND COMPULSORY ACQUISITION – THE COMMON GOOD

### Discussion

Under the Petroleum and Other Minerals Development Act 1960, there is provision for the Minister to exercise compulsory acquisition powers relevant to the activities referred to.

Since the Planning and Development Act 2000, many of the functions previously conferred on either the Minister for the Environment or public authorities in relation to confirmation of compulsory purchase orders has been vested in An Bord Pleanála. This is an external consent process like the one under the environmental impact assessment process.

In practical terms, compulsory acquisition orders and environment impact statements are submitted concurrently to An Bord Pleanála for the purposes of considering the public need to be met by the acquisition in question and the assessment of the impacts on the receiving environment. Concurrently, it is usual that issues relating to emissions control are the subject of a licence regime before the Environmental Protection Agency.

While there are some differences in terms of the procedures adopted, the essence of these procedures is for the developer to make an application to this independent body for consent or approval in relation to the activities it seeks to carry on in the context of onshore or foreshore activities.

## Comment/Analysis

There is no reason why the environmental 'controls' should not be extended to the offshore area (including the foreshore) and that the 'jurisdiction' of An Bord Pleanála and the EPA should not replace that of the Minister in terms of environmental or licensing regulatory regimes controlling the physical planning process and emissions arising either from exploration or prospecting and development of any oil or gas resources.

In this way, environmental protection and enforcement issues could stand independently, in the legal sense, from issues pertaining to fiscal return. This separation of powers and responsibilities is fully consistent with the overall objective that environmental assessment be kept separate from political and/or fiscal considerations as part of an overall regulatory structure for oil or gas prospecting or exploration.

## LEGISLATIVE OPTIONS: BEST PRACTICE — ALTERNATIVES

### Option 1: Extension to functions of existing decision-makers

Currently, there is a division in the environmental regulatory system between control of the physical planning process and emissions control. There has been some legal commentary in relation to the environmental 'gaps' that might arise in terms of environmental impact assessment given that two statutory bodies are responsible for such assessment.[3]

Under the present state of legislation, there is no reason why this regulatory system cannot be conferred on An Bord Pleanála or the Environmental Protection Agency and that their jurisdiction cannot be extended comprehensively to onshore, foreshore and offshore activities. This is particularly so in the context of EU directives for environmental impact assessment and strategic environmental assessment.

In terms of compulsory acquisition of land where the public need justifies such acquisition, there remains an appropriate mechanism for An Bord Pleanála to decide on an application for the compulsory acquisition of land, for example, by the Minister or any other public authority (whether on its own behalf or on behalf of or in conjunction with the private sector), in like manner as the provisions under Section 212 of the PDA, which gives local authorities the power to make compulsory purchase orders in conjunction with or following arrangements with third parties including the private sector. Those applications for compulsory acquisition are determined by An Bord Pleanála as an external consent body.

The structures created under Part 14 of the Planning and Development Acts can equally be applied in this regard.

## Option 2: Establishment of a New Specialist Body

The industry appears to regard as preferable a regulatory system that is a 'one-stop shop'. In May 2013, PWC produced a document entitled 'Making the Most of Our Natural Resources' commissioned by Providence Resources for offshore exploration in Ireland. In looking at the likelihood for commercial oil and gas in Ireland, this report considered the current structures in terms of licensing, fiscal, planning and environmental issues. It is suggested that the controversy in relation to the Corrib gas field had its origins in a planning system which it is suggested is less than perfect and provided little certainty to the oil industry. Comparison is made with the UK and Norway. PWC suggested that the planning and approval process would benefit from greater joined-up thinking.

In terms of environmental best practices, there is much to recommend the establishment of a specialist strategic infrastructure body responsible for oil and gas prospecting and exploration (the Hydrocarbon Infrastructure Agency). Such a body, under the chairmanship of a High Court judge, would be responsible for an independent environmental consent and licensing regime for the onshore, foreshore and offshore areas. A chairman appointed from the judiciary would give the agency both real and perceived impartiality in the decision-making process.

Such a body could be constituted along the lines of the strategic infrastructure division of An Bord Pleanála, to ensure the necessary public participation and technical evaluation of applications coming before it. Its jurisdiction would extend to both controlling the emissions arising from any activities, and the environmental considerations in terms of physical works associated with development in onshore, foreshore or offshore areas.

Such a body would be responsible for the enforcement of planning and licensing control to ensure the successful implementation of any conditions or restrictions imposed in any approval or licence granted, whether for drilling, prospecting or the development of resources.

Legislation establishing such an infrastructure division would give that body the power to appoint independent facilitators or mediators who could engage with stakeholders in relation to significant infrastructure projects in the oil and gas industry so that there would be early and effective community-wide engagement. The concept of environmental mediation is well established in other jurisdictions and the Mediation Bill currently being advanced gives further status to the role of mediation in dispute resolution. It is apt to include such a provision.

The Hydrocarbon Infrastructure Agency (HIA) would have the right to facilitate pre-planning applications by the developers and also pre-planning engagement with stakeholders in advance of regulatory applications being made. This is a power that is conferred in existing legislation on An Bord Pleanála and there is no reason for this not to be extended to an exploration, prospecting and development regime for the oil and gas industry.

Legislation establishing the HIA should also confer powers for compulsory acquisition of land on the Minister and/or the Commission for Energy Regulation in circumstances where all necessary consents/approvals are obtained or are in the process of being obtained, in order to give effect to and facilitate the implementation of the approvals/consents in like manner as compulsory acquisition powers conferred on public bodies where there is a public need to be met by the acquisition in question, supported at the policy level and the national, regional and local levels.

In line with other legislation, it would be a matter for the HIA, as an external consent body, to consider whether or not to confirm such a compulsory purchase order in relation to foreshore or onshore activities. Compensation for land acquired under such a regime should be subject to the same legislative provisions for compensation as pertain to other public authority compulsory acquisitions, where a clear public need is to be met by the acquisition in order to facilitate the exploitation of the natural resources if an appropriate fiscal regime is in place to ensure that the benefits of such resource exploration accrue to the developer and to the State in the manner envisaged in this book.

## Option 3: Extension of Functions of CER

The Commission for Energy Regulation has an expanded remit for health and safety regulation under the Energy (Miscellaneous Provisions) Act, 2006 and the Petroleum (Exploration and Safety) Act, 2010.

The functions of CER could be further expanded to deal with regulatory approval for onshore and offshore activities. This envisages a stand-alone structure within the Commission for Energy Regulation for environmental, emissions and planning approval in like manner as currently regulated by An Bord Pleanála and the Environmental Protection Agency. As there is regulatory expertise within the extant structures of An Bord Pleanála and the EPA, such structures can be established immediately by a secondment of appropriate members of the planning board or the EPA and/or its technical staff to create the necessary technical expertise for decision-making.

In the context of the creation of such structures within the Commission for Energy

Regulation, it is imperative that there is appropriate independence in the appointment of such members, not just to the board of the Commission for Energy Regulation but to the internal divisions within such structure dealing with planning, environmental and emissions approvals. In the event of the establishment of a specialist strategic infrastructure body within CER responsible for oil and gas prospecting and exploration, such a body ought to be politically 'independent' and be constituted under the chairmanship of a High Court judge or other 'independent' person responsible for its establishment and operation.

## MARITIME AREA AND FORESHORE (AMENDMENT) BILL 2013

The objectives of the bill appear to be to streamline proposed offshore development consent with the existing onshore planning process, to modernise the foreshore licensing regime and to regulate offshore natural gas storage. The bill proposes to amalgamate the foreshore, EEZ and continental shelf into one area called the 'maritime area' for the purposes of development consent. *However, developments relating to exploration and prospecting for petroleum will remain the responsibility of the Minister for Communications, Energy and Natural Resources.*

When applying for development consent in the maritime area, an applicant must obtain a maritime option from the appropriate minister and, once granted, apply for development consent from An Bord Pleanála or the planning authority, as appropriate. *If and when both the maritime option and planning consent has been granted, a developer may then apply for a foreshore lease/licence and/or apply for any other necessary licences as required.*

The bill also envisages a regulatory framework for offshore natural gas storage. Where a maritime option and development consent are granted, any successful applicant wishing to explore sites for natural gas storage and to carry out natural gas storage must also apply for any other appropriate consents, for example, an EEZ licence, petroleum authorisation, and safety permit.

An Bord Pleanála is assigned responsibility for development consents in the near-shore area, on the foreshore or in the wider maritime area which are deemed to be strategic infrastructure or which are of a class that require environmental impact assessments (under the EIA Directive) or appropriate assessments (under the Habitats Directive). An Bord Pleanála is also assigned responsibility for consenting to developments beyond the near-shore area and to carry out environmental impact assessments (EIAs) and/or appropriate assessments (AAs), where appropriate.

The bill eliminates duplication of the EIA and AA processes between different public or State authorities where consent is granted by the board under this bill.

The projects requiring approval of the board include large-scale projects in the maritime area, for example, extractive industry projects, new port developments, international energy connectors, renewable energy projects, marina developments and smaller-scale projects which do not require environmental impact or appropriate assessments located beyond the outer limit of the near-shore area.

The statutory procedures under the Planning and Development (Strategic Infrastructure) Act 2006 and associated regulations will apply to strategic infrastructure projects in the maritime area.

It will be necessary to apply to planning authorities for planning permission in respect of all proposed developments located within the near-shore area or partially on land and partially within the near-shore area which are not strategic infrastructure or do not require environmental or appropriate assessments.

Where a person wishes to develop, construct or operate an offshore natural gas facility it will require a planning authorisation by An Bord Pleanála, a gas storage licence, a petroleum authorisation, a foreshore licence or an exclusive economic zone licence, a permit under the Gas Interim Regulation Act 2002, and a safety permit. In effect, it is a precondition for obtaining consent to construct a pipeline under the Gas Interim Regulation Act 2002 and a safety permit from the CER that there is the relevant planning authorisation from An Bord Pleanála in the first place.

There will be consequential amendments to the Energy (Miscellaneous Provisions) Act 1995 recognising the new regime under the Planning and Development Act, the creation of renewable energy zones in the maritime area by the Minister for Communications, Energy and Natural Resources, the grant of maritime options for renewable energy projects, a form of 'licence to use the resource' and explicit provision avoiding duplication of EIA/AA where development consent has been granted by An Bord Pleanála.

## Overall Conclusions

The 2013 bill goes some way towards regularising the environmental impact assessment regime for onshore, part-onshore, near-shore, foreshore and offshore areas. It remains anomalous from an environmental perspective that the MCENR retains responsibility for environmental impact assessments for extraction and drilling purposes, even under the 2013 bill.

The 2013 bill will retain the system of multiple consent and licensing requirements and thus is limited to the physical planning process. It does not attempt in any way to address the invitation of the industry for a 'one-stop shop'.

Best practice supports the proposition that any fiscal return is separated from the environmental, planning and emissions-control regulatory systems. Any political decision to grant a licence for either drilling or exploration, whether onshore or offshore, can remain within the executive decision-making area, while environmental, licensing and planning regulatory approvals are given to an independent body exercising technical skill and competence.

It is submitted that the creation of a new specialist body under new legislation, referred to as Option 2 above, represents the optimum solution. In the absence of new legislation to this effect, the extension of functions to An Bord Pleanála and the Environmental Protection Agency of all consent/licensing/enforcement for drilling, exploration and production of oil and gas is the next available option to 'depoliticise' decision making.

## ABOUT THE AUTHOR

Dermot is a practicing barrister since 1987 and a senior counsel since 2000. He is a CIArb-accredited mediator.

He specialises in planning and environmental law, including compulsory acquisition of land, environmental impact assessment and statutory arbitration for public infrastructure projects.

Over twenty-five years, he has been retained and has advised on approximately 250 public and private infrastructure projects, which he has brought through the confirmation/approval process before An Bord Pleanála and the Environmental Protection Agency, including such projects as inter urban motorways, toll schemes, marine projects, landfill projects, wastewater and water-supply projects.

In his practice, he works on a day-to-day basis with property valuers, engineers and environmental consultants in relation to public and private infrastructure projects.

## NOTES

1. www.irishstatutebook.ie/1992/en/act/pub/0007/sched1.html#sched1

2. See also Directive 2008/56 on a framework for community action in the field of marine environmental policy (Marine Strategy Framework Directive)

3. See article by Garret Simons SC in 2013 *Journal of Planning and Environmental Law*

# 11.

# THE ECONOMIC IMPACT OF GETTING IT RIGHT

## Anna Hayes

Discovery of a significant concentration of a valuable resource, such as oil or gas, can have a profound impact on a country's development. There are several examples of such discoveries that led to disastrous consequences for the nation which owned the resources in the first place. What we are aiming to achieve in this chapter is to show the potential positive economic impact on the Irish people if the right legislative framework and the overall infrastructure is put in place before a significant discovery is confirmed.

Why not wait until we know for sure? Wealth and power are well-known factors that lead to corruption and, when exposed to these things, human beings are rarely able to resist the temptation. It is therefore important for Ireland, with strong potential for future discoveries of various natural resources, to have strong legal and administrative frameworks in place to handle any such discovery.

In this chapter we are not attempting to produce a strictly accurate analysis of the economic impact of oil discovery on an economy but rather to discuss how good it can be for the Irish people if the nation gets it right. We are not suggesting that developing a functional and effective infrastructure for the Irish economy to benefit from oil discovery is an easy or straightforward job. Only a few countries in the world managed to achieve success in this endeavour. Such success, however, is not accidental and is driven by clear understanding of the goals pursued by the nation and the defined plan of how such goals can and will be achieved in the short, medium and long term.

Unhappily, current debate, when there is any, is dominated by the dangerous misconception that planning a new national strategy for our natural resources should really begin in earnest only after there is a big oil strike. Such thinking, which dominates the establishment approach to Irish strategy, is misplaced, unworkable and high-risk when compared to a fulsome strategic development plan, which is well thought out, in advance of major discoveries.

## APPROACH TO THE ANALYSIS

The aim of this chapter is to look at the benefits that the discovery of commercially viable quantities of oil and gas can bring to the Irish economy.

The approach taken first looks at the primary financial contribution to the Irish economy. We first calculate the income that would be expected from the sale of Irish oil/gas if the estimates currently publicised by the various exploration and production companies operating within Irish territories prove to be accurate. At the same time, it is important to note that prices for oil are relatively high at the moment. We will look at the dynamics of oil prices in the past forty years to determine the appropriate scenarios for our projections. We would look at three scenarios for the starting production market price for crude oil – current, medium and low.

Once we have established the potential revenue that companies can hope to achieve from extracting oil from Irish territory, we will then discuss the various levels of revenue that can be received by the Irish people. We will start from estimating this revenue based on the current licensing regime and will then attempt to vary the individual components of the licences to show the potential benefit to the Irish economy.

The second part of this discussion is centred on the peripheral benefits that discovery of a natural resource can bring to the economy. Those are substantial, and critical for sustainable economic development when taken in aggregation. These benefits are not readily quantifiable when using publicly available information. However, the main goal of this discussion is to show the width and breadth of the positive and sustainable developments that can potentially be achieved by the Irish economy from establishing its own oil and gas industry.

The discussion and analysis in this chapter concentrates on the positive impact of commercial oil reserves on Irish territory. It is clearly a concern that any such discovery would be associated with significant environmental risk. Norway presents a good example of managing these risks and making sure that the production and distribution of oil is done in such a way as to maximise the financial benefit to the nation while making sure that the environmental aspects of any such activities are managed safely and effectively. For the purpose of our discussion, we will assume that Ireland will follow the Norwegian example and develop the risk management and safety framework to achieve the same results.

One would note that the term 'sustainable' is used frequently throughout this chapter. This is to emphasise that the economic development built on the basis of the approach of nation-oriented management of the natural resources can lead to a permanent shift in the overall quality of life for the Irish people as a whole. This is in contrast to temporary cyclical economic 'booms' experienced by Ireland in the past and based on temporary exploitation of perceived arbitrage conditions in the market. Such booms inevitably lead to economic crises, and a short period of economic prosperity for a select few is thus followed by prolonged periods of hardship for the nation as a whole.

When attempting to bring about a nation-centred framework for managing natural resources, the key emphasis is to ensure steady and consistent improvements in the quality of life for the Irish people in terms of both financial stability and the building up and maintenance of a stable and high-profile jobs market and education system.

## PRIMARY FINANCIAL GAINS: STATE REVENUE FROM OIL EXTRACTION AND SALE

Let us start from the amount of reserves we can potentially look at under the Irish territory and imagine the situation in the not-so-distant future when the technology progresses to the point that it makes exploration of the Irish resources commercially viable.[1] Several of the fields are already confirmed and are at the stage of either discovery or commercial production. Being cautiously optimistic, we can assume that not all of the declared prospects would turn out to be successful and some of them would even prove to be not viable for commercial production. Even if we assume that only half of the estimated natural resources can be commercially extracted, it still leaves us with a considerable endowment.

Sustainable development of any new industry means that there should be a period of development and accumulation of technical know-how. At the same time, when it comes to petrochemical industry, significant investment is required at the initial stages to ensure that the industry is set up in a safe and environmentally friendly way. It is also critical to ensure that the local suppliers get a chance to gain experience in the new areas of various operations related to exploration, extraction, transportation and re-fabrication of oil and gas products as well as any related and complementary areas.

All of the above means that production from any commercial field should be paced and controlled by the State at such a level as to allow the Irish contractors and the infrastructure to develop in line with the support required to accommodate the needs of the oil industry. What this means is that an Irish oil company should be formed to become a dominant player in the Irish petrochemical sector. It should be separate from the State to allow healthy economic and commercial development, but at the same time the State should take an active pro-national approach in supporting the new industry and the Irish oil-related activities.

Throughout this chapter we shall be looking back at the Norwegian experience, which is a proven 'best practice' when it comes to making a relatively new country with little industrial weight globally one of the world's wealthiest nations in the space of less than thirty years. This was achieved solely by proactive and nation-centred management of Norway's natural resources.

Any companies undertaking extraction and production work need to make significant capital investments in research and exploration of their fields. However, the fact that the oil and gas industry remains one of the most attractive industries in the world in terms of return on investment means that it can be safely said that only the prospect of solid profit can lead the companies to undertake any projects. The increased interest and activity that can be currently observed off the various coasts of Ireland indicates strong interest in and thus commercial potential of the Irish territories.

Before we go on to projecting the potential revenues from sale of the extracted assets, let us have a brief look at the history of oil prices in the past forty years. Figure 1 below shows historic annual average oil prices in US dollars from 1946 until now (adjusted for inflation).

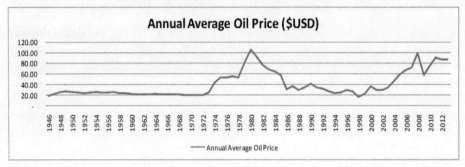

Figure 1

It can be seen that the prices follow a well-defined cycle and at the moment we are moving towards the peak. At the same time, the demand for oil-based products is high, so it is reasonable to assume that the prices are going to remain at least as high as in the past five years. However, given that the previous cycle appears to have reached its peak in approximately ten years and then took twenty years to bottom off before starting to rise again, we still adopt a relatively conservative approach to modelling cash flows, only allowing for a 2 percent increase in oil prices year-on-year, much below what oil 'peakers' predict is likely to happen next. Colin Campbell, the leading proponent of global peak oil and gas modelling, puts the peak behind us at 2005; others put it later, but few believe oil and gas to be self-regenerating. We use an assumption that price would increase in line with inflation, given the current inflation rates, and that it would stay relatively stable in real terms.

At the same time, considering that the price of oil is a volatile variable, we assumed the starting price at current, medium and low levels:

| Price Level | Price/Barrel (USD) | Price/Barrel (EUR) |
|---|---|---|
| Current: January 2014 | 106 | 78 |
| Medium: 2012 Average | 88 | 67 |
| Low: 10-year Average, 2002-12 | 70 | 53 |

Table 1

A simple cash-flow model has been used that took into consideration the initial oil prices and increases over the life of the project. Given the current market conditions and the low interest rates, it took a relatively conservative discount rate of 5 percent per annum for net present value calculations, which report future cash flows as a capital value in today's terms.[2]

Based on estimates of the amount of resources and the limits on extraction per day, it would take approximately seventeen years from the point when the oil is first extracted to deplete the reserves.

A company can comfortably spend between $200,000 and $700,000 per day in the pre-production stage. Referring to the Norwegian experience, we would allocate $4.5 billion for the initial capital outlay, with $2 billion and $2.5 billion spend in the first and second years respectively.

All of the calculations were initially performed in US dollars and then converted to euros using the conversion rate of €1.3194 for $1, which is the rate provided by the Central Bank of Ireland at the time of writing.

This is a very simplified model, allowing the total outlay for the capital investment for all projects initiated in Irish waters. While the actual cost to the companies is likely to be different, we believe it is a reasonable assumption at this point in time.

First let us look at the situation where the level of reserves discovered corresponds to the current state-supported projections (i.e. 10 billion barrels) and assume that with this level of reserves, Ireland would opt for relatively modest levels of daily production of 1 million barrels, similar to those currently maintained by the UK.[3]

Using all the assumptions, we can now compare six different regimes depending on the way the government can bring the oil revenues back to the State. The JOC report suggested that future pricing should rise to allow for an 80 percent State takeout, a figure broadly in line with mature oil extraction regimes. Let's envisage tapering up, accelerating if a giant field is discovered but initially targeting a 65 percent takeout, allowing the remainder to encourage risk-taking appropriate to Ireland's nascent stage of development.

- status quo – the current tax and licensing conditions

- introduction of royalties while the current tax and licensing conditions remain

- application of the Profit Resource Rent Tax (PPRT)

The following three scenarios look at measures that would allow the government to achieve a 65 percent government take:

- increased corporation tax to 65 percent

- application of PRRT and increased tax to 50 percent

- application of royalties and increased tax to 59 percent

A summary of the baseline scenario, with 10 billion barrels of reserves at 'low' prices, is provided in Table 2 below:

| Scenario | Current | With Royalties | With PRRT | Increased Tax | PRRT + Incr. Tax | Roy. + Incr. Tax |
|---|---|---|---|---|---|---|
| Corporation Tax (%) | 25 | 25 | 25 | 65 | 50 | 59 |
| PRRT (Yes/No) | N | N | Y | N | Y | N |
| Royalties (%) | 0 | 10 | 0 | 0 | 0 | 10 |
| Government Take (%) | 35 | 44 | 48 | 70 | 69 | 70 |
| Government Take (€, millions) | 58,513 | 80,816 | 89,589 | 152,133 | 148,101 | 149,025 |
| Current National Debt | 192,460 | 192,460 | 192,460 | 192,460 | 192,460 | 192,460 |
| Corp. Tax After Servicing Debt | 133,947 | 111,644 | 102,871 | 40,327 | 44,359 | 43,435 |
| IRR (%) | 100 | 91 | 93 | 71 | 75 | 69 |

Table 2
Scenario analysis – baseline scenario

Should the companies continue operating under the current regime, at most the Irish State can hope for 25 to 40 percent of the net revenues after costs and operating expenses have been taken into consideration and depending on the size of any given single operation. As a target figure we selected the level of national debt as of December 2012. The net national debt amounted to €192,460 million (or simply €192.5 billion).[4]

From Table 2 above we can see that the variation in licensing and taxation provides a gradual increase in the state revenues collected from oil production. Even with the level of government take as high as 70 percent, the internal rate of return on the companies' investments remains well above the current interest rates that can be earned in the financial markets.

Now that we have considered the baseline scenario and defined the main assumptions, we can go on and calculate the potential state revenue delivered by extracting the total amount of the reserve found using the cautiously optimistic reserve estimates as defined above. Taking oil prices at the rate of €78 per barrel,[5] the summary of the six scenarios is provided in Table 3 below.

Assuming that the State collects 25 percent of the revenues received from oil extraction, which are then fully saved and used for repayment of the national debt, even after all of the vast oil reserves have been fully extracted, there will still be over €53 billion worth of national debt to be repaid by the taxpayer.

This figure improves somewhat with the introduction of a 10 percent royalty rate for extraction and use of the Irish resources, bringing the total Irish take to €159,826 million.

While this could be a good development, if we look at the internal rate of return calculated for the overall process, it can be seen that the figure does not go below 150 percent at any point in time. This is allowing for the initial outlay of $4.5 billion and annual operational costs at 30 percent of the total gross production.[6]

| Scenario | Current | With Royalties | With PRRT | Increased Tax | PRRT + Incr. Tax | Roy. + Incr. Tax |
|---|---|---|---|---|---|---|
| Corporation Tax (%) | 25 | 25 | 25 | 65 | 50 | 59 |
| PRRT (Yes/No) | N | N | Y | N | Y | N |
| Royalties (%) | 0 | 10 | 0 | 0 | 0 | 10 |
| Government Take (%) | 25 | 36 | 40 | 65 | 65 | 65 |
| Government Take (€, millions) | 115,977 | 159,826 | 176,952 | 301,541 | 292,929 | 294,864 |
| Current National Debt | 192,460 | 192,460 | 192,460 | 192,460 | 192,460 | 192,460 |
| Corp. Tax After Servicing Debt | 76,483 | 32,634 | 15,508 | 109,081 | 100,469 | 102,404 |
| IRR (%) | 244 | 223 | 233 | 163 | 181 | 162 |

Table 3
Scenario analysis – current oil prices

Norwegian experience shows that when large reserves of oil are discovered, the industry can sustain the level of tax of up to 78 percent. At the same time, when looking at the government take in the rest of the world, 65 percent appears to be a more reasonable figure. It is also supported by a recent oil and gas taxation study undertaken by Deutsche Bank. Therefore, scenarios four to six allow for a total government take of 65 percent via different mechanisms.

At first sight, a simple increase in corporate tax rates produces the best result both in terms of maximising government take and allowing for relatively high IRR for the companies. The challenge with this approach is making sure that the costs allowed to be written off against the declared profits are strictly regulated and controlled such that the companies do not attempt to optimise their level of corporate tax. This, based on current rules, is a high-risk strategy allowing companies large scope for creative accounting. In September 2013 the EU announced an investigation into Ireland's corporation tax structures for multinationals because of the extraordinarily low rates of cash collected. This followed a period of harsh criticism of Ireland as a 'tax haven' during US Senate debates earlier the same year.

Some combination of an increased rate of corporate tax, tighter rules on offsets and the introduction of royalties should produce optimal results for the Irish people.

The current level of oil prices is very high but at the same time the companies are also operating in an environment of very low interest rates. Allowing for apparent cyclicality of oil prices and generally in the interest of providing some comparison, the following tables show the results of the same scenarios as above but calculated based on the medium and low levels of starting oil prices at the point of production.

| Scenario | Current | With Royalties | With PRRT | Increased Tax | PRRT + Incr. Tax | Roy. + Incr. Tax |
|---|---|---|---|---|---|---|
| Corporation Tax (%) | 25 | 25 | 25 | 65 | 50 | 59 |
| PRRT (Yes/No) | N | N | Y | N | Y | N |
| Royalties (%) | 0 | 10 | 0 | 0 | 0 | 10 |
| Government Take (%) | 25 | 36 | 40 | 65 | 65 | 65 |
| Government Take (€, millions) | 98,969 | 136,432 | 151,064 | 257,320 | 250,033 | 251,644 |
| Current National Debt | 192,460 | 192,460 | 192,460 | 192,460 | 192,460 | 192,460 |
| Corp. Tax After Servicing Debt | 93,491 | 56,028 | 41,396 | 64,860 | 57,573 | 59,184 |
| IRR (%) | 222 | 203 | 211 | 149 | 164 | 148 |

Table 4

Scenario analysis – medium starting oil price

With the medium level of oil prices, neither introduction of royalties at 10 percent nor PRRT provides meaningful improvement, leaving the Irish taxpayer with significant levels of national debt to pay at the end of the oil development. However, increasing the level of corporate taxation now seems to be by far the best course of action. For comparison, this is exactly the way followed by Norway in reclaiming oil revenues from the companies. The only exception is that the tax rate is significantly higher, at 78 percent. than that used for our analysis.

Changing the level of oil prices to the average of the past ten years (Table 5, below) does not produce any surprises. The most important point to note is the level of the internal rate of return for the scenarios. It remains consistently high and does not go below 130 percent even for the scenarios with the 65 percent government take under low oil prices.

While the level of 30 percent of gross revenue for operational costs may seem artificial, further variation of the levels of operational costs reveals that the company needs to spend well above 80 percent of its gross revenues on running its day-to-day activities before the IRR goes below 20 percent. Even at 20 percent this is still significantly higher than the current interest rate offered in the financial markets.

What this means is that the oil industry would remain an attractive investment for the companies even if the prices go down by 30 percent from the current level, the level of operational costs increases to 80 percent from the level assumed in the model and the Irish government increases its takeout to 65 percent.

| Scenario | Current | With Royalties | With PRRT | Increased Tax | PRRT + Incr. Tax | Roy. + Incr. Tax |
|---|---|---|---|---|---|---|
| Corporation Tax (%) | 25 | 25 | 25 | 65 | 50 | 59 |
| PRRT (Yes/No) | N | N | Y | N | Y | N |
| Royalties (%) | 0 | 10 | 0 | 0 | 0 | 10 |
| Government Take (%) | 25 | 36 | 40 | 65 | 65 | 65 |
| Government Take (€, millions) | 78,559 | 108,359 | 119,998 | 204,255 | 198,558 | 199,779 |
| Current National Debt | 192,460 | 192,460 | 192,460 | 192,460 | 192,460 | 192,460 |
| Corp. Tax After Servicing Debt | 113,901 | 84,101 | 72,462 | 11,795 | 6,098 | 7,319 |
| IRR (%) | 194 | 176 | 183 | 131 | 142 | 130 |

Table 5

Scenario analysis – low starting oil price

## DEBT OR DEVELOPMENT – DEPLOYING REVENUES

It's fair to ask whether it is such a good idea to invest all of the oil revenues into repayment of national debt. Let us ignore the peripheral benefits of establishing and maintaining the Irish oil industry and deal with the fact that in the situation where Ireland increases its take-out to 65 percent and there are successful discoveries, there will eventually be a surplus of cash coming into the economy from the sale of Irish oil and gas.

Let us first address the fact that while the oil cash is being accumulated and used for servicing the national debt, the rest of the economy can go about its business as usual without thinking of where to find extra tens of billions to cover the debt. At the beginning, there would be the need for significant investment and support for the newly established oil industry, but once the Irish oil industry has accumulated enough knowledge, competency and power and is operating at a certain level of independence, the revenues received can instead be redistributed to improve the condition of the Irish education system, healthcare, childcare, roads, sports and leisure facilities for the population, to name just a few areas.

Government can look at potentially encouraging small enterprises by providing them with tax breaks and other incentives. This would in turn create a virtuous circle within the economy when companies are doing better: they would require increased capacity and expand their need for human resources. This all means more jobs are created, more goods are produced and exported, and higher national revenue is generated within the economy. High revenues mean higher volumes of tax coming back to the State. Now remember that the government is using oil money to service the national debt, so the total tax take for the year can be put straight back into the economy.

Once the national debt is reduced to low-risk levels the oil and gas money can, itself, start to go directly into economic and social development. Surplus of cash in the economy is never a good idea as it inevitably leads to an increase in inflation, higher levels of prices, higher expected salaries and other things we have observed in the past that ultimately make the economy overheat.

This is really not the situation we want to develop and we again have a great example of dealing with such a situation – the Norwegian Fund for Future Generations. As the name suggests, it is a sovereign wealth fund that is managed by the State to provide for a good quality of life for Norwegian citizens, especially children.

Setting up a similar ring-fenced fund with clearly defined rules would allow the Irish economy to develop without overheating and damaging Irish society all over again, while ensuring that the nation feels safe in the knowledge that the 'rainy day' is covered.

## PERIPHERAL BENEFITS

While production is often seen as the main economic activity related to the oil and gas industry, it really is just the tip of the iceberg. In Norway only around 3 percent of the population is currently employed by the petrochemical and directly related industries.[7] However, the impact of developing a national oil and gas industry on the complementary service industries is enormous when all of the affected sectors of the economy are taken into consideration.

## CREATING JOBS

Discovery of large reserves of natural resources in the offshore territories does not automatically lead to job-creation opportunities for the original owner of the reserves (the Irish people), which is so badly needed in the current economic climate. Creation of the Norwegian national oil company Statoil, coupled with focused government policies with regard to involvement of the Norwegians in major developments, meant that over time the Norwegian industry accumulated enough know-how to compete in the international market of oil-related services and projects.

However, this does not happen overnight and significant state support is needed to ensure that the required infrastructure and human resources are available for the newly developed oil industry.

To ensure that the Irish retain the full benefit of the increased industrial activities off their coastlines, it is important to encourage the companies undertaking the development and exploration work to use local resources. This would allow gradual transfer of the technical knowledge and experience to the Irish and consequently lead to the development of an in-depth understanding of the issues related to managing and operating a national oil industry based on first-hand experience.

## DEMAND FOR HIGHER EDUCATION

The first step is always the most difficult. With little or no industry-related experience, many Irish workers are bound to be employed in relatively low-level and unskilled positions. While it means lower wages at the initial stage, this can also be a good selling point to the commercially minded companies, which would be able to lower their overhead costs. At the same time, opportunity exists for players like Statoil, the Norwegian State oil company, to provide assistance to the Irish people and train local resources in the first successful commercial projects. This would naturally lead to demand for more technical and specialised knowledge in various areas of business and science.

Ireland already has a well-established network of well-regarded universities, which would rise to the challenge of preparing the new generations of engineers, managers and scientists that would be driving Irish prosperity through oil and gas production.

This would provide opportunity for further funding options for the universities and ideally allow access to higher education for a wider pool of prospective students.

## EFFECT OF DISCOUNTED FUEL PRICES

Given that oil and gas extracted from the Irish offshore territories belongs to the Irish people, it is natural to expect a certain level of discount offered by the companies when selling Irish oil on the domestic market. To ensure that companies do not just sell Irish oil somewhere else, thus earning full market rates, a certain percentage of production should be allocated to domestic sale.

From this point on, there could be two options for managing the market. On the one hand the government can introduce additional levels of tax to ensure that the domestic fuel market is in line with the worldwide level of prices. This would mean that while the base oil prices are lower, a higher percentage of the selling price goes back into the government reserves and allows financing of the economically vital sections of the country and support of individual government activities.

This approach could be beneficial and in time would potentially allow full governmental sponsorship of the education system, healthcare system and other vital social systems, such as support for local and national public transport networks.

An alternative approach is to allow the lower prices to find their way to the end user. This would have a direct impact on the cost base of many businesses and would produce a 'ripple effect' for any sector of the economy that uses any form of transportation or other oil-related products.

One direct result of lower fuel prices would then be cheaper products produced in Ireland. Combined with a low corporation tax regime, this would make Ireland very attractive for both development of local industries and direct foreign investment. With cheaper prices for the same level of quality, Ireland would be in a position to compete in the world market with significant levels of success.

Now once the virtuous circle of cheaper production starts, this would lead to higher sales levels for the Irish businesses, increasing the need for expanded capacity and increasing production levels further. This in turn creates demand for more labour at various levels. Overall this would lead to the natural growth of the Irish economy through growth of the real sectors and not due to simply increasing prices for existing goods and services.

As more people go back to work and gain more experience, they would likely progress upwards along the business hierarchy and the overall level of disposable income would increase allowing people more scope to spend on items other than necessities.

With higher education, people become more concerned with keeping healthy and maintaining a certain lifestyle, leading to increased demand for agricultural products of better quality at relatively higher prices. This would boost the Irish farming and food industries. These lifestyle choices lead to increased demand for leisure and entertainment facilities and benefit the catering and hospitality industries along with potential investment into the infrastructure for physical and mental development for children, such as gymnastics, music and dance studious, stadiums and swimming pools.

It would be critically important to ensure that overall economic development is maintained and encouraged using the oil revenues as the driving force. The key to achieving maximum economic leverage from oil discovery is in viewing the Irish economy from the holistic perspective and ensuring that the benefits attributed to any significant resource discovery in general, and oil and gas in particular, are spread fairly and evenly across the various economic sectors. One of the crucial mistakes made by countries using their natural resources as the basis for their development is concentrating on developing that particular sector and neglecting the rest of the economy, thus creating the Dutch Disease effect. Inevitably, oil revenues will be fully exhausted, but the country can continue utilising the high levels of education, infrastructure and social protection.

## CONTRACTORS' NETWORK

The large international companies operating oil exploration projects rarely use contractors from their country of origin, i.e. a large American corporation is unlikely to ship their catering staff from the USA. People operating in the field would generate spending. Once the resource is extracted, it should be distributed to the production site. This would require development of the relevant infrastructure for transportation and distribution. There would be a strong case for using the local Irish construction, catering and other industries to accommodate those needs.

Following natural market laws of division of labour (just as it happened in Norway), the individual companies would start specialising in specific areas within their selected contracts. To allow this to happen, the State should be in a position to make the local offering competitive.

Upstream oil industry can produce all of the above benefits for the Irish economy. Instead of simply allowing the oil to be extracted with the help of the local population, Ireland could provide the necessary expertise, shipping and pipeline capacity as well as facilities for the varied midstream and downstream petroleum industries, such as petrochemical plants and oil refineries. Think of the shipyards that would need to be built to accommodate those demands and the deep divers who would need to work to put the pipelines in place. There would need to be engineers, geologists, project and risk managers working together to facilitate these developments. At the same time, Ireland would need to have access to the building materials, which (assuming that the oil is being sold at subsidised prices to the Irish producers) will be a lot more competitive than alternative sources.

It is easy to see that if it is organised and managed properly, the Irish experience of building its own oil-based economy can easily be as successful as that of Norway. The key to success is focusing on the maximisation of national wealth and ensuring that the Irish oil industry is given a chance to mature and develop with support and guidance of more mature players in the current market.

## ABOUT THE AUTHOR

Anna is a specialist within data analysis and modelling. Her academic background is in quantitative finance, mathematical and statistical modelling, and optimisation.

Anna gained a BSc in Finance and Management from Moscow University of Management, Russian Federation in 2002. In 2005 Anna was awarded an MSc in Logistics from Molde University College, Norway. The final thesis for this degree was published in the proceedings of the 16th Annual Conference for Nordic Researchers in Logistics, NOFOMA 2004, Linköping, Sweden.

In recent years, Anna has been applying her skills to the area of quantitative risk management within various industries. Anna has participated in and managed a number of projects in Ireland, the UK and other international locations for both financial and non-financial organisations. These projects allowed her to gain experience in quantitative analysis and the modelling of financial liabilities and risks for various private companies and public-sector organisations in Ireland, the UK, Russia, the UAE and Hong Kong.

Anna has been based in Ireland since 2010. She currently works for the actuarial team within one of the world's largest management consultancies.

## NOTES

1.   www.forbes.com/sites/markpmills/2012/09/18/america-take-note-technology-unleashes-black-gold-to-rescue-irelands-economy/

2.   'NPV compares the value of a dollar today to the value of that same dollar in the future, taking inflation and returns into account. If the NPV of a prospective project is positive, it should be accepted. However, if NPV is negative, the project should probably be rejected because cash flows will also be negative' www.investopedia.com/terms/n/npv.asp

3.   en.wikipedia.org/wiki/List_of_countries_by_oil_production

4.   www.ntma.ie/business-areas/funding-and-debt-management/debt-profile/ and www.ntma.ie/business-areas/funding-and-debt-management/debt-profile/ real time calculation here- http://www.financedublin.com/debtclock.php

5.   The price of a barrel of crude was $106 at time of writing

6.   csimarket.com/Industry/industry_Profitability_Ratios.php?ind=603

7.   Around 140,000 people are employed by petroleum-related businesses. kpmg.no/?aid=9668637 and www.ssb.no/a/english/minifakta/en/main_05.html#tab0505

# 12.

# PRICING: HOW MUCH WILL WE GET?

## Eilis Quinlan and Eddie Hobbs

How we price rights to exploit the hydrocarbon assets of the Irish people is the touchstone issue every time there is public debate. Pricing on its own, however, is just one part of Irish strategy, combining many other critical issues like:

- Who owns and controls the vital distribution infrastructure, especially offshore oil and gas pipe networks?

- What production-sharing devolves to the State?

- What controls and resources are in place by the industry regulator to ensure compliance, truthfulness and accuracy?

- What terms and conditions require licence-holders to develop a domestic Irish hydrocarbon industry involving everything from service vessels to refining and vital job creation?

Look through the existing licences and it is pretty clear that Ireland has no detailed strategy, merely a pricing policy – and that to be among the most generous in the world to corporates. There are precious few terms and conditions. The licence template looks like it was written over the shoulder of the Minister for Energy by industry during the pivotal year of 1987, when Ray Burke took the reins. The best way to grasp what that means is to consider what an Irish offshore exploration licence does *not* contain:

- No requirement to bring any oil and gas onshore. These can be delivered into international markets, to be bought back by Irish industry and consumers at international prices.

- No production-sharing at all. The State gets nada, not a sausage. Up until 1987, it would have automatically received 50 percent from each well.

- No share of sales, a cut off the top line, also known as a royalty. These disappeared during Minister Ray Burke's reign too.

- No improvement in Ireland's precarious end-of-the-line security-of-supply exposure in the event of an international oil and gas shortage, triggered by geopolitical deterioration in the unstable Middle East or in relationships between Russia and Europe.

- No time limits on tax write-offs, which if in place would incentivise industry to develop finds quickly.

Indeed, Ireland doesn't have a strategy. Instead, it merely has a corporation tax pricing regime that allows breath-taking scope for write-offs going back twenty-five years. Ireland ranks, in several studies, as among the most generous regimes in the world, affording exploration companies the cheapest terms to get access to our oil and gas assets. Ernst & Young provides a comprehensive annual report on global oil taxation regimes, where detailed comparisons can be made by tax experts across countries: in recent studies, Ireland's overall pricing has been identified as among the world's most generous. This is not by accident and, indeed, attempts were made to position Ireland as the cheapest place to drill, from a tax perspective, anywhere in the world.

Corporation tax was halved to 25 percent by Bertie Ahern as Minister for Finance in 1992 and allows for generous write-offs. Attempts to further halve it to 12.5 percent were shelved after disquiet following a pre-budget leak by the Fianna Fail/PD government. The rate stayed untouched until 2007, when Green minister Eamon Ryan introduced an extra tax of up to 15 percent depending on the ratio of costs in a field to production from it. But even at 40 percent, Ireland's take ranks as one of the most generous in the world, both in terms of the nominal rate of tax and the scope for delaying and minimising it.

Time and again we are told by the oil and gas explorers that cheap prices are the gateway to greater exploration. This was not borne out during the decade that followed Ray Burke's reversal of minister Justin Keating's regime, which had stood since the early 1970s.

It is logical that Irish pricing should reflect the higher risks associated with our waters and offshore geology, until larger and more numerous discoveries are made, but the current regime is a giveaway. Throughout the world, the nation-state participation ranges from 70 to 85 percent but still allows scope for industry to earn a beefy 20 to 30 percent per annum return. The take by nation-states comes from a combination of:

- Production Sharing – arrangements to cede ownership of the oil and gas extracted to the nation-state

- Royalties – a cut off the top on oil and gas revenues

- Corporation Tax – a tax on company profits

- Tight Accounting Rules – a set of conditions that restricts write-offs and punishes creative accounting like loading up subsidiaries with debt instead of equity, extracting the juice through interest charges

- Expert Oversight – experienced, informed and robust regulators that police compliance among some of the world's most powerful and controversial multinationals.

Continuously in press outings, industry spokespeople stress that the corporation tax rate of 25 to 40 percent will bring a tax bonanza of billions of euro to state coffers. This is simply untrue. Listen closely and you will even hear industry CEOs and chairpersons regularly swapping their chatter between 'we' the Irish and 'we' the shareholders of the exploration companies. It is not confusion, rather it is propaganda.

The truth is that at current pricing, we the people, the owners of these hydrocarbon assets, will get nothing, or next to nothing. At current pricing, the oil and gas would be better left in the ground until existing licences expire and a new generation of leaders emerge who are prepared to do what the Norwegians did in 1972 – wrest back control, with a fresh national strategy driven by a new way of thinking, prepared to look the powerful oil and gas lobby in the eye without blinking.

'Who extracts the rents on natural resources?' That is a question that has dominated world economics since the Industrial Revolution shifted from coal- to oil-based energy. Africa has been blighted by it, as powerful corporates positioned themselves with corrupt regimes to extract vast amounts of money that should otherwise have been deployed to develop public services and infrastructure. The economic rent is the return, over and above a reasonable return to the risk-taking explorer, that must find its way directly to the nation, if allegations of exploitation are to be avoided. That is not the case in Ireland.

Based on a model created by Standard Chartered Bank, and allowing for normal write-offs, a successful strike in Irish waters would yield a return of 46 percent per annum, doubling profits every nineteen months over the lifetime of a well for the licence-owner. This is excessive. Clearly economic rent cannot find its way to the Irish nation under these terms.

## What is Taxation?

It has been said that 'taxes are the price we pay for a civilised society' (Oliver Wendell Holmes, Jr). The purpose of taxation has always been to raise revenue to pay for the services that the State provides, although these services have changed over time. The rate which is applied by each tax depends on how much revenue the State needs to raise in order to meet its expenditure requirements. Taxes and duties are applied to revenues, income and gains made on the sale of capital assets. However, for the purposes of this chapter we will focus primarily on the taxation of corporates.

There are four fundamental principles that apply to all taxation systems, as outlined by Adam Smith in his book *The Wealth of Nations*[1]:

1. Economy: A taxation system should be easy to understand and the collection of taxes should not be expensive.

2. Certainty: Individuals and companies should know in advance the basis on which they will have to pay tax and when and how they will have to make the payment, or payments.

3. Convenience: The payment of tax should not be a cumbersome affair.

4. Equity: A tax system should be fair, or at least be considered to be so.

The world has developed considerably since the time Adam Smith wrote this book, and the commercial world is now a much more complex place. This is true of the taxes levied on commercial operations also. Given the innovative methods of tax-avoidance techniques and the complex anti-avoidance measures that governments need to implement to counteract these, Smith's first point is very difficult to achieve in a modern tax system. Complexity is difficult to avoid, although the introduction of 'General Anti-Avoidance Provisions' and the related recent Supreme Court judgement in the O'Flynn Construction case may go some way to removing the need for complex specific anti-avoidance provisions in the future.[2]

The Irish Revenue Commissioners could be considered to be adept at achieving points (2) and (3) (Certainty and Convenience). International evidence of this performance can be seen in 'Paying Taxes 2013: The Global Picture',[3] where Ireland was ranked sixth of 185 countries in terms of convenience of paying taxes. Ireland, however, hit the international headlines following a hot USA debate on multinational tax avoidance, as some senior US senators labelled Ireland a tax haven.

However, the idea of certainty would also seem to encompass the principle that a taxing authority would not apply taxes retrospectively, other than in rare instances. Retrospective legislation is not only contrary to this principle, it could also be subject to legal challenge on the basis that it may infringe the European Convention on Human Rights and may go against the concept of 'legitimate expectation' as found in the Marks and Spencer case.[4] As stated by Seely, the need to tax any windfall gain made by petroleum companies 'must be balanced against the need to give producers a degree of certainty in the fiscal regime when planning future investment decisions'.[5] However, it is worth noting that the UK government successfully introduced retrospective legislation to increase the tax rate on the petroleum industry in 1978 and 2005. In both instances the retrospective legislation was in response to a recent sharp rise in global oil prices, and a belief that the UK Exchequer was not receiving its fair share from its natural resources.

The last of Smith's points, and perhaps the most important, is that of equity. If a tax is perceived, rightly or wrongly, to be inequitable, then the ability of the tax to raise the intended level of income will be seriously diminished. The idea of fairness is often discussed in the media in relation to tax, particularly income tax. This concept is somewhat problematic because it is inherently subjective. One aspect of a tax system that is widely agreed to approximately represent 'fairness' is progressive taxation. A progressive tax levies a greater proportion of the total burden from that tax on those who are most capable of paying.

'Fairness' has been used frequently in the debate on the introduction of the Local Property Tax. However, fairness is also a concept that should apply to corporation tax. In general, our corporation tax system (along with the corporation tax systems of many other countries) is not very progressive. Very profitable enterprises continue to pay corporation tax at 12.5 percent, the same rate that applies to marginally profitable companies. This is in sharp contrast to our personal tax system, which applies income tax to employment income on a sliding scale.

Oil and gas exploration companies are always subject to a higher rate of tax (25 percent), and for more profitable companies, this can increase to 40 percent, despite earlier attempts to reduce the rate to 12.5 percent. The industry, much like development land speculation, is being singled out because these companies have the potential to make very large profits. It may also be an acknowledgement that the petroleum industry extracts a finite resource that ultimately belongs to the State, in the process of making profits. The State therefore may feel that the citizens (the ultimate owners of this finite resource) deserve a bigger share of the profits than would be possible under the lower corporate tax rate.

## IRELAND'S LOW CORPORATION TAX POLICY

Since the time of Adam Smith, the role of government has expanded to provide the environment in which the economy can grow, and thereby attempt to create full employment in the long run. For this reason, modern tax systems no longer solely deal with the levying of taxation. They also provide incentives to businesses, in the hope that these will encourage investment, instigate growth and thereby create employment. Incentives are common in modern tax systems, and Ireland currently has many examples. Ireland's 12.5 percent corporation tax rate is a well-publicised incentive that has been a cornerstone when it comes to attracting foreign direct investment.

In theory, lower tax rates for corporations should create more investment in the Irish economy, which should in turn increase employment, thus stimulating social and economic benefits. In our globalised economy, where companies can move easily between countries and can find equally well-educated employees in countries with lower cost bases, Ireland needs to remain competitive. Globalisation has led to increasing levels of 'tax competition' between nations, as governments are under pressure to offer a low corporate tax burden.[6] If the Irish government is to meet one of its objectives (maximising employment), it needs to provide incentives to companies to attract and retain investment in Ireland, such as the low corporate tax burden. The policy is widely accepted as being successful in attracting foreign direct investment: according to preliminary figures for 2012 released by the OECD, Ireland received the second highest inflow of foreign capital in the EU for 2012.[7]

## OIL AND GAS ARE DIFFERENT

But the two arguments (increasing employment levels and tax competition) outlined above in support of the lower corporation tax rate are not as relevant for the hydrocarbon industry for two reasons:

1. Based on the loose licence terms, it is highly unlikely that the industry will create any significant level of employment to reduce our high unemployment levels. Furthermore, any positions created are likely to be highly specialised and therefore could require mainly experienced international expertise. At the very least, any additional employment taxes, VAT, excise duties and so on arising from these activities are unlikely to compensate for the corporation tax foregone by having a lower corporation tax rate than is possible.

2. Petroleum is finite, with a low price elasticity of demand, thus making for a very valuable commodity. From an investor's perspective, their key concern will be their internal rate of return. Provided that our tax regime does not excessively diminish the returns to the industry, Ireland should continue to attract investors to Ireland and position ourselves to adjust new licence terms upwards if large, economically viable fields are confirmed by existing holders.

Taxpayers and their lobbyists always argue that investment is discouraged if tax rates are too high. This is because if the tax rates increase too much, it will no longer be viable for these companies to invest, as their potential return on the capital invested will be too low. the Laffer Curve,[8] a general economics representation, explains this scenario quite well.

This representation shows that there is a revenue-maximising level of taxation that will raise the greatest amount of tax from an income source. The idea is that with a 0 percent tax rate, no tax will be raised, simply because none has been applied. With a 100 percent rate of tax, no income will also be raised because there is no incentive to, in this case, extract the oil, as the government will take 100 percent of the profits. At some point in between is a tax rate that will raise the maximum amount of revenue for the Exchequer.

### The Laffer Curve

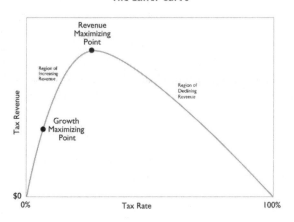

Figure 1

International research carried out by Standard Chartered found that, on average, government take is 49 percent of oil profits.[9] This figure is an average for the eight oil-producing countries researched. There are a number of factors that influence a government's ability to increase its tax take. Such factors can include, among others, the quantity of petroleum reserves, ease of extraction, the bargaining power of the parties, and the risks associated with oil exploration and extraction activities.

Capital Gains Tax needs to be considered separately to corporation tax. Companies are chargeable to corporation tax on any revenue/trading income they receive (after deducting allowable expenses). However, from time to time companies will sell some of the assets of the business. It is for this reason that Own Our Oil made a pre-budget submission to government in July 2013. Extracts follow here:

### *Capital Gains Tax: OOO Pre-Budget Submission*

Own Our Oil is today making a pre-budget submission to the Minister for Finance, Michael Noonan TD, because of concern about the possibility for the imminent sale of licences (or special-purpose companies who hold them) that have been purchased from the State for a few thousand euro, for hundreds of millions of non-recoverable euro. Own Our Oil is requesting that the government adjust the manner in which offshore oil and gas licences are taxed when offloaded to Oil Majors to recover Resource Rent immediately, i.e. supernormal profit.

OOO reminds the government that offshore oil and gas is the property of the people of Ireland and that the government is the custodian. Allowing for exploration and extraction costs and normal profits, currently in the range 20 percent to 30 percent pa internationally, any excess revenues ought to revert to its owners.

Under the current tax code that is not the case. The headline rate of tax on corporates comprising of corporation tax of 25 percent potentially rising to 40 percent by the addition of Resource Rent Tax, is misleading and allows the offshore oil and gas lobby to argue that a tax revenue bonanza would result from their success. Investigation by OOO tax experts however indicates that such is the scope for offsets from capital allowances, losses and 'farm out' relief, that any revenues collected by the State would be very small and would not arise for many years, if at all.

Own Our Oil is requesting the Minister for Finance in the October budget to remodel the tax regime specifically to deal with the potential imminent sale of Irish offshore oil and gas licences for supernormal profits, the resource rent that is properly the property of the people of Ireland, by:

- treating the licence sale in the same way as it would gains from the sale of development land by corporates (Part 22 Chapter 2, TCA 1997)

- disallowing exploration expenditure as a tax offset – to be carried forward instead by the new owners

- removing 'Farm Out Relief', the rollover of the gains into further exploration, minimising the risk of permanent loss to the State

- applying a Capital Gains Tax rate double the current rate, at 66 percent of the gain.

Own Our Oil reminds the government that surplus capital chasing finite oil and gas assets globally, aided by new deep-water exploration and extraction technologies, has led governments throughout the world to tighten tax policies.

By summer 2013, OOO was not too hopeful of the Irish government yielding to the logic of tightening up tax on the sale of assets in the industry, but this was a start. The challenge is in reaching a tipping point in both public and political opinion to recognise the benefits of acting in advance, and not after, a major find: a game-changer like the Ecofisk discovery in Norway.

## CORPORATION TAX

There is no question about a company's right to operate in a manner which maximises shareholder return. However, similarly there is no question of their legal and moral obligation to operate within the laws of those territories in which they operate. Effective corporate tax planning ensures that a company can achieve its objective of maximising shareholder return whilst ensuring compliance with tax legislation. Where a group of companies operate in a number of global economies, there is an incentive to use tax rate arbitrage across these markets to minimise taxes and duties, thus maximising shareholder return for the group.

One creative accounting method specifically targeted in the oil and gas exploration sector by informed regimes such as those of Ghana, is to set up subsidiaries with group loans rather than with equity, thus extracting the juice with excessive interest payments. The Ghanaian rules limit the use of intra-group finance. Irish rules are silent. Another is to apply intra-group services charges to subsidiaries for management, expertise, engineering, and so on, hollowing out the subsidiary and delaying the effect of corporation tax.

How multinationals avoid tax has become a hot issue in the USA and in the UK, where higher corporation tax rates have not yielded the revenues tax authorities had hoped for among their multinational behemoths like Google and Apple, both of whom are nominally exposed to Irish corporation tax of 12.5 percent but, in practice, pay a tiny fraction of that, due largely to the controversial practice of transfer pricing.

In its simplest terms, transfer pricing refers to the process by which a company arrives at a selling price for the transfer of goods or services between two related parties.[10] Through effective transfer pricing planning, a company can optimise where its profits are taxed. Here is a simple example of how this is done.

Company A and Company B are related parties. Company A is located in the USA, which has a headline tax rate of 35 percent (plus state taxes, which range from 3 to 10 percent). Company B is located in Ireland, with a headline corporation tax rate of 12.5 percent.

Company A manufactures a generic pharmaceutical painkiller at a cost of €5 and sells the product to Company B for €15, paying tax of €4 on the profit of €10 (assuming a 40 percent corporate-plus-state tax rate).

Company B packages the generic painkiller into its global-branded packaging at a cost of €1 per case and on-sells to third parties for €100 per case, paying tax of €10.50 on the profit of €84 generated.

Under this scenario, the group (i.e. Company A and B) has paid a total of €14.50 of tax per case. The alternative scenario is where Company A also packaged the products in the US and on-sells to third parties. The total profit earned, of €94, is thus taxed at 40 percent, i.e. €37.60.

Undoubtedly, selling the product to Company B to package and on-sell to third parties minimises the group's total tax liability and thus maximises shareholder return. However, given the incentive for companies to exploit tax-rate arbitrage, many tax authorities around the world have established transfer-pricing rules in an effort to ensure that the transaction price between Company A and Company B (and thus the profit earned by Company A) is at arm's length.[11] Transfer-pricing rules aim to ensure that all parties to a transaction earn a return that appropriately compensates them for the activities undertaken, the assets employed and the risk borne in the said transaction.

However, the issue facing tax authorities is to identify identical transactions and the market price of such transactions. In the absence of perfect comparables, there is leeway for companies to exploit what their perception of an arm's-length price is.

## NORWAY FINDS EVIDENCE OF TRANSFER PRICING ABUSES

Publish What You Pay Norway (PWYP) note in their research paper[12] the difficulties for tax authorities in evaluating whether a transfer price is in fact the market price. This research paper found evidence of mispriced crude oil in the petroleum industry. While they do point to some limitations in their research, PWYP found significant over- and under-pricing of crude oil transactions on the import of oil between the US and the EU from 2000 to 2010. An article[13] in the *International Tax Review* points to the increasing importance of transfer pricing in the petroleum industry.

In 2002, 24 percent of all imports into the US by the petroleum industry were by way of transactions with related companies; in 2011, that figure was 41 percent. They also state that the increasing importance of transfer pricing can be seen by the number of countries which have implemented transfer pricing legislation: in 1994, only twelve countries had transfer-pricing legislation; by 2012, fifty-four countries had implemented such legislation. The OECD in its report 'Addressing Base Erosion and Profit Shifting' (a report not specific to the petroleum industry) notes that one of the key risk causes of profit-shifting from a particular jurisdiction is that of transfer pricing. Importantly, they note that while they could not be conclusive on the magnitude of base erosion and profit shifting (BEPS), 'there is abundant circumstantial evidence that BEPS behaviours are widespread'.[14]

Detailed transfer pricing tax legislation was introduced in Ireland recently, effective from 1 January 2011. Ireland has two specific provisions relating to the petroleum industry that predate the new transfer-pricing rules. Disposals of petroleum between related parties must be at arm's length, and if not, the market value at the time of disposal is substituted. The other rule relates to appropriations of petroleum from one part of a business to the other: again, such a transfer must be at market value.

## CORPORATE TAX ON ACCOUNTING PROFITS

Accounting profits (per a company's financial statements) are not the same as taxable profits. Taxable profits are accounting profits, but after some tax adjustments (increase or decrease) depending on the provisions of the Irish corporation tax rules. The headline corporation tax rate is the rate of tax that is applied to the tax-adjusted profits of a company.

However, the effective tax rate is the rate of tax that applies when the tax payable, as calculated based on 'taxable profits', is compared to the accounting profits, i.e. the rate of tax that was 'effectively' applied to the accounting profits. That is:

- Headline rate of tax = Rate of tax applied to the taxable profits
- Effective rate of tax = Tax payable/Accounting profits.

Capital allowances are an example of a tax adjustment that will cause the effective rate to vary from the headline rate. Normally, revenue expenditure is only allowed as a deduction for tax purposes. Capital allowances are a tax deduction allowed for capital expenditure incurred. Capital allowances are a tax incentive provided by the government (i.e. the government forgoes an amount of tax revenue by allowing companies to take a deduction for capital expenditure) to encourage companies to incur capital expenditure (i.e. to invest).

The table below shows that the headline rate of corporation tax is not as important as the effective rate of tax. If tax-deductible expenditure is increased, taxable profits are reduced and therefore the headline corporation tax rate will be applied to a lower profit figure. This is an important point when considering how a company, through the use of transfer pricing (i.e. increasing its expenditure), could potentially reduce the tax it pays. It is also an important point when considering whether the taxation of profits is the most effective method of applying tax to companies in this industry.

|  | *Headline Tax Rate* | *Effective Tax Rate* |
|---|---|---|
| Income (oil sales, etc.) | 1,000 | 1,000 |
| Expenditure (purchases, salaries, royalty payments, interest expense on loans, other operating costs, etc.) | (300) | (300) |
| Accounting Profit | 700 | 700 |
| Capital Allowances | – | (200) |
| Taxable Profit | 700 | 500 |
| Corporation Tax @ 25% | (175) | (125) |
| After-Tax Profit | 525 | 375 |
| Headline Rate | 25% | 25% |
| Effective Rate | 175/700 = 25% | 125/700 = 17.9% |

Table 1
Headline Tax Rate/Effective Tax Rate

It is rare for a company ever to pay the headline rate of tax. Mostly accounting profits will be reduced by tax adjustments (such as capital allowances), but other tax adjustments may increase the effective rate of corporation tax: for example, an item of expenditure is deductible for accounting purposes, but not for tax purposes. While the Irish corporation tax rate in the industry is 25 percent (potentially rising to 40 percent), the effective rate of tax is likely to be far lower, at least for the early years of a project, when the companies write off the early capital expenditure, given the large capital allowances available.

## CORPORATE TAXATION OF THE IRISH PETROLEUM INDUSTRY

The profits of a company arising in its petroleum trade are subject to a headline corporation tax rate of 25 percent. A petroleum trade consists of any petroleum exploration or extraction activities, as well as the acquisition, enjoyment or exploitation of petroleum rights (Section 21A(1), Taxes Consolidation Act 1997).

Since 2007, Irish tax legislation has contained a provision which increases the corporation tax rate on certain profitable oil fields, i.e. oil fields subject to licences issued since 2007 which attain a certain level of profitability. This additional tax is referred to as a 'Profit Resource Rent Tax' (PRRT). PRRT operates as follows:

- As the cumulative profits (after corporate tax) from an oil field increase relative to the cumulative capital expenditures incurred in the field, a PRRT is applied to the taxable profits of the company.

- The PRRT rates range from 0 to 15 percent depending on the 'profit ratio' (i.e. the amount by which field profits exceed field capital investment) as follows:

  Profit ratio PRRT to apply to after-tax profits:

  - Less than 1.5 – 0 percent

  - More than 1.5 but less than 3 – 5 percent

  - 3 or more but less than 4.5 – 10 percent

  - 4.5 or more – 15 percent

- The PRRT is applied on a per-field basis. This means that losses incurred in other fields cannot be used to reduce the PRRT for profitable fields. However, there is a provision that allows certain related companies to transfer costs incurred by one company to the other company for the purposes of calculating the profit ratio.

- The PRRT only applies to licences and subsequent leases granted since 2007.

The expenditures used in calculating the profit ratio to determine whether the PRRT should apply are those from the three life-stages of an oil field: exploration, development and abandonment expenditures. These expenditures will be quite large and therefore it may take a long time for a petroleum company, even when exploiting a successful field, to start paying the PRRT.

## INTEREST AND OTHER FINANCE COSTS

Interest can be a significant cost for petroleum entities, and therefore if it is a tax-deductible expense, it may reduce profits significantly. Generally, an interest expense incurred on monies borrowed by a company for the purpose of its trade is, prima facie, a deductible expense. However, any interest expenses paid to a connected party that are greater than an arm's-length amount are not deductible for tax purposes. Specifically in relation to petroleum companies, any interest expense in relation to monies borrowed to fund petroleum exploration activities, and any interest expense in relation to monies borrowed to acquire petroleum rights from a connected person, are not deductible. These restrictions should result in a higher effective rate of tax than without the restrictions.

## CAPITAL ALLOWANCES

During the course of petroleum extraction activities, a petroleum company will incur large amounts of capital expenditure. This expenditure, referred to as 'Development Expenditure', would include, for example, the expenditure to build the oil rig and purchase the drilling equipment. Clearly the amounts involved here are very large. When a non-petroleum company, say a factory producing computers, incurs capital expenditure (such as purchasing a larger factory), they can claim capital allowances annually at 12.5 percent of the total cost incurred. This means that capital expenditure is normally written off over eight years. Irish tax legislation provides a 100 percent capital allowance to petroleum companies in the first year, i.e. the company is allowed to take a full deduction for its development costs as they are incurred.

An additional capital allowance is available in respect of petroleum exploration activities. These expenses are the costs associated with locating an oil field, such as the chartering of ships, the purchase of seismic equipment, or payments made to the Minister for Communications, Energy and Natural Resources for the granting of a licence to explore Irish territorial waters. The capital allowance granted in year 1 is 100 percent of the exploration expenses incurred. In order to claim this allowance, the petroleum company must be carrying out petroleum extraction activities, i.e. the allowance is only available when the company begins to extract oil or gas. However, once the company does qualify for this allowance, it will be entitled to an upfront allowance representing all explorative expenditure (both successful and abortive) incurred in the previous twenty-five years.

This exploration expenditure can be transferred to a related company in two circumstances. Firstly, where the exploration company disposes of the asset that was created through the incursion of this exploration expenditure, the purchasing company can take a deduction for the exploration expenditure (not exceeding the amount paid by the purchasing company in acquiring this asset). Secondly, the exploring company is permitted to transfer the exploration costs it incurred to an oil-extracting company in the same group, so that the oil-extracting company is deemed to have incurred the expenditure itself.

Under the terms of a petroleum extraction lease (licence), a petroleum extraction company will be required to dismantle its structures in the oil field. Again, such costs will be very large, given the scale of the operation, the highly specialised equipment involved and the location of the oil drilling operations. Irish tax legislation provides a further allowance for the capital expenditures incurred in dismantling the oil operations, referred to as 'Abandonment Expenditure'. The allowance provides for the 100 percent write-off of all Abandonment Expenditure against the profits of the year in which the costs were incurred, as well as the profits of the three preceding years.

## TAX LOSSES

Losses arising in a petroleum trade can be set against trading profits and chargeable gains of the current and immediately preceding year, with any remaining losses available to be carried forward indefinitely to shelter future trading profits from the same trade. Furthermore, losses arising in the petroleum trade of one company can be surrendered to another group company to set against the profits and chargeable gains in its petroleum trade. Due to the 100 percent upfront capital allowances, combined with the unrestricted carry-forward of trading losses, corporation tax is not likely to be paid until the later years of an oil-extraction project.

Losses arising in a petroleum trade are subject to 'two-way ring-fencing' provisions. This means that losses arising in a petroleum trade cannot be offset against profits in a non-petroleum trade, and vice versa. This is to prevent the (potentially significant) trading losses in a petroleum trade from reducing the tax liability of other trades. The same 'two-way ring-fencing' provisions apply in the case of losses arising on non-trading income and chargeable gains as well as in the case of two companies surrendering losses between one another ('group loss relief'). This should ensure that all forms of income earned by a petroleum company in a non-petroleum trade cannot be sheltered by losses from a petroleum trade, and vice versa.

## CAPITAL GAINS TAX

Any capital gain arising from the disposal of petroleum-related capital assets (including the disposal of an oil exploration licence) will also be subject to corporation tax, but at the capital gains tax rate of 33 percent. As such gains are brought into the corporation tax computation, it is possible that losses (including certain losses incurred by group companies) or capital allowances (in certain instances) in relation to other petroleum activities could be used to shelter such gains.

A 'farm-out' is the process whereby a petroleum exploration company with a licence in a petroleum field disposes of its interest in that field to a petroleum extraction company, who will then extract the petroleum. Significant gains could arise from the disposal of such a licence. Irish corporation tax legislation provides a deferral of the payment of corporation tax on chargeable gains arising on the disposal of a petroleum licence, once the proceeds of the disposal are applied to other petroleum exploitation activities within three years or longer if the Minister for Communications, Energy and Natural resources allows it. Theoretically the deferred tax should eventually be paid upon the disposal of any asset created by this new investment in exploration activities. The relief is to provide an incentive for petroleum entities to invest further capital in Irish oil exploration activities, which may in turn result in the discovery of other petroleum fields and thereby increase the future corporation tax take of the State. However, as any future exploration activities may or may not be successful, it is the Irish taxpayer who ultimately assumes the investment risk of the reinvested proceeds. This, set against increased recent activity in Irish waters, is one of the reasons why Own Our Oil made its pre-budget submission on Capital Gains Tax in 2013.

## INTERNATIONAL TAX PRACTICE

There are a large number of oil-producing countries worldwide. Each country has its own pricing regime tailored to that country's particular needs. Most countries impose a variety of taxes on different aspects of the petroleum companies' operations. The combination of these different taxes will result in the overall 'government take' for that country.

'Government take' can be described as the percentage of petroleum profits that are taken by a government. Some countries have very high levels of 'government take' (up to 98 percent) while others have very low levels of taxation. A government will generally be able to apply higher rates of taxation to the petroleum industry in countries that have larger reserves of oil, where those oil reserves are very accessible, and where the country is a net oil exporter.[15]

Comparisons between the Irish tax system and those of many oil-producing nations is complicated for two reasons. Firstly, the taxation systems and the types of taxes applied can vary quite considerably from country to country. Secondly, varying social, economic and political influences may have impacted on the forms and levels of taxation that have developed in other countries, so a comparison based solely on taxation rates does not provide a true benchmark of the level of taxation that should apply to the petroleum industry in Ireland.

## UK Comparison

If oil is found off County Antrim, how would the pricing differ from oil found off County Donegal? The Irish tax system is comparable to the UK's tax system in terms of geography and structure – although not pricing. The UK's petroleum industry began in the late 1960s with the discovery of North Sea oil and as a result the UK has a well-established petroleum industry today.

### Corporation Tax Rate

Ireland applies a headline rate of corporation tax of 25 percent to oil exploration and extraction activities. The UK applies a rate of 30 percent. Other petroleum-related activities, such as oil refining and marketing, are subject to the 12.5 percent rate of tax in Ireland, while from 2014 these activities in the UK will be subject to 21 percent corporation tax.

The UK also applies a further level of corporation tax, referred to as the 'Supplementary Charge Tax'. This tax is calculated on profits (as with the normal corporation tax rate), but these profits are adjusted upwards, as no deduction is allowed for financing costs (such as interest, finance charges on leases, and so on). The UK reduces the burden of this tax in certain instances in order to encourage investment in more challenging oil fields. The Supplementary Charge is applied at a rate of 32 percent. Ireland does not apply such a tax.

The UK applies a third form of taxation to profits, 'Petroleum Revenue Tax' (the name is a bit misleading as it is not a tax on revenue). This tax head is similar to the Irish Profit Resource Rent Tax (PRRT) in that it is calculated on a field-by-field basis. However, it differs from the Irish PRRT in a number of ways. The Petroleum Revenue Tax in the UK only applies to older fields (licences issued pre-1993). It is not based on accounting profits, rather on profits calculated in accordance with UK statutory provisions. For example, finance costs are not deductible when calculating profits for Petroleum Revenue Tax. The UK system does provide some reliefs from this tax.

Petroleum Revenue Tax losses can be carried forward or back indefinitely, and oil allowances are provided to reduce the burden on marginal fields for the first ten years. The Petroleum Revenue Tax is charged at 50 percent of the statutorily calculated profits, but this tax is tax-deductible for the purposes of calculating the two other corporation taxes (corporation tax and supplementary charge tax). Irish PRRT ranges from 0 to 15 percent, but for PRRT to apply, the oil field must first reach a certain level of profitability.

### Interest and Other Finance Costs

For the purposes of the charge to corporation tax in both Ireland and the UK, only certain interest expenses are allowed to be deducted (i.e. interest on monies borrowed for oil extraction purposes (not exploration) and interest on monies borrowed to acquire a licence from a third party (not a related party)). These restrictions also apply to the PRRT in Ireland.

Interest and other finance costs are not deductible for the purposes of calculating the UK Supplementary Charge Tax, and interest is not deductible for the Petroleum Revenue Tax. This restriction has the effect of taxing larger profits than would be the case if the petroleum entities were allowed to deduct such finance costs. Ireland does not have a Supplementary Charge Tax or a Petroleum Revenue Tax.

## Capital Allowances

As with the Irish regime, the UK provides an allowance of 100 percent for exploration costs prior to production and development costs as they are incurred. However, if such assets to which the allowance relates are sold or cease to be used for exploration or extraction activities within five years of acquisition, the allowance is clawed back. Ireland does not have this clawback provision.

Both the UK and Irish regimes also provide for a 100 percent allowance for decommissioning costs at the end of the lease term. However, for the purposes of the Supplementary Charge Tax in the UK, the allowance on decommissioning is limited to 20 percent of the costs incurred. The UK system is currently more generous in one aspect, as it allows such decommissioning costs to be used to reduce taxable profits as far back as 2002, while the Irish system only permits a three-year carry-back period beyond the year in which the costs are incurred.

## Tax Losses

The treatment of trading losses in Ireland and the UK appears to be quite similar except in the case of Petroleum Revenue Tax in the UK, which has an indefinite carry-back and carry-forward period. The UK provides a 'Ring-fence Expenditure Supplement', which effectively increases the value of a petroleum company's losses in the years that such a company can neither use the losses nor surrender the losses to a group company. The losses are increased by 10 percent each year this relief is claimed, and the relief can be claimed for up to six years. This relief is not available in Ireland.

## Capital Gains Tax

Capital gains on the disposal of assets by a petroleum company are effectively subject to corporation tax in Ireland at 33 percent and in the UK at 30 percent. The rate in the UK is reduced to 26 percent for companies not involved in exploration or extraction activities.

Companies involved in exploration or extraction activities will be subject additionally to the Supplementary Charge Tax at 32 percent.

In the UK, chargeable gains on the disposal of licences (and assets transferred as part of the licence transfer) are ring-fenced. This means that chargeable gains on the disposal of a licence cannot be reduced by previous capital losses unless these losses arose on the sale of other licences. This narrow ring-fencing ensures that the disposal of licences should result in a corporation tax charge for the disposing company.

Ireland has a wider ring-fencing rule for chargeable gains, which encompasses all petroleum-related assets, such as licences, exploration or development assets, and shares in companies deriving their value from petroleum activities. The Irish system therefore provides more opportunities to use losses against chargeable gains arising on the sale of licences. The narrow ring-fenced losses in the UK can be used to offset non-ring-fenced gains ('one-way ring-fencing'), while this is not allowable under the Irish two-way ring-fencing rules.

The UK system provides an exemption from corporation tax ('reinvestment relief') where the proceeds for the disposal of oil assets (except licences) are invested in other 'oil assets'. These oil assets have a broad definition and cover exploration expenditure and the purchase of licences, among other assets. Ireland does not offer this reinvestment relief.

In Ireland, investment in oil exploration activities using the proceeds from a licence 'farm-out' is sufficient to obtain a deferral of corporation tax on the disposal of a petroleum licence. Taxable gains on 'farm-outs' are also capable of being deferred in the UK, where the consideration for the disposal is used to acquire certain assets. These assets are more restricted than under the reinvestment relief, and do not include exploration expenditure.

The UK provides an exemption from capital gains tax on the disposal of a company by a parent company which holds at least 10 percent of its shares. A similar relief is available in Ireland; however, companies in the petroleum industry are specifically excluded from this relief.

## Transfer Pricing

The UK and Ireland both have transfer-pricing legislation in place, as well as additional market-value rules in relation to appropriations between different aspects of a petroleum company. However, the UK has additional specific transfer-pricing rules for the petroleum industry that we do not have in Ireland. The Irish system requires that transfers of petroleum between related parties take place at market value. The determination of this market value is not specified. By contrast, the UK tax authorities have strict valuation rules and maintain a database of values of common crude-oil types, as a means of ensuring the correct market value is used. Furthermore, the UK tax authorities have implemented a 'nomination scheme'.[16] This is to prevent petroleum organisations reducing their liability to Petroleum Revenue Tax and involves a complex system of nominating oil sales contracts in advance of deliveries. Overall, the UK TP regime is more focused and more sophisticated in relation to the petroleum industry, when compared to the new Irish TP regime.

## Other

The UK also provides a number of incentives to the petroleum industry. Both Ireland and the UK offer tax reliefs to companies (not exclusive to the petroleum industry) investing in R&D activities. The R&D relief would appear to be more generous in Ireland but this is available to all companies and is the result of government policy for the last number of years to increase the levels of R&D being carried out in Ireland.

Overall it is pretty evident that the government take from a petroleum company operating under an Irish licence would be lower than that of a comparable company in the UK.

## OTHER INTERNATIONAL COMPARISONS IN BRIEF

Detailed comparisons can be made by accessing the Ernst & Young guide on global oil and gas regime pricing across more than one hundred countries reflecting localised geology, development, political systems and locations. The following is a high-level overview of the situation in some of these countries.

## Portugal[17]

Portugal has a headline corporation tax rate of 25 percent plus a local surcharge of 1.5 percent. The aggregate headline rate can increase to 31.5 percent depending on profit levels. Portugal does not apply royalties and restricts the use of losses significantly. Firstly, it does not allow the indefinite carry-forward of losses: the carry-forward period is restricted to five years. Secondly, the amount of losses that are allowed to be offset against profits in any one year are restricted to 75 percent of those profits, meaning that at least 25 percent of tax-adjusted profits in any year should be subject to tax. Due to the potentially large losses that are created by the significant capital allowances in the early years of a petroleum field, restricting the quantity of losses that can be used against profits in any one year should ensure that corporation tax is paid throughout the life of the oil field.

## Peru

Peru has a headline corporation tax rate of 30 percent and also applies royalties of 5 to 20 percent. A petroleum company operating in Peru is required to distribute 5 percent of its pre-tax profits among its employees. Capital allowances in any one year are 20 percent of the cost in respect of equipment used in the petroleum industry. A full deduction for exploration and development expenditures incurred prior to production are allowed either over the life of the oil field or on a straight-line basis for a minimum of five years. A corporate tax payer has a choice of how they wish to use any tax losses. The losses can either be carried forward unrestricted to set against the profits of the subsequent four tax years, or the losses can be carried forward indefinitely, but the losses available in any one year are restricted to 50 percent of the tax-adjusted profits.

## Canada

Federal corporate tax of 15 percent and provincial corporate tax rates of 10 to 16 percent apply to the taxable profits of all companies in Canada. Petroleum companies must also pay royalties at a rate between 10 and 45 percent, depending on the province in which the oil well is located, the productivity of the well, and the sales price of the oil. Canada offers a form of capital allowances to petroleum companies. The percentage of capital costs that can be taken as a deduction in any one tax year are 10 percent (cost of oil and gas rights), 25 percent (oil and gas equipment), 30 percent (development expenditure) and 100 percent (exploration expenditure). There is also a 10 percent allowance for costs associated with acquiring foreign petroleum rights and exploration and development costs in fields outside Canada. Tax losses can be carried back three years and forward twenty years to offset against tax-adjusted profits. There is no group loss relief in Canada.

## POTENTIAL CHANGES TO THE IRISH REGIME

The following points may be considered as part of any detailed review of the Irish petroleum industry.

- The risks of transfer pricing and the fallacy of only taxing an enterprise based on their tax-adjusted profits needs close attention. As highlighted by the OECD report, base erosion and profit-shifting techniques are commonly used to reduce tax liabilities of corporations. A potential solution would be to implement a system that requires petroleum companies to pay a royalty relative to their level of production. This would tax revenues, and not profits, which could potentially be subject to manipulation through the use of profit-shifting techniques. The UK rules of transfer pricing, at the very least, should be copied.

- There may be merit in changing the formula used to establish whether a company is to be subject to the PRRT. An amended formula could be based on the cumulative revenues from a particular field, rather than cumulative profits from a particular field, which is currently the case. Alternatively, the PRRT could be abolished in favour of a tax similar to the UK's Petroleum Revenue Tax.

- As noted previously, the UK applies an additional corporation tax level (the 'Supplementary Charge Tax'). Introducing a further corporation tax charge in Ireland or raising the current rate of corporation tax on petroleum activities may be beneficial.

- It may be possible to extend the restrictions on deductibility of interest and finance charges, in order to increase the effective rate of tax for the petroleum industry. For example, the restrictions could be extended to interest on monies borrowed to undertake petroleum exploitation activities or to interest on monies borrowed to acquire petroleum rights from all parties, connected and unconnected.

- A restriction on the number of years that losses can be carried forward by petroleum companies makes sense, or, at least, a restriction on the use of losses each year to ensure that a minimum amount of profits is taxed throughout the life of a petroleum field.

- The various capital allowances provided under Irish tax legislation to petroleum companies all allow a 100 percent write-off of capital costs in year 1. The write-off period could be extended so that large write-offs were not available in the first year. This would have the effect of reducing the amount of losses allowable as a deduction against taxable profits in any one year. As with the losses, this may ensure that corporation tax was received over the life of an oil field, rather than later in the project.

- Currently, successful and abortive exploratory expenditure for twenty-five years is deductible. It is questionable whether such a long period of time is necessary, logical or equitable.

- There may be merit in narrowing the Irish ring-fencing rules in relation to chargeable gains in order to ensure that capital allowances, trading losses and group losses are not available to shelter such gains. Alternatively, the legislation could be amended so that disposals of licences are subject to capital gains tax rather than corporation tax, as outlined in the Own Our Oil pre-budget submission, 2013.

## WHAT ABOUT EXISTING LICENCES?

The use of retrospective legislation may need to be considered to extend any tax increases to licences issued pre-2007. Retrospective legislation goes against the basic principle of certainty in taxation, and it has also been said potentially to be contrary to the European

Convention on Human Rights. However, companies and individuals across Ireland are living in very different circumstances compared to 2007, and the pivot in 1987 by Minister Ray Burke, who was subsequently jailed on corruption charges related to planning, is a mitigating factor. The UK has increased tax rates retrospectively on the petroleum industry in response to large increases in oil prices. In order to avoid the need for such retrospective legislation in future, it may be worth considering the inclusion of mechanisms in our legislation which would automatically increase the tax rate applied to the petroleum industry at times when increases in global oil prices may create windfall gains for the industry.

## CONCLUSION

Getting the balance right between Irish pricing and Irish risks to exploration companies is not easy. The situation is complicated by Irish geology, depth of waters, weather, planning and international competition but especially by the apparent callowness of the Irish establishment since Justin Keating's thinking and pricing was dismantled by Ray Burke. This book is dedicated to the memory of Justin Keating for good reason: he grasped, absorbed and implemented the lessons from the dramatic Norwegian overhaul in 1972.

Irish pricing has to reflect Irish risks and where we stand along the development curve, but it should also reflect the will of the Irish people not to be exploited and, instead, to regain control over our oil and gas endowment for this and future generations. As part of a belt-and-braces overhaul of Irish strategy that includes changes to the planning system and a development plan for a domestic hydrocarbon industry, Irish pricing first needs to be repositioned and then tightened in line with audited data on new discoveries. Meanwhile, Irish expertise needs to grow, funnelled through a national oil exploration company that partners and learns from private companies, over time. All of this needs to happen with an overarching framework that gives environmental protection priority.

In this chapter, a number of tactics have been identified to tighten up on the scope for creative accounting. All make sense, including the submission to the Minister for Finance on Capital Gains Tax, but the real hot issue is the implementation of production-sharing and royalties for future licences. These, in combination with an overhaul of Irish strategy, recommend themselves highly despite industry bleating to the contrary.

Production-sharing would allow the State a share in every barrel of oil or cubic metre of gas extracted. Royalties would allow for a percentage on every sale from these national resources. Neither currently exist; both bypass the labyrinthine world of tax avoidance and bring certainty to revenue flows. We end, not being overly prescriptive – the right balance needs to be struck at the right time, like coinciding with a major new discovery – but one thing is absolutely clear: the existing pricing regime is exploitative, is of questionable origin and marks a shameful giveaway of Irish assets to private industry for a handful of coloured beans.

## About the Author

Eilis Quinlan is a fellow of the Association of Chartered Certified Accountants. She is also a registered auditor who runs a successful accountancy practice in Naas, County Kildare. Eilis holds an accredited mediator award from the Mediation Forum of Ireland and a certificate in computing from DCU. She is also a member of MENSA.

Eilis is currently president of the North Kildare Chamber of Commerce and a director and past chairman of the Irish Small and Medium Enterprises Association. Her main expertise lies in the areas of taxation advice, small-company development and corporate finance. Eilis is a non-executive director of a number of limited companies and charities, and she also sits on various committees in a bid to encourage local business growth.

Eilis is a regular contributor to national television and radio programmes.

In 2009 Eilis was appointed by then Minister Michael Martin to the government's advisory Management Development Council. In 2010 Eilis was voted Kildare Business Woman of the Year, and was also runner-up in the Irish Business Woman of the Year that same year.

Outside of business, Eilis enjoys many interests including horses (show jumping, racing and polo) and was a member of the Irish International Amateur Showjumping Team from 1997 to 2001, winning the Irish National Championships in 2001, after which a bad fall ended her showjumping career. Eilis played the cello with the National Youth Orchestra of Ireland and the RTÉ Symphony Orchestra.

Eilis enjoys cooking, theatre, music of all kinds, especially classical, and travel, but most of all, relaxing with friends, her husband and family, including her two grandchildren, over a Sunday roast.

## Notes

1.  Smith, Adam. 1776. *The Wealth of Nations*

2.  *The Revenue Commissioners v. O'Flynn Construction Ltd and Others* (2011) ITR 113

3.  The World Bank/IFC, PwC, 'Paying Taxes 2013 – The Global Picture'

4.  Case C-446/03, *Marks & Spencer plc v David Halsey (HM Inspector of Taxes)*

5.  Seely, Antony. 2012. 'Retrospective Taxation: Earlier Debates.' House of Commons Library, pg 12

6.  OECD. 2013. 'Addressing Base Erosion and Profit Shifting.' OECD Publishing, pg 28. dx.doi.org/10.1787/9789264192744-en

7.  OECD. 2013. 'FDI in Figures.' www.oecd.org/daf/inv/FDI%20in%20figures.pdf

8.  www.cato.org/blog/question-week-whats-right-point-laffer-curve

9.  Standard Chartered (2012). 'Global Crude Oil – A Compass for Fiscal Change.'

10. There is no standard international tax definition of 'related-parties', however it can generally be assumed to apply to two parties which have a 50% or greater common shareholding, either directly or indirectly

11. 'This valuation principle is commonly applied to commercial and financial transactions between related companies. It says that transactions should be valued as if they had been carried out between unrelated parties, each acting in his own best interest.' stats.oecd.org/glossary/detail.asp?ID=7245

12. Publish What You Pay (Norway) (2012). 'Lost Billions – Transfer Pricing in the Extractive Industries.' www.pwyp.no/sites/all/files/1008a-PWYP_TransferPricing_ENG_DOWNLOAD.pdf

13. International Tax Review. 2012. 'Transfer Pricing – Transfer Pricing in the Oil and Gas Sector: A Primer'

14. OECD. 2013. 'Addressing Base Erosion and Profit Shifting.' OECD Publishing, pg 15. dx.doi.org/10.1787/9789264192744-en

15. Standard Chartered. 2012. 'Global Crude Oil – A Compass for Fiscal Change'

16. KPMG. 2012. 'A Guide to UK Oil and Gas Taxation.' www.kpmginstitutes.com/global-energy-institute/insights/2013/pdf/guide-to-uk-oil-and-gas-taxation.pdf

17. 'Portugal Tax Guide 2012.' www.claytonmckervey.com/attach/worldwide-tax-guide-portugal.pdf

# 13.

# MY OIL AND GAS FILMING IN NORWAY
## Scott O'Connor

*Scott O'Connor was so irked about Ireland's oil and gas giveaway that he travelled from Dingle, County Kerry, with his one-man camera crew to visit Oslo in 2011, producing a documentary of remarkable clarity and insights from the streets of the Norwegian capital. You can view Scott's film on Own Our Oil's website. This is his story.*

## NERVES OVER THE WORLD'S MOST EXPENSIVE PIZZA

The world's most expensive pizza sat looking at us on the countertop of an Oslo bar. We sat, looking at each other.

'Are they just going to tell us to F off?' Aidan asked me nervously. I couldn't answer him with any degree of honesty because I didn't know. The questions we were about to ask the Norwegians might be construed as confrontational. As I looked around the bar, I couldn't help imagining some of their faces contorting or becoming incensed as they slowly construed that we were accusing them of stealing Ireland's oil money. In the bag at our feet was a small video camera we had borrowed and a microphone that looked like it came in a cracker. The tripod that protruded from the bag was little more than a silver twig with arbitrary plastic bits stuck to it. And the notebook in the front pocket was blank where it was supposed to have six short and clearly written questions. Ill-equipped and ill-prepared, we both resigned ourselves to nerves and apprehension. My feeble attempts to hide this fact were lost on Aidan.

'Don't worry man, sure what of it if they do,' I said rhetorically.

'What if they do what?' he said.

'Tell us to F off.'

'Why would they tell us to F off?'

We had just begun sharing the pizza when the sound of Scandinavian undulations came from behind Aidan. Amidst the gentle-sounding language we heard the voice say 'Irish coffee' to the bar-girl. Like some nervous reaction, Aidan spun on his stool to face what was a normal-looking man, probably in his sixties. As if his dramatic spin, long hair and goatee weren't enough to throw the man, Aidan said:

'My mate's grandfather invented Irish coffees, you know.' As with the other ten or fifteen times that Aidan has grasped this opportunity in his life, the retort he received was jovial and utterly sceptical.

'Ah yes, very good,' replied the man. I empathised with the stranger, an unsolicited information breakout from Jesus with an Irish accent, claiming ties to the first man to combine whiskey, coffee and cream in the same cup.

'No, no, no, he really did,' persisted Aidan. Again the man politely feigned laughter, while I could see the calculations he was making as to Aidan's sobriety.

'He really did, I'm telling you, his name was Joe Jackson.'

As the man walked away from us, I only spoke two words to Aidan. They were: 'nice' and 'start'. We finished the world's most expensive pizza slowly, but the pace at which we did so had nothing to do with the price.

The prospect of abject failure really sucks when you're deciding whether or not to do something. It sucks exponentially if the prospect comes to mind when you've only just begun. Your whole river of enthusiasm can be polluted beyond restoration. In the quiet moments I had when Aidan went to the gents, I could afford to be downright negative about the future of this trip. I could envision the remaining hours of this day, sidling up to strangers and sheepishly asking them loaded questions about where their nation gets its money from. And, in turn, I could envision the three days after that not bothering at all, and just making snide jokes to each other in order to fog our failings while we waited for the plane back to what we were now calling 'Owe-land'. Would any of this messing with this video camera really contribute, or was it merely a fun idea that would have been better left as something we had just talked about.

Perhaps I had now become beset by the stark reality that we hadn't a clue what we were doing. I never believed that 'things' change because of popular movements. History, time and time again, says that it is small groups, good or bad, that direct the world, and that the masses are merely a conduit for their misadventure. Yet here I was making a video on the premise that if enough people were incensed by it, they might actually do something. If we ever got this video done, would they even watch it? Would an amateur video about 'political stuff' really rile anyone up in Ireland, or would it just be adding one more chunk of agitation to the puke bag of unproductive commentary that I so greatly disgust?

Aidan returned: 'Right come on, let's go and ask these assholes for our fish back.'

We paid what felt like a day's wages for the pizza and stepped outside to light some smokes. We must have looked quite grim, until a voice reached over to us from the many high tables under the canopy of the bar.

'Hey! You were right. I believe you.' We turned to see the Irish-coffee man waving his iPhone jovially and indicating that he had been Googling.

'You are from Ireland, yes?'

Yes, we told him, with utter delight. Aidan couldn't help himself, and asked the man if he had ever been there.

'Ah yes, in the eighties, on the seismic,' said the man.

For a moment I thought the man had actually said 'seismic'. 'Seismic? As in oil and gas exploration?' I asked him.

'Yes, on the seismic for oil, and gas.' He followed by making hand gestures, outlining the Norwegian coast, over the North Sea, Derry and down the west coast. As his hand passed over the place where I live, a visceral memory pierced me and a thought came to mind: right, let's make this bloody video.

## THE MADDENING

This bloody video had started as a single cynical thought two months earlier. A thought born from many things: years of contempt for the decadence of the Celtic Tiger (the only animal I've ever been glad to see become extinct); then a mere moment's respite before I witnessed my whole country fall into the jaws of those merciless businesses owned by those we call the bondholders. But the final push came when I learnt about what is done with oil and gas in this country. This led to what I call 'the Maddening', a term I use to describe the moment when Irish people perceive exactly how badly they are being shafted when it comes to their natural resources.

My own maddening began quite bluntly on a windswept road in west Mayo when I saw a member of the Gardaí throw a girl into a ditch. What had started out as a surf trip, to one of the most beautiful parts of Ireland, became a journey into the ugliest parts of the Irish State. The long drive home granted me the opportunity to view the bigger picture. What I saw wasn't just farmers being thrown into the ditch, but along with them our natural resources, our justice system, and all regard for our nature and citizens. The voices of those who aimed to defend such acts with jobs statistics, I could only view as the voice of aggressive stupidity.

The event had left me with a spiralling mass of emotions. Two days later, and I still felt knotted; the Thursday after that, I felt even more so. There was guilt and there was anger, but mostly there was frustration: what could I do? That particular evening I couldn't even finish a single thought before a worse one barged in. Worst of all, I really couldn't concentrate on work or anything else. Clearly this was driving me mad. So, as one does in such times, I went to bed.

As I curled up to sleep that night, I could see the strobing images of the brutality that was merely a physical manifestation of the government's attitude on this whole issue. Ever since Burke and Ahern did their thing, it had been: 'Get back, you bastards, and stay back. We're doing stuff behind this fence.' These images became overdubbed by Oscar Wilde, who misquoted himself to me: 'The hottest places in hell are reserved for those who, in a time of moral crisis retain neutrality.'

If the sweaty heap I woke up in was anything to go by, I'd definitely say that the Maddening had intensified during the night. At this point I didn't really give a rat's about Irish people and had a more pressing challenge in quelling my infuriation. If it was Oscar who had presided over my descent into sleep, it was the words of my mother which did so on my rising from it. Through my many, many years of being an asshole, I'd say my teenage ones were the most outstanding. All during this time, her mantra 'Don't get bitter, get better' had seemed so redundant to me, but now – how much the phrase she had put in my head meant to me.

All I was doing was getting bitter. I began thinking. Maybe, if Irish people knew that a bunch of strangers in Norway were getting more out of this than them, they'd at least pay attention. After all, aren't we always going on about our penchant for begrudgery? In fact, don't we nearly boast about it, like Irish begrudgery is the best begrudgery in the world or something. But maybe if they saw that they could do something about it, they would.

I pulled up some basic figures: estimated value of Corrib gas field, €13 billion; total Statoil share, 38 percent; state ownership of Statoil, 78 percent; number of adults in Norway, 4.6 million. I did some rudimentary calculations and came up with the inaccurate yet approximate estimation that every adult in Norway will get four grand from the field. If this tax appraisal of the current oil and gas regime in Ireland was correct, then Irish people would only be getting 4 percent, which worked out at just €167.74 for every adult. That kind of money would be lost on the inefficiencies of the State. Nothing, I thought. What a bloody joke. However, I didn't dwell on it. There had been enough internal griping in the last forty-eight hours, and now I was deeply compelled to do something about it. 'What if I lashed up a video on YouTube explaining this?' I thought. Then I returned to reality: no one would watch that, it is boring to most, and it's nothing that hasn't been said before. Then I cynically thought: 'What if I just went to Norway and asked them for the money back?' The notion amused me at first, but quickly the idea became quite clear – to the point that I had imagined all the questions you could ask a Norwegian on the street. I needed a catalyst if I was going to do this … someone who is brazen, likes riling people, a born agitator. Then it became obvious: Aidan Killian, stand-up comedian. I picked up the phone, selected 'Aiding'.

'What's the crack?'

'Ughhhhhh,' was all I heard, and that went on for a while.

'Yeah yeah, listen do you want to go to Norway?'

'Yeah, for what?'

'I'll explain to you on the way.'

It was that simple, and I booked the flights there and then. In a month's time we would fly to Oslo, and in the meantime I could get back to my work. Which is exactly what I didn't do. I kept finding myself on some oil industry blog or the Government's DCENR Petroleum Affairs Division (PAD), website. Many of the news articles related to Ireland's resources are calamitous, and while they are initially infuriating to anyone who possesses the most basic facts, they ultimately become amusing. While the broadsheets would predominantly report on companies like Providence Resources in a mealy-mouthed manner, the financial news would read like a sales pitch for the very same company. One would tell you that the risks for the company were large and the prospects poor when it suited the agenda, while the other would have you thinking about investing in a sure thing. The pattern of: 'There is probably nothing there', then 'There is a bonanza on the way' is one that I couldn't see ending as long as Tony O'Reilly's newspapers were writing about his oil company.

We needed somewhere to stay, so I chanced sending an email out to all sorts of Norwegian organisations – none of which I knew. The subject of the email simply read: 'Couch?' To my amazement, a lady called Marie Frogner from an environmental organisation called the Neptune Network rang me one day. She had seemed sceptical during the phone call, which is why I was flabbergasted when I received an email from her, the attachment to which was a hotel receipt for a double room, booked and paid for. I almost wanted to give it back: it seemed way too much. This was my first taste of Norwegian kindness and support, which has its own unique character. The email reminded me that I had heard that Norway had offered Ireland help with its resources in the 1980s. I have yet to find a diplomatic letter to the effect, but given that it's probably in a landfill, that is to be expected. All we needed now was a video camera and a microphone. Feeling great about the hotel thing, I left off acquiring both of these essentials until seven hours before takeoff. I very much wish I had not done so, given the fumbling that was to come.

## THE TRUTH OUTS IN THE FIRST INTERVIEW

The Irish-coffee man quickly matched our own level of astonishment when we told him we were making a video about Ireland's oil and gas, but before any further scepticism could seep in, I asked him if we could interview him. He agreed, albeit he still seemed slightly bemused. I clumsily set up the tripod and handed Aidan the microphone, which he took from me as though it had a disease.

'OK, ready?' he asked me. His question might have helped inspire confidence if the mic had actually been plugged in, rather than a cable dangling from his hand. As I fumbled for the mic port, the levels of awkwardness began rising. When I eventually did rig the gear, I peeked up to find that they were staring at me like a pair of shy kids. Then I realised I was probably looking back in a similar fashion. For a split-second all three of us floated in an embarrassed limbo together, each one praying: 'Please God will someone take control of this situation.'

'OK?' Aidan asked again.

'Eh, yeah, go,' I said, hoping that I had things set right.

Aidan began. 'OK . . . eh, you've been to Ireland looking for oil. Can you tell us about that stuff?' The Irish-coffee man nearly fell off his stool, blasted, as it were, by the broadness of the question. And I, in turn, nearly threw up, given how far removed the question was from the ones Aidan and I had discussed over and over. But timidly, the oil man worked out his own way to tell us about his experiences, working, as so many of his nation have famously done, at sea. He explained his thoughts on 'the Porcupine', its similarities and its differences to the North Sea geology, and how he thought that many of the discoveries had been capped. I soaked up every word. It hardly mattered that I had the camera recording it all.

Before I left, I had transcribed pertinent facts and figures from the internet into my little notebook. The ones from the DCENR Petroleum Affairs Division declared what it called 'non-viable' wells. In other words, wells which are known, but are not producing. Here now I heard a man talking about finding such wells in the 1980s. It makes you think, when all you've heard in the mainstream media is a repetitious string of bent statistics portraying Ireland's fossil prospects as poor. The most glaringly fraudulent of which is to claim that Ireland's strike rate has been dismal since 1970. What they are not telling is that almost no 3D seismic data existed for the Irish territory in the pre-mobile-phone era, which is when the vast majority of these failed exploration wells they are referring to were drilled. From 1995 onwards there was a surge in the amount of highly accurate 3D data collected, and an increase in the strike rate followed. Most importantly, these 'non-viable' wells sat in the statistics like an ice cream just waiting for a politician to lick them. Was the viability of an oil well in the 1980s the same as it is now? No, the fact is with the increased oil prices and the game-changing drilling technology of the last ten years, 'viable' is now as far down as 4,000 metres. Were the oil lobby, the PAD and Pat Rabbitte using the quarter-century-old version of the term, or the present-day meaning? If they are using the former, they'd be well to do some basic searches, although I'm certain such information is unavailable on Teletext.

Our spirits were lifted walking away from the bar: 'Irish coffee' had lit a fire in us. He had accommodated our amateurism, eased our apprehension and generally been a really nice man. The coincidence of meeting him was a good omen, but then when 250,000 of his nation's people work in the energy sector, it was by no means outrageous. We were still shaky in our confidence as fledgling vox-poppers, but we had set our sights on nailing these interviews, and I was adamant that I wasn't going to stop until I had filled the camera's drive with as much of a cross-section of the Norwegian public as it would carry. The idea was that if every sort of a person featured in the video, it would show that, whatever they were saying, they were all saying it: we hadn't just cherry-picked the answers from the types we thought would give them to us.

Our next two interviews went down like lead balloons. We had plenty of enthusiasm – maybe too much. It was our technique that was atrocious. However we weren't deterred, and gladly we didn't revert to the two cowering ducks that we had been back on the bar stools. I kept thinking: 'Look, it can't be that hard.' But before we could address the difficulties facing our interviews, we had addressed the fact that most people didn't want to be in them. It's not easy to arrest people in the street with a video camera, but I quickly realised some of the basics that made it easier.

Mental notes:

1) make it clear you're not a weirdo

2) establish quickly that you're not selling anything

3) smile even though it hurts your face, and

4) keep Aidan hidden until they agree.

By doing this, the agreements started to outnumber the declines, and we managed to do about two or three more. However, our list of questions was long-winded and laced with talk of oil industry tax breaks and alien Irish politics: launching straight into them put people on edge or bemused them, and we had to simplify. So we stopped, and went to find the hotel.

## Nobody Has a Clue

The interviews that first day made us realise that in our naivety we had presumed that the average Norwegian might actually be aware of what their state oil company was up to in Ireland – and that they would know something as to what they stood to gain financially from Ireland's property. They don't. It was Aidan who'd made this point best when pacing around the hotel room: 'They haven't got a f**kin' clue what we're on about, Scott.' Our expectation was akin to expecting that most Irish people, for example, would know that our country gleans tax of €90 million in arms trading annually, which can be used to pay for, say, hospital laundry – they don't. I think I put this best when trying to compare the camera menus to the blasted manual. I said: 'Nobody has a f**kin' clue about this sh*t Aidan, nobody has a clue about lots of sh*t . . . including us.'

On reflecting, for the rest of the evening, in this manic sort of foul-mouthed way, Aidan and I also had to admit that because most Irish people were oblivious to the terms that the State gives to oil and gas companies, we might just have to explain all of this in the video. A daunting avalanche appeared. In it we could see ourselves having somehow to convey tax breaks, politics, geology and every other thing that could wither a viewer's interest.

'Our video won't have a hope against anything with a cat in it,' said Aidan at one point in the debate. Yet without such explanations, it was hard to give a context in which these Norwegian answers would make any sense at all. We could feel that people at home might just think: 'What's this got to do with us?' Then again this was why we were here; it had everything to do with 'us'. The fact that they didn't know that the government was in the process of giving away control of the most promising regions of our seabed was the thing we needed to explain. The fact that the current terms would benefit another country more than us. We should know, and felt by right that there should be a hiatus on the hand-out, until a wide public discourse of the facts took place in our society. It's just too big a deal not to. Whatever about the terms.

We were at breakfast the next morning when Aidan pointed out the other quite obvious problem we were facing. 'They were nervous,' he said. Indeed, everyone we had interviewed since 'Irish coffee' had been taken aback when we bombarded them with such heavy questions. We had come off accusatory without the intention to do so: 'Where d'ya get yer money from?' And while the initial idea for the video came from asking these people for our money back, we really only wanted to explain things to people in Ireland. And to do it in the most simple, accessible way we could.

I was mainly thinking about the sheer quantity of food laid out on the nearby buffet when Aidan suggested: 'Let's just ask them some throwaway questions. You know, to make 'em relax.'

'Good idea,' I said, as I noticed the complexity of this conveyor-type toasting machine they had in the buffet area.

'OK, let's ask them something stupid . . . like . . . like . . . what's Norway famous for.' I nodded in agreement.

'Then . . . what's Ireland famous for, and then we hit them with the real questions.' It made sense: it was a kind of friendly ambush. He went through it again.

'Right, what's Norway famous for: they'll say fjords or something. Then what's Ireland famous for: and they'll say Guinness or something. And then – bang – why is Norway so prosperous.'

'Then we ask them the rest.'

'Yeah,' he said, and together we reeled off the following questions.

Was Norway always such a wealthy nation?

Who gets the money from the oil?

What would you do if your government gave it away and the people got little or nothing?

We felt good.

'I have another idea,' I said. 'Let's get a rake of that meat and bread there and make a heap of sandwiches to bring with us.' As we exited the breakfast hall, heaps of sandwiches discreetly bailed under our arms, I could imagine Aidan's suggestion working . . . and it wasn't long before it did.

Back on the street, the first guy we tried it on answered 'trolls' for Norway's most famous thing, and 'little green men' for Ireland's. Aidan told him that they were called leprechauns, and the man laughed more than when he had said little green men. Now relaxed, Aidan asked him the reason about the country's wealth and he simply answered 'Oil'. We both felt like we had hit upon something, and Aidan kept it going.

'So, were you always a rich nation?'

And he answered: 'No, we were a poor nation before the oil.'

'Who gets the money from the oil?'

And he said: 'We get the money.'

'What if your government gave it away and you got nothing?'

And he went: 'Ha ha ha.'

From that point until the camera batteries ran out that evening, everyone we interviewed gave pretty much the same responses to these six simple questions. The only thing the Norwegians really disagreed on was whether we were more famous for Guinness, leprechauns, music or fighting.

The fact that everyone had given such definite and consistent answers made quite an impression on us. As hard as we tried, we could not find a single person who didn't know fundamentally what they were entitled to from their resources. Many even chose to elaborate vastly for us, giving us insights. One restaurant owner we asked for an interview initially said he was in a rush, yet twenty minutes later he was pounding out facts and figures on wealth distribution from oil and how it was managed in their *massive* sovereign wealth fund.

It made us feel a bit small after a while, especially when we were eating our sandwiches on the green across from the guy's bustling restaurant. Given the Irish situation, we felt a bit like we'd climbed out of a primordial tree and sat down at a picnic for the socially enlightened of Scandinavia. We didn't even want to tell interviewees about our oil deal, lest they all started laughing at us. Then maybe call their friends over to laugh at us some more: 'Ha ha ha, come come, look at these obscure little wallies from Ireland, they give their oil away for next to nothing, sprinkled with a few jobs.' If they had not been such friendly people, we may have become ratty. Such demoralisation was bound, sooner or later, to be directed towards home.

## MESSAGES FROM THE €540 BILLION NOTE

'We, don't, even, talk about this at home, man,' lamented Aidan. 'Jesus, when was the last time you heard a sixteen-year-old girl tell you (putting on a D4 accent) 'Like yeah, we only spend like 4 percent, the rest goes in like the sovereign wealth fund and stuff.'

I was looking for a cigarette paper in my wallet when I pulled out a note I had. It was a €540 billion note made to look like the real thing by the Shell To Sea campaign. Printed on the back were facts and figures. Among them: 'Norway will benefit more from Irish gas than Ireland will.'

'We should be giving one of these to everyone we interview,' I said.

Aidan took a few and began reading one dramatically.

'Ten billion barrels of oil.'

'Government giving it away.'

'Corrupt politician Ray Burke changed the law.'

'Our oil and gas deals are not set in stone. Other countries have renegotiated theirs.'

'We can take it back.'

'€540 billion . . . €540 billion . . . €540 billion!' I gave him a clap.

'Sure we could give Goldman Sachs their blood money and still have enough left over for a fleet of space rockets,' he said, walloping his knee.

'I'd feckin love to go to space,' I said. 'And it's sad, because we probably actually could build satellites or something. All this goddamn talk of attracting foreign investment chasing its tail. Yet, we could be saying: come to Ireland, we have a cheap and secure energy supply and our economy is backed by oil. We could give farmers diesel for next to nothing and make our food exports more competitive. We could do all that. But instead, all we are saying is that we are just another debt-ridden state, with a worse energy policy than war-torn Nigeria.' He grimaced.

'But there's something else, you know, Aidan. When you think about it, there's all this hullabaloo in certain circles about this potential for €540 billion worth of oil and gas, right? And the government says: 'Hey look, if a few wells come good, we'll hike the tax take.' But what if there isn't any more? What if the reserves of the Corrib, Barryroe and Dalkey is all we've got? Then what? Then we would have given away control of the nation's energy security for bugger all. At which point it's not about money, it's about fate.'

It was 2011, we were thirty years old, saturated with IMF debts that weren't ours; both of us had lost friends to emigration, and both of us were sick to death of the apathy at home.

'I just can't understand why there isn't bloody war,' said Aidan. 'Why the whole country isn't on the streets.' He started doing impressions of Kenny meeting the Troika, winking profusely and shaking hands like the village idiot.

'I dunno either,' I said regretfully.

'Maybe we just don't understand debt as a nation,' he lamented, and then got angry.

'Those bastard bondholders. They never had a bigger bonanza . . . payin' off their bets with our sweat, Jesus Christ. I just don't think that people join the dots and realise they're the ones paying it. You'd think now more than ever that they'd be all over all of this oil and gas, as a means to pay it back.' To most of us, money only comes in one form: work. Unless you have something valuable in your possession, the only way you're getting it: effort.

'Look at it this way . . . get out the calculator there.' I rummaged in my pocket and pulled out my phone.

'What's minimum wage?' he asked.

'Eight euros, I'd say.'

'Right, well if a lady working on the supermarket till is earning eight quid an hour, and she's saved up €10,000, what's that in hours?' I pressed the buttons and divided 8 into 10,000.

'1,156 hours, not including tax and all that.'

'Well, she doesn't really have ten grand in her bank, she has stored 1,156 hours of work going bleep . . . bleep . . . bleep . . .' He raised his eyes and started swiping imaginary corn-flakes boxes making the bleep sound.

'If she gets up, drinks a pint of milk and opens her letters to find that she still owes 200k on her mortgage, she will have to do another . . . go on . . . 8 into 200,000?' he instructed me.

'23,121,' I replied.

'She'll have to do another 23,121 hours of bleeps for the bank before she owns the house, and a fair few more bleeps before she owns another pint of milk.'

'Girls don't drink pints of milk for breakfast, Aidan.'

'Whatever, they might.'

'Go on . . .'

'And every single one of her bleeps is taxed. So how many bleeps does she do for roads and hospitals and that? But more importantly, how many of those bleeps is she doing for some for-eigner she never met, who probably lives on a super yacht.' He was right: in a sense she had two employers, one being the supermarket and the other being this bondholder man on the yacht.

'She should at least know who he is, since she probably paid for his towels.' He was right again, thinking back: the parties 'denigrated' their own politics in 2009, when they wouldn't even tell this cash-register lady who her new shadow employers were.

'So there she is, bleeping away, one bleep for a bank, one bleep for roads, and one bleep for your man's luxury towels. And all the while the only other thing she owns of any worth is sitting beneath the sea, a billion years of dirty auld oil. And oh look! What's this, here comes the oil industry just ready to suck her oil out of the sea, then sell it back to the bus company that she both paid for, and uses to go to work to do more blasted bleeps.' He began working the till again, swiping more imaginary cornflakes while he made worn-out faces.

'You forgot her milk there,' I said, handing him an imaginary pint. It was a good way of putting it. A payment docked from every hour of work that every Irish person would do until every penny was paid off. A payment that had, through the most immoral and corrupt means, become enmeshed in all our day-to-day labours. Yet conversely, all this Irish oil potential, and a virtual national silence on the matter.

The next day we met Karine Finne from the Neptune Network, who took us out to the countryside. We interviewed farmers, stopped mountain bikers and ran after a few people on peculiar ski blades. She was cool with the whole thing, patiently watching us, as a display of amateurism unfolded before her, the likes of which I'm sure she had never seen before. Later she invited us to her home. We interviewed her daughter and ate half their food. Thanks to Karine's wisdom, we got a sense of how people might react to lots of things we'd been wanting to ask but hadn't. Most importantly, the fact that Norwegians were going to get more from Irish gas than us. And thanks to Karine's suggestion, we went to the grounds of the Norwegian Palace, which presides over Karl Johan's gate, with precisely that in mind.

We sat on the grass watching people stroll by almost as if hunting for the stereotypes we had not yet interviewed.

'Look at them all, not a care in the world, and half of Europe in torment,' said Aidan

'I know, it's like another world. I bet their prime minister isn't a clown's arse.'

'Why do we get them all? I mean consistently in our government, all these winking eejits over and over?' He lay back on the grass, sighing, and said 'I dunno, maybe we Irish deserve what we're getting'. I think what he was getting at was the idea that a nation of sheep will beget a government of wolves.

'I dunno either Aidan, maybe if you listen to several hundred hours of talk radio, and if you still feel conflicted you could read an eleven-hundred-page treatise on western democracy.'

'And remain no better able to answer the question,' he pointed out. What I was avoiding was an earnest question: why is it that the government of my country always seems to be doing the wrong thing? And at whose door should we really lay the blame? This is something which has confounded me for a long time.

'It might be far simpler to consider the whole thing with maths, Aidan, rather than reams of political theory.'

'Oh yeah,' he said, in a quizzical yet cynical manner.

'Yeah actually,' I said. 'The majority of Irish people are not represented by the government, they never are, and anyone can prove it with sums.' I pulled out my notebook, in which I had copied results of the 2011 general election from www.fairocracy.com.

'Right! Fine Gael 801,729 votes, Labour 431,856 votes, together 1,233,585 votes. Number of people eligible to vote in Ireland 3,198,765.' Using the calculator on my mobile, I tallied the votes in percentages.

'Twenty-five percent Fine Gael, 13 percent Labour, 38 percent Combined. There's your answer. Next time you get angry at the government, remember that the vast majority of us didn't vote for them.'

Just under 2 million Irish people, nearly two-thirds of us, sidelined every four years. The figures made us squirm in their simplicity. With numbers like these, it is naive to expect to live in a society of contentment or fairness. It's far more likely that you'll live in a society that feels as though 60 percent of you are permanently pissed off.

'Is it any wonder we've the second-worst deal in the world on oil and gas?' Aidan said with profound sentiment, then laughed, reflecting on the absurdity. I spotted a group of young lads go and sit on a wall down the way.

'We should ask them there – we have no young lads.' Aidan nodded in agreement, then eased further back into his grassy bed and closed his eyes.

'It gets worse, you know, Aidan. Rabbitte got in on 12,500 votes. I mean, come on, 12,500 ticked boxes. D'you think it's democratic, that an issue of such monumental national importance is being decided on by a man that has fewer supporters than Shelbourne Football Club?' Aidan laughed again. I checked: the young lads were still sitting on the wall.

'And it gets worse again. Behind him is a department of unelected civil servants who we never get to talk to, but the oil lobby does,' Aidan grunted, and we were quiet for a time.

'Come on, let's go and get these guys before they leave,' I said.

'Before they spend all our money on drink,' jested Aidan, but he didn't even open his eyes. 'Do you think they'd go to the offy for us and buy us a few cans?'

We sat a while longer in the sun, as did the group of young lads. I thought heavily about the defeatists; the ones I've heard who on one hand agree we need a better deal but on the other are certain we can never get it. It reminded me of a man my girlfriend and I picked up one time, somewhere near Ennis, a town I once went to school in. He was an older gentleman who spoke with all the authority and stateliness of a male Mary Robinson and was only too happy to conversationally tear at the powers that be. But much to my disappointment, he was clearly resigned to an ideal that nothing would ever change, frequently using the term 'deeply entrenched' to describe the government. But it is not a trench that this small group of people inhabit, it is a sandcastle, beyond which laps a public tide that has merely lost its moon.

## THE NEW APPROACH

Eventually Aidan did get up when I arrived back over to him from the young lads on the wall and gave him a kick in the shoe. It's great being behind a camera: you get to view all the nuances of life like you're hidden. I felt really envious of all five of them sitting up there on the wall hunched over just kicking it with their heels. Each one vying for biggest baboon, laughing and pucking each other. The joy of deliberate stupidity, the joke that just keeps on giving. But even they couldn't keep it up for long. The turning point came when one of them broke ranks and said something intelligent in response to one of the questions, and then smartness became the new accolade among them, and they all began vying for the position of most informed. Aidan had asked all the usual questions and I was about to switch off to save battery power when he broke the routine, and this time, unfettered, he explained that they stood to gain more from Ireland's resources than we currently did. And not caring, he followed by asking simply: 'Do you have anything to say to the people of Ireland.' There it was: it had finally been asked. They understood it perfectly . . . were silent for a moment and then one of them just blurted out: 'Thanks, Ireland!'

We were so amused by the young lads' answer that it now became a routine question in our interviews. Explaining the disparity, and then changing between: 'Do you have anything to say to the people of Ireland?' and 'Have you any advice for Irish people?' Many people either thanked Ireland for their gift of oil or made suggestions as to why and how Ireland should act in regard to the matter. One man answered 'Protest, of course!' – with much indignation. After which Aidan mumbled something bitter about Irish people and protest-ing. I would have known what he was saying if I hadn't been doing the exact same myself. Greece was in flames, Spain was beginning to riot, and Ireland was conducting the great mumble protests of 2011.

'Well, they're going to be angry when they hear this lot.'

'Yeah, but where can one go with that anger? What can one do with that impulse? Why give it to someone if you don't offer any solution to go with it?'

Ever since we'd first had this video idea, we had talked and thought much about its pur-pose. Yes, if it ever got finished, it would probably inform people. And if it came out the way I envisaged, then it would probably anger them as well. Anger that I could unfortunate-ly only see being directed in a literal sense at a laptop. Every activist these days wants to make 'the video'. We live in the age of 'awareness making', where knowing about a problem has superseded solving it. I was traipsing around these streets with Aidan and our borrowed video gear, because I was as mad as hell that Ireland's politicians – and, it has to be said, its people – were neglecting our resources and everything that stood in the way of extracting them. I had felt massive anger when I learnt about all this, but I had also felt helpless to do anything about it. Now I was sure we were doing something about it, but was that thing we were doing only going to stimulate outrage in people? Unbinding us from the feeling of helplessness, only to bind others to it?

We sat in silence. The question 'What can people do to change these terms?' loomed over us, more unresolved than ever. It had come up so many times, and yet every solution we thought of seemed not only ineffective but utterly useless. At the most floppy end of the spectrum was the option to make a petition, and at the hard end was a call for a street rally. Neither one seemed that effective – which is why we began thinking about all sorts of other things. All manner of publicity stunts, a European people's initiative – for which we needed one million signatures – and a letter-writing campaign of monumental proportions, which seemed ambitious to the point of fantasy.

'I suppose the good thing is that the Irish government has given such ridiculously good terms to the oil companies,' said Aidan. I got kind of annoyed.

'What are you on about?'

'Well, what we get is so unbelievably sh*t, like worse than Cameroon or wherever you said, that it's not going to be hard to get people riled up about it. I mean, if the terms were just crappy, but still, say, similar to France or somewhere, then people wouldn't be so bothered, would they? And we wouldn't have any chance to change it at all.'

'Yeah, if only the people got the same deal as the oil company.' I was thinking about what we had both just said when I realised something that should have been completely obvious.

'Aidan, listen, if the deal is so damn good for these companies, why don't we just set one up ourselves, like the Norwegians did. Then we'll be the ones getting the absurdly good deal and the tables will have been turned.' He made the sound 'Pfffffff' – and the face that goes with it.

'Never work, man.'

'It already has,' I said. And he looked at me absurdly.

'What do you think Statoil is? A company, just like any other in Norway – subject to all the same laws. Sure it's 78 percent owned by the State, and it gets preferential treatment from the Ministry of Oil, but it is a regular company all the same.' The cogs of belief jerked inside his head, then stopped abruptly again.

'OK, so we've got a people's oil company. Then what?'

'We put together a board of trustworthy people. Then we offer Norway a share of the company, and then we tender for the blocks, same as the rest of those companies do.' A spark showed in his eyes, and he put out his hands as though he was holding hope.

'What if they deny the application, though?'

'I'd like to see the government dismiss the application of a company owned by the people. It would cause . . . well, fallout.'

## NORWEGIAN COP

At the hotel, Aidan received an email from two Norwegian girls he had met in Thailand. He responded, saying we would meet them. We did so that evening: we had dinner outside a restaurant and walked around a bit.

The girls took us to sit on the grassy hilltop of Akershus Fortress overlooking the bay. Habitually now, I peeled the velcro on the camera bag. The sound of which at this stage made Aidan recoil and emit a Pavlovian groan.

'Go on,' I said, throwing him the mic. He was disgusted.

'Ah, come on, not another one. Will you relax a minute?'

The girls were coy, the interview was a farce, and we just ended up having a bit of a laugh.

It was still light when a policeman came up the hill and asked us to leave. Not because we were doing wrong but because the fortress was being closed for the evening. We were gathering our things when, bucking the trend, Aidan said 'I'm going to ask him for an interview', and shot off down the hill in pursuit of the cop. Aidan and cops . . . it made me wary. His last interaction with the force had been only weeks ago. He had been in the midst of sawing a wheel-clamp off a car when a Guard appeared above him and asked him: 'Are you all right there?'

Aidan looked up and replied: 'Yeah, I'm fine thanks, I nearly have it off.'

I bagged the camera and hastened down the hill after him.

The policeman turned out to be a pretty courteous guy, and his answers were much the same as those of everyone else we had met: Prosperity? Oil. Past? Poor. Resources? Everyone's.

That was, until he was asked: what would you think if your government gave all your resources away and you, the people, got nothing? He laughed and then, astoundingly, replied: 'Highly unlikely, I'd say, but I guess that would be sort of a reason for a war . . . wouldn't it?' Aidan turned to me, grinning from ear to ear. It was a remarkable and surprising response, and one I wish the public-bashing Gardai of north-west Mayo could have heard. When we wrapped up the interview, Aidan jokingly remarked: 'Well, that's it, I suppose we have to go home and start a war.' To which the policeman responded: 'Well, try not to get drunk before you do!' We laughed.

'That reminds me,' said Aidan, 'we never asked you what Ireland was famous for.'

'James Joyce,' he said, and the pair of us began laughing uncontrollably. Then, slightly confused, as our laughter faded we struck up a conversation. Like all policemen, he was eager to know who we were and what we were up to, so we told him: Ireland fecked, erroneous debts, youth emigration rising, oil prospects high, government morality low, national apathy index holding strong, and all of this we were going to solve with a video camera and a YouTube account . . .

I told him: 'Besides everything that Aidan told you about the economic injustice around our natural resources, there are social ones too. I'd like to ask you . . .' It was difficult to sum up all of what I wanted to ask him in a sentence, and I stuttered a bit. But he was nice: he knew there was a cop question coming, and he was helping me ask it.

'Yes,' he said, coaxing me along.

'OK, look, behind this it seems that every branch of the law sides with the oil companies – most prominent of which have been the police. They have beaten both locals living in proximity to a high-pressure refinery and the people who cared enough to go there and support them.'

He gave me a likely look – and fair enough, I still find it hard to believe myself when I recount the things I've seen. I never thought they could happen in Ireland. But it does every week, and I wanted to impress this upon him, so he would give me an honest answer. He took what I said as fact – at least for the sake of the question to come. So I asked him: 'If the situation became like that here, and you got orders to go and defend the interests of an oil company, would you?' He thought hard about it before pointing to the wall of the fort only twenty yards from us and said: 'The Nazis executed many of the Norwegian resistance right there.' True enough, the Germans held the fort during the Norwegian occupation and had executed many. When the war was over, Norway in turn executed eight of their own for conspiring with the Nazis. He continued: 'My grandparents sympathised with the Germans.'

We could tell that this was a difficult thing for him to have said, and were confused as to why he had said it. He was emotional when he went on to explain the rest. What I took from it was that his grandparents were from a valley and essentially cut off not only in a physical sense but in terms of knowledge too. In their ignorance, they had given their support to something which turned out to be a massive error in judgment. Now, today, here he was, a peacekeeper with a knowledge of Irish literature and an ability to answer a question with an improvised parable. Fair play to him, I thought: he hadn't answered the question but he had thought about it, and what a nice man. Parting company, none of us would have believed that in a matter of weeks, and only a short walk from where we were standing, the bombs of Anders Breivik would shatter a five-storey building, and this man would probably be at the forefront of dealing with the massacre that followed that day.

We went out that night. Ten-euro cans of Guinness started to get lost in us as we went deeper and deeper into the morality of the Irish State. I tried to describe my feelings on the matter, but as with all three-pint politics, my points got all wound up like spanners in my washing-machine mouth. The only one that fell out was that I was slightly drunk. Aidan did-n't care anyway: he was busy making his own points, with his index finger. 'Jeez, check her out.' You can only talk about this stuff for so long, so we went outside and sat with a few people smoking fags, drinking and talking about regular stuff. Yet I still felt like we had work to do. We interviewed each other for the laugh, asking all the usual questions, but never pressed 'record'. Later that evening, as the bars were closing, I found Aidan on a wall. He was in good spirits until I said: 'You know what would be great is if we had some interviews with drunk people. I mean if they can make sense in that state, well we've really covered all the angles.' At this stage, we had recorded everyone from schoolgirls to grandmothers, from Rastas to financial traders, and there was a clear theme to their responses. But perhaps, lubri-cated by alcohol, something different would come out. Aidan nearly screamed at the idea.

'No, no, no . . . I'm not doing any more.'

'You are, come on,' I said but he was adamant, worn out and ready to go.

'Come on,' I tried again, ripping the velcro on the bag.

'No.'

I couldn't persuade him, but I knew what might. Marching up the street, I found the prettiest girl I could. She agreed to the interview, and the guy she was with came too. But when we returned, Aidan was no more enthusiastic than he had been before. I gave him the mic but he stayed put, sat on the wall, hunched over like he was my reluctant teenage son, whom I had dragged on holidays. He began reeling off the questions to the pair in a monotone. Leprechauns, trolls, oil, gas . . . The fella did most of the answering until she cut across him.

'I think that you should demand that the Irish government have at least over 51 percent shares,' she said, before the guy cut back across her. Lit up by her words, Aidan bounced off the wall, physically excluding the guy from the conversation, and pointed the microphone to the girl. 'Go on,' he said to her.

'So that all of the revenue that comes from the oil companies, at least a percentage of that goes straight back into any kind of welfare programme that benefits society as a whole, because you as a people own your country: you own the natural resources.'

Aidan was still talking about her at breakfast, referring to her as 'the Princess of Joy' and insisting that I did too. Every time I tried, we ended up in hysterics. Aidan was besotted, and I had a mild hangover, which made sandwich duty at the buffet both difficult and obvious. Even I felt jaded at the prospect of more interviews, so we decided to do just a couple. It was sunny again, so we agreed that, if we got enough interviews, we'd go to the Viking museum. We checked ourselves and our sandwiches out of the hotel.

## THOUGHTS FROM THE VIKING MUSEUM

Strolling around Oslo's Viking museum, you will find a glass cabinet down the back with beautiful antiquities from Ireland. I was stood staring at it, like a cabbage, musing over all that was becoming clear to me. I couldn't help thinking that perhaps the Vikings hadn't stolen these treasures at all and that maybe the Celts had just given them away. I imagined some half-witted chieftain who cared more for his self-preservation than his tribe's well-being. When Eric the Red showed up, the ball-less chieftain sent down a welcoming committee of his equally ball-less Druids. They promptly wrote up some licences in Brehon law, entitling Eric to all the lovely things he could carry.

Eric was delighted, bemused and upset, given that he got no fight, at all. When Mike Cunningham, former director of Statoil E&P, Ireland, said 'No country in the world gives as favourable terms to the oil companies as Ireland', he might have been channelling the spirit of my imaginary Eric, who, sailing away, must have thought: 'No kingdom on the earth gives as favourable terms to raiders as Éire.'

When some of the tribespeople stood up to challenge the chieftain on what had happened, the chieftain responded by saying: 'Sure what's wrong with you, if we didn't give it him, no one would have taken it. Eric risked a lot coming here, what with the cost of boats and swords, and sure didn't he pay a handful of you to help him carry the treasure down to the pier?' Incensed by the absurdity of the chieftain's anti-logic, two of the tribesmen got a video camera and . . . I stopped the imagination right there.

We ate our 'complimentary' sandwiches on the deck of a beautiful wooden schooner that carried visitors across the fjord – to and from the city. Long picnic benches ran its length, dressed with neatly folded woolly blankets. I sat beside Aidan, so that his face wouldn't spoil the pleasant view, and began asking him for his opinion about Goldman Sachs, bonds, and credit default swaps all at once. The response he gave me was memorable and profound. Letting out a sigh, he simply replied 'I don't care' and stared across the fjord. Had I not known Aidan, I might have thought that his answer was curt, or dismissive. But quite the opposite. Aidan is adept in his knowledge of economics and the social fibre of law, both of which are central columns on which his stand-up is built. Having also given up his high-flying job in Japan as a financial trader, for something more meaningful and less well paid, he knows both sides of the monetary divide. To me, his answer summed up a consensus among an entire sector of Irish-born people at that moment in time. It is not that he didn't care, at all, it is that he cared so much that he couldn't bring himself to talk about it.

'I don't care' meant 'Don't say anything lest I explode'. It is with leisure that we can discuss things that do not affect us: other people's woes and other eras' struggles. Matters that are dear to us, however, often cause shouting and blood-rush. This serene boat jaunt was no place for either, and I got the sense that nature and the afternoon sky had trumped human trifles. He had stumped me, in a way that I enjoy, and had explained something to me not by what he had said but by who he is. My next question to him was 'Coffee?' I went to the wheel-house shop to get him one, and leave him staring across the fjord.

The sandwiches were lovely, and they were free. Just like Ireland's oil will be to Exxon Mobil. I mean to say that there was a certain effort invested in making them, and pilfering them, but essentially they were on the house. It is extraordinarily important for anyone who wants to learn from Norway's experience of managing resources, that they understand the mindset of the people in the late sixties. To them this resource was not an opportunity for exploiting, it was an opportunity for enabling. To enable their whole society to have something to work at, to enable their whole society to be secure and independent, and to enable future generations to have more than just a job.

Oil and gas was a just jumping-off point for Norway, and today they own 1 percent of the entire global stock market, and have over $800 billion in their people's wealth fund – but that's not what impresses me. What does is that the country did its best to adhere to one sentence written in the seminal 'White Paper No. 25' in 1974. It said: 'Wealth from oil should be used to develop a qualitatively better society.' It is a tremendous attitude towards people and nature. The application of which leads to the development of welfare, environment, equality, local politics. In essence: everything that I could see around me now from this boat, and much, much more that I could not, all this was financed by oil, not by excessive, unrealistic borrowing.

\*

All that summer I could feel the impact that Oslo had made on my pocket, yet my wallet was still bulging with €540 billion notes. The footage from our four days in Oslo had sat idle, on a black hard drive in my desk drawer, for months. Every time I went to get a stapler or a scissors, I felt sharp pangs of procrastinator's guilt, and closed it quickly. But eventually I pushed on.

\*

Three weeks later it was finished, after many evenings replaying clips, watching the faces of Norwegians and listening to the sounds they made over and over and over. Something had become clear to me: ask anyone in Norway why they are so prosperous, and the sound of three letters – 'O' 'I' 'L' – will be fired back at you. But I found that the real truth to our questions was not in the words with which they answered, but the manner in which they replied. A manner that is sensible, a tone that is assertive and an overall expression of fairness which has permeated their national character and their attitude to their natural resources. Of course they would 'give it back'!

### ABOUT THE AUTHOR

Scott O'Connor is an ordinary Irish citizen who couldn't sit by and simply do nothing about the mismanagement of Ireland's natural resources, which he saw as 'social demolition whereby we the people gain little more than the economic rubble'.

In an attempt to highlight the matter to the Irish public, he decided to make a video to illustrate the absurdity of the fact that the Norwegian people are set to benefit more from the Irish people's property than the Irish themselves are. The video which Scott made with his cohort Aidan Killian went viral and had received close to 100,000 hits on *YouTube* at the time of writing. *YouTube* analytics for the video showed that more than 90 percent of those views were from within Ireland, and demonstrated that a large portion of the Irish public are tuning into this issue and are compelled to change it for the better. Tens of thousands of people, equally infuriated. They signed up in droves to show support on his website, which is now part of OOO.ie.

# 14.

## STRATEGIC CONSIDERATIONS

### Chris Sanders

Ireland is generously endowed with energy resources. These have not, however, been favoured in the Age of Fossil Fuels, but they do promise to bless Ireland in the new age that is dawning. Ireland has coal, oil and gas but not in abundance, nor is it easy to exploit. Urbanisation and industrialisation therefore have been dependent on imported energy, a fact that has handicapped Ireland's competitiveness vis-à-vis neighbours such as the UK. This geological reality has ramifications for Irish political realities. Remarkably, given the central importance of energy, national energy policy has been notable for the narrowness of the national discussion on the subject – the long-running dispute over the Corrib gas field notwithstanding. This may seem at odds given the ballyhoo over carbon emissions and climate change, but at rock bottom the truth is that there is precious little discussion. The result is that the issue has been left to the 'experts' while the rest of us get on with our business.

This is a mistake. Why? Because the experts and those who employ them, however well-meaning, work and think in the milieu to which they have been trained, towards objectives which are not openly discussed or necessarily in the public interest. Nowhere is this more so than economics. The standard public policy analysis is singularly unsuited to devising an inclusive policy for energy. Few would dispute the need for a policy, but its very importance in a societal sense may inform the lack of an informed public discussion.

The world, and not just Ireland, is facing an unprecedented crisis. The marginal unit of energy available for use has been rapidly becoming more expensive in terms of the energy required to find, produce, process and deliver it. Just about everyone understands that there is a global, or at least OECD, banking and financial crisis. But few people understand the link between the financial crisis and the underlying supply of energy to the world economy. This linkage is straightforward and readily understood: our monetary system is based on debt creation, which, in turn, depends on a consensus that debt can be serviced and repaid. If the flow rate of energy to the real economy – that is, agricultural and industrial production – is constrained, then the consensus supporting debt growth cannot be maintained, simply because the energy available to enable the growth required to service debt growth isn't there.

This is ultimately the problem behind the current EU crisis – the collision between the political priority of salvaging the banking sector from the ruins of its collapse in 2008 and the energetic limits to real GDP growth. The Irish government promised that year to underwrite the entire balance sheet of the banking sector and gave priority to bondholders over other creditors. This was a reckless policy in light of its aftermath: a deep and deepening recession evidenced by the ongoing collapse in Irish petroleum consumption and the steady downtrend in electricity production since 2007.

**Ireland: annual oil consumption and rate of change**

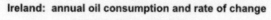

BP Statistical Review of World Energy

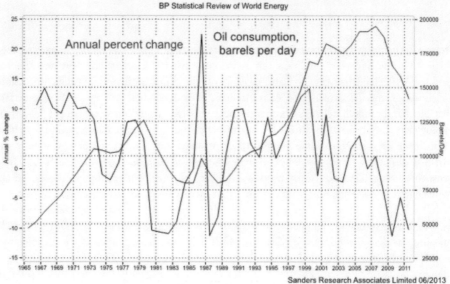

Sanders Research Associates Limited 06/2013

This brings to mind the proverb, 'As the pie gets smaller, the table manners get worse.' Ireland should take note of the tragedy in Cyprus, which just happens to hold title to a rich gas find off its southern shore and to possibly others in the immediate environs off its coast. The Cypriot economy's dependence on banking and the Eurozone could be seen as its downfall. Cyprus further risks losing control over its only natural resource endowment that might help it extricate itself from its financial chains. Likewise, Ireland's dependence on finance, construction and outside capital in the Celtic Tiger years haunts it today. Its sovereignty compromised by membership in the Eurozone, it is unclear if Ireland can maintain control over its own natural resources.

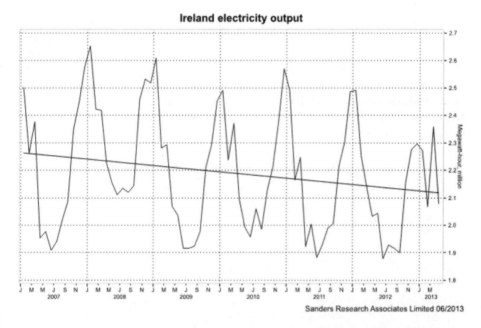

**Ireland electricity output**

Sanders Research Associates Limited 06/2013

In this chapter we shall see why more debt is not the way forward, why Ireland's energy problem is part of a larger resource issue and needs to be addressed in that context, why it is vital to win the intellectual debate that is currently dominated by economists, and why this can lead us to a holistic and productive national strategy that is inclusive, consensual and in the long run far cheaper and more humane than the strategy we appear to be following. We begin with the geopolitics of global energy.

## THE GEOPOLITICS OF GLOBAL ENERGY

In 1971 Richard Nixon's administration closed the Fed's gold window and suspended US dollar gold convertibility, ushering in an era of floating exchange rates that is with us still. This action is usually attributed to the government's preference for financing through debt its war in Vietnam and the raft of new social legislation called the Great Society. Although this is true as far as it goes, it is incomplete. At least as important was the end of American energy independence, when US domestic oil production peaked in 1970. This was the coup de grace for the US balance of payments, which went into deficit and has remained there ever since.

Dire warnings of global collapse turned out to have been wrong or at least premature by forty years. The US intensified its military and financial involvement in the Persian Gulf region and, over the course of the 1970s, oil discoveries in Alaska, the Gulf of Mexico and the North Sea were brought on stream. It is no accident that the long bear market in shares that began with the crisis of 1970-71 ended with the beginning of production from these provinces. Not only were these huge deposits of petroleum, but they were geographically located under the umbrella of NATO and the American fleet, which also controlled the maritime supply lines for the distribution of oil around the globe. The doomsayers were wrong not because the problem they saw was non-existent but because the US was able to impose an imperial, that is to say a NATO, solution on the world. Its alliance with Saudi Arabia ensured that the world trade in oil outside of the Communist Bloc would be denominated in dollars. Thus was born the petro-dollar standard. Instead of gold, countries could convert their dollar export earnings into oil. The US was only too happy to oblige their need for dollars, and its banking system profited from the recycling of dollars from oil earnings into loans to developing countries, US Treasury and Agency bonds and, in more recent years, highly speculative real-estate lending. The damage that this did to US manufacturing was long-term and profound. The consensus that enabled this to happen was only possible with the destruction of organised labour as an effective political force in the US and the UK.

The fall of the Soviet Union in the 1980s occurred in the context of a temporary collapse in Soviet oil production. This was part of a larger energy crisis in the Eastern Bloc due in part, we now know, to western sabotage of the Soviet pipeline network and greatly worsened by the catastrophe at Chernobyl.[1] With oil production from the Gulf of Mexico, Alaska and the North Sea rising throughout this period, the centre of gravity of the world energy net was firmly in Western control.

In retrospect, however, it is plain that the seeds of the current global crisis were sown during the 1970s. Unsurprisingly, the trigger for those seeds to fruit was again oil, with the production of the big three – Alaska, the Gulf of Mexico and the North Sea – peaking in 2001-3. World stock markets reacted predictably by falling sharply over the same period, only to recover with the advent of the 'Greenspan Put', a policy euphemism coined by the markets for then chairman of the US Federal Reserve Alan Greenspan, who tied US interest rates and monetary policy to the stock market.

The decline of Western, that is to say OECD, oil production has meant a permanent shift in the axis of the world energy system to the Persian Gulf, Central Asia and Russia. Critically, this means that the American fleet no longer exercises absolute control of the world's energy distribution net as overland pipelines to supply China and the Far East and to link Western Europe to Russia have been, and are being, built outside of the control of NATO armed forces or Western oil majors. This is reflected in institutional arrangements such as the creation of the Shanghai Cooperation Organisation (SCO) for trade and defence issues in 2001, involving Russia, China, Kazakhstan, Kyrgyzstan and Uzbekistan. The SCO's observer membership includes India, Iran, Pakistan, Afghanistan and Mongolia.

Russia and China have complemented the SCO with other initiatives. Notably, they have forged an economic and financial alliance with fellow BRICS Brazil, India and South Africa that includes the creation of a BRICS development bank. China has concluded currency-swap arrangements with nineteen countries including US allies Japan, Australia and the UK as well as a number of bilateral trade agreements. These represent a necessary step towards the use of the yuan as an international reserve currency. Concretely, what this means is that, increasingly, international trade in hydrocarbons is denominated in currencies other than US dollars and also in gold.

With the decline in world conventional oil production has come a shift in the composition of the world energy mix to make up the production shortfall relative to demand. Unconventional oils such as 'tight oil' from shale and limestone formations, ultra-deep-water crude bitumen, biofuels and natural gas liquids (NGLs) are forming a bigger proportion of world all-liquids production. Natural gas production is climbing too, and here again the Russians have been busy, forming, along with Qatar and Iran, the Gas Exporting Countries Forum in 2008, which now includes eleven members and controls over 70 percent of the world's gas reserves, 38 percent of world pipeline shipments and more than 85 percent of liquefied natural gas (LNG) production.

Taken together, these developments constitute the biggest shift in the world balance of power since the Allied victory in 1945. If there ever was a true unipolar moment after the fall of the Soviet Union, it didn't survive the peak in North Sea oil and gas production except perhaps in the minds of those NATO planners who dreamt up the occupation of Afghanistan and Iraq. Today, some trillions of dollars and millions of lost and ruined lives later, Iraqi oil production is back where it was just before the American invasion in 2003. Libyan production has plummeted since the destruction of the Gaddafi government. The US, which long desired a pipeline route out of Central Asia to the Indian Ocean untroubled by Russian interference, still has no pipeline, though another may well be built that terminates in India and China. Russia has built pipelines direct to Germany across the Baltic Sea and crossing Asia to the Sea of Japan.

And, as if all that isn't enough, Gazprom recently signed a deal with Israel to market LNG produced in Israel's new deep-water Mediterranean gas field. Both the US and the EU have long hoped to build a pipeline from Azerbaijan to Europe to rival Russia's pipelines. The so-called Nabucco pipeline is intended to do just that, but the consortium formed to build it is finding sources of gas to fill it problematic. Without Iranian gas it is unlikely that this will happen, though deep-water finds in the eastern Mediterranean have fuelled hopes that this could be a solution. This seems increasingly remote now that Gazprom is in the picture.

What this demonstrates is not just the importance of the location of production, but the geopolitical and commercial importance of distribution. World War II was won by an alliance between the world's two largest oil producers, Russia and the United States, and the boundaries of their post-world war zones of influence were largely drawn by their ability to supply oil. The collapse of Russian oil production in the late 1980s wrecked the Soviet Union and its alliance structure. Russia's restoration on the world geopolitical stage is largely due to the rebuilding of its hydrocarbon industry on its own terms, under the control of the Russian state. The crucial moment in that development was the breakup of Yukos Oil nearly a decade ago and the absorption of Yukos into state gas producer Rosneft. While usually explained as a political vendetta by Vladimir Putin against Yukos boss Mikhail Khodorkovsky, what really drove the Russian government's action was a Yukos supply contract negotiated with China that, if allowed to go forward, would have meant the loss of control by Russia to a foreign-controlled corporation of not just oil and gas production but also of exports. This explains, to a large extent, the visceral hostility in the West to Putin, especially in Britain, whose nationals dominated the board of the Gibraltar holding company that controlled Yukos.

**Russia: oil production**

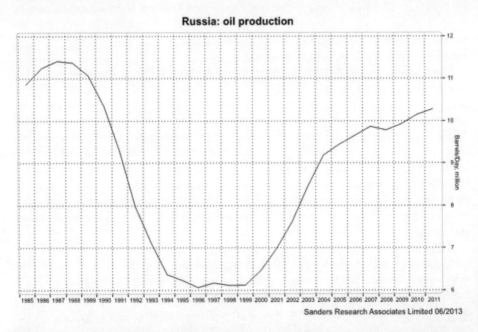

Sanders Research Associates Limited 06/2013

The purchase of BP/TNK by Rosneft in early 2013 and the assumption by BP of a seat on the Rosneft board signals the end of that episode and the beginning of a new era in Eurasian energy developments. Gazprom and Rosneft have signed supply contracts with China, effectively completing the original Yukos deal, but this time in a context controlled by the state between two countries united in military and commercial collaboration by their partnership in the SCO and the BRICS. That times have changed is clearly evidenced by the United Kingdom's negotiation of an extension of the trans-Baltic gas pipelines between Russia and Germany across northern Europe to the UK.

These developments have deep implications for existing world political, institutional and financial arrangements. The place to be these days for the international corporate set is not Davos, but the BRICS and SCO summits, but they do not seem to have figured that out yet.

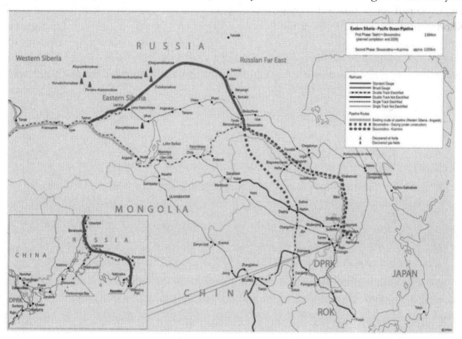

Russian Eastern Siberia – Pacific Ocean (ESPO) Pipeline (to be completed 2013-14)
Source: The Economic Research Institute for Northeast Asia[2]

Closer to home, what this means is that the marginal supplier of energy to Europe remains Russia and the GECF (Gas Exporting Countries Forum), over which Russia exercises the key influence. The completion last year of a gas pipeline from Siberia to the Sea of Japan (to be followed by an oil pipeline) and a large LNG facility at its terminus places Russia in a unique position to influence world energy pricing. It also sets the current hoopla over tight oil and gas produced by 'fracking' shale and limestone formations in a different context than the usual hyperbole about a new world 'energy revolution' and North American energy independence.

The facts are considerably less exciting. North American gas at the present price level circa $4/MMBtu is priced at about half the level needed to make it an economic proposition. The markets, if not the mainstream press, understand this very well, which is why dry gas drilling in shale formations in the United States has more or less stopped altogether (the current marginal gas production is associated with tight oil production). Dry tight gas won't flow unless the US begins to export LNG. Given its low price, this is bitterly opposed by US industrial consumers and underlines the fact that even if the US becomes a meaningful gas exporter, development of this resource is dependent on international, not domestic, pricing and demand.

The replacement of dollar-gold convertibility with a de facto petro-dollar standard in the 1970s was possible because Iran and Saudi Arabia were both US allies and the Persian Gulf was an American lake. Since the Iranian Revolution in 1978, Iran and the US have periodically been at loggerheads, leaving American control of the Gulf largely dependent on the Saudi alliance and an unofficial regional alliance between the Saudis, Egypt, Israel and Turkey. The stability of this arrangement has depended on a multitude of factors, but one above all – Saudi Arabia's gigantic oil reserves and its ability to perform as world swing producer.

Over the last ten years questions have arisen about Saudi production and spare capacity. American investment banker Matt Simmons focused attention on the issue in his 2005 book, *Twilight in the Desert*, in which he questioned Saudi reserve and production capacity figures and correctly forecast a peak in Saudi production.

Two facts inform the outlook for Saudi production: the dominance of output from the supergiant Ghawar field and the fact that for all intents and purposes there is no more oil to be found in that country. Ghawar is gigantic, accounting for more than 5 percent of *global* oil production and more than 30 percent of Saudi production. Oil began to flow from Ghawar in the early 1950s, making it quite elderly in oil-field terms. Production levels have been maintained by the early and vigorous use of enhanced recovery techniques, a euphemism for water flooding and horizontal drilling. Some reports in recent years have put the water cut – the percentage of water to oil produced – as high as 55 percent. Ghawar is by far the biggest oil field in history. Its oil column was originally 1,500 feet high. Today it is less than 150 feet.

With Ghawar in decline, Saudi Arabia needs to bring new production online to make up for the shortfall from its biggest field. This is easier said than done, but the Kingdom has managed to keep production more or less flat since 2005. In the longer term, to sustain today's production levels new oil needs to be found. This isn't going to happen, as a chart of cumulative Saudi oil discovery versus cumulative exploration wells makes clear. Saudi Arabia is a busted flush.

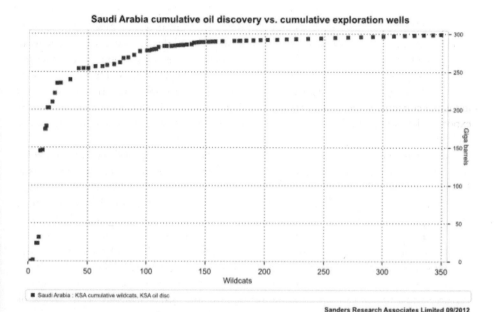

**Saudi Arabia cumulative oil discovery vs. cumulative exploration wells**

■ Saudi Arabia : KSA cumulative wildcats, KSA oil disc

Sanders Research Associates Limited 09/2012

The geopolitical significance of this fact cannot be overstated. *The world oil industry no longer has a swing producer. Any increase in world demand therefore can be expected to result in higher prices and, perhaps even more problematic, much higher price volatility.*

Much hope is invested in technological solutions to the problem of declining conventional petroleum production. Because of its unique chemistry and portability, oil has been, since its production began in the nineteenth century, primarily a transport fuel which is simply unrivalled and for which no perfect substitute exists. All of the alternatives being developed today are vastly more capital-intensive than conventional oil. The first wells in Pennsylvania and Texas have been characterised as 'poking a straw in the ground'. Contrast this to ultra-deep offshore exploration and production: the ships alone cost a billion dollars each, and they drill far more dry holes relative to productive ones than used to be the case on shore. This brings us to a subject closely connected to the geopolitical characteristics of developments in the energy world, something we might call the complexity conundrum.

## The Complexity Conundrum

All of us understand the idea of complexity in the sense of a situation or of a household appliance we are trying to assemble with unclear instructions from the manufacturer. Most of us have probably not thought of complexity in the sense of it being a problem-solving tool. But in fact that is exactly what it is. From the beginnings of animal husbandry and the invention of the plough to Roundup Ready corn, the history of agriculture has been one of ever-increasing 'complexification' in the quest for higher and more dependable yields. Similarly, the production of goods and services has increased in complexity. Imagine the difference between cottage weavers and modern capital-intensive fabric and dye manufacturing. Or think of the difference between the business of a medieval gold merchant and a contemporary transnational bank: book ledgers versus massive computer data centres. Not only is production more capital-intensive, it is globally distributed and specialised.

From this perspective, the economic and political development we call globalisation is in fact 'complexification' aimed at increasing economies of scale and lowering unit labour costs. In this sense it has been very successful and is widely perceived as such. What is less widely understood is that complexity is directly correlated to energy use. Increased complexity requires increased consumption of energy. The industrial *sine qua non* of complexification is the IT industry, whose voracious demand for electric power is exponential. Energy consumption in IT is the obverse of Moore's law. As a rule of thumb we may say that halving the cost of processing power requires very roughly a doubling of required direct and embedded energy.[3]

Every student who has completed a basic biology course ought to know that systems that display exponential growth expand exponentially until they overshoot their available resource base and collapse.

Clearly, economists don't study biology. This brings us to the intellectual problem.

## THE INTELLECTUAL PROBLEM

Contemporary mainstream economics as practised in the financial and public sectors has as its basis the idea that human economic life is subject to laws of cause and effect not unlike those that govern the physical world. This is not unreasonable as we shall show, but is oddly a premise honoured by contemporary economists more in its breach than its observation.

The operative problem in economics is the proposition that price will marry supply and demand and that by extension there is neither a 'problem' with resource availability nor with the disposal of wastes. For a high enough price either more resources will be produced or substitutes found or invented. Waste disposal, insofar as it is considered at all, is just another business, a proposition that ignores the actual physical complications associated therewith. It is not at all clear how the price mechanism can solve this particular challenge. In the last three years we have witnessed the largest (and ongoing) industrial accidents in history: BP's Macondo well blowout in the Gulf of Mexico and the triple meltdown at Japan's Fukushima Daiichi nuclear power plant (NPP). In neither case has the 'waste problem' been contained, much less solved, a matter that we shall return to later in this chapter.

The importance of these examples to the discussion here is that they are both evidence that in the oil and nuclear industries the risks of catastrophic failure are unsupportable by the industries and even the societies involved. Why? Because they are so costly as to be, for all intents and purposes, insusceptible to material mitigation or remediation. They are, in short, examples of the complete failure of economic theory, according to which none of this should have happened.

The root problem here is the presumption that the money economy is the real economy rather than a representative abstraction thereof. Because of this, we have become, to paraphrase Oscar Wilde, a civilisation that knows the price of everything and the value of nothing. To illustrate the point, the market price of oil and gas is the price that clears short-term supply and demand. This mechanism has nothing to do with the *value* of either resource, or the opportunity cost of the destruction of a resource such as the ecosystem of the Gulf of Mexico in order to produce them.

This is not a new problem, but over the last two centuries the availability of cheap and abundant energy has relegated its resolution to the benches of the economic pitch, making career advancement increasingly dependent on the mastery of dogma rather than reason, with all that this implies for public policy. This has left the advancement of the field to those not captivated by economic dogma, which means it has been left largely to biologists and ecologists studying natural systems, among which is our economy, to advance our understanding.

The economy that we actually inhabit is in fact a complex flow of matter and energy through a series of conversion processes during which a certain amount of energy is 'lost' in the form of, say, heat and at the end of which we are left with 'waste' materials as a result of conversion. The economic output of this process is the result of the conversion of matter and energy into useful goods and services. This process is governed by the law of the conservation of matter and energy, which basically tells us that what goes in must all come out, albeit in altered form. Further, there is a 'loss' of energy during the process in the sense that the lost energy is not lost, it has simply become unusable. The loss of energy in a system is referred to as an increase in the entropy of the system.

This is a simple but extremely important point because it means that the *real* cost of economic activity is not monetary but energetic. As energy economist and historian Vaclav Smil has put it, energy is the one true currency.

This has profound consequences.

To begin with, it means that decision-making on the basis of monetary pricing is tricky at best and even dangerously misleading. Another way of putting this is that the risk of capital misallocation is very high, which results in a higher increase in the entropy of our economic system. The Gulf of Mexico and Fukushima NPP accidents represent surges in systemic entropy. The best we can hope to achieve is to minimise this loss.

Early attempts by economists to measure relative inputs to the economy left out this reality altogether. Real explanatory value had to wait until the early 2000s, when Robert Ayres, a physicist, and Benjamin Warr, a mathematician, published papers and subsequently a book in which they modelled the US economy using a mass-flow process.[4] This simply means that they modelled the actual material and energetic inputs and outputs to the economy, in the process arriving at a result that mirrors actual GDP over more than a century almost exactly.

This represents a major intellectual advance in our understanding of the economy, not least because energy is an enormously more important input to economic activity than is understood by conventional economists, who estimate this contribution to be only some 5 percent in an advanced industrial economy *based on price*. Ayres and Warr estimated this contribution to be around 45 percent based on actual inputs.

This brings us to a related problem, energy quality.

## ENTROPY AND NET ENERGY YIELD

It follows from the foregoing discussion that change in real economic output is a function of the rate of entropy change in the system. Real output can only be increased by decreasing the rate of energy loss in the process of mass conversion into useful output. Increasing total energy consumption without fully offsetting efficiency gains will increase the rate of entropy growth. This is in fact exactly what has happened over the course of the last century. Most of the economic growth of that period is explained by increased consumption of primary energy resources rather than by gains in the efficiency of energy use.[5]

This will no doubt disturb the contemporary technophile consensus, but real-world examples abound. One of the most striking is modern industrial agriculture. This is at bottom a process that converts hydrocarbons from oil and gas into units of edible energy in a ratio of 10:1. It is difficult to conceive of any process that could be less efficient and more wasteful. The advent of genetically modified organisms (GMO) has pushed this ratio even further, one suspects, given the higher chemical inputs required and lower yields that GM agriculture is achieving. That said, industrial agriculture is profitable in a monetary sense largely because it has dispensed with labour on the farm and enjoys large economies of scale. Monsanto's business model is the *reductio ad absurdum* of this development, seeking to monopolise seed production by patenting genetic profiles in order to control the rate of profit. As has been repeatedly shown over the years, large-scale intensive organic gardening produces higher yields but is not as 'profitable'.[6]

With the peak of world conventional oil production has passed the era in which total primary energy consumption could be increased at will. The reason for this is twofold: not only can oil not be produced at increasing rates but the energetic value of other primary energy forms is lower. Gas, for instance, has about 60 to 80 percent of the calorific value of oil, and coal some 50 percent that of gas. Volumetric estimates of resources in place ignore both the lower embedded energy content of the resources yet to be produced as well as the greater difficulty and therefore the higher energetic cost of extraction, transport and conversion to useable form.

What this means is that at the margin it is necessary to invest more energy to produce a given net output of energy, that is to say the net energy yield (NEY) available to us is falling. This has also been termed energy return on (energy) investment (EROI). The graphic below shows why this matters urgently.

**The Energy Sink**

Source: Sanders Research Associates Limited following Mearns, Hall & Murphy

It is a characteristic of the intersection of natural resource exploitation with the money economy that those resources that are easiest and cheapest to get are the ones that are extracted first. As time goes by the physical, labour and energy capital intensity of exploitation increases. The increase is not linear, but exponential. We call this the Energy Sink. As primary energy becomes more difficult to find and produce, the process of doing so becomes more costly both in terms of money and more importantly *in terms of the energy required*.

Consider that a century ago onshore conventional petroleum in the US had an EROI of some 100:1. Today that return is more like 12:1. In energy terms its price has increased by

8.3 times. Today, when we replace onshore conventional oil using processed tar sands with an EROI of 3:1,[7] the marginal energy cost rises by another four times.

A common misconception is that as long as the EROI of an energy resource is positive it makes sense to exploit the resource. This isn't true. Without a significantly positive EROI the real capital accumulation that society needs in order to function as it has been accustomed is impossible. A few moments' study of a mass-flow diagram of the economy shows clearly why this is so. If the net energy yield of our available primary energy resources is falling, the process of net energy production requires a greater and greater share of net energy available to society to be diverted to that process, co-opting first discretionary sectors and finally non-discretionary sectors, at which point society is in a state of collapse. The present pricing mechanism of the energy industry simply does not capture this fundamental relationship at all.

This brings us to the crux of the matter from the standpoint of the economy: the relationship of energy use to money.

## ENERGY AND MONEY

Ayres' and Warr's ground-breaking work shows us that energy consumption and economic growth are directly and positively correlated. It also shows us that it isn't just a matter of the rate of change of gross energy consumption but of the efficiency with which that primary energy is sourced and used.

We can express this algebraically using Fisher's output identity, familiar to all students of basic macroeconomics:

$$PQ=MV \quad (1)$$

P is prices, Q is output, M is the money stock and V is the velocity of monetary circulation. Based on the forgoing discussion we can substitute energy (E) times an efficiency of use coefficient to obtain:

$$P(Ee)=MV \quad (2)$$

E is gross energy consumption and e is an efficiency coefficient. The relationship between money and energy is best illustrated by solving for prices, P:

$$P=\frac{MV}{Ee} \quad (3)$$

A few minutes' contemplation of these relationships tells us a lot. The first is that increasing money supply to try and support economic growth if energy supply is constrained is inflationary. Secondly, the flow of energy (E) is not simply gross energy consumed but rather the net energy produced for consumption in the system. Therefore the quality of energy is vitally important. Increasing the efficiency with which net energy is consumed can help, but there is little reason from historical experience to think that it can fully offset the decline in E, much less reverse it. This leads us to the third observation, which is that any increase in M, assuming constrained Ee can only be offset by a decrease in velocity V, meaning a decrease in transactional volume in the economy.

This, in fact, is a pretty good template for understanding the current predicament of the world economy, and especially the OECD part of it. The policy response to the collapse of the financial system in 2008 has been to increase money-supply growth by increasing the amount of debt in the system to plug the hole left by the destruction done to bank balance sheets. The relationships above explain the focus on 'austerity' as the preferred fiscal policy approach: constraining velocity is a technical euphemism for increasing unemployment and decreasing disposable income. The policies used to achieve this are zero or near-zero interest rates and quantitative easing (QE). These policies now being pursued aggressively by the world's biggest central banks have a number of consequences.

Savers worldwide are being impoverished as the low yield on government bonds decimates pension funds and annuities. This of course represents a growing drag on demand. But capital formation is also being damaged by the zero-rate policy and QE. By preventing, or at least significantly delaying, any resolution of losses (that is to say, by keeping insolvent financial institutions alive) there is in effect a massive distortion of prices, beginning with bonds themselves. Bonds rise in price when interest rates fall, and vice versa. Investors usually think of this in terms of the value of their bond holdings, or assets. However, in a heavily leveraged world it is well to remember that liabilities also become more expensive when interest rates fall.

The impact of this is to severely distort the capital structure of the corporate sector. If these policies were truly temporary then this might not be an issue. The fact that they have now been in place for years is quite another matter. Not just pensions but insurance too faces a problem: how to hedge long-term liabilities with bonds that are at all-time highs in price and lows in yield.

The severity of the global downturn can be seen in the impact on global cash flow, which has fallen to a deficit of some 6 percent of world GDP. Any economy with export dependency, be it China or Ireland, can only look at this and wonder: what is going to happen to my markets?

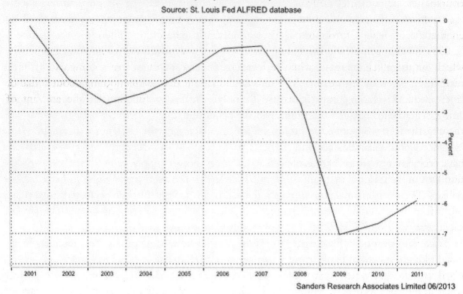

**Global cash flow (surplus/deficit) as % world GDP**

Source: St. Louis Fed ALFRED database

Sanders Research Associates Limited 06/2013

## THE POLITICAL CONUNDRUM

Plato in his *Republic* characterised the principal political divide in society as between those with wealth and those who labour for them. Not much has changed. The same divide bedevils us today. What has changed, and profoundly so, is the way in which the classes relate. This is due primarily to the change in energy availability over the last 200 years.

In the world before the Age of Fossil Fuels (AFF), energy for economic and other purposes came primarily from wood, wind, rivers and tides, and, of course, human and animal muscle. With the advent of coal, theretofore unimaginable levels of energy were made available for use and economic activity and capital accumulation expanded exponentially along with the rate of coal production. This pattern has been repeated with the exploitation of oil since the end of the nineteenth century.

Before the AFF, economic energy was drawn largely from human labour. The logic of profit and capital accumulation dictated a highly unequal distribution of the proceeds of that labour, the most extreme example of which was indentured servitude and slavery. Since the beginning of AFF, that logic has been inverted in a process in which human and animal labour has been largely replaced with energy derived from fossil fuels. Labour historically being the greatest cost of production, it has been easier to shed it than to pay for it. This of course is simply a financial calculation intended to increase the rate of profit and has nothing to do with the underlying real economic calculus, which is energetic. As we have seen, energetic costs have soared, but old ideas and habits die hard.

This can be seen clearly in contemporary notions of productivity and competitiveness, which 'improve' (i.e. increase) when real wages fall. In reality these are nothing except technical terms for relationships between output and labour that tell us nothing about actual or true productivity and competitiveness. These are instead a function of the amount of entropy generated by the economic process. Logically, the higher the entropy generated thereby, the less productive the process.

Once again, examples abound, but perhaps the most compelling is agriculture. As we have seen, contemporary economics deals with problems of resource exhaustion and pollution by simply ignoring them: in the economists' language these problems have been 'externalised'. What this means in practice is that costs are not borne by the entity generating them but rather by society at large. Perhaps even more important, these externalities are for the most part not factored in at all.

Thus, erosion caused by the destruction of soil structure by chemical fertilisers, mechanised ploughing, sowing and reaping and the extravagant use of water are costs not recognised in industrial agriculture, which is nonetheless profitable. The one-off use of aquifer water in North America, North Africa and the Arabian Peninsula is another example. These activities are all very energy-intensive and destructive of long-term agricultural productivity even though they are profitable in the narrow formal sense of the term as used by mainstream economists. The fact that intensive organic gardening produces higher *yields* is discarded because as a process it is labour-intensive.

Though not generally couched in such terms, this choice has little to do with feeding people per se and everything to do with the politics of industry and land ownership. It has been possible to ignore this for a long time because the issue of feeding people and creating jobs has been at bottom a question of being able to 'dial up' more energy on demand.

Those days are gone, but we are left with institutional and political structures that were formed in an era of fossil energy abundance. Chief amongst institutional structures is the multinational corporation, which faces unprecedented challenges to its raison d'être. Inexorably rising real energy costs are inhibiting the process of capital accumulation, rendering the very notion of competitive markets moot. What is left is a strategy of monopoly and regulatory capture which at bottom can only be perpetuated through the state's legal monopoly on sanctioned violence. Unfortunately there is collateral damage to the legal system upon which consent to that monopoly rests.

How long will populations accept higher taxes, lower real wages and fewer public services? This is the real issue for national security.

## THE IRISH DILEMMA

As a small, open economy and member of a large supranational currency bloc, Ireland in the best of times would find it challenging to manage its way through the vagaries of the economic cycle. These are not the best of times, and as discussed are unlikely to improve due to the inexorable global squeeze on energy supplies. The problem is compounded for the Irish because, quite apart from Ireland's size, it has surrendered control of critical components of national sovereignty to foreign interests. These include, notably, control over its currency and even legal control over aspects of its banking system. How else to explain the otherwise incomprehensible decision of the Fianna Fáil-Green coalition to guarantee all bank liabilities? The decision was correctly if ineffectually criticised at the time it was made five years ago. Ireland simply does not have the resources to make good on the promise. As we now know, the decision was welcomed by the foreign holders of Irish bank debt for whom an Irish default is problematic given their effective insolvency and size relative to their national economies. Ireland's action in effect volunteers her population to help carry the burden of those losses through higher taxes and, thanks to membership in the Eurozone, a savage internal devaluation to restore 'competitiveness'.

**Ireland: all sectors outstanding debt securities (euros)**

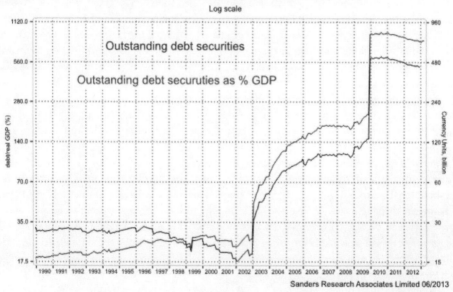

Log scale

Outstanding debt securities

Outstanding debt securuties as % GDP

Sanders Research Associates Limited 06/2013

To listen to the present Fine Gael-Labour coalition, the country has 'turned the corner'. If this were true, no doubt the Taoiseach would grant more press conferences. As we showed above, the oil statistics do not lie: petroleum consumption continues to plunge. It is doubtful that the average citizen is aware of the parlous state of the national balance sheet. Some €700 billion in debt outstanding exists, almost all of it incurred since Ireland joined the euro. This represents nearly five times GDP.[8]

While the drama of the 2007-08 collapse is hard to ignore, it was apparently not hard to ignore the explosive build-up of debt that began after Ireland joined the Eurozone, with debt growth far outpacing growth in GDP. Nor does it seem that it was hard to ignore the trend downward in industrial employment that also began in 2002. There is no sign that this is ending, nor any sign of plans to try to arrest the decline. Also in trend decline since the turn of the century has been employment in agriculture, forestry and fishing. Although employment in the sector has grown in the last two years, it is still too early to say whether or not this represents a trend change or a temporary correction within the overall decline. Astonishingly, the banking, finance and real-estate sector employment has been quite resilient. This is, of course, due to the equally astonishing unproductive direct and indirect subsidy being thrown at the sector at a time when productive government subsidy for regional and local LEADER programs,[9] health and education are being cut.

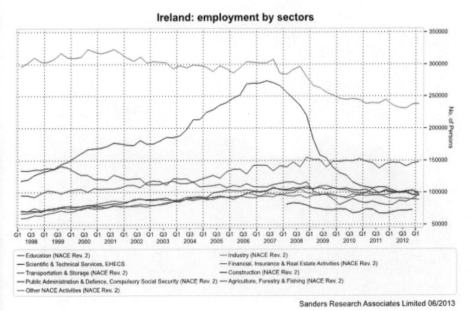

**Ireland: employment by sectors**

Sanders Research Associates Limited 06/2013

Ominously, its relatively small proportion of total employment notwithstanding, employment in logistics – that is, what gets goods to your door – has begun to drift lower. Taken along with the continued drop in fuel consumption, this suggests that real economic activity is not just stagnating but continuing to decline.

It is hard to avoid the conclusion that the Irish economy in fact entered a long-term recession beginning at the turn of the century that was disguised by EU spending, the surge in construction spending and a speculative boom in real estate that drove a boom in lending. The finance to make this possible was sourced from foreign lenders, an unfortunate fact of life that has considerably narrowed the 'acceptable' policy options for the current generation of Irish leadership.

## THE RESOURCE DILEMMA

World oil exports peaked in 2005 along with conventional oil production, squeezed not just by falling OECD demand, but by growing demand in many oil-exporting economies and falling production rates. The message could not be clearer to countries dependent on imported oil. The days of cheap oil are over. The only cap on price from now is going to be related to demand.

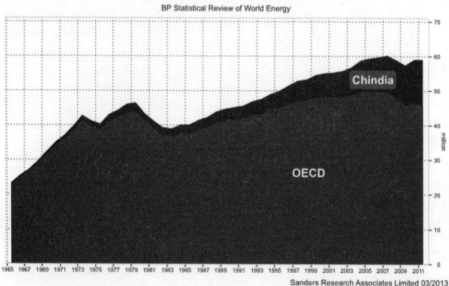

**OECD and Chindia oil consumption**

BP Statistical Review of World Energy

Sanders Research Associates Limited 03/2013

304

At the world level, demand restraint is coming from the OECD, whose falling oil consumption has accommodated rising demand from China and India (Chindia).[10] This has implications for everyone, not least because a trend such as this is not extendable indefinitely. For countries with endowments of oil and gas it is clear that it makes more sense to husband those resources rather than succumb to the temptation to monetise them as quickly as possible. In the contemporary world the cheapest way to 'produce' oil and gas is to find ways to not use them.

Management of Ireland's oil and gas endowment does not suggest that the government has taken this on board. This is a national strategic issue of utmost importance.

## Irish National Strategy

Current policy exerts no influence whatsoever over the rate of extraction. From the producer's point of view, it makes sense to lift the oil and gas as quickly as possible to maximise the *financial* return. Current policy allows them to offset exploration and development costs against tax, leading to the ridiculous conclusion that the Irish state might effectively not gain any benefit at all. Nor does there appear to be any intention of developing a domestic refining capability that would create jobs and prevent the equally ridiculous result under current policy of Ireland shipping its oil to refineries abroad from which it can buy it back. With the revenues and profits from oil and gas production privatised and the resource exported, Ireland nets virtually no benefit at all.

The size of the recoverable resource in place at Barryroe off the southern coast has been estimated to be 311 million barrels of oil and 207 billion cubic feet of associated gas.[11] These are extremely modest amounts in global terms representing *just four days' world consumption of oil and even less in terms of gas*. However, for Ireland the amounts are significant, being six years' oil consumption at current rates and more than a year's supply of natural gas. In financial terms that amounts to roughly *€24 billion worth of oil and €1.6 billion worth of gas*. With an annual trade deficit in oil of more than €5 billion, Ireland needs Barryroe.[12]

Ireland also needs whatever else can be found in the way of producible oil and gas under its seabed. The problem here is one of geology and statistics. No giant field (capable of producing more than 1 million barrels a day) has been found worldwide since the 1970s. Ireland would do well to find even a handful of Barryroe equivalents. *The prospects are small enough in international terms that the oil majors are highly unlikely to find it an attractive prospect relative to the risks and technical challenges. Thus it is to smaller exploration companies that Ireland must turn. This needs to be done in such a way that the conflict between national and corporate interests is resolved in a manner favourable to the nation.*

## Prospering in a New World Order:
## Some Strategic Conclusions

As we have seen, the world financial crisis has decisively broken the link between money and energy. The debt-based monetary system that has been the basis for the world economy since the early nineteenth century is decidedly unsuitable for a world in which cheap energy is no longer freely available.[13] It is abundantly clear that new monetary arrangements will need to be negotiated at the international level and that no system that does not take into account the interests of China, and particularly Russia, is likely to be a success. The problem in monetary terms is simply that in such a heavily indebted, energy-constrained world, realistic debt service and debt repayment is impossible. Zero interest rates and quantitative easing merely delay the inevitable. They are nothing but strategies to buy time.

Russia and China understand this perfectly well, which is why they are pushing ahead on their own with plans for a new international investment bank and with full convertibility of the Chinese yuan.[14] When this happens it is highly likely to be backed by gold or a combination of gold and possibly an energy component.

This matters for Ireland, for whom Eurozone membership must be counted less than successful. It has for better or for worse served as cover for a massive misallocation of investment capital into unneeded housing and real-estate speculation. Part of Ireland's strategy going forward necessarily must involve a re-examination of its national currency arrangements. The legacy system with which we are today burdened is one in which those who control debt creation have determined how resources are allocated between countries and between social classes. It is no longer workable. Going forward it is going to be those who control who gets how much energy who have that power. It follows that Ireland should not leave that power in the hands of the companies that exploit its national energy endowment.

It follows too that Ireland ought to conduct a thorough energy audit of its economy. This should be done not in the framework of conventional national accounting, which is a price-based methodology, but rather by the construction of a mass-flow model of the economy that begins with material and energetic inputs and ends with material and energetic outputs. This is not pie-in-the-sky thinking: the intellectual framework already exists and has been applied to both the US and Japanese economies by Ayres and Warr. This would give us a considerably truer picture of the sources and uses of energy for the economy and enable us to make better-informed choices about our future.

Ireland actually has a considerable non-hydrocarbon energy endowment of renewable energy in the form of wind, direct sunlight (harvested with PVC panels), tidal energy and agriculture. Indigenous primary energy production today is dominated by these renewables, especially wind. The steep decline in electricity generated with indigenous natural gas reflects the production decline of the Kinsale field off Cork and should be reversed when the offshore Corrib field comes on stream. Perhaps the most important thing to take away from this chart is the strategic reality that we are far from a 'solution' to our energy challenge.

### Ireland: Indigenous energy production

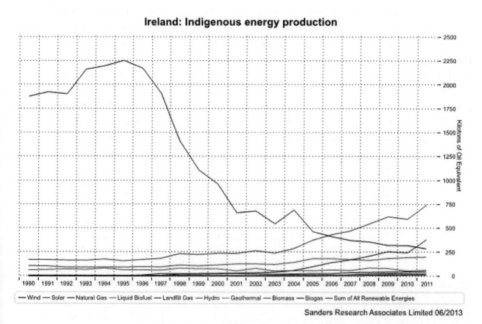

Sanders Research Associates Limited 06/2013

There are, however, principles that would serve us well to be mindful of. One is that the Irish people come first. This ought not to be controversial, but it will undoubtedly be so, however much lip service is paid to it. This is ironic, given the energetic sources of our crisis. People represent a source of energy, and as we have seen, labour-intensive agriculture produces higher yields than fossil-fuel-intensive agriculture. Ireland has long been an exporter of her people, arguably the most important indigenous energy resource of all.

This brings us to the second principle, which is that the national discussion needs to be open and inclusive and based on physical realities, not economic or dreamy abstractions. Irish GDP is an inaccurate abstract representation of the true state of the economy, which is more accurately represented by employment and energy consumption and production. These are all in multi-year downtrends that show no sign of reversing.

And this brings us to the third conclusion, and the end of this chapter as well. There needs to be national recognition that we face an epochal crisis, not just a bad business cycle. Apparent national priorities such as the return of Ireland to the international bond markets, the sale of national assets or the withdrawal of services from rural areas that actually are key to a real national recovery are not just artefacts of an age that is past but are damaging to the country. To recognise this and to act on it requires courage, not just from politicians, but from the people whose expectations have been perhaps overinflated during years of easy money. The Irish have never been short of courage. Now's the time to use it.

## ABOUT THE AUTHOR

Chris Sanders is the managing director of Sanders Research Associates Limited (SRA), an Irish open-source research and intelligence company. He has spent more than thirty years in capital markets and investment management in Europe and the Middle East, founding SRA in 1997 to fill the gaps left by mainstream economic and market analysis. His work today is focused especially on the politics and economics of resource depletion. For ten years he was a guest lecturer in international economics at the School of Public Administration at the University of Gothenburg in Sweden. He now lives and works in Ireland.

## NOTES

1. Reed, Thomas. 2005. *At the Abyss.* Presidio Press

2. www.erina.or.jp/en/Asia/map/image/VSTO0905.jpg

3. www.lowtechmagazine.com/2009/06/embodied-energy-of-digital-technology.html

4. Ayres, Robert and Benjamin Warr. 2009. *The Economic Growth Engine: How Energy and Work Drive Material Prosperity.* Edward Elgar Publishing Limited

5. *Ibid.*

6. See Joe Studwell's *How Asia Works* for a full analysis of the successful application of intensive gardening as part of a larger program for economic development in Taiwan, Korea, and Japan

7. Sanders Research Associates Limited

8. $210 billion in 2012. www.tradingeconomics.com/ireland/gdp

9. leaderpartnership.ie/about/

10. www.bp.com/en/global/corporate/about-bp/statistical-review-of-world-energy-2013/2012-in-review.html

11. www.fxcentre.com/news.asp?3051351

12. 90 million barrels per day in 2011 www.indexmundi.com/energy.aspx, 120 bcf of gas

for the whole year in 2011 www.indexmundi.com/energy.aspx?product=gas& graph=consumption

13. For an excellent discussion of this subject, see Richard Douthwaite's 'The Supply of Money in an Energy Scarce World' in *Fleeing Vesuvius*, FEASTA, New Society Publishers, 2011

14. www.breitbart.com/Big-Peace/2013/03/30/China-Russia-Coalition-Creates-Alternative-to-IMF-World-Bank, www.ibtimes.com/china-russia-currency-agreement-further-threatens-us-dollar-248338, www.bloomberg.com/news/2013-03-25/brics-nations-plan-new-bank-to-bypass-world-bank-imf.html

# 15.

# BY THEIR WORDS YOU SHALL KNOW THEM

## Press Cuttings

### POLITICIANS

#### Ray Burke

I've come here today to defend my personal integrity, the integrity of my party [Fianna Fáil], of this government, and the honour of this House [the Dáil]. I have come to reassure the public that I have done nothing wrong. There were no rules in place in 1989. I have bared my soul to this House today. I am being judged on 1997 rules for a contribution that I received in 1989 when there were no rules in place. Whatever comes out of the woodwork from now on, the line is in the sand, as far as I'm concerned.

I move on to United Nations, to Europe and anybody who had anything to ask had the opportunity in Leinster House to do it today . . . I have no doubt that the representatives would have had plenty of stories given to them, by every crank in Christendom, but from now on, we move on . . . no more scapegoats.

—Ray Burke[1]


I have met representatives of more than twenty companies from around the world – some were operating here before, some were here and others were never in Irish waters. As well as my own contacts with these oil companies, there have been a considerable number of contacts between officials of my department and representatives of other companies.

—Ray Burke[2]

I must say I liked Ray Burke. He was friendly, good company, generous. You could never put your hand in your pocket for a drink when Ray was around. I didn't know where he got 'the walking-around money' as he called it. We knew he was bold but we didn't realise how bold. We didn't know about all the corruption behind the generosity.

—Sean Duignan[3]

For decades he [Ray Burke] was advanced to us as a man worthy, not just of our votes, but of the highest offices in the land – yet all along he was corrupt.

—*RTÉ*[4]

The planning tribunal investigated him for years, the Criminal Assets Bureau raided his house, the Revenue Commissioners made a €600,000 settlement with him and he's now in jail. Yet when it comes to Ray Burke and his dark secrets, we may only have scratched the surface.

The irony is that, for all the time he has spent in the public glare over recent years, only a fraction of the decisions Burke took during his lengthy political career have undergone thorough public scrutiny.

But large swathes of his career have never been the subject of detailed public hearings. Decisions he made as a Minister in various portfolios have also attracted controversy, but few have been the subject of detailed investigation. At this late stage, these matters may never be investigated. Many of the controversies date back several decades, so any relevant documents or records would be scarce. Some of the main figures involved have passed on.

The law of diminishing returns may apply.

As Minister for Energy in 1987, Burke significantly eased the terms for oil companies prospecting off the Irish coast. Royalties were abolished and the State relinquished any stake in an eventual oil or gas find.

His move effectively reversed the terms introduced by the Labour energy minister, Justin Keating, in 1975, which had given the State the right to take a stake of up to 50 percent in any discovery, and also allowed for the payment of royalties.

—*Daily Mail*[5]

It is a mark of the odd way in which we conduct our affairs that a man who was labelled corrupt by a planning tribunal continues to live on the generous state income of €103,838 per year.

It has been estimated that since his premature retirement from politics, Burke –

once described as an 'honourable man' by Bertie Ahern – has cost the State €1m in pensions alone.

'Did ye hear,' he once declared to political correspondents in Leinster House when his planning dealings were attracting unwelcome attention, 'I'm the most interviewed deputy in the House.'

'That's great, Ray,' said a journalist.

'Yeah, by the f**kin' guards,' Burke replied.

—Kim Bielenberg[6]


## Justin Keating

If the oil remained in the ground, my heart wasn't broken – it wouldn't get less valuable, it would get more valuable, as has happened . . .

The oil crisis weakened my hand a lot . . . there was a worldwide recession . . . It was a very sharp crisis that we survived without people knowing how desperate it was in `73. But if you have the oil, as the companies had, if you have the tankers, as the companies had, if you can play supply on the global scale, we had very few cards in our hands. We had to beg them 'Please, don't let us run out', and in the goodness of their hearts, they didn't let us run out. But we had no clout – they had all the clout. Then.

I came to realise that we couldn't abdicate our authority and power and responsibility and give it to the big oil companies.

So we started to develop some expertise and perhaps the most important thing we did was to look at the situation in the North Sea: Britain wasting their resource because the big companies were so powerful and Norway using it brilliantly, so that they have now secured their future. They had a far-sighted government – very patriotic, independent, determined to do the best for themselves. They introduced what I think was a brilliant policy . . .

Make big mistakes in service industry and it dies and goes away. Make big mistakes with natural resources and that's it – there is no rehearsal and there is no second choice – it's gone . . .

I would like to add this thought – which is a thought about the future: if we waste this resource, it will be a crime against Irish people. We are in danger of doing it.

—Justin Keating[7]

## Bertie Ahern

Defending Ray Burke's appointment to Cabinet in Ahern's first government in 1997, after questions about Burke's suitability were raised: 'I've looked up every tree in north Dublin.'[8]

*

My discussions with Ray Burke at any time before appointing him Minister were on the basis that he had done nothing wrong. I had asked Ray Burke, in the terms of donations, had he got donations and was there anything wrong. In terms of that, Ray Burke had made it very clear that any money that he had got were donations to his constituency and that there was no wrongdoing whatsoever involved with any of those.

—Bertie Ahern[9]

In the light of the Flood Tribunal Report, it is now clear that the Taoiseach [Bertie Ahern] and the Dáil were deliberately misled by Mr Burke, and that his conduct deserves all of the public criticism made of him. The Taoiseach repeats his disgust at Mr Burke's betrayal of the public trust and reiterates his condemnations of Mr Burke's conduct.

—Bertie Ahern[10]

On 30 September 1987, Mr Burke announced new fiscal terms that included the exemption of all oil and gas production from royalty payments, a 100 percent tax write-off against profits on capital expenditure for exploration, development and production extending back 25 years and the abolition of all other state participation in oil and gas development. Electing to leave corporation tax at 50 percent, he told the press that, after considering a reduction, he had decided that such a move would be 'over-generous'. Five years later, the then Minister for Finance, Bertie Ahern, cut the oil-industry corporation tax to 25 percent.

—Centre for Public Inquiry[11]

## Pat Rabbitte

[Ray Burke] circumscribed himself by saying that he wouldn't answer questions about contributions other than this particular donation (£30,000 received in 1989) . . . and therefore I think we are still at a loss . . .

—Pat Rabbitte[12]

Rabbitte also said there wasn't 'much reality' to suggestions that Ireland's resources are being given away – but said he is open to changing the licensing terms if necessary.

—thejournal.ie[13]

We are convinced that debate, objectively analysed by the media, will clearly demonstrate that the proper development of Ireland's mineral resources under public ownership has the potential to change the face of the nation. It is difficult to grasp the enormous potential of the Irish industry, when traditionally we have been taught that this country is endowed with no such wealth. All that is necessary now is the political will on the part of our government to ensure that this enormous wealth is exploited on behalf of the Irish people.

The present controversy is very lop-sided in the sense that those with a vested interest in development of Irish resources appear to have access to unlimited finance for public-relations purposes. Generally speaking, the media has been less than anxious to explore the other side of the story.

The Land Acts and the 1940 Minerals Act vest the ownership of all of the minerals under the Irish soil in the State. The minerals under the ground belong to the people of Ireland and not to any private company. The government is seriously contemplating giving our resources away.

Whatever government action is decided upon will not only determine the extent to which the Irish people as the owners will benefit, but may set a precedent for government policy on future discoveries of resources. The mining companies are quick to underestimate the value and to imply that there are circumstances which will preclude major profit-making. This is not surprising, but it is significant that the government has completely accepted what the companies have to say . . .

This calculation by the government is wrong, because:

a. It accepts the mining companies' figures, which are too low

b. It draws a direct comparison between the cost of . . . two mines . . . quite different as engineering operations.

c. It makes no allowance for the probable increase in [resource] prices . . .

Moreover, the policy is wrong because (as pointed out by C. J. Haughey), a good accountant can arrange a company's books so that profits are absorbed into costs . . .

1. Could it (the State) make available the capital from the public sector when such scarce financial resources are needed for more important social goals?

2. Could (the State) attract the technology expertise and enterprise to establish a viable industry?

3. Is the industry large enough to warrant national management? . . .

One argument, lately used by Senator Brian Lenihan, is that state intervention, even to the extent of taxing the profits from the extractive stage, would frighten away the foreign investors 'we so desperately need to provide jobs for our people' (especially in marginal constituencies) . . .

Mr John Teeling . . . predicted on November 8th that [the resources in question] would eventually be big enough to take on the world's largest companies . . .

If the companies believe it more profitable to export the unrefined ores, they will do so without establishing in Ireland . . . only a fraction of the wealth-generating potential will remain within the Irish economy . . .

Our mineral resources represent the potential for real take-off and development of the Irish economy. Proper development of the minerals could lead to long-term massive benefits, rather than short-term marginal benefits as at present . . . 'The government must govern in the long-term interests of the country and not fashion policy to deal with the short-term exigencies. The development of a national resource is a long-term business, as anyone who has worked in it will testify. It needs the continued and long-term attention of government, consistent policies and a stable fiscal environment' . . .

Obviously, the tax situation was an anomaly . . .The State already owns the minerals – why should it give the wealth away . . . for any . . . deal with a private company? . . .

The fact that the geological structures which have yielded fields of oil and gas in the North Sea are repeated in several places in the seabed around Ireland means that further such finds here are a probability rather than a possibility . . .

The government already possesses the legal powers and the moral, political and economic justification to retain the ownership and control of the minerals . . . The only thing it may lack is the political will to secure the most just and equitable solution for the Irish people . . .

*Proposals*

1. That . . . the government should retain its exclusive ownership of the mineral rights . . . and not relinquish them to any private company.

2. That all government negotiations . . . [with any] private company should cease forthwith . . . Mianrai Teoranta should be recapitalised and reactivated by the State so as to be able to exploit the extremely valuable deposit . . . on behalf of all Irish people.

—Union of Students in Ireland (Pat Rabbitte, President), 1973[14]

[Pat] Rabbitte said: 'I think it's a pity that this canard about Norway has been flown and has captured some imagination'. . . . He said that comparisons to Norway were like 'comparing apples with oranges' and people who were responsible for this comparison 'should have recanted but didn't'.

—thejournal.ie[15]

If ever there was a doubt about the undesirability of a dominant position in such a sensitive industry then the conduct of Independent Newspapers over the weekend removed that doubt. Journalists and columnists were used in such an overkill to defend the economic interests of their proprietor that the public were given a glimpse of what abuse of dominant position means in practice.

—Pat Rabbitte, on Tony O'Reilly being linked to donations to Ray Burke[16]

\*

Whatever about the tits on Mrs Murphy's cow, to be honest deputy, that contribution is about as much use as tits on a bull.

—Pat Rabbitte on fracking, to TD Mattie McGrath[17]

### Dick Spring

*Erstwhile Labour Party leader, who in 1985–86 first amended Justin Keating's 1975 terms to remove state participation and royalties on oil and gas fields of less than 75 million barrels*

In a Dáil speech in September 1987 the leader of the Labour Party, Dick Spring, described Mr Burke's revisions as 'an act of economic treason'.

—Centre for Public Inquiry[18]

### Tommy Broughan

*Labour energy spokesperson, prior to Labour being elected into the government of the 31st Dáil*

Although the focus at present has been on the dispute over the Corrib gas pipeline and the ongoing incarceration of the five Rossport residents, the wider issues of the management of Ireland's natural resources and the financial return to the Irish State for such assets needs to be urgently examined.

The current measures in place in Ireland for licensing oil and gas exploration are some of the most advantageous to international oil companies in the EU and across the world. The corresponding return to Irish citizens for what is a critical national resource is extraordinarily low in comparison to other states.

In 1975 my great predecessor and then Minister for Industry and Commerce, Justin Keating, established a comprehensive strategy for regulating oil and gas exploration in Ireland that corresponded to best international practice. This included a 50 percent state shareholding in any discovery plus royalties of 6 to 7 percent. However, the changes imposed by Ray Burke as Energy Minister in 1988 and in 1992 by then Minister for Finance, Bertie Ahern, and Energy Minister Bobby Molloy resulted in the present inadequate system.

At present the Irish government has no stake in any such developments (unlike the Norwegian and Danish states), earns no royalties from the process and has a very low oil-tax regime.

Many other states have successfully changed the terms of their exploration licences and fiscal regimes, and as circumstances change, periodically review the measures in place. The UK's North Sea fiscal regime was changed in the 2002 British budget to increase the return to the British state on oil and gas exploration and extraction.

When the Dáil resumes in the autumn I will be pressing for a similar review of the management of Ireland's oil and gas natural resources and the Labour Party will propose any necessary legislation.

—Tommy Broughan[19]

## Cian O'Callaghan

*Councillor, former Mayor of Fingal – ex-Labour*[20]

Minister Pat Rabbitte TD argues that Ireland's tax take on our oil and gas 'compare[s] favourably with all similar countries but not with Norway'. This is complete nonsense.

A report by the US Government Accountability Office in 2007 found that Ireland has the second-lowest government take on oil and gas deposits of 142 countries studied. The Department of Communications, Marine and Natural Resources reported in 2006 that average government takes range from 25 to 90 percent across the world. They further found that the European average government take excluding Ireland is between 35 to 65 percent. The assertion that the Irish government take, at 25 percent, compares favourably only rings true for the corporations that wish to exploit our resources. For the rest of us it represents an insane act of economic treason, offering to give away some €750 billion worth of oil and gas over the coming decades at the worst possible terms and conditions for the Irish people and the Irish economy.

—Cian O'Callaghan[21]

## Finian McGrath
*Independent* TD

I wish to challenge all the previous governments on their records as regards our oil and gas reserves. We never got to the bottom of the deals signed with oil and gas companies, particularly during the time of former minister Ray Burke. Were back-handers given and did the major parties receive significant donations from these companies? These are legitimate questions which should be answered immediately, and our people deserve the truth. We must get all the facts regarding these big companies.

I say to the government to get off the stage, to listen to the facts and to look at the wording of the motion and to come up with new ideas. We should not simply hand it over, willy-nilly. I support the motion for a complete review of the licensing and revenue terms and the immediate revocation of consents given pending such a review. I hope the Minister, Deputy Rabbitte, takes note of this part of the motion. I also support the establishment of a State oil and gas mineral exploration company holding a 51 percent majority share in oil and gas finds, with its own research facility which would collect full and up-to-date information. This is a very sensible proposal with regard to job creation in particular.

The motion also proposes the imposition of a 50 percent tax on oil and gas profits and a 7.5 percent royalty, and that the revenues accruing would provide towards the resources for long-term and sustainable growth in place of the current indenture to the EU and IMF because of the unsustainable bank debt. The motion proposes that we use the resources for the benefit of the majority of the people of this country. These are sensible proposals and all Members should support them.

The Minister asks what can be done as we cannot find any oil or gas. There is a surrender mentality at work. We need new ideas. We need to go out and do the business.

We need our oil and gas and we need new ideas for economic development. We also need common sense and we need to use the resources for our people . . .

—Finian McGrath[22]

## INDUSTRY VOICES

### Oh Really, O'Reilly?
### Tony O'Reilly, Sr

The seismic material which identified areas of potential finds was provided initially by state geologists. According to Ivan Fallon's biography, *The Luck of O'Reilly*, O'Reilly believed that there was a simplistic public notion in the 1970s that 'Irish oil and minerals belonged to the Irish people at large'.

—politico.ie[23]

Says O'Reilly, in a broad Irish accent, 'There are t'ree [sic] reasons why Ireland is doing so well. First we have very computer-literate children. We have the lowest tax rate, 10 percent for corporates, in Europe – probably the world . . .' And then, with the timing of a natural actor, O'Reilly delivers the punchline. 'And most importantly we're robbing the bloody Germans blind!'

'We [Ireland] have rejected our neutrality, something we wore as a badge on [sic] honour, to become part of the EU. Now prosperity has made sovereignty a more complex and subtle thing.'

—*New Zealand Herald*[24]

Media magnate Sir Anthony O'Reilly has escaped a Mahon Tribunal grilling over a £30,000 payment to Fianna Fail, £20,000 of which was pocketed by the disgraced Ray Burke.

The tribunal had planned to question Sir Anthony and executives of his then private investment vehicle, the Fitzwilton Group, over the 1989 payment later this year. The tribunal wanted to establish if Mr Burke performed any favours for Fitzwilton while he was Minister for Communications. When the company said it had given money to Mr Burke for Fianna Fail, party fundraisers contacted the Minister, who presented them with a bank draft for £10,000. When they asked for the balance, Mr Burke told officials: 'That's as much as you're getting. Good luck.'

—*Daily Mail*[25]

*The Burke controversy. An independent story? Have Tony O'Reilly's Irish interests got themselves linked to a controversy over donations to political parties?*
Cheque number 9922 was a ticking bomb at the heart of the country's political

establishment, but no one heard it. Nine years on, it has exploded under Ray Burke, the man who received the cheque and is now a disgraced ex-minister. Caught in the blast wave is Tony O'Reilly, the billionaire tycoon who dominates Ireland's newspaper industry. The payment to Burke was by Fitzwilton, a company chaired by O'Reilly. Now a tribunal investigating political sleaze, which will examine the payment, is to question O'Reilly.

Opposition politicians, under parliamentary privilege, have called on O'Reilly to explain his view of Fitzwilton's cheque. Four months after receiving the cheque Burke gave seven licences to a different O'Reilly company. Pure coincidence, said an O'Reilly spokesman.

Those who claim a link are begrudgers, intent on smearing the man who controls the *Independent* and *Independent on Sunday* in Britain. The allegations have fuelled a near-hysterical reaction from O'Reilly's Irish media empire, Independent Newspapers. An unprecedented blitz of editorials, opinion pieces and news reports have denounced the allegations and those who made them. The invective against O'Reilly's accusers is withering, sustained and coordinated – an awesome onslaught from a group that controls two-thirds of the market.

The sheer scale of the group, dwarfing in relative terms Rupert Murdoch's News International, is intimidating and unhealthy, said Pat Rabbitte, a member of parliament and former cabinet minister.

—*The Guardian*[26]

[O'Reilly] told Forbes in a 1983 interview that being Ireland's biggest media baron had helped him in his quixotic oil quest. 'Since I own 35 percent of the newspapers in Ireland, I have close contact with the politicians. I got the block he [the geologist] wanted.'

—*Forbes*[27]

### Tony O'Reilly Jr

I view it as a type of offshore property company. Our focus is to create more value tomorrow than we have today. There is no doubt that this is the best time to be in the oil and gas industry.

—Tony O'Reilly Jr[28]

There are proven fields.

—Tony O'Reilly Jr[29]

I'm not concerned about oil prices at all . . . when we are looking at our projects, we are looking at numbers in the 20s and 30s (dollars per barrel) as the economic cut-off . . . but obviously we are looking at a higher price deck going forward. People still are consuming . . . so even if it is down a little bit, we're still coming off high with Brent at €100.

—Tony O'Reilly Jr[30]

Barryroe is a big discovery that the market didn't believe. It's a waxy crude – when it was discovered in the `70s by Esso, it was a technological challenge, but also a financial challenge, because you need $30 to $35 price deck to justify the investment. That's why it was never developed before. So what have we done? We came in and we shot 3D and that de-risked the whole 'compartmentalisation' argument. We'll deliver 1,800 barrels a day. Barryroe is a hugely important well for us . . . it also is important at unlocking other plays in the Celtic Sea. It also de-risks Ireland . . . We don't need hundred-dollar pricing to make the Irish model work; we certainly do feel we probably need $40.

—Tony O'Reilly Jr[31]

As an Irish company, Providence has a policy to utilise Irish workers as appropriate. Unfortunately, there are no Irish rig owners (yet) so naturally we have to use international contractors. Hopefully that will change as the industry develops. Likewise, there are limited support service operators – so again, we have to take resources where we can get them from for now . . . The fiscal terms are appropriate for the current state of the industry.

—Tony O'Reilly Jr[32]

Of course you need regulation. But you don't need over-regulation. What we need is appropriate regulation.

—Sean Fitzpatrick[33]

As Providence's technical director, John O'Sullivan, explained to me, modern technology means that oil can be put into 'tanker-ready form' at the rig. There's no need to pipe it ashore. Once in the tankers, the oil from Dalkey could be shipped to Milford Haven in the UK or Rotterdam, he said.

—irishoilandgas.wordpress.com[34]

## David Horgan

We'll worry about the taxes whenever there is something to worry about, and be in no doubt that every Irish minister is going to change the rules if we have a bonanza.

—David Horgan[35]

Very simple – the government has got people onto the dancefloor and given them a few drinks – let's see what happens.

—David Horgan[36]

Providence should be able to go back all the way to Atlantic Resources in the 1980s . . . in their case, they have probably spent a billion dollars, so there would be a lot of write-offs before they have to pay any tax . . . we don't expect that Ireland is the sort of country that will go back on its promises – Ireland is too respectable a country for that.

—David Horgan[37]

Once you have a bonanza, then you change the tax rates to a fair proportion – but you don't do it retrospectively.

—David Horgan[38]

Everyone's for progress as long as it doesn't involve change . . . Beware of industry insiders when they're telling you that something that is in their best interest is also in your interest.

—David Horgan[39]

Oil has gone up to $120 a barrel. Technology has leaped ahead [and] has made possible the development of a discovery that was first made in the `70s. Esso found it [Barryroe] in 1973 and it flowed at 780 barrels, which was uneconomic. Then it was drilled by Marathon in 1978 and it flowed at about twice that. This [development] in turn is flowing at about twice the rate that Marathon was able to flow it at, but a series of problems have been solved . . . the main one is that they have been able to use 3D seismic to get a better photograph and that enables them both to see what's there and to tap it by a new development called horizontal drilling – in the old days you couldn't do that, now you can – and then lastly they developed a technique that the waxy oil doesn't freeze in the pipe – it flows like normal oil. Put those three things together, adding the very favourable tax rates in Ireland – it really should be economic. Basically, as long as the oil price stays at $60 or better this should be an economic discovery. Ireland has very attractive taxes.

—David Horgan[40]

We are generous [in Ireland] in the sense that our terms are the best of any hydrocarbon province in the world [for corporates], so that's a good start. In the `70s there was interest, but they found nothing, basically.

Ireland got a bad name because when people explored, they were looking for North Sea-type targets. Now the industry knows so much more, technology has moved on, the oil price is higher, and the government has improved the fiscal terms to now being the best of any hydrocarbon province.

I would love that the Irish Exchequer had a big slice of the cake. Right now, there is no cake.

[Corrib] has been a factor. In every meeting that you have, it comes up. But Ireland is not the only country that has resource nationalism and has difficult community relations, so if you explain [to people with whom one meets] the history of Mayo, Mícheál Mac Daibhéid and how Mayo is special, and then you contrast it with Cobh and there wasn't the same difficulty over forty years serving Kinsale out of the port of Cobh, then people say, 'Well, that is like the difficulties that you have in Nigeria or Russia.'

—David Horgan[41]

When the point was made during a discussion on RTÉ that Ireland's licence conditions are too generous, Petrel Resources geologist Dave Naylor agreed that a country should get the best result it can. Also, the application of new ideas, technologies and techniques raises the chances of success – so that would be a reason to make Ireland more attractive, without the generous terms.[42]

### Brian O'Cathain

*CEO of Petroceltic*

Corrib will never pay tax.

—Brian O'Cathain

### Mike Cunningham

*Former director of Statoil Exploration Ireland*

No other country in the world has given such favourable terms as Ireland.

—Mike Cunningham

## MEDIA COMMENTATORS

### Fintan O'Toole

The State is about to sign away almost all our resources on terms by far the worst in the developed world. Sometimes, you have to consider extraordinary things. I want to suggest . . . that the State is simply incapable of dealing with one of the key challenges and opportunities facing Irish people: getting the best for the Irish people from the potentially huge resources of oil and gas off our shores.

—Fintan O'Toole[43]

### Harry McGee

*Irish Times Political Correspondent*

If a head-hunting team began a trawl to find the most suitable person to be minister for communications, energy and natural resources, it is likely they would choose . . . somebody who is not Pat Rabbitte. A perception has grown that the department is not a natural fit for him, outside the communications and media part of the portfolio.

—Harry McGee[44]

## Dr Tom O'Connor

*Lecturer in economics and public policy at CIT, author of* The Soul of Irish Indifference

The obsequious Irish trusted their masters and were driven by a combination of media spin and naked individualism to do so. The fact that homelessness was increasing and hundreds were on hospital trolleys was of secondary importance. The cultural conditioning was coming home to roost.

Then there is the effect of mushroom information on the Irish where they are kept in the dark by politicians and fed with shite. A major inhibitory factor to protest is that people believe the government spin that there aren't any alternatives and they themselves are powerless!

The information gap created by reading tabloids and the press-release 'manufactured' *Six One News* means Irish people don't know of alternatives: that for example a 5 percent gross tax could provide health insurance for all with no waiting lists, or that there is €8 billion in untapped taxes to make up most of the fiscal savings going forward, which would hit the wealthy only without spreading the pain to those who can least afford it. Under these circumstances, demoralised people prefer to sit on the sofa. Another spur to protest is lost. Adding up all the factors explains why Irish people endure such suffering without significant protest.

—Tom O'Connor[45]


## ADVISORS


## Thomas Pringle

*Independent member of the Joint Oireachtas Committee on Communications, Natural Resources and Agriculture*

The tax rate is too low. Companies reap the benefit of discoveries while there is no dividend for the public.

—Thomas Pringle[46]


## James Gogarty

*A former executive at the building firm JMSE, delivered a bribe to Mr Burke in 1989*[47]

James Gogarty accompanied Michael Bailey, from another firm, to Burke's home with at least £30,000 – mostly in cash. Gogarty told the tribunal that on the way to the house he asked:

'Will we get a receipt for this money?'

Bailey replied: 'Will we f\*\*k!'

In his heyday Burke was the quintessential clientelist operator, who based his popularity on doing favours.

—Kim Bielenberg[48]

## PriceWaterhouseCoopers

*'Important message' from the PwC report on our oil and gas, commissioned by Providence Resources*

Important message to any person not authorised to have access to this report.

Should any unauthorised person obtain access to, and read this report, by reading this report such person accepts and agrees to the following terms:

1. The reader of this report understands that the work performed by PwC was performed in accordance with instructions provided by our client and was performed exclusively for our client's sole benefit and use.

2. The reader of this report acknowledges that this report was prepared at the direction of our client and may not include all procedures deemed necessary for the purposes of the reader.

3. Further, the reader agrees that this report is not to be referred to or quoted, in whole or in part, in any public or legal agreement or document and not to distribute the report without PwC's prior written consent.

(Note: Which is a pity, because on pg 63, the report outlines what business will be given to non-Irish companies.)

## Alan McCrae

Head of energy tax at PricewaterhouseCoopers UK, suggested that the government consider getting rid of capital-gains tax where producing oil or gas assets are sold. His argument is that this would get rid of a tax barrier for anyone who wants to exit, making them more transferrable and helping to make the regime here more attractive.[49]

### Dr Alfred Kjemperud

A 25 million bbl field in Ireland gives the same profit after tax for the oil company as a 144 million bbl field in Indonesia.

—Dr Alfred Kjemperud, The Bridge Group[50]

### Norges Geologiske Undersøkelse

A letter (reproduced below) from Norway's national institution for knowledge on bedrock, mineral resources, surface deposits, and groundwater to the Norwegian Ministry of Foreign Affairs in answer to a question raised during a UN conference in Geneva on 25 February 1958 read, in part:

One can ignore the possibility of finding coal, oil or sulphur on the continental shelf along the Norwegian coastline.

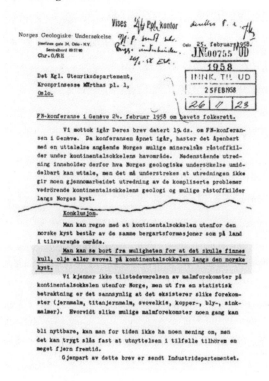

# NOTES

*All quotations cited in this book, including in this chapter, are available at ownouroil.ie/quOOOtes.*

1.   www.youtube.com/watch?v=UesOWVRdWLU

2.   As quoted in the Centre for Public Inquiry Fiosrú November 2005 Vol1 No2 p.59 www.ownouroil.ie/images/resources/Centre_Public_Inquiry.pdf

3.   Former Government Press Secretary and former broadcaster, 'Wise Guy: The Ray Burke Story- RTÉ Scannal' http://www.rte.ie/tv/scannal/RayBurke.html

4.   www.youtube.com/watch?v=_-YgMpFxu3c

5.   Daily Mail July 5th 2007. www.indymedia.ie/attachments/mar2012/ahern_burke_oreilly_dossier_19982011.pdf

6.   Independent.ie 19th November 2011. www.independent.ie/opinion/analysis/the-cricketloving-excon-paid-103000-a-year-by-taxpayers-26794239.html

7.   In an interview with Richie O'Donnell – 2008. Video is on OOO.ie

8.   www.thejournal.ie/will-we-fk-the-mahon-tribunal-in-quotes-374774-Mar2012/

9.   www.youtube.com/watch?v=MD5ICE2kzyM

10.  www.youtube.com/watch?v=MD5ICE2kzyM#t=9m13s

11.  Centre for Public Inquiry, Fiosrú publication November 2005, Vol1 No2 pg 59 http://www.ownouroil.ie/images/resources/Centre_Public_Inquiry.pdf

12.  www.youtube.com/watch?v=UesOWVRdWLU#t=6m39s

13.  www.thejournal.ie/pat-rabbitte-fracking-ireland-931018-Jun2013/

14.  irishlabour.com/pamphlets/Mines-USI.pdf

15.  businessetc.thejournal.ie/ireland-norway-oil-909379-May2013/

16.  As quoted in the *Guardian* 15 June 1998, regarding the controversy around Tony O'Reilly being linked to donations to Ray Burke. www.indymedia.ie/attachments/mar 2012/ahern_burke_oreilly_dossier_19982011.pdf

17.  www.breakingnews.ie/discover/udderly-bizarre-mcgrath-asks-rabbitte-to-count-the-tits-on-murphys-cow-611195.html

18.  As quoted in the Centre For Public Enquiry's Fiosrú publication November 2005, Vol. 1, No. 2 pg 59

19. www.labour.ie/press/2005/08/12/full-review-of-irish-oil-gas-regime-necessary/

20. www.independent.ie/regionals/fingalindependent/news/ocallaghan-quits-labour-over-unfair-and-unjust-policies-29458451.html

21. paddyhealy.wordpress.com/2011/08/20/labour-councillor-rubbishes-rabitte-on-oil-and-gas/

22. Dail debates, 19 April 2011. debates.oireachtas.ie/dail/2011/04/19/00022.asp

23. politico.ie/index.php?option=com_content&view=article&id=2126:tony-oreilly-more-mega-millions&catid=219:media&Itemid=1242. See also: Fallon, Ivan. 1994. *The Luck of O'Reilly*, Warner Books, pp 311-312.

24. *New Zealand Herald,* 1 October 2000. www.nzherald.co.nz/nz/news/article.cfm?c_id=1&objectid=153340

25. www.indymedia.ie/attachments/mar2012/ahern_burke_oreilly_dossier_19982011.pdf

26. www.indymedia.ie/attachments/mar2012/ahern_burke_oreilly_dossier_19982011.pd7

27. www.forbes.com/sites/christopherhelman/2012/10/16/amid-irish-outcry-billionaires-son-to-drill-for-oil-in-bonos-backyard/2/

28. As quoted in the Centre For Public Enquiry's Fiosrú publication November 2005, Vol. 1, No. 2, pg 72. www.cym.ie/documents/Centre_Public_Inquiry.pdf

29. www.bloomberg.com/video/67852252-providence-resources-tony-o-reilly-interview.html

30. www.bloomberg.com/video/providence-says-hasn-t-sought-partner-for-oil-field-mn~XEWm8SWCAp2yvzVTvKw.html

31. 50th Oilbarrel Conference, 16 February 2012. www.youtube.com/watch?v=j_yARrMwb4o

32. www.rigzone.com/news/oil_gas/a/127176/Oil_and_Gas_Whats_In_It_For_The_Irish/?all=HG2

33. wp.sme.ie/ireland-2/leadership-and-integrity/sean-fitzpatrick-interview/

34. irishoilandgas.wordpress.com/2011/07/03/oil-companies-plan-to-export-directly-from-irish-oil-fields/

35. In a discussion on Newstalk radio. www.youtube.com/watch?v=U8rKOziuimM#t=6m50

36. In a discussion on Newstalk radio. www.youtube.com/watch?v=U8rKOziuimM#t=6m50

37.  www.newstalk.ie/player/listen_back/8/976/08th_May_2013_-_Moncrieff_Part_1

38.  In a discussion on RTÉ's *Today With Seán O'Rourke*, 11 September 2013

39.  On *Prime Time,* 23 September. www.rte.ie/player/ie/show/10201359/

40.  On *Prime Time*, 15 March 2012. www.rte.ie/news/player/2012/0315/3229548-interview-chief-executive-of-petrel-resources-david-horgan/

41.  On *Today with Pat Kenny,* 28 May 2013. soundcloud.com/williamhederman/today-with-pat-kenny-28-may

42.  http://www.rte.ie/news/player/2012/1113/20106862-prospects-for-big-oil-finds-off-the-irish-coast/

43.  *Irish Times,* 16 August 2011. www.billtormey.ie/2011/08/20/fintan-otoole-v-pat-rabbitte-rounds-1-fintan-kicks-pat-around-the-ring-round-2-pats-left-hook-puts-fintan-on-the-floor-and-angelo-dundee-throws-in-the-towel-he-wants-to-preserve-fintans/

44.  *The Irish Times, 4* January 2013. www.irishtimes.com/newspaper/ireland/2013/0104/1224328423425.html January 2013 via www.shelltosea.com/content/rabbitte-insists-he-good-fit-his-department-and-excited-about-future-0

45.  irishexaminer.com/business/features/why-we-sit-on-sofas-rather-than-take-to-the-streets-237484.html

46.  www.ft.com/intl/cms/s/0/e3142470-bcaf-11e2-9519-00144feab7de.html?siteedition=uk#axzz2rgbyskgj

47.  www.breakingnews.ie/ireland/tribunal-whistleblower-james-gogarty-dies-aged-88-221064.html

48.  www.independent.ie/opinion/analysis/the-cricketloving-excon-paid-103000-a-year-by-taxpayers-26794239.html

49.  irishtimes.com/business/sectors/energy-and-resources/tax-debate-on-oil-and-gas-needs-to-await-delivery-1.1436741

50.  www.ccop.or.th/ppm/document/CAEXV5/CAEXV5DOC03_kjemperud.pdf

# 16.

## EPILOGUE
### Eddie Hobbs

All over the place, from the popular culture to the propaganda system, there is constant pressure to make people feel that they are helpless, that the only role they can have is to ratify decisions and to consume.

—Noam Chomsky[1]

The establishment (let's be specific: that nexus of relationships that exists between the DCENR and private exploration businesses, many of them owned by non-tax residents) rely on our apathy. They don't want to hear the voice of the people except to ratify their common thinking, their way of doing things, their idea of the status quo. The Irish people are to remain uninterested, bored and fed a low dosage of learned helplessness.

But now that you've read this book, do you feel different? You now know what we know – the only question left is, what are you prepared to do about it? For sure it's not black and white. Exploitation of resources from a first-world country is hardly going to be. Instead it is subtle, opaque, coded.

There has been no publicised oil strike, therefore no oil. The multi-billion-euro gas pipeline investment at Corrib is purely speculative; there is no network of gas fields off Ireland's north-west. There are no governing principles that define national strategy and set the parameters around development. There is merely a pricing policy. This is to pass the economic rent, the super profits from your natural resource endowment, to a small group of private investors, who, in turn, will flog it to big oil at the first available opportunity.

The DCENR represents the State, the Trustee, tasked with acting as guardian of the Irish people's natural resource endowment, but its strategy is to do nothing, to await developments, and then rely on native cunning to jack up pricing for new licences as soon as a real winner makes the headlines. That's it.

Strike oil today and you can double your profits every year and a half for decades to come. You can take Irish oil in Irish waters off your platforms straight into international refineries. The Irish have to buy it back at international market prices – for as long as the field lasts. There are no requirements for Irish jobs, Irish infrastructure, Irish production-sharing or discounts for Irish consumers or businesses. We rely on the integrity of high-powered accountants on oil company payrolls not to screw us further by exploiting the creative accounting trail-blazed by large multinational corporations through Irish law. I don't know about you, but that gets me angry – angry enough to do something.

Except for Justin Keating, no Minister has really stood up for the Irish people on this matter: perhaps they are trapped by a short-term electoral cycle that fails to reward long-term strategic thinking. What's followed has been a queue of servitude. Meanwhile, permanent government officers remain faceless, work through their entire civil service careers and drift into retirement, without adequate performance-measurement and without consequences. There is no reward for taking risks, for challenging the paradigm within, there is just apathy in a secretive world unchanged since inheriting an Edwardian civil service model from Dublin Castle. Meanwhile the Joint Oireachtas Committee Report reveals an unambitious, uninformed and leaderless political class on this crucial subject.

Still, there is no hiding from the fact that government policy is reckless. Norwegian Helge Ryggvik has warned: don't give away too much in the first round, take time to set up a legal framework flexible enough for the State to tighten rules when conditions change, strategic agreements and decisions made in the early phase in an oil region's development have decisive implications.

In an interview about homelessness on *Newstalk* with Pat Kenny as 2013 closed out, Jesuit priest Father Peter McVerry challenged us – have we lost our sense of outrage? Rather, I'm betting that it merely sleeps, that the inherent Irish character is to fight. In 2013, the most widely read article in the *Irish Times* for the entire year was a rerun of a German feature piece on Ireland's baffling and illogical approach to offshore hydrocarbons, which was first published by Germany's largest daily newspaper and included an interview with Own Our Oil. Outsiders are shocked at Irish government policy, at Irish State servitude and apathy, but so too, I believe, are many Irish people, deeply concerned about how state services are to be hollowed out for at least another decade of debt servitude.

At the height of the Celtic Tiger, RTÉ's *Rip-Off Republic* tapped into a deep feeling of unease with how Ireland is run. That unease, exacerbated by the capitulation to powerful Irish banks and their faceless bondholders, remains. Ask yourself, isn't there a quiet sense of outrage, a feeling that we deserve better, a determination that this must never happen again? The political class remains largely unchanged, dominated by long-serving insiders whose contemporaries lost heavily to international bank bondholders because of atypical servility, callowness and incompetence.

But there is time – we do not have to lose our offshore oil and gas, nor accept the current version of trusteeship. There is a separation between the owners of our offshore natural resource endowment – the people – and our trustee, the State. It's time that, as owners, we set new rules of engagement. Irish national strategy towards offshore oil and gas must change. The publication of *Own Our Oil: The Fight for Ireland's Economic Freedom* bookends what has gone before, the old debate dominated by industry and officialdom one-liners, soft media interviews, unchallenged broadcasts leading to an acceptance of the status quo – learned helplessness. There is a new debate starting with deeper insights, better information and committed experts contributing voluntarily to an organisation whose sole objective is to raise awareness and increase public knowledge. But more is needed – to paraphrase the African proverb, when the herd stands together, the lion lies down hungry.

You can make a difference. Tell your family, friends and community about how you feel, what you've learned. Pass the book around, email your network with links to the condensed and free e-book at www.ownouroil.ie/ebook. Can you speak in public? Contact Own Our Oil, become an advocate – one speech, two, a multitude, it doesn't matter, so long as you act. We'll get you slides, videos and support. Have you skills like broadcasting, song-writing, marketing, lobbying, raising funds, administration or advocating? If so, join us by emailing eddie@ownouroil.ie.

Whatever you do, however you react to this book, I hope you feel better-informed, more curious and, above all, no longer neutral. Thanks for reading.

—Eddie Hobbs, February 2014

## NOTES

1. Chomsky is an American linguist, philosopher, cognitive scientist, political commentator and activist. www.youtube.com/watch?v=kO60mOzv7QA

# 17.

## ODE OUR OIL

### Dominic Sherlock

Ireland's an enigma – a real paradox.
Proud, hardy people, tugging their forelocks.
We're favourite when we're underdogs – we punch above our weight:
A long, ancient history, but a mere infant State.
So at times it's important to keep perspective grounded –
It's less than a century since our nation was founded.
Though there are chapters to regret from our more recent past
The opportunity is here to build a future to last.

Irish people have achieved wherever they roam
But now it's time to bring that expertise home
And back ourselves to do what's best for our land
Not just grumble and moan, but to take a stand.

Our woes today are just history repeating
Though you might not know it from the media's bleating
About Troika, and bailouts, and a property crash
Which has resulted in the export of all of our cash.
We're left high and dry, politicians wring their hands
And stand idly by while others plunder our lands –
The exact same thing happened in 1845:
Irish people must struggle or emigrate to survive.

The Great Irish Famine was a man-made plight
Simplistically blamed on bad potato blight.

But while the Irish were starving and dying in millions,
Some were making the modern equivalent of billions
By exporting all of our natural produce.
The parallels here, we hope you'll deduce
Are stark when you see that much of our wealth
Has been exported again – this time by stealth.

But that's just the start – to make matters worse
We're going to be haunted again by the curse
Of our subservient Irish mentality –
Indifferent, disenfranchised, drowned in apathy.
Because we've given away our mineral resources
On deals struck in Bertie's tent at the horses.

Some might shrug their shoulders, thinking nothing can be done –
With that attitude the west will never be won.
But you've taken the first step of opening this book
And once you've taken the time to look
You'll realise that we've got to stand up for our nation –
Not just for ourselves, but the next generations.

Change comes from the grass-roots, not the 'political elite' –
Some of whom are publicly proven tax cheats
Whose primary focus was their own pension plans
And they feathered their nests at the cost of our land.

One of them subsequently did time in jail –
The rest of them seem to escape without fail.
But there's no time to point fingers nor apportion the blame
Fixing the problem is Own Our Oil's aim.

Nowhere else in the world is so much given away
To corporates who decide what tax they *won't* pay
Through loopholes and write-offs and lack of reporting
On the exact quantity of what they're exporting.
Norway, when faced with the same tough decision,
Saw through the oil barons' threats and derision.
So they founded a fund for their sovereign wealth,
Which guarantees their country's financial health.

At the moment all Ireland gets is the bill
For a cleanup if there is another oil spill
Like the one just off Cork back in '79
Because industry was left to its own devices that time.

What we can't afford to gamble with is our oil and gas
Of which we are told our endowment is vast.
Yet they say it's unproven and that we should wait
'Til production has started to have a debate
On what we should get, but by then it's too late
So *this* is the time to determine our fate.

Because once it's been licensed, there'll be no come-backs
Nor chances to change the rate of the tax –
Nor more importantly still to secure our supply –
From foreigners our very own oil we must buy.
And at market prices, we needn't point out –
We get no concessions, of that there's no doubt.

But will our grandkids look back at this time and wonder
Why the hell we did nothing to stop the plunder –
Of the wealth which off our shores has been found?
Under current conditions it's best left in the ground.
And if you're opposed to all fossil fuel
And don't want it extracted at all, well then you'll
Realise the pillage is happening irrespective of whether
You want to prevent more change to our weather.
But if we take back control of what gets drilled, where,
We can then start to mitigate damage to our air
And to our waters, our wildlife and land.
Divided we'll fall, together we'll stand.

From Vikings to Cromwell to bondholders and now
Once again to external forces will we bow?
Whatever happened to our national pride?
We've got to stand up and dig deep inside.
Even Cromwell left Connacht as our alternative to hell –

But this current deal has sold the west as (a) well.
We simply can't let it come to that.
This government of wolves that we sheep begat
Are answerable to us, though it seems there's a lack
Of political will to take our wealth back.

But the power to change that is now in (y)our hands
All that's needed is enough people taking a stand.
So we hope you will give Own Our Oil consideration
As one way to stem the flow for our nation.
And if not, then perhaps you will see your own way
To make a positive change for our country today.

To wrap up, we'll echo Mandela, the late –
'Sometimes it falls on a generation to be great.
YOU CAN BE that great generation –
Let your greatness blossom' for the sake of our nation.

Dominic was kindly invited by Irish singer-songwriter Declan O'Rourke to speak about Own Our Oil before each of Declan's December 2013 gigs in the Republic of Ireland. To get the message across in a way which wasn't a lecture, Dominic delivered a localised version of the above poem, tailored to each of the regional audiences. The feedback received at those gigs was overwhelming and it was highly encouraging to see the interest that the people of Ireland have in this issue.

The support, encouragement and volunteer force amassed through OOO.ie, by email and in person, made this book possible and will form the basis of where Own Our Oil goes from here to get a better deal for Ireland.

We would like to thank the thousands who have stood up to be counted – this movement is for you and by you. Together, we will build a brighter future for Ireland.

# 18.
## SOURCES

### CHAPTER 4

Embassy of Denmark, Oslo. 2009. 'Overview of the Norwegian Oil and Gas Industry.' www.offshorecenter.dk/filer/files/Project/Internationalisering/OCD%20report%20 (Norway).pdf

Flower, Merlin. 2009. 'Oil Drilling – An Expensive Business.' www.oil-price.net/en/articles/oil-drilling-expensive-business.php

Karl, Terry L. 2007. 'Oil-led Development: Social, Political and Economic Consequences.' Stanford University: Center on Democracy, Development and the Rule of Law. iis-db.stanford.edu/pubs/21537/No_80_Terry_Karl_-_Effects_of_Oil_Development.pdf

National Treasury Management Agency. 2013. 'Debt Profile.' www.ntma.ie/business-areas/funding-and-debt-management/debt-profile

OECD. 2013. OECD Statistics Database. stats.oecd.org

PWC. 2013. 'Report highlights employment and tax benefits potential to Ireland of oil and gas industry.' www.pwc.ie/press-release/press-release-10-05-2013.jhtml

PWC. 2013. 'Making the most of our natural resources.' www.providenceresources.com/uploads/pwcoilandgasreport-final-may2013.pdf

### CHAPTER 8

Bunreacht na hÉireann (Constitution of Ireland). 1937. Government Publications

Daly, Mary E. 1981. *Social & Economic History of Ireland Since 1800.* Edco

Duffy, Paul. 2004. 'The Pre-History of the Shannon Scheme.' *History Ireland,* Issue 4, Volume 12

Ferriter, Diarmaid. 2007. *Judging Dev.* Royal Irish Academy

Fisk, Robert. 1985. *In Time of War: Ireland, Ulster and the Price of Neutrality.* Paladin Books

Foster, R.F. 1988. *Modern Ireland 1600–1972.* Penguin Books

Gilmartin, Mary. 2012. 'The Changing Landscape of Irish Migration.' NIRSA, NUI Maynooth

Hickey, D.J. and J.E. Doherty. 2003. *A New Dictionary of Irish History from 1800.* Gill & MacMillan

Hix, Simon. 1999. *The Poitical System of the European Union.* MacMillan Press

Jackson, Alvin. 2003. *Home Rule: An Irish History 1800-2000.* Weidenfeld & Nicolson

Johnson, David. 1985. *The Interwar Economy in Ireland.* Dundalgan Press

Lyons, F.S.L. 2005. *Charles Stewart Parnell.* Gill & MacMillan

McDowell, Andrew. 2006. 'Globalisation and the Knowledge Economy – the Case of Ireland.' Forfás

Murphy, John A. 1975. *Ireland in the 20th Century.* Gill & MacMillan

Patterson, Henry. 2006. *Ireland Since 1939: The Persistence of Conflict.* Penguin Books

www.merrionstreet.ie

www.ria.ie

## CHAPTER 10

Ernst & Young. 2012. 'Global Oil and Gas Tax Guide, 2012'

Feeney, Michael. 2012. 'The Taxation of Companies: 2012'

Stamp Duty Consolidation Act, 1999

Taxes Consolidation Act, 1997